IELTS
雅思核心词汇
精讲精练

宋鹏昊　编著

浙江教育出版社·杭州

音 频

图书在版编目(CIP)数据

雅思核心词汇精讲精练 / 宋鹏昊编著. -- 杭州：
浙江教育出版社, 2024.4
ISBN 978-7-5722-7386-5

Ⅰ. ①雅... Ⅱ. ①宋... Ⅲ. ①IELTS – 词汇 – 自学参
考资料 Ⅳ. ①H313

中国国家版本馆CIP数据核字(2024)第036003号

雅思核心词汇精讲精练
YASI HEXIN CIHUI JING JIANG JING LIAN
宋鹏昊　编著

责任编辑	赵清刚
美术编辑	韩　波
责任校对	马立改
责任印务	时小娟
文字编辑	刘　畅
封面设计	李　倩
版式设计	李　倩
出版发行	浙江教育出版社
	地址：杭州市天目山路40号
	邮编：310013
	电话：（0571）85170300 – 80928
	邮箱：dywh@xdf.cn
印　　刷	三河市良远印务有限公司
开　　本	710mm×1000mm　1/16
成品尺寸	168mm×240mm
印　　张	23.5
字　　数	357 000
版　　次	2024年4月第1版
印　　次	2024年4月第1次印刷
标准书号	ISBN 978-7-5722-7386-5
定　　价	58.00元

雅思考试作为一项设计科学、应用广泛的语言能力测试，正在受到越来越多考生的青睐，让不同地区、不同年龄的考生能在统一标准下对语言能力进行评估。想在雅思考试中获得理想分数，自身的语言能力自然是最重要的影响因素。而作为构成语言的最基本要素，词汇往往是很多雅思考生学习过程的开端，也是后续备考高效进行的前提。因此，一本科学策划、精心编写的词汇书，能够使学习的效果更好、效率更高。

本书首版于 2018 年 1 月出版，受到了众多考生的喜欢，因其选词精准、讲解全面，成为很多同学"人生中学完的第一本词汇书"。在与大家的互动中，我也收获颇丰，于去年启动了新版的策划和编写，并高质量地完成了这本全新的作品。本书主要有以下特点：

首先，本书选词精准，覆盖全面。我们按照"考什么，学什么"的原则，针对性地建立雅思真题语料库，并通过词频和内容等多个维度筛选单词，最终精选出 1,600 个词条。同时，通过对每个词条的扩展，将更多核心词汇融入书中，将全书覆盖词汇量控制在 7,000 词左右，既重点突出，又覆盖全面。

其次，本书对每个词条做了精细讲解，配备了与雅思考试语言风格一致的例句，并从用法、同义词、反义词、同类别词汇、扩展词等多个角度进行讲解。书中也收录了部分真题中的原句，使大家在学习词汇的同时，提前适应真题的语言风格和难度。

最后，本书针对学习方法进行了讲解，并在每个单元配备了练习题。学习方法篇在本书开头部分，针对考生们提问最多的问题进行了逐一解答，比如考雅思需要多少词汇、从哪些角度学习词汇、词根及词缀的作用等。每个单元的练习题主要用于强化和检验学习效果，通过完成练习，也能够进行查漏补缺。

雅思学习的过程，除了学习语言知识、提升语言技能外，对考生的规划能力、信息分析能力、抗压能力、执行能力、反思能力都会带来全方位的提升。很多考生可能会将本书作为备考的第一个环节，以平和且自信的心态，认认真真完成每个单元的学习，这必然会是一个圆满的开端。我也相信，一本专业且实用的词汇书，能为备考者带来很大帮助。希望每一位考生都能取得理想分数，实现自己的追求和梦想！

宋鹏昊

使用说明

收录主词条或其派生词在真题中出现的句子或用法，提前适应真题难度。

扫码收听单词录音，地道英式发音，边听边记，提高效率。

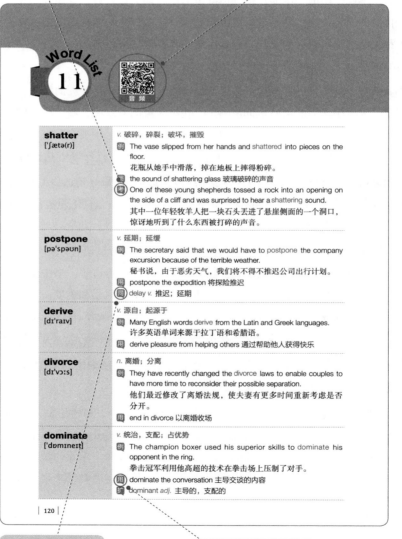

Word List 11

音频

shatter [ˈʃætə(r)]	*v.* 破碎，碎裂；破坏，摧毁 例 The vase slipped from her hands and shattered into pieces on the floor. 花瓶从她手中滑落，掉在地板上摔得粉碎。 用 the sound of shattering glass 玻璃破碎的声音 真 One of these young shepherds tossed a rock into an opening on the side of a cliff and was surprised to hear a shattering sound. 其中一位年轻牧羊人把一块石头丢进了悬崖侧面的一个洞口，惊讶地听到了什么东西被打碎的声音。
postpone [pəˈspəʊn]	*v.* 延期；延缓 例 The secretary said that we would have to postpone the company excursion because of the terrible weather. 秘书说，由于恶劣天气，我们将不得不推迟公司出行计划。 用 postpone the expedition 将探险推迟 近 delay *v.* 推迟；延期
derive [dɪˈraɪv]	*v.* 源自；起源于 例 Many English words derive from the Latin and Greek languages. 许多英语单词来源于拉丁语和希腊语。 用 derive pleasure from helping others 通过帮助他人获得快乐
divorce [dɪˈvɔːs]	*n.* 离婚；分离 例 They have recently changed the divorce laws to enable couples to have more time to reconsider their possible separation. 他们最近修改了离婚法规，使夫妻有更多时间重新考虑是否分开。 用 end in divorce 以离婚收场
dominate [ˈdɒmɪneɪt]	*v.* 统治，支配；占优势 例 The champion boxer used his superior skills to dominate his opponent in the ring. 拳击冠军利用他高超的技术在拳击场上压制了对手。 用 dominate the conversation 主导交谈的内容 拓 dominant *adj.* 主导的，支配的

列举同义词及反义词，帮助考生灵活应对同义替换。

给出常见词组及搭配，帮助考生掌握单词用法。

提供贴近雅思考试难度的例句，
结合具体语境，高效记忆单词。

discount ['dɪskaʊnt]	*n.* 折扣 *v.* 打折；贬损；忽视 例 The store offers generous discounts on electronic goods at New Year. 这家商店在新年期间对电子产品给出了很大折扣。 用 get a discount 得到折扣 discount prices 折扣价 a discount shop 一家折扣商店
metaphor ['metəfə(r)]	*n.* 比喻；隐喻 例 Metaphors are often used in literature and also in everyday sayings. 隐喻经常在文学作品和日常用语中使用。 用 the writer's striking use of metaphor 这位作家对隐喻的独到运用
accommodation [əˌkɒmə'deɪʃn]	*n.* 住处；住宿 例 The accomodation situation on the new campus was excellent; they had built new dormitories with improved bathroom facilities. 新校区的住宿条件非常好，他们新建了宿舍，改善了浴室设施。 用 temporary accommodation 临时的住处 扩 accommodate *v.* 容纳；使适应；提供住处
helicopter ['helɪkɒptə(r)]	*n.* 直升机 例 The rescue team arrived quickly in a helicopter to aid the stranded hikers. 救援队乘坐直升机迅速赶到，救助被困的徒步旅行者。 用 a police helicopter 一架警用直升机 a helicopter pilot 一位直升机驾驶员
admire [əd'maɪə(r)]	*v.* 钦佩；赞美，称赞 例 I've always admired famous singers who genuinely have creativity and talent; not just those that can look good on stage. 我一直很欣赏那些有创造力和才华的著名歌手，而不是单单喜欢那些在舞台上看起来很好看的人。 用 admire the way he handled the situation 佩服他处理这种局面的方式 扩 admiration *n.* 赞美；钦佩
landlord ['lændlɔːd]	*n.* 房东；地主 例 The landlord increased the rent by twenty percent, much to the shock of most of the tenants. 房东把租金提高了百分之二十，这让多数房客非常吃惊。 用 negotiate with the landlord 与房东协商 类 rent *n.* 租金 tenant *n.* 租户

| 121 |

列举丰富的派生词及同
根词，横向扩充词汇量。

归纳在语义上属于相
同类别的单词，全面
增加词汇储备。

目 录
CONTENTS

学习方法篇

　　在开始学习每一个核心词汇前，我们要先对词汇学习有足够的了解，并形成正确的观念。这样做不仅可以帮助你提升效率，还可以让学习过程更加顺畅，少走弯路。本篇基于雅思词汇的常见问题进行讲解，你将了解到考雅思需要学多少词汇、需要重点学习哪些词汇、从哪些角度学习词汇、词根词缀的作用、如何高效完成词汇学习，并理解词汇学习是贯穿雅思备考全程的。本部分讲解中的很多内容会在后面的备考过程中用到，而对这些问题的理解也会为之后的学习奠定坚实的基础。

当我们希望学会一种知识或掌握一项技能时,对其有正确的认识是非常重要的第一步,学习雅思词汇自然也是如此。了解词汇学习的规律,采用正确的方法,不仅可以提升效率,事半功倍,更重要的是,可以减少学习过程中的挫败感。很多考生在整个英语学习过程中没有完整地学完过任何一本词汇书,很大程度上也是由于没有建立对词汇学习的正确认识,进而导致学习过程不顺利以至放弃。本篇内容将会集中解答考生在词汇学习中最关注的问题,帮助大家建立理性的认识,这会对后面的学习大有帮助。

 考雅思要学习多少词汇

雅思考试主要考查考生在学术和生活情境下使用英语进行沟通的能力,词汇范围比较广,也没有所谓"大纲词汇"和"超纲词汇"的说法。但是,我们依然可以通过科学的方法,从过往的考试中找到规律,确定哪些词是需要优先学习的,这也是本书编写的基本思路。

首先,我们将剑桥雅思官方发布的真题集和各类主流试题集进行整理和分析,用到了国内外几乎所有能够见到的雅思相关素材,建立起超过 100 万词的试题"语料库"。这个库"非常雅思"。通过将相同单词归类,语料库中的词汇数量共计 15,000 个左右,每个单词对应了相应的出现频率。例如,the 出现了几万次,紧随其后的是 of、to、in 这类词。

之后,对这约 15,000 个单词作进一步的合并。例如:将单复数形式进行合并,也就是把 river 和 rivers 归到一个词条下;将英美写法进行合并,也就是把 colour 和 color 归到一个词条下;将 -ing 和 -ed 形式进行合并,也就是把 watching 和 watched 归到一个词条下。

最后,将词汇进行分类处理,选出本书需要收录的词条。基本方法为:去除功能词汇,如 the、of、in、not 等;去除专有名词,如人名 James Barrett、地名 Vitcos 等;保留内容词汇,如 carbon dioxide、legislation 等;将内容词汇按词频排序,保留高频词汇;通过例句、同义词 / 反义词、扩展词等方式,收录其他核心词;结合听、说、读、写不同科目特点,进一步扩展词条。

通过以上方式,这本词汇书做到了既精简又全面,通过 1,600 个词条,完成了对雅思考试核心词汇的收录,并配备了相应的练习。

 需要重点学习哪些词汇

由于雅思考试没有所谓的"大纲词汇",我们就需要找出简单的标准,来说清楚需要重点学习哪些词汇。我认为可以通过两个标准回答这个问题。

第一条标准：本书中的词汇全部熟练掌握。本书针对雅思真题进行了详细分析，精选了词条，并通过对词条的讲解进一步扩展了词汇量。如果能将本书中收录的单词全部熟练掌握，便具备了后续使用听、说、读、写不同科目真题进行学习的基础。反过来讲，如果本书中的单词还没有熟练掌握，那么后续的学习会非常困难，很可能出现由于无法顺利进行听、说、读、写的学习而重新开始词汇学习的情况。因此，强烈建议考生不要在自身英语基础不够扎实的情况下，跳过词汇而直接进入具体科目的学习。

第二条标准：剑桥雅思真题集中的词汇全部熟练掌握。雅思真题无疑是备考过程中最重要的素材。在完成每套题目的练习后，考生就要进入对该套题目进行学习的环节，其中要做的第一件事便是整理生词，包括听力文本中的生词或听错的词、阅读文章和题目中的生词、写作文章中会用到的词，以及口语回答中会用到的词等。在考试前，将做过的真题中出现的核心词全部掌握，是获得理想分数的基本条件。

在学习单词这件事上，很多考生会陷入一个误区。在考试中，究竟是该追求单词几乎全认识、文章都能看懂或听懂，还是追求在有生词且文章没太看懂或听懂的情况下，也能通过一定的方法或技巧把题目做对。在这件事上，我们的追求一定是前者。这显然是一种更加稳妥和高效的选择，并且第二种情形实际上是很难实现的。原因在于，如果有能力在文章没太看懂或听懂的情况下把题目做对，那付出的时间和精力足够把单词学得很扎实了。雅思考试是对语言能力本身的考查，看懂、听懂是最为简单有效的应对方式。

The **conviction** that historical **relics** provide **infallible testimony** about the past is rooted in the nineteenth and early twentieth centuries, when science was **regarded** as **objective** and value free. As one writer **observes**: 'Although it is now **evident** that **artefacts** are as easily **altered** as **chronicles**, public **faith** in their **veracity endures**: a **tangible relic** seems ipso facto real.' Such **conviction** was, until recently, **reflected** in museum **displays**. Museums used to look – and some still do – much like **storage** rooms of **objects packed** together in **showcases**: good for **scholars** who wanted to study the **subtle** differences in **design**, but not for the **ordinary** visitor, to whom it all looked alike. **Similarly**, the information **accompanying** the **objects** often made little **sense** to the lay visitor. The **content** and **format** of **explanations** dated back to a time when the museum was the **exclusive domain** of the scientific researcher.

以上段落来自剑桥雅思真题。从中可以看出，用粗体标记的单词，就属于我们所说的"核心词汇"，这也是本书在收录单词时的标准。同时，也可以看出，如果不认识这些单词中的大多数或无法快速反应出其词义，则很难理解文章内容。并且，由于这是文章的第一段，会对整篇文章答题的心态产生影响。因此，将词汇书中的单词熟练掌握，将真题中的核心词熟练掌握，是备考雅思的最优选择。

笔者经常建议考生将学习单词和背单词作为两件事对待。学习单词的过程是慢下来、有深度的，而背单词的过程是快速的、不需要深度而是需要通过重复完成的。很多考生之所以感到背单词非常困难，很大程度上是由于没有进行前期学习单词的过程，面对大量生词不断机械重复，缺少对单词的理解，效率自然很低。因此，先对单词进行全面学习，之后大量、快速、重复背单词，是掌握词汇较好的路径，这也会给之后听、说、读、写不同科目的学习打下好的基础。

以下是学习雅思词汇的主要角度，也是除单词的音标和释义之外，本书编写时用来扩展词条的主要角度。

例句 在书中以符号 例 表示。在不同的语境下重复见到同一个单词，才能达到好的学习效果。在最初的学习阶段，就要将单词放到语境中进行学习。因此，除音标和释义之外，本书中每个词条的例句也都是需要学习的，而例句中往往也会重复出现其他雅思核心词汇，这也是为了增加重复次数，方便考生进行学习巩固。例如：

impart

例 The wise teacher sought to impart valuable life lessons to her students.
这位明智的老师设法向学生传授宝贵的人生经验。

absorb

例 Plants thrive when they absorb plenty of nutrients from the soil.
当植物在土壤中吸收大量养分时，它们就会茁壮生长。

除了词条 impart 和 absorb 外，以上例句中的 seek、valuable、thrive、nutrients、soil 等雅思核心词也都需要考生一并学习和掌握。

用法 在书中以 用 表示。单词的用法是非常重要的学习内容，各类常见搭配以及不同语境下的用法都会在这部分出现，以帮助考生更好地学习。例如：

artificial

用 artificial intelligence 人工智能 artificial light 人造光

facilitate

用 facilitate the development of tourism 促进旅游业的发展

maximum

用 the maximum speed 最快速度 the maximum volume 最大音量

同义词/反义词 在书中分别以 同 和 反 表示。由于同义替换在考试的各个科目中都会出现，并且这也是语言学习中非常重要的能力，所以本书中一些词条下会列出该词的同义词或反义词。例如：

cease *v.* 停止

同 stop *v.* 停止

反 continue *v.* 继续

fringe *n.* 边缘

同 edge *n.* 边缘 margin *n.* 边缘 brink *n.* 边缘

反 centre *n.* 中心

派生词/同根词 在书中以 扩 表示。根据词根、词缀进行的扩展都会在这个条目下出现，以帮助考生了解单词的变体，同时利用词根、词缀扩展单词量。例如：

sustain *v.* 持续

扩 sustainable *adj.* 可持续的（后缀 -able 表示形容词，含义为"可……的"）sustainable development 可持续发展

同类别词汇 在书中以 类 表示。单词在语言中不是孤立出现的，往往会与一定的主题和语境有关，因此本书将语义上属于相同类别的词汇列举在同一个词条下，作为扩展词汇的角度之一。例如：

tissue *n.* 组织

类 cell *n.* 细胞 muscle *n.* 肌肉 bacterium *n.* 细菌

真题中的考试范例 在书中以 考 表示。学习词汇最终是为了更加从容地应对考试，因此本书在一些词条下会给出雅思真题中包含该词或其派生词的句子或短语的示例，以更好地衔接词汇学习与真题备考。例如：

current

考 the current unprecedented global warming 如今空前的全球变暖现象

distinguish

考 Two things distinguish food production from all other productive activities. 两个因素将粮食生产与所有其他生产活动区分开来。

练习 在每个单元后，均设置了两种针对本单元词汇的练习，要求考生分别对单词的中文释义和英文释义进行匹配。通过这种交互，考生可以强化学习效果，也可以作为对本单元词汇掌握情况的检验。

说到词根、词缀，很多考生似乎并不陌生，但在实际学习中并没有很好地使用。作为构成单词的基本要素，不同的词根、词缀进行组合，形成了一个个完整的单词。词根、词缀的主要作用是帮助我们理解单词是如何构造的，从而更加快速地记忆，并且更加有深度地理解，同时由于词根、词缀会在不同词汇中重复出现，随着不断学习，会大幅提升词汇学习的效率。我们对于词根、词缀的态度应该是放在词汇中学习，作为有效的辅助工具来使用，而并非孤立地学习和记忆词根、词缀。在多数情况下，词根、词缀有如下作用。

词根 表示一个单词的核心含义，单词最终的含义往往是基于词根的含义引申出来的，有些词根本身也是单词，有些词根不是完整的单词。例如，mit 这个词根表示的含义为 send，那么其构成的很多单词都是基于这个含义引申出来的，比如 emit，前缀 e- 表示 out 的意思，因此基于前缀和词根的含义，我们可以更快地理解 emit 的含义为"发射，发送"。

前缀 主要起到辅助表示单词含义的作用，具体来说，常见的作用有以下三个。

第一，前缀可以表示方向。很多前缀都带有与方向有关的含义，例如：

前缀 im- 和 in- 都表示 in 的含义，而前缀 ex- 表示 out 的含义，在构词时，由于 port 作为单词表示"港口"，作为词根表示 carry，所以 import 和 export 就分别表示"进口"和"出口"的意思。

前缀 pre- 表示 before 的含义，post- 表示 after 的含义，构词时，由于单词 war 表示"战争"的意思，所以 prewar 和 postwar 就分别表示"战前的"和"战后的"的意思。

第二，前缀可以表示数字。很多前缀都带有与数字有关的含义，例如：

前缀 uni- 表示 one，单词 form 表示"形式"，因此单词 uniform 表示"制服"或"统一的"，这两个意思也是有一定联系的，制服的作用就是使人们在形式上保持一致。

前缀 bi- 表示 two 的意思，单词 lingual 表示"语言的"，因此 bilingual 表示"双语的"；而词根 cycle 表示"转"的含义，因此我们也就清楚为什么 bicycle 表示"自行车"了。

第三，前缀可以表示否定。很多前缀都带有与否定有关的含义，例如：

前缀 im-、in-、un-、dis-、mis- 等都可以表示否定的含义，因此我们见到的很多单词由于加上否定前缀而产生了含义的变化。例如单词 possible 表示"可能的"，而 impossible 表示"不可能的"；单词 fortunate 表示"幸运的"，而 unfortunate 表示"不幸的"；单词 understand 表示"理解"，而 misunderstand 表示"误解"。

后缀 同样起到辅助表示单词含义的作用，具体来说，常见的作用有以下两个。

第一，后缀表示词性。一些后缀可以表示单词的词性，例如：

后缀 -ment、-tion 往往表示名词，由于动词 move 表示"运动，移动"，所以 movement 表示名词"运动"；动词 educate 表示"教育"，所以 education 表示名词"教育"。

第二，后缀表示类别。一些后缀可以起到表示单词所属类别的作用，例如：

后缀 -er、-ar、-or 都可以用来表示人或物，由于动词 teach 表示"教学"，所以 teacher 表示"教师"；动词 contain 表示"包含，含有"，所以 container 表示名词"容器"。

以上是词根、词缀的一些基本作用，在单词构造的过程中，还有下面这些常见的构词规则，在学习中也会不断地遇到。

连接符 i, u

在单词构成中，经常遇到不表示含义的字母 i 或 u。例如单词 annual 中，词根 ann 表示 year，后缀 -al 表示形容词，而中间的 u 只起到连接作用，不表示任何含义，单词 annual 表示"年度的，每年的"。

加强 一般通过"字母 a"或"a＋辅音"或"a＋辅音双写"表示加强

加强是指基于词根含义进行引申，常见形式是单词开头通过"字母 a"或"a＋辅音"或"a＋辅音双写"来表示。例如 access，构成为 ac＋cess，基于词根 cess 的含义，引申为"进入"。advocate 的构成为 ad＋voc＋ate，这里的 ad 表示加强，基于词根 voc 的含义，引申为"提倡，支持"。

同化 辅音字母之间同化

在词根、词缀连接的地方，会发生同化现象。例如单词 legal 的否定前缀 im- 或 in-，会由于 legal 的首字母为 l，而被同化为 il-，因此其否定词为 illegal；同样地，relevant 的否定词为 irrelevant。

缩写 常见于元音字母

在构成单词时，原单词中的元音可以缩写，例如 school 中的 oo，在 scholar 中被缩写为 o。

音变 发音口型类似的字母之间可以转换

由于英语本身是拼音文字，发音类似的字母之间往往可以发生变换，因此元音字母 a、e、i、o、u 之间经常可以变换，而 u、v、w，或者 l、n、r 之间，由于发音方式类似，也可以在构词时进行变换。例如单词 language 的构成为 lang＋u＋age，词根 lang 表示"舌头，语言"，与词根 ling 一致，因此形容词 lingual 表示"语言的"。

除了上述词根、词缀和构词规则外，也可以从词源的角度了解词根的来源，语言的背后往往是文化和思维方式，一些词根背后可能是一段有趣的神话故事。随着对词汇的学习越来越全面，能够既知道每个词的含义和用法，也了解这个词的来源和构成，那无疑会让你对英文的理解更加深入，也对英文背后的文化产生越发浓厚的热情。

五　如何高效完成词汇学习

很多考生在词汇学习中，经常由于方法不当而陷入低效学习的状态。比较常见的学习误区有以下三种：第一，有不少考生没有对词汇进行深入学习，而是从一开始就单纯以背单词的心态进行机械记忆，导致学习效率低下；第二，有的考生无法持续学习，要么没有及时复习，导致遗忘，要么在完成一周左右的学习后出现学习的间断，之后再重新学起；第三，有些考生希望通过一两次学习和背诵就能够掌握单词，而忽略了词汇需要通过大量重复才能真正掌握这一事实，对于半生不熟的词产生挫败感，影响学习效率。针对这些问题，笔者给出以下三点建议，作为学习本书时需要重点关注的学习策略。

首先，先学单词，再背单词。学习单词指的是使用本书，将每一个词条和与之相关的例句等信息全部逐词逐句学习，全面学习一个单词的同时，也将例句和扩展信息中的单词进行有效学习。这样做之后，就能够基本完成对词汇的学习和理解，基于理解的背诵才是效率更高的选择。建议将书中每个词条至少完整地学习一遍，尽量学习两遍以上，这个阶段的特点是注意学习深度，尽量比较慢地进行；而随后便是快速反复背诵记忆的过程，这个阶段的特点是注意遍数和速度，每个词条至少重复四五遍，这个过程可以比较快速地进行。之后进入到与真题相关的听、说、读、写各科目学习阶段时，也会不断遇到书中的核心词，如果有一时回忆不起来的情况也属正常，把真题中的生词整理出来并且增加学习遍数，也是顺利掌握词汇的必要过程。

其次，及时复习，减少遗忘。很多考生在学习过程中，总是容易高估自己一天之内能做的事情，而忽视了每天学习一点、日积月累持续学习的巨大成效。在学习词汇这件事上，不少考生并不是没有能力很好地记忆单词，而是学习几天之后就会放下，停下几天之后，前面学过的也就会忘记很多。与记忆相对的便是遗忘，而根据大量研究的结果，在学习知识后的第一天，也就是24小时内，遗忘的量是最多的，随后遗忘会缓慢发生，遗忘的数量会逐步递减。因此，有效的学习策略便是在学习之后的当天以及第二天马上安排复习，之后可以每间隔几天复习一次，或者规律性地安排在第二天、第四天、第七天进行复习。总之，学习是持续的过程，即使每天的学习量并不多，只要能够持续进行，也会产生好的效果。

最后，不同情境，增加重复。词汇的学习会经过几个不同的阶段，每个阶段也会有不同的感受。第一阶段，往往会对单词完全没有印象。一些单词学习过几天后，很多考生再看到时完全没有印象，出现这种情况往往是因为这是一个纯生词，并且在学习时没有太多的深入理解，只进行了单纯的机械背诵。第二阶段，有印象但是无法反应出其含义。这个阶段往往出现在对词汇进行了学习但重现的遍数不够多时，典型的特征是知道自己曾经学习过，但无法回忆出含义，此时如果看到其含义，会马上反应过来。很多考生出现挫败感往往是在这个阶段，这是最容易放弃学习的阶段，也是必然要经过的阶段。第三阶段，一般能够反应出单词的含义但无法主动使用词汇。第四阶段，一般看到单词无需反应就能够理解含义，并且能够在口语和写作的表达中有效使用词汇。造成以上不同阶段不同反应的根本原因是学习和重复的遍数不同，通过单词书、听力、阅读、主动表达等各种不同情境增加与词汇"见面"的次数，是增加学习效果的最有效途径，一般对于雅思核心词汇而言，每个单词"见面"10次左右，就能够达到在考试中游刃有余的状态。

六　词汇学习贯穿备考全程

一些考生认为，在备考初期完成词汇学习后，之后的备考就可以一马平川，只需要掌握各种解题方法即可，这种想法在现实中是不成立的。实际上，词汇的学习是贯穿整个备考过程的。

首先，尽管书中针对每个词条都进行了详细讲解，并且提供了一些练习，但考生依然需要在随后的真题训练和学习阶段不断重复学习词汇，以最终熟练掌握词汇。此外，由于听、说、读、写不同科目考试的形式和话题不同，考生需要在后面的备考阶段有针对性地总结和学习词汇。

其次，如果把备考分成三个阶段，那么每个阶段实际上都有针对性的任务。具体而言，初期需要做的是完整学习至少一遍，之后不断快速刷单词和背诵；中期需要做的是在学习真题的过程中不断整理重要的、不熟悉的单词，并反复背诵掌握；考前需要做的是拿出词汇书和生词本，标注已经掌握的词，记忆不熟悉的词，反复进行直至所有单词都学会为止。

最后，对于雅思考试而言，对词汇的熟练掌握是成本最低的提升能力的方法，基于扎实的词汇能力，各种语言技能的提升也会效率更高。

以上就是笔者针对词汇学习中一些核心问题的解答，希望你能够保持平和的心态，养成持续学习的习惯，通过每天的积累，最终在雅思考试中取得理想的分数。这种"做成一件事"的经历，也会对你在生活中面对的其他挑战产生潜移默化的正向影响，无论是在信心上、策略上，还是习惯上，能够把事情做成的人总是能够积极有效地获得更加接近自身期望的生活。

核心词汇篇

　　如果把掌握学习方法的过程作为认识层面的学习，那么本篇就是针对行为层面的学习了。在本篇中，你会学习共计 32 个单元、1,600 个核心词条的内容。由于例句和扩展部分也会包含大量核心词，所以在完成全部内容的学习后，你已经与绝大多数在真题中会遇到的单词见过面了。在学习这些词汇时，强烈建议按照"先学一遍、再刷许多遍"的方式进行，也建议你及时复习，减少遗忘，以及在不同情境中增加重复的次数，这在前面的讲解中都有提及。希望这本书可以陪伴你开启一段充实的雅思备考之旅。

ecosystem [ˈiːkəʊsɪstəm]	*n.* 生态系统
	例 The ecosystem in the pacific ocean is suffering from extensive damage due to pollution. 太平洋的生态系统正在遭受污染带来的严重损害。
	用 maintain the integrity of the ecosystem 维持生态系统的完整性 the forest ecosystem 森林生态系统
	扩 ecology *n.* 生态学 ecological *adj.* 生态的
	考 significant long-term changes to the local ecosystems 对当地生态环境深远的长期影响
underline [ˌʌndəˈlaɪn]	*v.* 强调；在……下面划线
	例 It's a good study strategy to underline the words in a reading passage that you don't understand. 划出阅读文章中不理解的单词是一种很好的学习策略。
	用 underline the positive words 划出表示积极意义的词
	同 emphasise *v.* 强调
proficiency [prəˈfɪʃnsi]	*n.* 精通，熟练
	例 His level of oral English proficiency was excellent after his years overseas. 在海外生活多年后，他的英语口语已经非常熟练。
	用 a certificate of language proficiency 语言水平证书 proficiency test 能力测试
	扩 proficient *adj.* 熟练的
	考 a high level of proficiency 高度熟练
scenario [səˈnɑːriəʊ]	*n.* 设想，可能的情况；剧情梗概；场景
	例 The worst case scenario is that you will have to look for another job next year. 最坏的情况是你明年需要另找一份工作。
	用 a nightmare scenario 极坏的可能
	考 It's scenarios like these that many researchers are working to avoid. 许多研究人员都在努力避免这种情况。

staircase ['steəkeɪs]	*n.* 楼梯；楼梯间
	例 She climbed the spiral staircase to reach the top of the tower. 她爬上螺旋形楼梯，到达塔顶。
	用 walk down the staircase 沿楼梯往下走
	考 Leonardo wanted the city to be built on several levels, linked with vertical outdoor staircases. Leonardo 希望这座城市建立在几个不同的层次上，彼此之间用垂直的外部楼梯连接起来。
rooftop ['ruːftɒp]	*n.* 屋顶
	例 They enjoyed the beautiful view from the rooftop terrace of the skyscraper. 他们从摩天大楼的屋顶露台欣赏美丽景色。
	用 the rooftops of a few small villages 一些小村庄的屋顶
	考 Rooftops covered with grass, vegetable gardens and lush foliage are now a common sight in many cities around the world. 覆盖着青草、菜园和繁茂枝叶的屋顶是当今世界上许多城市里的一个常见景象。
irrigation [ˌɪrɪ'geɪʃn]	*n.* 灌溉；冲洗
	例 The new irrigation systems used in farming mean that a lot of crops can be watered regularly with much less manual effort. 耕种过程中使用的新灌溉系统意味着很多作物可以在花费更少人工的情况下得到定期灌溉。
	用 irrigation channels 灌溉渠
	扩 irrigate *v.* 灌溉
	考 improved irrigation systems 经过改进的灌溉系统
embrace [ɪm'breɪs]	*v.* 拥抱；包含；接受
	例 Today, artists and musicians are embracing new technologies to produce interesting and innovative works. 如今，艺术家和音乐家们接受使用新技术来创作有趣而新颖的作品。
	用 embrace new rules 接受新的规则 embrace every aspect of the subject 包含这一学科的各个方面
	同 hug *v.* 抱，拥抱 accept *v.* 接受 contain *v.* 包含
	考 Observation of iconoclasts shows that they embrace novelty while most people avoid things that are different. 对求新逐异者的观察表明他们会接受创新，而大多数人会避开新奇的事物。

enlighten [ɪnˈlaɪtn]	*v.* 启发；阐明；照亮
	例 She felt enlightened by his informative and interesting presentation. 他的讲述信息充实，妙趣横生，这使她感觉受到了启发。
	用 enlighten the studies of origins of myths 将有关神话起源的研究阐述清楚
	同 shed light on 照亮；启发
	扩 enlightening *adj.* 有启发作用的
rotate [rəʊˈteɪt]	*v.* （使）旋转，（使）转动
	例 Rotate the handle about 180 degrees to open the door of the safe in the office. 将把手转动180度来打开办公室保险箱的门。
	用 rotate the wheel 转动轮子
	扩 rotation *n.* 旋转，转动
recover [rɪˈkʌvə(r)]	*v.* 恢复，康复；重新获得
	例 After taking the medicine for a few weeks she recovered from her illness. 在服药几周后，她从疾病中恢复过来了。
	用 recover your sight 恢复视力
	同 restore *v.* 恢复，修复 regain *v.* 恢复；重新获得
	扩 recovery *n.* 恢复，复原
approach [əˈprəʊtʃ]	*v.* 接近，靠近 *n.* 方法，途径；接近
	例 As the storm approached everyone in the region was put on high alert. 随着暴风雨临近，该地区的每个人都处于高度警觉状态。
	用 adopt a different approach 采取不同的方法 the approach of spring 春天的来临
	同 means *n.* 方法；途径
	考 I've got very interested in all the different approaches that film directors take. 我对电影导演使用的各种不同方法都很感兴趣。
reset [ˌriːˈset]	*v.* 重置；重新设定
	例 Whenever I have problems with my computer I always reset it by turning it off and then on again. 每当我的电脑出现问题，我总会通过关机后再打开的方式来重启它。
	用 reset the watch to local time 把手表调成当地时间

interface
['ɪntəfeɪs]

n. 界面；接口 *v.* 相互作用；连接；交流

例 The latest version of this software has an impressive, user-friendly interface.
这款软件的最新版本拥有令人印象深刻且用户友好的界面。

用 the user interface 用户界面
the interface between computer and printer
计算机和打印机之间的接口
the way we interface with the environment
我们与环境相互作用的方式

扩 preface *n.* 序言

identify
[aɪ'dentɪfaɪ]

v. 确定；识别；认同

例 They couldn't identify the source of the strange smell that was coming into the office from outside.
他们无法确定从外面进入办公区的奇怪气味的来源。

用 identify a link between diet and cancer 找到饮食与癌症间的关联

扩 identification *n.* 识别；身份证明 identity *n.* 身份；同一性
identical *adj.* 同一的；相同的

考 identify the most appropriate innovation strategy to use
确定最适合使用的创新策略

panic
['pænɪk]

n. 恐慌，惊慌 *v.* （使）恐慌

例 I always get into a panic when I have too much work to do and very tight deadlines.
我在有太多事情要做、期限又很紧的时候，总会陷入恐慌。

用 a moment of panic 一时惊慌 be in a state of panic 处于惊恐中

考 I know I've got to look calm even if I'm in a panic.
我知道即使我很恐慌，我也要看起来很冷静。

swift
[swɪft]

adj. 敏捷的；迅速的

例 Time was running out so she was forced to make a swift decision.
时间所剩无几，所以她不得不迅速作出决定。

用 swift current 湍急的水流

考 Perhaps most impressively, the Model B was amazingly swift.
也许最令人印象深刻之处在于，B模型的速度快得简直神奇。

allege
[ə'ledʒ]

v. （未经证实地）宣称，断言

例 The media have alleged that the criminal stole the diamonds with no help from an accomplice.
媒体宣称罪犯在没有同伙帮助的情况下偷走了钻石。

用 be alleged to have assulted him 被指控袭击了他

扩 allegation *n.* （无证据的）说法，指控

cease [siːs]	*v.* 停止，结束 例 I wish he would cease behaving in this argumentative manner during meetings. 我希望他能够停止这种在会议中好争辩的行事方式。 用 cease strike action immediately 立即停止罢工 同 stop *v.* 停止 反 continue *v.* 继续
fringe [frɪndʒ]	*n.* 穗，流苏；刘海儿；边缘 例 The school requires that pupils cannot have a long fringe, or strange hairstyle. 学校规定学生不能留长刘海儿或奇怪的发型。 用 on the northern fringe of the city 该市的北部边缘 同 edge *n.* 边缘 margin *n.* 边缘 brink *n.* 边缘 反 centre *n.* 中心
converge [kən'vɜːdʒ]	*v.* 汇聚；聚集 例 As they flow south and pass by the city the two rivers converge into one huge river. 当两条河流向南流动经过城市时，它们汇成了一条大河。 用 converge slowly 缓慢交汇 反 diverge *v.* 分开；分歧 扩 convergent *adj.* 会聚的；趋同的 convergent lines 相交的线条 convergent opinions 一致的观点 考 Reaching some gravelly coastline in the Arctic, upon which other arctic terns have converged, will serve its larger purpose as shaped by evolution: finding a place, a time, and a set of circumstances in which it can successfully hatch and rear offspring. 去到北极某个沙砾遍地的海岸，其他北极燕鸥都集结在了那里，这将让它达成那个由进化所塑造出来的更远大目标：找到某个地点、某个时间和一系列环境条件，它可以在其间成功地孵化和养育后代。
reflect [rɪ'flekt]	*v.* 反映；反射；反省 例 It's about time you sit down and reflect on your own behaviour. 对你而言，是时候坐下来反思一下自己的行为了。 用 reflect the bright afternoon sunlight 反射午后明媚的阳光 扩 reflection *n.* 反映；思考 考 reflect on their job prospects 反思他们的工作前景

origin [ˈɒrɪdʒɪn]	*n.* 起源；原点；开端
	例 Charles Darwin studied the origin of the human species and became famous for his works on evolutionary biology and the history of our planet.
	查尔斯·达尔文研究人类物种的起源，并因其在进化生物学和地球历史方面的著作而闻名。
	用 theories about the origin of life 有关生命起源的各种理论
	扩 original *adj.* 原始的；最初的 originality *n.* 独创性；原创
	考 But the origin of coconuts discovered along the west coast of America by 16th century sailors has been the subject of centuries of discussion.
	但是16世纪海员们在美国西海岸发现的椰子的起源成为几个世纪以来讨论的主题。
undermine [ˌʌndəˈmaɪn]	*v.* 破坏；逐渐削弱
	例 She always says things to contradict me and undermine my opinions.
	她总是说些反驳我的话，动摇我的观点。
	用 undermine her authority 毁掉她的权威
depletion [dɪˈpliːʃn]	*n.* 消耗；损耗
	例 Depletion of the ozone layer leaves the earth's surface increasingly exposed to harmful radiation from the sun.
	臭氧层的损耗使地球表面越来越多地暴露在来自太阳的有害辐射之下。
	用 ozone depletion 臭氧损耗 the depletion of fish stocks 鱼类资源损耗
mercury [ˈmɜːkjəri]	*n.* 汞，水银；水银柱
	例 The temperature dropped, and the mercury in the thermometer fell to record lows.
	温度下降了，温度计中的水银柱降到了历史最低点。
	用 the chemical symbol for mercury 汞的化学符号
	考 Mercury's one of the 120 or so elements that make up all matter, and it has the symbol Hg.
	汞是构成所有物质的120种元素之一，它的符号是Hg。
damp [dæmp]	*adj.* 潮湿的 *n.* 湿气，潮气；沼气 *v.* 使潮湿；减弱，抑制
	例 The rain left everything damp and cool, creating a refreshing atmosphere.
	雨水使一切都潮湿凉爽，营造出一种清新的气氛。
	用 damp clothes 潮湿的衣服
	a cold and damp cottage 一间又冷又湿的小屋

overcome [ˌəʊvəˈkʌm]	*v.* 克服；战胜
	例 She had been through a lot of difficulties, but had overcome them bravely. 她经历过许多困难，但都勇敢地克服了。
	用 overcome weakness, despair and fear 战胜软弱、绝望和恐惧 overcome difficulties 战胜困难
transcribe [trænˈskraɪb]	*v.* 抄录；把……转成（另一种书写形式）
	例 The translator was given the task of transcribing the text into pinyin first. 翻译人员的任务首先是把文本译成拼音。
	用 transcribe the conversation completely 将对话完全抄录下来
	扩 describe *v.* 描述；描写 prescribe *v.* 规定；开处方
	考 Individual systems can play chess or transcribe speech, but a general theory of machine intelligence still remains elusive. 单独的系统可以下棋或转换语音，但是仍然没有一套关于机器智能的宏观理论。
scale [skeɪl]	*n.* 规模；等级；刻度；比例 *v.* 攀登；改变……的大小
	例 The scale of the problem is now universally recognized. 这一问题的严重性已经被广泛认识到。
	用 underestimate the scale of the problem 低估问题的严重性 evaluate performance on a scale from 0 to 9 按0到9来评估表现
bullet [ˈbʊlɪt]	*n.* 子弹
	例 The detective found a bullet casing at the crime scene, a crucial piece of evidence. 侦探在犯罪现场发现了一个弹壳，这是一个至关重要的证据。
	用 bullet wounds 枪伤
appliance [əˈplaɪəns]	*n.* （家用）电器，器具
	例 The sale of electrical appliances this year has increased considerably. 今年电器的销售有了相当大的增长。
	用 household appliances 家用电器
credential [krəˈdenʃl]	*n.* 资格，证明；文凭，资格证书
	例 His impressive credentials earned him the job as a senior manager. 他令人印象深刻的资历为他赢得了高级经理的工作。
	用 provide him with credentials 向他提供证明

cue [kju:]	*v./n.* 暗示，提示 例 The director gave her a cue, and she delivered her lines with confidence. 导演给了她一个提示，她自信地说完了台词。 用 a cue for more champagne 意味着要喝更多香槟 同 hint *v./n.* 暗示，提示
permanent ['pɜːmənənt]	*adj.* 永久的，永恒的；不变的 例 After doing several part-time jobs during the summer, she was now ready to find something permanent. 在暑假期间做了几份兼职工作之后，她现在准备找一份固定工作。 用 a permanent job 一份固定工作
faculty ['fæklti]	*n.* 科，系，院；能力；全体教员 例 He studied Japanese and English language in the faculty of translation. 他在翻译学院学习了日语和英语。 用 the faculty of understanding complex issues 理解复杂问题的能力 a faculty meeting 全体教师会议 faculty members 全体教师
transient ['trænziənt]	*adj.* 短暂的；暂住的；临时的 例 The spring in his region was really lovely, but occasionally there were transient cold spells. 他所在地区的春天非常美丽，但偶尔也会有短暂的寒潮。 用 a city with a large transient population 有大量流动人口的城市 同 temporary *adj.* 临时的，暂时的 反 permanent *adj.* 永久的，永远的
stumble ['stʌmbl]	*v./n.* 蹒跚，踉跄 例 He stumbled on the roots of trees as he made his way through the dark woodland. 他在黑暗的树林中行走时，被树根绊了一下。 用 stumble over a rock 在石头上绊了一下 stumble across 偶然发现，无意中发现 考 He and his companions later entered the cave and stumbled across a collection of large clay jars, seven of which contained scrolls with writing on them. 他和伙伴们后来钻进了洞穴里，无意中发现了一堆大瓦罐，其中的七个里面装着写了字的卷轴。

elderly ['eldəli]	*adj.* 上年纪的，老年的 例 A lot of elderly people like to gather in local parks and engage in morning exercise, square dancing or playing chess and other games. 很多老年人喜欢聚集在当地的公园里，参与晨练、广场舞或者下棋等活动。 用 an elderly couple 一对老年夫妇　elderly relatives 年长的亲戚
campaign [kæm'peɪn]	*n.* 运动；活动；战役 例 The advertising campaign was elaborate and very costly. 这次广告宣传活动是精心策划的，并且花费巨大。 用 an anti-smoking campaign 一场反对吸烟的运动 a campaign against ageism in the workplace 一场反对在工作场所存在年龄歧视的运动 考 The campaign focused on New Zealand's scenic beauty, exhilarating outdoor activities and authentic Maori culture, and it made New Zealand one of the strongest national brands in the world. 这场宣传活动集中突出了新西兰的优美风景、各种激动人心的户外项目和原汁原味的毛利文化，它将新西兰塑造成了世界上最强有力的国家品牌之一。
formula ['fɔːmjələ]	*n.* 公式，方程式；方案 例 Many perfumes are made following a chemical formula that has been tested many times. 许多香水都是按照经过多次测试的化学公式制成的。 用 the formula for carbon monoxide 一氧化碳的分子式 扩 formulate *v.* 规划；用公式表示
intersection ['ɪntəsekʃn]	*n.* 交叉；十字路口 例 When the traffic lights broke, the policeman directed the traffic at the intersection. 当交通灯损坏时，警察在十字路口指挥交通。 用 a busy intersection 一个繁忙的道路交叉口
manifest ['mænɪfest]	*v.* 证明；表明，显示 例 He was concerned about her because she was manifesting signs of depression and frustration. 他很担心她，因为她表现出了抑郁和挫败的迹象。 用 manifest a pleasing personality on stage 在舞台上展现出令人喜爱的个性 同 demonstrate *v.* 证明；表明 考 manifest in different ways 以不同的方式呈现

depression
[dɪ'preʃn]

n. 沮丧；抑郁；萧条

例 After seeing a therapist for a a number of years she eventually recovered from her depression.
经过数年的治疗，她终于从抑郁中恢复过来。

用 suffer from severe depression 患严重抑郁症

扩 depress *v.* 使沮丧；使萧条

考 It's most commonly used to treat depression.
它最常用于治疗抑郁症。

slide
[slaɪd]

v./n. 滑动，滑行；降低，衰落

例 You can slide the front seats backwards if you need more legroom in the car.
如果在车里需要更多的腿部空间，你可以将前面的座位向后滑动。

用 slide into decline 出现衰落 slide towards bankruptcy 走向破产

sensation
[sen'seɪʃn]

n. 感觉；轰动；感动

例 Floating in zero gravity in space is said to be a very strange sensation.
据说在太空中失重漂浮是一种非常奇怪的感受。

用 a sensation of falling 一种坠落的感觉

扩 sensational *adj.* 轰动的；令人震惊的

考 Blind people report that so-called "facial vision" is comparable to the sensation of touch on the face.
盲人报告所谓的"面部视觉"类似于触摸脸部的感觉。

undertake
[ˌʌndə'teɪk]

v. 承担；从事；保证，承诺

例 He undertook a number of complicated tasks and spent much of his free time trying to improve the business.
他承担了许多复杂的任务，并花了大量空闲时间试图改善业务。

用 undertake a task 承担一项任务

考 Algorithms are capable of learning from data to undertake tasks that previously needed human judgement, such as reading legal contracts, analysing medical scans and gathering market intelligence.
算法有能力从数据中学习，从而承担先前需要人类判断力才能完成的各种任务，例如阅读法律合同、分析医疗扫描结果以及收集市场情报。

slab [slæb]	*n.* （石、木等硬质材料的）厚板
	例 The mason laid the concrete slab as a foundation for the building. 泥瓦匠铺设混凝土石板作为建筑物的基础。
	用 pave slabs 铺路石板 smooth stone slabs 平整的石板
	考 For reasons which remain unclear, Djoser's main official, whose name was Imhotep, conceived of building a taller, more impressive tomb for his king by stacking stone slabs on top of one another, progressively making them smaller, to form the shape now known as the Step Pyramid. 出于至今仍不明确的原因，左塞尔的股肱之臣，名叫Imhotep，想到了要为自己的君主建造一座更高、更令人一见不忘的墓葬：将石板一层层地堆叠起来，每层面积逐步缩小，所构成的形状就是现在为人们所知的阶梯金字塔。
convince [kən'vɪns]	*v.* 说服，使信服
	例 She would not change her opinion, even though he tried to convince her multiple times. 她不会改变自己的看法，尽管他多次尝试说服她。
	用 convince the public 让公众相信
physiology [ˌfɪzi'ɒlədʒi]	*n.* 生理学；生理机能
	例 The physiology of athletes is closely linked to their performance and achievements in the field. 运动员的生理机能与他们在运动场上的表现和成就密切相关。
	用 the department of anatomy and physiology 解剖生理学系

Exercise 01

一、中文释义练习

请选择单词正确的中文释义。

_____ 1. slab   A. 楼梯   _____ 11. undermine   A. 战胜
_____ 2. proficiency   B. 场景   _____ 12. mercury   B. 水银
_____ 3. staircase   C. 石板   _____ 13. overcome   C. 破坏
_____ 4. scenario   D. 灌溉   _____ 14. transcribe   D. 资格
_____ 5. irrigation   E. 熟练   _____ 15. credential   E. 转录

_____ 6. enlighten   A. 启发   _____ 16. permanent   A. 永久的
_____ 7. approach   B. 边缘   _____ 17. faculty   B. 全体教员
_____ 8. swift   C. 宣称   _____ 18. formula   C. 承担
_____ 9. fringe   D. 敏捷的   _____ 19. manifest   D. 公式
_____ 10. allege   E. 接近   _____ 20. undertake   E. 表明

二、英文释义练习

请选择单词正确的英文释义。

_____ 1. underline   A. to move or turn around a central fixed point
_____ 2. rooftop   B. a sudden feeling of fear that cannot be controlled
_____ 3. rotate   C. the outside part of the roof of a building
_____ 4. recover   D. to draw a line under a word or sentence
_____ 5. panic   E. to get well again after being ill or hurt

_____ 6. reflect   A. continuing for only a short time
_____ 7. appliance   B. to make sb. believe that sth. is true
_____ 8. transient   C. to throw back light, heat or sound from a surface
_____ 9. sensation   D. a feeling that you get when sth. affects your body
_____ 10. convince   E. a machine that can do a particular thing in the home

音频

aggravate ['ægrəveɪt]	*v.* 加重，加剧，恶化
	例 The way his sister dealt with the problem did not help at all, but only aggravated the already difficult situation. 他姐姐处理问题的方式没有任何帮助，只是加剧了已经很困难的情况。
	用 aggravate the conflict even further 使冲突加剧
	同 worsen *v.* 加剧，变坏
speculate ['spekjuleɪt]	*v.* 推测，猜测
	例 It's important to look at the scientific facts and not speculate too much based on random opinions found on social media. 重要的是要着眼于科学事实，而不是根据社交媒体上的随机观点进行过多推测。
	用 speculate about the reasons for her resignation 推测她辞职的原因
	扩 speculation *n.* 推断
persist [pə'sɪst]	*v.* 坚持；持续
	例 If symptoms persist then it is advised that you see your doctor again for more tests. 如果症状持续，建议你再去看一下医生，做更细致的检查。
	用 those who persist in their dreams 坚持梦想的人
	扩 persistence *n.* 坚持；持续
disperse [dɪ'spɜːs]	*v.* 分散；传播
	例 As the smoke began to disperse on the stage, the band came on. 当舞台上的烟开始散去时，乐队登场了。
	用 disperse quickly 很快散开
visual ['vɪʒuəl]	*adj.* 视觉的，视力的
	例 He was a huge fan of the visual arts, and particularly liked dance and live performances. 他是视觉艺术的超级粉丝，尤其喜欢舞蹈和现场演出。
	用 visual depiction of violence 对暴力的视觉描绘
	扩 visualise *v.* 使可见；想象

context ['kɒntekst]	*n.* 环境，背景；上下文，语境 例 It's important to learn about the historical context to understand events. 了解历史背景对理解事件是很重要的。 用 in the context of Britain in the 1960s 以20世纪60年代的英国为背景 扩 contextual *adj.* 上下文的 考 Thus, by strategically displaying more dominant laughter when the context allows, low-status individuals may achieve higher status in the eyes of others. 因此，当情景允许的时候，通过策略性地展示出更多支配性笑声，身份地位低的人就有可能在其他人的眼中营造出更高的身份地位感。
plough [plaʊ]	*v.* 犁（田）；耕（地）*n.* 犁 例 The fields had been ploughed with a state-of-the-art modern tractor, and were ready for planting. 田地已经用最先进的现代拖拉机犁过，可以进行播种了。 用 a carefully ploughed field 一片仔细犁过的田地
entrepreneur [ˌɒntrəprəˈnɜː]	*n.* 企业家；主办者 例 An entrepreneur is more than just a risk taker and a visionary business person. 企业家不仅仅是一个冒险者和一个有远见的商人。 用 entrepreneur spirit 企业家精神
consolation [ˌkɒnsəˈleɪʃn]	*n.* 安慰，慰藉 例 Her friends offered words of consolation and support during her time of grief. 在她悲伤的时候，她的朋友们纷纷表示安慰和支持。 用 a few words of consolation 几句安慰的话
alternative [ɔːlˈtɜːnətɪv]	*adj.* 可供替代的；另外的 *n.* 可供选择的事物 例 He felt he had no alternative but to confront her directly about the issue, in hope they could resolve it honestly. 他觉得自己别无选择，只能直接面对她，希望他们能有诚意地解决问题。 用 a vegetarian alternative on the menu 菜单上的素食者选择 扩 alternate *adj.* 轮流的，交替的 *v.* 轮流，交替 alternation *n.* 轮流，交替 考 alternative explorations 其他的探索方法

explicit
[ɪk'splɪsɪt]

adj. 明确的，清楚的

例 He was highly explicit in detailing the needs and requirements of the project.
他非常明确地详细描述了项目的需求和要求。

用 very explicit directions on how to get there
清楚地说明了去那儿的路线

反 implicit *adj.* 含蓄的；不清楚的

algebra
['ældʒɪbrə]

n. 代数；代数学

例 The algebra class focused on solving complex mathematical equations and expressions.
代数课的重点是解决复杂的数学方程和表达式。

用 difficult algebra questions 很难的代数题

ambiguity
[ˌæmbɪ'gjuːəti]

n. 含糊，不明确，模棱两可

例 The poem's ambiguity made it difficult for me to understand the author's viewpoint.
这首诗模棱两可，使我很难理解作者的立场。

用 avoid ambiguity 避免含糊不清

vacant
['veɪkənt]

adj. 空的；空缺的；空闲的

例 The business closed down and they moved everything out, leaving the space vacant.
业务关停，他们搬走了所有物品，让这里空无一物。

用 vacant properties 未被占用的房产

扩 vacancy *n.* 空白；空缺

tropic
['trɒpɪk]

n. (the ~s) 热带；回归线

例 The tropics located south of the equator are noted for heat and humidity almost the entire year round.
赤道以南的热带地区以几乎全年的炎热和潮湿而闻名。

用 protect tropic forests 保护热带雨林

扩 subtropics *n.* 亚热带 subtropical *adj.* 亚热带的

devote
[dɪ'vəut]

v. 致力于；奉献于

例 He was a great father and he devoted all his free time and energy into educating his daughter.
他是一位伟大的父亲，将所有的空闲时间和精力都投入到教育自己的女儿上。

用 devote herself to her career 全力倾注于她自己的事业

扩 devotion *n.* 奉献；贡献

deadline ['dedlaɪn]	*n.* 截止日期，最终期限
	例 The deadline was too tight and she worried she would not be able to meet it. 最后期限太紧张了，她担心自己无法完成。
	用 meet the deadline 赶上最后期限
	考 miss the deadline 错过截止日期
capital ['kæpɪtl]	*n.* 资金，资本；首都，省会；大写字母 *adj.* 首都的；大写的；可处死刑的
	例 We don't really have enough capital to invest in new premises or expand the office. 我们确实没有足够的资金来投资新的办公场地或扩大办公区。
	用 capital expenditure 资本投资 capital and labour 资方与劳方
	考 Travel and tourism is the largest industry in the world on virtually any economic measure including value-added capital investment, employment and tax contributions. 从包括增值资本投资、就业和税收贡献在内的任何经济指标来看，旅游和旅游业几乎都是全世界最大的产业。
consensus [kən'sensəs]	*n.* 一致，共识
	例 Eventually, after multiple meetings, all sides reached a consensus. 最终，经过多次会议，各方都达成了共识。
	用 a general consensus 普遍共识 an attempt to reach a consensus 一次达成共识的尝试
congestion [kən'dʒestʃən]	*n.* 拥挤；拥塞
	例 Traffic congestion is a major problem in my city, and leads to long commutes. 交通拥堵是我所在城市的一个主要问题，导致了长时间的通勤。
	用 traffic congestion and pollution 交通拥塞和污染
juvenile ['dʒuːvənaɪl]	*adj.* 青少年的 *n.* 青少年
	例 His early psychology research focused mainly on juvenile delinquency. 他早期的心理学研究主要集中于青少年犯罪。
	用 juvenile crime 青少年犯罪
	考 Upon their release, the juvenile tortoises quickly spread out over their ancestral territory, investigating their new surroundings and feeding on the vegetation. 一经释放，这些幼龟马上在它们祖先的土地上四散开去，四处探索它们的新环境，品尝植被食粮。

provision [prə'vɪʒn]	*n.* 提供；供给；规定；条款
	例 The government places a high priority on the provision of effective public services for the elderly. 政府优先为老人们提供有效的公共服务。
	用 housing provision 住房供应 the provision of specialist teachers 配备专业教师
	扩 provide *v.* 提供
motivate ['məʊtɪveɪt]	*v.* 刺激，使有动机，激发
	例 It's very hard to motivate some young children to study, especially if they are strong-willed, creative and energetic. 鼓励一些儿童学习非常困难，尤其是在他们想法坚定、喜欢创造且活力十足的时候。
	用 a highly motivated student 一名学习积极性很高的学生
	扩 motivation *n.* 动机，动力
veracity [və'ræsəti]	*n.* 真实，准确；诚实
	例 The witness's testimony was questioned due to doubts about the veracity of their statements. 由于怀疑证人陈述的真实性，他们的证词受到了质疑。
	用 the veracity of the story 故事的真实性
vanish ['vænɪʃ]	*v.* 消失
	例 As the ship sailed off into the mist we watched its stern vanish into the night. 随着船只驶入雾中，我们看着船尾消失在夜色中。
	用 the vanishing woodlands of Europe 即将消失的欧洲林地
	同 disappear *v.* 消失
	反 appear *v.* 出现
notion ['nəʊʃn]	*n.* 观念；想法，见解
	例 Nobody had the faintest notion what the abstract painting was about. 没有人知道这幅抽象画是关于什么的。
	用 a management system based on the notions of equality 建立在平等观念基础上的管理体系
	考 An alternative to this notion of genetic programming is to see the teacher-subjects' actions as a result of the social environment under which the experiment was carried out. 与这种基因说不同的观点是将那些扮演教师的试验对象的行为看作是进行试验的社会环境所造成的。

commodity [kə'mɒdəti]	*n.* 商品；货物；日用品
	例 Crude oil is probably one of the world's most important commodities. 原油或许是世界上最重要的商品之一。
	用 a drop in commodity prices 商品价格的下跌
	考 It was named the Silk Road after its most precious commodity, which was considered to be worth more than gold. 之所以叫做"丝绸之路"，正是以其最珍贵的商品而得名，它被视为比黄金更贵重。
instil [ɪn'stɪl]	*v.* 灌输，培养；滴注
	例 The teacher sought to instil a love for learning in her students through engaging lessons. 老师试图通过引人入胜的课程向学生灌输对学习的热爱。
	用 instil a winning attitude in the kids 给孩子们灌输胜利的心态
	考 The second group—those who had been instilled with a "growth mindset"—were subsequently far more likely to put effort into future tasks. 第二组——那些被灌输了"成长性思维"的孩子——接下来会明显更乐意去为未来各种任务投入精力。
collocation [ˌkɒlə'keɪʃn]	*n.* 搭配；组配；组合
	例 It's very important to improve your knowledge of common collocations in English. 提高对英语中常用搭配的认识是非常重要的。
	用 the basic notion of collocation 搭配的基本概念
creep [kriːp]	*v.* 爬行，匍匐；蔓延
	例 The hunter stealthily crept through the undergrowth as he approached the deer. 猎人蹑手蹑脚地穿过矮树丛，走近那只鹿。
	用 creep downstairs 小心地下楼
ecology [i'kɒlədʒi]	*n.* 生态；生态学
	例 Focussing on ecology should be a top priority for all countries today, if we are going to solve significant climate issues. 如果我们要解决重要的气候问题，关注生态应该是当今所有国家的首要任务。
	用 human ecology 人类生态学
	扩 ecological *adj.* 生态的

opulent ['ɒpjələnt]	*adj.* 豪华的；富有的；大量的
	例 The luxurious palace displayed opulent decorations and furnishings. 这座豪华的宫殿拥有华丽的装饰和陈设。
	用 add an opulent touch to a formal dinner party 给正式晚宴增加一种奢华感
adverse ['ædvɜːs]	*adj.* 不利的；相反的；敌对的
	例 She had an adverse reaction to the medicine so the doctor recommended another. 她对这种药有不良反应，所以医生推荐了另一种药。
	用 an adverse effect on our research programme 对我们研究方案的不利影响
	扩 adversity *n.* 逆境；不幸
emotion [ɪ'məʊʃn]	*n.* 情感；情绪
	例 He was filled with emotion after watching the moving film. 看了这部感人的电影后，他感慨良多。
	用 the split between reason and emotion 理智与情感分离
	扩 emotional *adj.* 情感的；有感染力的
	考 a particular technique for learning based on emotions 一种基于情感的特殊学习方式
excursion [ɪk'skɜːʃn]	*n.* 远足；旅行；游览；离题
	例 Team-building excursions are a great way for people in the same company to get to know each other, and learn to work together better. 团队建设远足是一个很好的方式，可以让公司内的人互相了解，并学习更好地一起工作。
	用 go on an excursion 去旅行
sympathy ['sɪmpəθi]	*n.* 同情；赞同
	例 I don't have much sympathy for people who are always complaining all the time about problems that they cannot solve. 我不会太同情那些总是抱怨自己无法解决问题的人。
	用 be in sympathy with 支持；与……意见一致 express sympathy for sb. 表达对某人的同情
	扩 sympathetic *adj.* 同情的；有同情心的
	考 The person who deserves most sympathy is the French astronomer Guillaume Le Gentil. 最值得同情的人是法国天文学家Guillaume Le Gentil。

upgrade
[ˌʌpˈgreɪd] v.
[ˈʌpgreɪd] n.

v. 升级；改善；上升 *n.* 升级；提升

例 It's important to upgrade your phone every few years or it starts to get slow and full of bugs.
每隔几年升级一下你的手机是很重要的，否则它就会变得反应慢，总是出问题。

用 upgrade the town's leisure facilities 改善镇里的休闲设施
upgrade the status of teachers 提升老师的地位

---

symphony
[ˈsɪmfəni]

n. 交响乐；和声

例 I love listening to classic music, especially long, epic symphonies.
我喜欢听古典音乐，尤其是长篇史诗般的交响乐。

用 Beethoven's Fifth Symphony 贝多芬的第五交响曲

考 She usually plays with symphony orchestras, and apparently this is her first time with a jazz band.
她通常在交响乐团演出，显然这是她第一次在爵士乐队演出。

---

adolescent
[ˌædəˈlesnt]

adj. 青春期的；青少年的 *n.* 青少年

例 Some say that the adolescent period of one's life is the most challenging, but fun.
有人说，人生的青春时期是最具挑战但也最有趣的时期。

用 adolescent experiences 青春期的经历

扩 adolescence *n.* 青年期；青春期

---

stripe
[straɪp]

n. 条纹，线条；类型

例 The zebra's black and white stripes are said to confuse predators in the wilderness.
据说斑马的黑白条纹可以在荒野中迷惑捕食者。

用 entrepreneurs of all stripes 各类企业家

考 Its most distinguishing feature was the 13–19 dark brown stripes over its back, beginning at the rear of the body and extending onto the tail.
它最显著的特征是背部有13到19条黑棕色条纹，从身体的背部一直延伸到尾巴。

---

cosmetic
[kɒzˈmetɪk]

adj. 美容的；装点门面的 *n.* 化妆品；装饰品

例 The national health service cannot provide cosmetic surgery services.
国民保健服务不能提供整容手术服务。

用 the cosmetics industry 化妆品行业
a cosmetic company 一家化妆品公司

clay
[kleɪ]

n. 黏土，陶土

例 The potter molded the clay into a beautiful vase, shaping it with skilled hands.
陶工用熟练的双手把黏土捏成了一个漂亮的花瓶。

用 a large piece of clay 一大块陶土

考 He did dozens of studies in clay for the sculpture, and these were cast in bronze and issued in editions of seven to nine copies each.
他为这组雕像做了几十次黏土研究，这些（雕像）都是用青铜铸成的，每个版本有7到9个副本。

current
['kʌrənt]

adj. 现在的；最近的；流通的 *n.* 水流；电流；趋势

例 The current climate for those interested in getting into engineering is a very positive one.
对于那些对工程学感兴趣的人而言，当前的形势是非常积极的。

用 a budget for the current year 今年的预算 electrical current 电流

扩 currency *n.* 货币；流行

考 the current unprecedented global warming
如今空前的全球变暖现象

element
['elɪmənt]

n. 元素；成分；自然环境

例 Customer relations is an important element of marketing job in the company.
客户关系是公司营销工作的重要元素。

用 a key element in our decision 我们决策时考虑的主要因素

考 He wants to preserve an element of uncertainty in his music, making our brains beg for the one chord he refuses to give us.
他想在音乐中保留不确定的元素，使我们的大脑渴望那些他没有使用的和弦。

anecdote
['ænɪkdəʊt]

n. 轶事，奇闻，秘史

例 He began his presentation by telling a personal anecdote from his experiences overseas.
他用讲述自己海外经历中一件个人轶事的方式开始了自己的演说。

用 amusing anecdotes about his brief career as an actor
关于他短暂演员生涯的趣闻逸事

tilt
[tɪlt]

v./n. 倾斜；倾侧

例 It was quite fashionable in the 1940s for women to wear their hats at a tilt.
在20世纪40年代，妇女歪戴着帽子是很时髦的。

用 the abrupt tilt of the hill 山势的陡峭

genuine ['dʒenjuɪn]	*adj.* 真实的，真正的；真诚的
	例 He made genuine and sincere attempts to resolve the dispute. 他为解决争议作出了真挚而充满诚意的尝试。
	用 genuine concern for others 对他人真诚的关心
	同 authentic *adj.* 真实的；真正的
duplicate ['dju:plɪkeɪt] *v.* ['dju:plɪkət] *adj.&n.*	*v.* 复制；重复 *n.* 副本；复制品 *adj.* 复制的；二重的
	例 He made a duplicate of the document so that he could keep one copy for himself, and give the other to HR. 他复印了文档，以便自己保留一份，另一份交给人力资源部。
	用 a duplicated form 一份复制的表格
	扩 duplication *n.* 重复；复制
intimate ['ɪntɪmət]	*adj.* 亲密的；私人的 *n.* 知己；至交
	例 I only discuss private and personal issues with my intimate friends. 我只和自己亲密的朋友讨论私人问题。
	用 on intimate terms 关系紧密
subsequent ['sʌbsɪkwənt]	*adj.* 随后的；后来的
	例 The family skills in the trade were passed on to subsequent generations. 家族的贸易技能一代一代传了下来。
	用 subsequent events 后来发生的事 subsequent experiments 随后的实验

Exercise 02

一、中文释义练习

请选择单词正确的中文释义。

_____	1.	persist	A. 另外的
_____	2.	visual	B. 坚持
_____	3.	plough	C. 视觉的
_____	4.	alternative	D. 代数
_____	5.	algebra	E. 犁

_____	11.	collocation	A. 青春期的
_____	12.	creep	B. 陶土
_____	13.	emotion	C. 情感
_____	14.	adolescent	D. 爬行
_____	15.	clay	E. 搭配

_____	6.	vacant	A. 空的
_____	7.	consensus	B. 一致
_____	8.	juvenile	C. 青少年的
_____	9.	motivate	D. 准确
_____	10.	veracity	E. 刺激

_____	16.	element	A. 元素
_____	17.	cosmetic	B. 倾斜
_____	18.	tilt	C. 美容的
_____	19.	intimate	D. 亲密的
_____	20.	subsequent	E. 后来的

二、英文释义练习

请选择单词正确的英文释义。

_____	1.	speculate	A. to form an opinion without knowing all the facts
_____	2.	disperse	B. a person or thing that makes you feel better
_____	3.	consolation	C. to move apart and go away in different directions
_____	4.	deadline	D. a point in time by which sth. must be done
_____	5.	congestion	E. the state of being crowded and full of traffic

_____	6.	vanish	A. made or decorated using expensive materials
_____	7.	commodity	B. a product or a raw material that can be bought
_____	8.	opulent	C. the feeling of being sorry for sb.
_____	9.	sympathy	D. to make an exact copy of sth.
_____	10.	duplicate	E. to disappear suddenly in a way that you cannot explain

音频

moisture [ˈmɔɪstʃə(r)]	*n.* 潮湿；湿度；水分 例 The plants thrived in the garden thanks to the rich soil and ample moisture. 由于土壤肥沃，水分充足，花园里的植物长得很茂盛。 用 the skin's natural moisture 皮肤的天然水分 考 Wood expands as it absorbs moisture from the air and is susceptible to pests. 木材在吸收空气中的水分时会膨胀，容易受到害虫的侵害。
advent [ˈædvent]	*n.* 出现，到来 例 The advent of the Internet revolutionized the way people communicate and access information. 互联网的出现彻底改变了人们交流和获取信息的方式。 用 the advent of new technology 新技术的出现
offspring [ˈɒfsprɪŋ]	*n.* 后代，子孙；产物 例 The female of this particular species of duck usually gives birth to at least ten offspring. 这种特殊物种的雌性鸭子通常会孕育至少十个后代。 用 the problems parents have with their teenage offspring 父母与青少年子女之间的问题
astray [əˈstreɪ]	*adv.* 离开正确的路（或方向），迷路 例 The lost hiker realized he had wandered astray from the marked trail. 迷路的徒步旅行者意识到他偏离了标记的路线。 用 lead him astray 把他引入歧途
chew [tʃuː]	*v./n.* 咀嚼 例 You don't chew your food enough and that's why you get indigestion. 你没把食物嚼烂，这就是你消化不良的原因。 用 chew gum 嚼口香糖

diesel ['diːzl]	*n.* 柴油；内燃机，柴油车
	例 The truck ran on a powerful diesel engine, providing the necessary power for heavy-duty tasks. 这辆卡车由一台强大的柴油发动机驱动，为重型任务提供必要的动力。
	用 diesel cars 柴油汽车
pastime ['pɑːstaɪm]	*n.* 娱乐，消遣
	例 It's important that people have hobbies, interests and pastimes. 人们有爱好、兴趣和娱乐活动是很重要的。
	用 his favourite pastime 他最喜欢的消遣
release [rɪ'liːs]	*v.* 释放；公开；发表 *n.* 释放；发布，发行
	例 There was great anticipation before the release of the new model of smartphone. 在新型号的智能手机上市销售前，人们有很大的期待。
	用 release a prisoner 释放囚犯 release further details about the accident 透露事故的更多细节 new products released onto the market 投放到市场的新产品
	考 release aerosol sprays into the stratosphere 将喷雾剂释放到平流层
loop [luːp]	*n.* 环状物；回路；环线
	例 The trail formed a loop, allowing hikers to return to the starting point without retracing their steps. 这条小路形成了一个环线，使徒步旅行者可以回到起点，而不用折返行走。
	用 tie a loop of rope around his arm 在他的手臂上用绳子系一个圈
passive ['pæsɪv]	*adj.* 被动的；消极的
	例 He is quite passive in meetings and doesn't give his opinions openly. 他在会议上很被动，从不公开发表意见。
	用 passive acceptance 被动接受
	反 active *adj.* 主动的；活跃的
	扩 passively *adv.* 被动地；消极地
precedent ['presɪdənt]	*n.* 先例，前例
	例 The judge's strict ruling and sentence set a precedent for similar, future cases. 法官的严厉裁定和判决为今后类似的案件开创了先例。
	用 set an important precedent for dealing with similar cases 为处理类似案件开创重要先例

resilience [rɪˈzɪliəns]	*n.* 恢复力，复原力；弹性
	例 Despite facing numerous challenges, her resilience helped her bounce back stronger than ever. 尽管面临许多挑战，但她的韧性使得她比以往任何时候都更坚强。
	用 the misconception of resilience 对复原力的误解
	扩 resilient *adj.* 有承受力的，有复原力的
	考 They help control problem insects and increase the health and resilience of the forest. 它们有助于控制问题昆虫以及增加森林的健康度和复原能力。
diagnose [ˈdaɪəgnəʊz]	*v.* 诊断；判断
	例 The test is designed to diagnose a range of similar diseases. 该测试旨在诊断一系列类似的疾病。
	用 be used to diagnose a variety of diseases 被用于诊断多种疾病
	扩 diagnosis *n.* 诊断；判断
	考 It is probable that many undiagnosed children exist in the education system with "invisible" disabilities. 也许有很多未确诊的孩子带着"未知"的残疾接受教育。
receptive [rɪˈseptɪv]	*adj.* 接受的；容纳的
	例 He gave an impressive speech, and the audience was very receptive. 他发表了一次令人印象深刻的演讲，听众很接受他讲的内容。
	用 always receptive to new ideas 总是愿意接受新观点
	扩 receive *v.* 接收；收到 reception *n.* 接待；接待处
ideal [aɪˈdiːəl]	*adj.* 理想的；完美的 *n.* 理想；典范
	例 Her manager was impressed when she came up with an ideal solution to the problem. 当她想出一个解决问题的理想方案时，受到了经理的关注。
	用 the ideal candidate for the job 这项工作的理想人选
	扩 idealism *n.* 理想主义
	考 focus more on interpersonal and moral ideals such as justice and impartiality 更加关注人际和道德规范，例如公正和公平
rely [rɪˈlaɪ]	*v.* 依靠；信赖
	例 She was not very independent and often relied on help from her parents. 她不是很独立，经常依赖于父母的帮助。
	用 rely on 依赖于

proper ['prɒpə(r)]	*adj.* 合适的，适当的
	例 When learning to write in Chinese it's important to learn the proper order of the strokes. 学习写汉字时，学会正确的笔画顺序是很重要的。
	用 follow the proper procedures for dealing with complaints 按正当手续处理投诉
	同 appropriate *adj.* 合适的
	反 improper *adj.* 不合适的
lateral ['lætərəl]	*adj.* 侧面的，横向的
	例 You have to train yourself in lateral thinking to solve the kinds of puzzles in that reasoning test. 你必须训练自己的横向思维来解出推理测试中的各种题目。
	用 lateral movement of the bridge 大桥的横向移动
impart [ɪm'pɑːrt]	*v.* 传授，告知；赋予，给予
	例 The wise teacher sought to impart valuable life lessons to her students. 这位明智的老师设法向学生传授宝贵的人生经验。
	用 impart an Eastern flavour to the dish 给菜肴添加一种东方风味
	考 Research suggests that when adopting a first-person viewpoint we focus on "the focal features of the environment" and when we adopt a third-person, "observer" viewpoint we reason more broadly and focus more on interpersonal and moral ideals such as justice and impartiality. 研究显示，当采用第一人称视角的时候，我们会专注于"此场景的焦点特征"；而当我们采取了一种第三人称的"观察者"视角时，我们会进行更广角的分析，会更多关注人际和道德规范，例如公正和公平。
sanitary ['sænətri]	*adj.* 卫生的，清洁的
	例 The sanitary conditions in the new hospital are fantastic. 新建医院的卫生条件非常好。
	用 sanitary facilities 卫生设施
	考 Those who could afford to live in more pleasant surroundings moved out, and the area became one where the vast majority of people lived in extreme poverty, and suffered from appalling sanitary conditions. 那些能够负担起更好环境的人们搬走了，剩下的绝大多数人生活得极其贫困，并且忍受着极其恶劣的卫生条件。

fossil ['fɒsl]	*n.* 化石；老顽固，思想僵化的人 例 Some fossils are over a billion years old and are found in the rocks of cliffs by the seaside. 有些化石已经存在了超过10亿年，在海边悬崖的岩石中被发现。 用 fossil fuels 矿物燃料
academic [ˌækə'demɪk]	*adj.* 学术的；理论的；学院的 例 The course is aimed at improving academic English for postgraduate study. 这门课程旨在提高研究生的学术英语水平。 用 academic qualifications 学术资历 a purely academic question 一个纯理论问题 an academic career 学术生涯 扩 academy *n.* 学会；学院
texture ['tekstʃə(r)]	*n.* 质地，纹理 例 The fabric had a soft and smooth texture, pleasing to the touch. 这种织物质地柔软光滑，摸起来很舒服。 用 the soft texture of velvet 天鹅绒柔软的质地
era ['ɪərə]	*n.* 时代，年代，纪元 例 The Renaissance era brought forth a remarkable flourishing of art, culture, and scientific advancements. 文艺复兴时期带来了艺术、文化和科学发展的显著繁荣。 用 the end of an era 一个时代的结束 考 Although the Renaissance is renowned as an era of incredible progress in art and architecture, it is rarely noted that the 15th century also marked the birth of urbanism as a true academic discipline. 虽然文艺复兴时期最为著名的是艺术和建筑领域令人惊叹的诸多进步，但很少有人注意到，15世纪同时也标志着城市研究作为一门真正的学术科目的诞生。
reliable [rɪ'laɪəbl]	*adj.* 可靠的；可信赖的 例 I just want a good, reliable car, nothing flashy or too expensive. 我只想要一辆不错的、可靠的车，不需要太花哨或者太贵。 用 a reliable friend 一个可信赖的朋友 a reliable witness 一位可信的目击证人 考 It is a more reliable source of energy than wind power. 这是一种比风能更为可靠的能源。

shrewd [ʃruːd]	*adj.* 精明的，机敏的
	例 The shrewd businessman always made wise investment decisions. 精明的商人总是做出明智的投资决策。
	用 a shrewd judge of character 看人看得很准
	同 subtle *adj.* 机智的；敏锐的
grand [grænd]	*adj.* 壮丽的；宏伟的
	例 The grand mansion stood imposingly on top of the hill just outside the town. 那座宏伟的大厦雄伟地矗立在城外的山顶上。
	用 a grand strategy 一项宏伟战略
	同 magnificent *adj.* 壮丽的；宏伟的
administration [ədˌmɪnɪˈstreɪʃn]	*n.* 管理；行政；实施；行政机构
	例 Human Resources is a key department in the administration of a big company, and deals with recruitment and employee management. 人力资源是大公司行政管理的关键部门，负责招聘和员工管理。
	用 administration costs 行政费用
	扩 administrate *v.* 管理；支配 administrator *n.* 管理者
drawback [ˈdrɔːbæk]	*n.* 缺点，不利条件
	例 The main drawback of mobile phones is that they are very addictive for young people. 手机的主要缺点是很容易让年轻人上瘾。
	用 a major drawback of the new system 新系统的一大弊端
	同 disadvantage *n.* 缺点
complicate [ˈkɒmplɪkeɪt]	*v.* 使复杂化
	例 He always got flustered in stressful situations and then complicated things unnecessarily. 他在紧张的情境中总是很慌乱，并毫无必要地把事情复杂化。
	用 complicate the situation 使情况复杂化
	扩 complicated *adj.* 复杂的；混乱的
sphere [sfɪə(r)]	*n.* 范围，领域；球体，球形
	例 The earth is not a perfect sphere but is slightly oval-shaped. 地球不是一个完美的球体，实际上它略微呈现椭圆形。
	用 the sphere of international politics 国际政治领域
	扩 atmosphere *n.* 大气层 hemisphere *n.* 半球

surplus ['sɜːpləs]	*n.* 剩余；盈余；贸易顺差 *adj.* 剩余的；过剩的
	例 It was an especially good harvest this year and there was a huge surplus of grain by the end of the season. 今年是收成特别好的一年，到季末都有大量粮食富余。
	用 be in surplus 出现过剩 a surplus of teachers 教师过剩
	反 deficit *n.* 赤字；亏损 shortage *n.* 短缺
trap [træp]	*n.* 陷阱；圈套；困境 *v.* 设陷阱；使陷入圈套
	例 The skilled hunter set a trap in the forest to catch the elusive animal. 熟练的猎人在森林里设了一个陷阱来捕捉那只难以发现的动物。
	用 a fox with its leg in a trap 一只被夹子夹住腿的狐狸
	考 The device has a very simple filter to trap particles, and this can easily be shaken to remove them. 该设备有一个非常简单的过滤器用来过滤颗粒物，通过晃动过滤器就可以轻松去除颗粒物。
gravity ['grævəti]	*n.* 重力，地心引力；严重性
	例 The section of the rocket will apparently be pulled down to earth by gravity and land in the middle of the Atlantic Ocean. 显然火箭的这一部分会被重力拉回地球，并在大西洋中部着陆。
	用 Newton's law of universal gravity 牛顿万有引力定律
	同 seriousness *n.* 严重性
	扩 grave *adj.* 严重的，重大的 aggravate *v.* 使恶化，使变严重
cube [kjuːb]	*n.* 立方体；立方
	例 The package contained a perfect cube of colourful building blocks. 包裹里装着一个完美的彩色积木立方体。
	用 cold water with ice cubes in it 加冰块的冷水
	考 This glass has five times the strength of standard glass, and when it does break it shatters into tiny cubes rather than large, razor-sharp shards. 这种玻璃的强度是普通玻璃的五倍，破碎时裂成细小颗粒而不是锋利的大块碎片。
conscience ['kɒnʃəns]	*n.* 道德心，良心
	例 He had a guilty conscience about having cheated in the examination. 他因为在考试中作弊而感到内心愧疚。
	用 trouble his conscience 使他良心不安

deduce [dɪˈdjuːs]	*v.* 推论，推断；演绎出
	例 We can deduce from these figures that the business is declining this season. 我们可以从这些数字中推测这个季度业务会下滑。
	用 deduce a lot from what people choose to buy 从人们选购的东西作出多方面推断
	同 infer *v.* 推论，推断
comprehend [ˌkɒmprɪˈhend]	*v.* 理解，领悟
	例 I find it difficult to comprehend the difficult formulas and equations in physics. 我发现理解物理学里那些很难的公式和方程是非常困难的。
	用 unable to comprehend 无法理解
	扩 comprehension *n.* 理解，包含 comprehensive *adj.* 综合的，广泛的
	考 make AI's decision-making process easier to comprehend 让人工智能的决策过程更容易理解
retreat [rɪˈtriːt]	*v.* 撤退；后退；隐退 *n.* 撤退；后退；僻静处；静修
	例 The peaceful retreat offered meditation and relaxation sessions all the year round. 这个宁静的静修处一年四季都提供冥想和放松课程。
	用 retreat from the room 从房间里退出来
ballet [ˈbæleɪ]	*n.* 芭蕾舞剧；芭蕾舞
	例 She dreamed of becoming a prima ballerina in a prestigious ballet company. 她梦想成为一家著名芭蕾舞团的首席芭蕾舞演员。
	用 ballet shoes 芭蕾舞鞋
monster [ˈmɒnstə(r)]	*n.* 怪兽，怪物 *adj.* 庞大的，巨大的
	例 In mythology, the dragon is often portrayed as a fearsome monster. 在神话中，龙经常被描绘成可怕的怪物。
	用 a monster with three heads 一个三头怪兽 prehistoric monsters 史前怪物
erupt [ɪˈrʌpt]	*v.* 爆发；喷发
	例 The volcano in The Canary Islands erupted last week, but caused no harm. 加那利群岛的这座火山上周喷发了，但没有造成伤害。
	用 erupt from the crater 从火山口喷出
	扩 eruption *n.* 爆发；喷出

surround [sə'raʊnd]	*v.* 围绕；包围 例 He hated being surrounded by lots of other people when he was shopping or in a busy place. 当他在购物或者在人多的地方时，他讨厌被很多人围绕着。 用 tall trees surrounding the lake 环湖的大树 扩 surrounding *adj.* 周围的；附近的
poll [pəʊl]	*n.* 投票；民意测验 *v.* 对……进行民意测验；获得（票数） 例 The poll showed that 80% of the population supported the policy proposal. 民意调查显示80%的人支持这项政策建议。 用 carry out a poll 进行民意测验 be ahead in the poll 票数领先 同 survey *n.* 调查 ballot *n.* 投票表决
frequent ['friːkwənt]	*adj.* 频繁的；时常发生的 例 He made frequent visits to his grandmother in hospital when she was sick. 当他的祖母生病时，他经常去医院看望她。 用 frequent visitors to this country 经常来到该国的访客 扩 frequency *n.* 频繁；频率 frequently *adv.* 频繁地
conversely ['kɒnvɜːsli]	*adv.* 相反地 例 We are not going to have enough onions to last the year, while potatoes, conversely, are in a major surplus. 我们将没有足够的洋葱维持一年，相反，土豆会有很大的富余。 用 or conversely 或者相反地 扩 converse *adj.* 相反的
forecast ['fɔːkɑːst]	*v./n.* 预测，预报 例 The weather is forecast to be dull and wet for the next fortnight, so they will probably delay their hiking trip. 天气预报说未来两周的天气将阴冷潮湿，所以他们可能会推迟徒步旅行。 用 sales forecasts 销售预测 同 predict *v.* 预测 foresee *v.* 预测
genius ['dʒiːniəs]	*n.* 天才；天赋 例 Einstein was most certainly a genius—his discoveries have formed the basis of most physics that we study in schools today. 爱因斯坦无疑是一个天才，他的发现构成了我们如今在学校学习的大多数物理学的基础。 用 a mathematical genius 一个数学天才

initial [ɪˈnɪʃl]	*adj.* 最初的，开始的；（字母）位于词首的
	例 His initial attempts at the game were weak, but he quickly improved with practice. 他最初在比赛中表现不佳，但通过练习很快获得了进步。
	用 in the initial stages 在最初阶段 my initial reaction 我的最初反应
	扩 initially *adv.* 开始，最初 initiate *v.* 开始；发起 initiative *n.* 措施，倡议；主动性
atom [ˈætəm]	*n.* 原子
	例 Two atoms of hydrogen combine with one atom of oxygen to form a molecule of water. 两个氢原子和一个氧原子结合组成一个水分子。
	用 the splitting of the atom 原子的分裂 two atoms of hydrogen 两个氢原子
	扩 atomic *adj.* 原子的
	类 molecule *n.* 分子 neutron *n.* 中子 particle *n.* 微粒，颗粒；粒子 proton *n.* 质子

Exercise \03

一、中文释义练习

请选择单词正确的中文释义。

_____ 1.	moisture	A. 娱乐	_____ 11.	surplus	A. 芭蕾舞
_____ 2.	offspring	B. 释放	_____ 12.	trap	B. 剩余
_____ 3.	diesel	C. 后代	_____ 13.	conscience	C. 良心
_____ 4.	pastime	D. 潮湿	_____ 14.	cube	D. 陷阱
_____ 5.	release	E. 柴油	_____ 15.	ballet	E. 立方体
_____ 6.	resilience	A. 质地	_____ 16.	initial	A. 最初的
_____ 7.	fossil	B. 恢复力	_____ 17.	atom	B. 围绕
_____ 8.	texture	C. 壮丽的	_____ 18.	erupt	C. 相反地
_____ 9.	grand	D. 化石	_____ 19.	surround	D. 爆发
_____ 10.	reliable	E. 可靠的	_____ 20.	conversely	E. 原子

二、英文释义练习

请选择单词正确的英文释义。

_____ 1.	loop	A. a similar action or event that happened earlier
_____ 2.	diagnose	B. a shape like a curve or circle made by a line
_____ 3.	precedent	C. to say exactly what an illness is
_____ 4.	impart	D. to pass information or knowledge to other people
_____ 5.	complicate	E. to make sth. more difficult to understand or deal with
_____ 6.	gravity	A. to form an opinion based on the evidence available
_____ 7.	deduce	B. to move away from a place or an enemy
_____ 8.	retreat	C. a statement about what will happen in the future
_____ 9.	forecast	D. the force attracts objects in space towards each other
_____ 10.	frequent	E. happening or doing sth. often

interplay
['ɪntəpleɪ]

n. 相互影响，相互作用

例 Our personalities develop through a complex interplay of genetic and environmental factors.
我们的个性是在遗传和环境因素复杂的相互作用下形成的。

用 the subtle interplay of colours 色彩的相互掩映

考 the interplay of nature and nurture in determining our personalities, behavior, and vulnerability to disease
先天和后天在决定我们性格、行为和对疾病易感性方面的相互作用

lavatory
['lævətri]

n. 盥洗室，厕所

例 He knows that the nearest public lavatory is at the station.
他知道最近的公共厕所在车站。

用 a bathroom and a lavatory upstairs 楼上的浴室和卫生间

stable
['steɪbl]

adj. 稳定的；牢固的；持久的

例 Some people believe that working in a big, established company is more stable than in a smaller one.
有些人认为在规模大的知名公司工作比在小公司工作稳定。

用 stable prices 稳定的价格

同 steady *adj.* 稳定的

扩 stability *n.* 稳定；稳定性

breed
[briːd]

v. 繁殖；养育，培养 *n.* 品种；类型

例 They decided to adopt a rescue dog rather than buy a specific breed from a breeder.
他们决定收养一只救援犬，而不是从饲养员那里购买特定的品种。

用 a new breed of entrepreneurs 新型的企业家

drift
[drɪft]

n. 漂流，漂移；流动；趋势 *v.* 漂流，漂移；漂泊

例 The boat raised its anchor and started to drift with the tide.
船起了锚，开始随着潮汐漂流。

用 a population drift away from rural areas 农村地区的人口外流

acrobat ['ækrəbæt]	*n.* 杂技演员
	例 The skilled acrobat amazed the audience with breathtaking stunts. 熟练的杂技演员以令人惊叹的特技使观众兴奋不已。
	用 an acrobat in a circus 马戏团的一名杂技演员
lens [lenz]	*n.* 镜头；透镜，镜片
	例 The photographer adjusted the camera lens to capture the perfect shot. 摄影师调整了镜头以捕捉完美的画面。
	用 camera with an adjustable lens 带有可调节镜头的照相机
parcel ['pɑːsl]	*n.* 包裹；一批；一块土地 *v.* 包起来，打包
	例 Her admirer delivered the small parcel and quietly left it in the reception room. 她的仰慕者送来了小包裹，悄悄地把它放在会客厅里。
	用 a parcel and some letters for you 你的一个包裹和几封信
sensor ['sensə(r)]	*n.* 传感器
	例 Cars almost all have sensors today so that the vehicle can warn you if you are too close to another car or an obstacle while parking. 如今，几乎所有的汽车都装有传感器，停车时，如果你离另一辆汽车或障碍物太近，汽车就会发出警告。
	用 light sensor 光传感器 temperature sensor 温度传感器
susceptible [sə'septəbl]	*adj.* 易受影响的；易感动的
	例 Older people are more susceptible to infections than younger people. 老年人比年轻人更容易被感染。
	用 the most susceptible to advertisements 最容易受广告影响
sanction ['sæŋkʃn]	*v./n.* 制裁，处罚；许可，批准
	例 The government imposed economic sanctions to pressure the neighbouring country. 政府实施经济制裁以向邻国施压。
	用 trade sanctions 贸易制裁
praise [preɪz]	*v./n.* 赞扬，称赞
	例 It is important to give children praise for good work, so they remain motivated. 对孩子好的表现给予表扬是很重要的，这样他们可以保持积极性。
	用 full of praise for his progress 对他的进步进行夸赞

dissertation [ˌdɪsəˈteɪʃn]	*n.* 专题论文，学位论文
	例 She dedicated months to research and writing to complete her doctoral dissertation. 为了完成博士论文，她花了几个月的时间进行研究和写作。
	用 write a dissertation 写一篇论文
	考 If I choose that option, I don't have to do a dissertation module. 如果我选择了那个选项，我就不必做论文模块了。
plank [plæŋk]	*n.* 木板；政策准则
	例 The circus performer balanced skillfully on the wooden plank, showcasing his agility. 马戏演员熟练地在木板上保持平衡，展示了他的敏捷。
	用 a wooden plank 一条木板
	考 More recent archaeological hypotheses have them transporting the bluestones with supersized wicker baskets on a combination of ball bearings and long grooved planks, hauled by oxen. 更近期的考古学假设是：他们用超大号的藤条篮子盛放这些蓝灰砂岩，放在由球型轴承和有凹槽的长木板组合成的运输工具上，用牛群拖拽。
equivalent [ɪˈkwɪvələnt]	*adj.* 相等的；等价的 *n.* 等价物
	例 She was a fantastic cook, and her dishes were equivalent in quality to those in some of the best restaurants. 她是一位出色的厨师，她做的菜的质量与一些最好餐馆里菜的质量相当。
	用 be equivalent to 相当于，等同于
	扩 equivalence *n.* 均等；相等
	考 According to its proponents, geo-engineering is the equivalent of a backup generator. 对于其支持者而言，地质工程就相当于一个备用的发电机。
particle [ˈpɑːtɪkl]	*n.* 微粒；粒子
	例 There was not a particle of evidence to support his viewpoint. 没有一点证据支持他的观点。
	用 a particle of hot metal 热金属微粒
	考 The reader must remain a tantalized spectator rather than an involved participant, since the appropriate language for describing the details in much of science is mathematics, whether the subject is expanding universe, subatomic particles, or chromosomes. 读者只好全程做一个跃跃欲试而不得的旁观者，而不是加入其中的参与者，因为描述大部分科学领域中细节内容的恰当语言是数学语言，无论话题是膨胀宇宙、亚原子粒子，还是染色体。

statistics [stə'tɪstɪks]	*n.* 统计；统计学；统计数字 例 The statistics come from a recent study by Oxford University research team. 这些数据来自牛津大学研究团队最近的一项研究。 用 official statistics 官方统计数字
interpersonal [ˌɪntə'pɜːsənl]	*adj.* 人际的；人际关系的 例 Interpersonal relationships across cultures are key to developing sound global skills in today's world. 在当今世界，跨文化的人际交往能力是培养全球化技能的关键。 用 interpersonal skills 人际交往技巧
valid [valid]	*adj.* 有效的；有根据的；合法的 例 Your passport must be valid for at least six months to apply for a visa. 你的护照必须有至少六个月的有效期才能申请签证。 用 valid passport 有效的护照 反 invalid *adj.* 无效的 扩 validity *n.* 有效性，效度
hull [hʌl]	*n.* 船体；外壳 例 The hull of the ship had been severely damaged by the accident. 这艘船的船体在这次事故中被严重损坏。 用 wooden hull 木质船体 steel hull 钢质船体
chaos ['keɪɒs]	*n.* 混沌；混乱 例 Without strict regulations and rules schools would fall into total chaos. 没有严格的规章制度，学校就会陷入一片混乱。 用 economic chaos 经济混乱
embody [ɪm'bɒdi]	*v.* 体现；收录，包含 例 The actor's performance perfectly embodied the character's emotions. 演员的表演完美地体现了角色的情感。 用 embody the proposal in a draft resolution 将提议包含在一份决议草案中
incentive [ɪn'sentɪv]	*n.* 激励，刺激 例 The company offered him an extra bonus as an incentive. 公司给他一笔额外奖金作为激励。 用 tax incentives 税收激励

motif [məʊˈtiːf]	*n.* 主题，主旨；装饰图案，装饰图形 例 The ancient rug was decorated with a beautiful flower motif. 这块古老的地毯上装饰着美丽的花朵图案。 用 wallpaper with a flower motif 有鲜花图案的墙纸
pharmacy [ˈfɑːməsi]	*n.* 药店，药房；药剂学 例 The pharmacy near his home was open 24 hours, which was convenient when he needed to buy medicine at night. 他家附近的药店24小时营业，这在晚上需要买药时很方便。 用 modern pharmacy 现代制药学 扩 pharmaceutical *adj.* 制药的
grateful [ˈɡreɪtfl]	*adj.* 感谢的，感激的 例 She was incredibly grateful for all the wonderful gifts they had given her for her anniversary. 她非常感激他们送给自己的结婚纪念日礼物。 用 grateful for a chance to relax 庆幸有机会放松一下
adequate [ˈædɪkwət]	*adj.* 充足的；适当的 例 Adequate water intake is necessary for the body to function properly. 充足的水分摄入是身体正常运转所必需的。 用 an adequate supply of hot water 充足的热水供应 反 inadequate *adj.* 不足的；不充分的 扩 adequately *adv.* 足够地 考 have adequate sanitation services 有充足的卫生服务
calcium [ˈkælsiəm]	*n.* 钙 例 Consuming foods rich in calcium is essential for maintaining strong and healthy bones. 食用富含钙的食物对于保持强壮健康的骨骼是必不可少的。 用 aid the absorption of calcium from food 帮助从食物中吸收钙
priority [praɪˈɒrəti]	*n.* 优先事项；优先级 例 His top priority for the new company was to improve staff motivation by organising team-building activities. 他在新公司的首要任务是通过组织团队建设活动来提高员工积极性。 用 top priority 最重要的事项 our first priority 我们最优先的事项 考 Fragile mountain forests should be given priority in research programs. 研究项目应当首先考虑脆弱的山地森林。

envisage [ɪnˈvɪzɪdʒ]	*v.* 设想，想象，展望
	例 They could not envisage the challenges that lay ahead. 他们无法想象到出现在面前的挑战。
	用 envisage working with him again 想象再与他一起工作
	扩 envision *v.* 想象；预想
efficiency [ɪˈfɪʃnsi]	*n.* 效率，效能；功率
	例 The new manufacturing process improved efficiency, reducing production time and costs. 新的制造工艺提高了效率，减少了生产时间和成本。
	用 improvements in efficiency at the factory 工厂效率的提高
	扩 efficient *adj.* 高效的 proficient *adj.* 熟练的
	考 Engineers are tasked with changing how we travel round cities through urban design, but the engineering industry still works on the assumptions that led to the creation of the energy-consuming transport systems we have now: the emphasis placed solely on efficiency, speed, and quantitative data. 工程师们的任务是通过都市设计来改变我们在城市中的流动方式，然而工程建筑业仍然在这样的一些理念下运转，最终形成了我们目前所拥有的这些消耗能量的交通系统：重点全盘放在了效率、速度和量化数据上。
stitch [stɪtʃ]	*n.* 针脚，一针；缝线 *v.* 缝，缝补；缝合
	例 The surgeon would pick up his instruments, probe, repair, and stitch up again. 外科医生会拿起器械进行探查、修复，然后再缝合。
	用 keep the stitches small and straight 针脚尽量缝得小而直
appraisal [əˈpreɪzl]	*n.* 评价；估计
	例 The end of year performance appraisals should be out some time in the middle of this month. 年终绩效评估应该会在本月中旬公布。
	用 detailed critical appraisals of her work 对她作品的详细评论
	扩 appraise *v.* 评价；估价；估计
neural [ˈnjʊərəl]	*adj.* 神经的；神经系统的
	例 They say that if you take vitamin B regularly, this improves the performance of the neural networks in your brain. 他们说，如果定期服用维生素B，这将改善你大脑中神经网络的状态。
	用 neural pathways in the brain 大脑的神经通路

crown [kraʊn]	*n.* 王冠，冕；王位，王权 例 The king placed the jeweled crown on his head, symbolizing his authority. 国王把镶有宝石的王冠戴在头上，象征着他的权威。 用 a crown of flowers 一个花冠 考 He argues that tooth crowns and roots have a high genetic component, minimally affected by environmental and other factors. 他认为齿冠和齿根包含极高的遗传因素，受环境和其他因素影响最小。
pretend [prɪ'tend]	*v.* 假装，伪装 例 She was incredibly sad but she pretended to be happy so not to worry her family. 她非常伤心，但还是假装高兴，为了不让家人担心。 用 have to pretend all the time 总是需要假装 扩 intend *v.* 想要，有意 attend *v.* 参加，出席
compulsory [kəm'pʌlsəri]	*adj.* 强制的；义务的；必修的 例 Studying science and math at middle school level is compulsory in most countries. 在大多数国家，中学阶段的科学和数学都是必修课。 用 compulsory education 义务教育 compulsory redundancy 强制裁员 反 voluntary *adj.* 自愿的；志愿的
category ['kætəgəri]	*n.* 种类，分类；范畴 例 There is a special category in the tax form for people who have part-time employment. 在税务清单上有一个特殊类别，是为那些有兼职工作的人准备的。 用 three main categories 三大类 同 class *n.* 类别；阶层
prototype ['prəʊtətaɪp]	*n.* 原型；雏形 例 The final product was not yet complete, but the prototype had successfully performed during the trials. 最终产品尚未完成，但原型产品在试验期间成功运行。 用 the prototype of the bicycle 自行车的雏形 考 Prototypes of medical-diagnosis programs and speech recognition software appeared to be making progress. 医学诊断程序和语音识别软件的原型似乎正在取得进展。

milestone ['maɪlstəʊn]	*n.* 里程碑；划时代事件 例 Finally getting his master's degree was an important milestone in his academic life. 最终取得硕士学位是他学术生涯中一个重要的里程碑。 用 a milestone in the history of cinema 电影史上的一个里程碑
eventually [ɪ'ventʃuəli]	*adv.* 最后，终于 例 After a lot of effort and trial and error he eventually managed to solve the problem. 经过大量努力和反复尝试，他最终成功解决了问题。 用 arrive at the hotel eventually 最终到达了旅馆 反 initially *adv.* 最初地 扩 eventual *adj.* 最终的，最后的 考 Eventually, Rome's navy became the largest and most powerful in the Mediterranean, and the Romans had control over what they therefore called Mare Nostrum meaning "our sea". 最终，罗马海军成为地中海区域最大、最强的军队，罗马人征服了这片他们称为Mare Nostrum的海域，意为"我们的海"。
chamber ['tʃeɪmbə(r)]	*n.* 室，腔；房间；会议厅 例 The courtroom was a large, dark chamber at the end of the hall. 法庭在大厅尽头，是一个很大的、光线暗的房间。 用 leave the council chamber 离开会议厅 考 the burial chamber of the tomb 陵墓的墓室
virtue ['vɜːtʃuː]	*n.* 美德；优点 例 It was a surprise to many that the Olympic athletes displayed such virtue in praising and encouraging their opponents. 令许多人吃惊的是，奥运会运动员在赞扬和鼓励他们的对手方面表现出了如此的善意。 用 the virtues of the Internet 互联网的好处 同 advantage *n.* 优点
inhale [ɪn'heɪl]	*v.* 吸入；吸气 例 When doing yoga exercises it is important to control how you inhale and exhale. 做瑜伽练习时，控制你的吸气和呼气是很重要的。 用 inhale fresh air 呼吸新鲜空气 同 breathe in 吸气；吸入 反 exhale *v.* 呼气；发出

terrestrial [təˈrestrɪəl]	*adj.* 地球的；陆地的，陆生的 例 It is said that these terrestrial plants do not grow at all in water. 据说这些陆生植物完全无法在水中生长。 用 terrestrial life forms 地球上的生命形态 考 other large terrestrial mammals 其他大型陆生哺乳动物
accustom [əˈkʌstəm]	*v.* 使习惯，使适应 例 When one moves away from home, it takes time to accustom oneself to a new environment. 当一个人离开家后，使自己适应新环境是需要时间的。 用 accustom herself to the tight bandages 使她自己习惯那些紧绷的绷带
disguise [dɪsˈɡaɪz]	*v.* 伪装；掩饰 *n.* 伪装物；伪装 例 I love old detective stories where the secret agents wear all sorts of different disguises. 我喜欢早期的侦探小说，里面的秘密特工会使用各种各样的伪装。 用 disguise her surprise 掩饰她的惊奇 同 conceal *v.* 隐藏，隐瞒
define [dɪˈfaɪn]	*v.* 下定义；使明确；规定 例 It is difficult for people to really define what they mean by happiness. 人们很难真正定义他们所谓的幸福是什么。 用 be difficult to define 很难界定 考 Here is how some of today's "explorers" define the word. 以下是如今一些"探索者"对这个词的定义。
collision [kəˈlɪʒn]	*n.* 碰撞，相撞；冲突 例 There was a slight collision but my car was undamaged. 虽有轻微碰撞，但我的汽车没有损坏。 用 a collision between two trains 两列火车相撞事故 考 That would alleviate the need for many of the unnecessary manoeuvres that are carried out to avoid potential collisions. 那样就能减少许多不必要的为了避免碰撞而做出的躲避动作。
syndrome [ˈsɪndrəʊm]	*n.* 综合症状，综合征；并发症状 例 His anxiety syndrome was always something he struggled with after the conflict. 他总是在发生矛盾后受到焦虑症状的困扰。 用 Middle East Respiratory Syndrome 中东呼吸综合征

Exercise 04

一、中文释义练习

请选择单词正确的中文释义。

_____	1. interplay	A. 镜头
_____	2. lavatory	B. 盥洗室
_____	3. stable	C. 相互影响
_____	4. drift	D. 漂流
_____	5. lens	E. 稳定的

_____	11. hull	A. 充足的
_____	12. chaos	B. 药店
_____	13. pharmacy	C. 混沌
_____	14. adequate	D. 钙
_____	15. calcium	E. 船体

_____	6. sensor	A. 相等的
_____	7. susceptible	B. 颗粒
_____	8. equivalent	C. 统计
_____	9. particle	D. 传感器
_____	10. statistics	E. 易受影响的

_____	16. envisage	A. 设想
_____	17. neural	B. 陆地的
_____	18. virtue	C. 综合症状
_____	19. terrestrial	D. 优点
_____	20. syndrome	E. 神经的

二、英文释义练习

请选择单词正确的英文释义。

_____	1. acrobat	A. something that encourages you to do sth.
_____	2. dissertation	B. an entertainer who performs difficult acts at a circus
_____	3. praise	C. words that show approval of or admiration
_____	4. incentive	D. the quality of doing sth. well with no waste of time
_____	5. efficiency	E. a long piece of writing on a particular subject

_____	6. priority	A. the first design from which other forms are developed
_____	7. category	B. something that you think is more important than others
_____	8. chamber	C. a separated space in the body or in a machine
_____	9. prototype	D. a group of things with particular features in common
_____	10. define	E. to say or explain what the meaning is

miserable ['mɪzrəbl]	*adj.* 悲惨的；痛苦的
	例 The weather was cloudy again and it made him feel miserable. 天气再次变得阴沉，这使他感觉很悲伤。
	用 miserable housing conditions 恶劣的住房条件
	扩 misery *n.* 痛苦；不幸
embed [ɪm'bed]	*v.* 嵌入；插入；内置
	例 When he shot the arrow it hit the door and embedded itself into the wood. 他的箭射中了门，并嵌入了木头里。
	用 an embedded sentence 一个嵌入的句子
rehearse [rɪ'hɜːs]	*v.* 排练，预演，彩排
	例 When people put on a big performance they often rehearse for a long time beforehand. 当人们上演一场大型演出时，他们通常事先排练很长时间。
	用 rehearse for the opening ceremony 为开幕式排练
tag [tæg]	*n.* 标签；称呼 *v.* 贴标签；把……称作
	例 She wrote her name on a tag and attached it to her school sports bag. 她把名字写在一个标签上，并把它贴在学校的运动背包上。
	用 wear name tags 佩戴姓名标签
extinct [ɪk'stɪŋkt]	*adj.* 灭绝的；已消亡的
	例 Quite a few species of animals have become extinct over the past twenty years. 在过去二十年里，相当多的动物物种已经灭绝了。
	用 an extinct species 一个已灭绝的物种
	扩 extinction *n.* 灭绝
	考 The species was declared extinct by the Tasmanian government in 1986. 该物种在1986年由塔斯马尼亚政府宣告灭绝。

assignment [ə'saɪnmənt]	*n.* 分配；任务；作业 例 He had only a month left to complete his final assignment for the course. 他只剩下一个月时间来完成这门课的最后一项作业。 用 complete three written assignments per semester 每学期完成三项书面作业
meadow ['medəʊ]	*n.* 草地，牧场 例 The vast meadow was filled with colourful wildflowers and buzzing bees. 广阔的草地上遍布着五颜六色的野花和嗡嗡作响的蜜蜂。 用 water meadows 岸边的草地 考 After being comprehensively defeated on the meadows outside the city by the Parliamentarian army, the 21-year-old king found himself the subject of a national manhunt, with a huge sum offered for his capture. 在城外草地上遭受了议会军的全面击溃之后，这位21岁的君主发现自己成了全国上下追捕的对象，为捉拿他而设下了重金悬赏。
talent ['tælənt]	*n.* 才能，天才，天资 例 He had a natural talent for music and picked up the piano very quickly. 他对音乐很有天赋，很快就学会了弹钢琴。 用 have great artistic talent 很有艺术天赋
trivial ['trɪviəl]	*adj.* 琐碎的；不重要的 例 They never argue about anything serious, but only really trivial little things. 他们从不为严肃的事情争论，只会争论一些琐碎的小事。 用 a trivial detail 细枝末节
hectare ['hekteə(r)]	*n.* 公顷 例 The farm covered several hectares of land, providing ample space for cultivation. 这个农场占地数公顷，有充足的种植空间。 用 in just one hectare of rainforest 在一公顷的雨林里
invest [ɪn'vest]	*v.* 投资；投入；授予 例 It is unwise to invest in real estate in these insecure economic times. 在这种经济不稳定的时期投资房地产是不明智的。 用 invest heavily in public transport 对公共交通投入大量资金 扩 investment *n.* 投资；投入

versatile ['vɜːsətaɪl]	*adj.* 多才多艺的；通用的，万能的 例 She is able to do a diverse range of jobs in our team, so she really is a versatile member of the organization. 她可以在我们团队中做各种各样的工作，所以她确实是组织中多才多艺的一员。 用 a versatile actor 一名多才多艺的演员 扩 verse *n.* 诗歌 universal *adj.* 普遍的；一般的
demolish [dɪ'mɒlɪʃ]	*v.* 拆除；破坏 例 They were renovating the entire old part of the city, and they demolished a lot of buildings in the process. 他们正在翻新城市的整个老城区，并在这一过程中拆除了很多建筑。 用 demolish part of the wall 破坏了一部分墙体
endorse [ɪn'dɔːs]	*v.* 背书；认可，赞同 例 The report was endorsed by the college professor and then submitted for final approval and publication. 报告得到了学校教授的背书并随后提交以完成最终审核和发布。 用 be endorsed by the college 得到学院认可 扩 endorsement *n.* 背书；认可
calibrate ['kælɪbreɪt]	*v.* 校准，精确测量 例 The scientist meticulously calibrated the instruments to ensure accurate measurement readings. 科学家仔细校准仪器以确保准确的测量读数。 用 instructions on how to calibrate a thermometer 关于校准温度计的说明 扩 calibration *n.* 校准
conceive [kən'siːv]	*v.* 构思；设想；怀孕 例 Many people today cannot conceive of what it would be like to live without a mobile phone. 今天许多人无法想象没有手机的生活会是什么样子。 用 be conceived as 被作为；被理解为 扩 receive *v.* 接收 考 It is difficult to conceive of vigorous economic growth without an efficient transport system. 如果没有有效的交通体系，很难想象会有强劲的经济增长。

statue ['stætʃuː]	*n.* 雕像，塑像
	例 They erected a huge stone statue of the hero in the town square, to commemorate the great deeds he did for the country.
	他们在城市广场上竖立了一座巨大的英雄雕像，以纪念他为国家所做出的伟大事迹。
	用 pull down a statue 推倒一座雕像
elect [ɪ'lekt]	*v.* 选举；选择
	例 The president was elected through a series of parliamentary elections last month.
	总统通过上个月的一系列议会选举被选出。
	用 an elected representative 一名选出的代表
	扩 election *n.* 选举；选择
affluent ['æfluənt]	*adj.* 富裕的；丰富的
	例 His parents were very affluent and owned several houses in different areas of the city.
	他的父母非常富裕，在这个城市的不同区域拥有几套房产。
	用 a very affluent neighbourhood 一片富人区
	同 prosperous *adj.* 繁荣的，兴旺的 wealthy *adj.* 富有的
invoice ['ɪnvɔɪs]	*n.* 发票，账单
	例 The accountant prepared the invoice, detailing the products purchased and the total amount due.
	会计准备了发票，详细说明了购买的产品和应付总金额。
	用 send an invoice for the goods 发送费用清单
weed [wiːd]	*n.* 野草，杂草
	例 She diligently removed the weeds from her flowerbeds to maintain their neatness and beauty.
	她勤奋地清除花坛中的杂草，以保持花坛的整洁和美丽。
	用 be overgrown with weeds 杂草丛生
integrate ['ɪntɪɡreɪt]	*v.* 整合，合并；（使）加入，融入
	例 Transport planning should be integrated into the new urban reforms that they are working on for the city.
	交通规划应被纳入他们正在为城市进行的新的改革中。
	用 integrate successfully into the Italian way of life 顺利融入意大利的生活方式中
	扩 integration *n.* 整合，合并 integrated *adj.* 完整的

browse [braʊz]	*v.* 浏览，翻阅 例 She loved to browse through antique shops, searching for hidden treasures. 她喜欢逛古董店，寻找隐藏的贵重物品。 用 browse through the newspaper 翻阅报纸
illuminate [ɪ'luːmɪneɪt]	*v.* 阐明，说明；照亮 例 The whole field was illuminated by the firework display. 整片田地都被烟火照亮了。 用 illuminate the stadium 照亮体育场 扩 illumination *n.* 阐明，说明；照亮 考 illuminate the path 照亮道路
mathematics [ˌmæθə'mætɪks]	*n.* 数学；数学运算 例 It's important to have a strong basis in mathematics if you want to study physics. 如果你想学习物理，有扎实的数学基础是很重要的。 用 a professor of mathematics 一位数学教授 类 accounting *n.* 会计学 finance *n.* 金融学 engineering *n.* 工程学 anthropology *n.* 人类学 psychology *n.* 心理学 physiology *n.* 生理学 marketing *n.* 市场营销 statistics *n.* 统计学
prevail [prɪ'veɪl]	*v.* 流行；普遍存在；战胜 例 It is important that logic prevails over emotion when making important business decisions. 重要的是在做重要的业务决策时，逻辑要胜过情感。 用 prevail among certain social groups 在某些社会群体中很盛行 扩 prevailing *adj.* 普遍的；流行的
inborn [ˌɪn'bɔːn]	*adj.* 天生的 例 Some talents, like a natural aptitude for music, seem inborn in individuals. 有些天赋，比如音乐天赋，似乎是天生的。 用 an inborn talent for languages 天生的语言才能
arable ['ærəbl]	*adj.* 可耕种的；耕作的 例 The fertile soil in the region made it ideal for arable farming and crop cultivation. 该地区肥沃的土壤使其成为耕种和作物种植的理想地点。 用 arable farms 耕作农场

spoil [spɔɪl]	*v.* 溺爱；破坏，糟蹋
	例 She really believed that the new, modern building was ugly and spoilt the whole view. 她真的认为这座新的、现代化的建筑很难看，破坏了整片景观。
	用 spoil your appetite 破坏你的食欲

luxury ['lʌkʃəri]	*n.* 奢侈；奢侈品 *adj.* 奢侈的
	例 He tended to enjoy staying in luxury hotels rather than cheap guesthouses. 他喜欢住豪华酒店，而不是廉价旅馆。
	用 a luxury hotel 一家豪华酒店
	扩 luxurious *adj.* 奢侈的
	考 Humour may be a luxury, but the mechanism behind it is no evolutionary accident. 幽默或许是一种奢侈品，但是其背后的机制并非进化中的意外。

split [splɪt]	*v.* （使）分裂；分开 *n.* 裂缝；分裂；分歧
	例 He split the log in half with the axe, so that it would fit in the wood burner. 他用斧头把木头劈成两半，从而使其可以放到烧木头的炉子里。
	用 split neatly into two groups 恰巧分成两类

discipline ['dɪsəplɪn]	*n.* 学科；纪律；训练
	例 He had an admirable sense of discipline and respect for his teachers. 他有令人称赞的纪律性，并且尊重老师。
	用 strict discipline 严格的纪律

intact [ɪn'tækt]	*adj.* 完整的；未受损伤的
	例 It was amazing that the medieval tower remained intact after so many hundred years. 令人惊讶的是这座中世纪的塔几百年之后仍然完好无损。
	用 remain intact 保持完整
	同 undamaged *adj.* 未受损伤的

pervasive [pə'veɪsɪv]	*adj.* 遍布的，无处不在的
	例 Violence and crime are pervasive problems in some cities in the world. 暴力和犯罪是世界上一些城市中普遍存在的问题。
	用 the pervasive influence 无处不在的影响
	扩 pervasively *adv.* 广泛地

fabric ['fæbrɪk]	*n.* 织物，布料；结构，构造
	例 The curtains were made of a thick, soft fabric that made the room look comfortable and warm. 窗帘是由一种又厚又软的织物制成的，这使房间看起来既舒适又温暖。
	用 cotton fabric 棉织物
	考 Perkin quickly grasped that his purple solution could be used to colour fabric, thus making it the world's first synthetic dye. Perkin很快发现他的紫色溶液可以用来为纺织品染色，从而制作出了世界上最早的合成染料。
spontaneous [spɒn'teɪnɪəs]	*adj.* 自发的；自然的
	例 She was always making spontaneous decisions without much consideration. 她总是不经过深思熟虑就自发地做出决定。
	用 burst into spontaneous applause 自发地鼓掌
	扩 spontaneously *adv.* 自发地；自然地 simultaneous *adj.* 同时的
exacerbate [ɪg'zæsəbeɪt]	*v.* 使加剧，使恶化；激怒
	例 If you do not take your medicine, your condition will exacerbate, and you will feel worse. 如果不吃药，你的情况会恶化，而且你会感觉更差。
	用 be exacerbated by racial divisions 因种族分裂而恶化
	同 aggravate *v.* 使严重；使恶化
	考 Noise in classroom can only exacerbate their difficulty in comprehending and processing verbal communication with other children and instructions from the teacher. 教室中的噪音只会加剧他们理解和处理与其他儿童的言语交流以及教师发出的指令时的困难。
dubious ['djuːbɪəs]	*adj.* 可疑的；有疑虑的
	例 His dubious claims raised doubts about the authenticity of his story. 他令人生疑的说法使人们对他故事的真实性产生了怀疑。
	用 be dubious about the whole idea 对这整个想法持怀疑态度
steady ['stedi]	*adj.* 稳定的；不变的
	例 She was not quick at learning the piano, but she was making slow, steady progress. 她学钢琴学得不快，但一直有缓慢而稳定的进步。
	用 five years of steady economic growth 经济稳定发展的五年
	同 constant *adj.* 持续的；稳定的 stable *adj.* 稳定的

character ['kærəktə(r)]	*n.* 性格，品质；特性；角色
	例 Micheal was an interesting character with a great sense of humour and sharp intellect. Michael是一个有趣的角色，他有很强的幽默感和敏锐的才智。
	用 have a strong character 个性强
	扩 characteristic *adj.* 独特的，特有的

vein [veɪn]	*n.* 静脉；叶脉；纹理
	例 The nurse was having trouble finding the vein in her arm to administer the injection. 护士很难找到她手臂上的静脉来进行注射。
	用 inject glucose into the patient's vein 将葡萄糖注射入病人的静脉

anticipate [æn'tɪsɪpeɪt]	*v.* 预料，预期
	例 The cost of the rennovations turned out to be a lot higher than they had anticipated. 翻新的费用比他们的预期高出很多。
	用 anticipate the result 预料结果
	扩 anticipation *n.* 预期；期待

deputy ['depjuti]	*n.* 副手，副职；代理人；代表
	例 The deputy took charge in the absence of the sheriff, ensuring law and order in the town. 警长不在时，副警长负责维护镇上的法律和秩序。
	用 the deputy head of a school 副校长

olfactory [ɒl'fæktəri]	*adj.* 嗅觉的
	例 Dogs are well-known for having incredibly heightened olfactory senses. 众所周知，狗有令人难以置信的灵敏嗅觉。
	用 olfactory cell 嗅觉细胞 olfactory nerve 嗅觉神经 olfactory organ 嗅觉器官

assimilation [ə,sɪmə'leɪʃn]	*n.* 同化；吸收
	例 It can take generations for an immigrant culture to reach a level of assimilation with a host culture. 移民文化可能需要几代人的时间才能达到与所在国文化出现同化的程度。
	用 the rapid assimilation of new ideas 对新思想的迅速吸收
	扩 assimilate *v.* 同化；吸收

merchant	*n.* 商人；批发商
['mɜːtʃənt]	例 The Tang Dynasty was a period in Chinese history when merchants from all over the world visited China.
	唐朝是中国历史上一个世界各地商人都会访问中国的时期。
	用 a wholesale merchant 一个批发商
	扩 merchandise *v.* 买卖，交易

transition	*n.* 过渡；转变；转换
[træn'zɪʃn]	例 The transition from a primary to secondary school is usually quite a big and daunting step for children.
	对孩子们而言，从小学到中学的转变往往是巨大且艰难的一步。
	用 the transition from school to full-time work
	从学校到全职工作的过渡

plagiarism	*n.* 剽窃；剽窃作品
['pleɪdʒərɪzəm]	例 They are implementing new measures to try to prevent students from engaging in plagiarism.
	他们使用新的方法试图阻止学生参与抄袭。
	用 plagiarism scandal 抄袭丑闻

embark	*v.* 上船，上飞机；着手，开始
[ɪm'bɑːk]	例 The explorers and their crew were excited to embark on a new adventure together.
	探险者和他们的船员兴奋地一起开始了新的冒险。
	用 embark on a new career as a writer 开始一个作家的新生涯

heritage	*n.* 遗产；传统
['herɪtɪdʒ]	例 The building is protected because it is a cultural heritage site, so it must be maintained in a particular way.
	由于属于文化遗址，这栋建筑得到了保护，因此它必须以特定的方式进行维护。
	用 rich cultural heritage 丰富的文化遗产

Exercise 05

一、中文释义练习

请选择单词正确的中文释义。

_____ 1. embed   A. 嵌入
_____ 2. extinct   B. 分配
_____ 3. assignment   C. 灭绝的
_____ 4. trivial   D. 公顷
_____ 5. hectare   E. 琐碎的

_____ 11. prevail   A. 分开
_____ 12. arable   B. 织物
_____ 13. split   C. 流行
_____ 14. exacerbate   D. 可耕种的
_____ 15. fabric   E. 使恶化

_____ 6. demolish   A. 破坏
_____ 7. endorse   B. 野草
_____ 8. calibrate   C. 背书
_____ 9. weed   D. 浏览
_____ 10. browse   E. 校准

_____ 16. dubious   A. 遗产
_____ 17. anticipate   B. 过渡
_____ 18. merchant   C. 预期
_____ 19. transition   D. 商人
_____ 20. heritage   E. 可疑的

二、英文释义练习

请选择单词正确的英文释义。

_____ 1. rehearse   A. to practise a play in preparation for a performance
_____ 2. invest   B. to buy property in the hope of making a profit
_____ 3. invoice   C. a list of goods that have been sold showing the price
_____ 4. integrate   D. to make sth. clearer or easier to understand
_____ 5. illuminate   E. to combine things so that they work together

_____ 6. spoil   A. training people to obey rules and orders
_____ 7. discipline   B. existing in all parts of a place or thing
_____ 8. pervasive   C. developing gradually in an even and regular way
_____ 9. steady   D. using or copying someone else's idea or work
_____ 10. plagiarism   E. to give a child everything that they ask for

elbow [ˈelbəʊ]	*n.* 肘，肘部；弯处
	例 She accidentally bumped her elbow against the table, causing a momentary jolt of pain. 她不小心把胳膊肘撞在桌子上，引起一阵酸痛。
	用 fracture his elbow 他肘部骨折
compact [ˈkɒmpækt]	*adj.* 小型的，袖珍的；简约的；紧凑的
	例 It was a new design of suitcase for the frequent traveller, and was compact, stylish and very light to carry. 这是一种专为经常旅行的人设计的新手提箱，简约、时尚、携带轻便。
	用 a compact camera 一台袖珍照相机
overlap [ˌəʊvəˈlæp] *v.* [ˈəʊvəlæp] *n.*	*v.* 部分重叠，交叠 *n.* 重叠部分
	例 The tiles on the roof overlap one another to prevent water seeping into the house. 屋顶上的瓦片相互交叠以防止水渗到房子里。
	用 considerable overlap between the two subjects 两门科目间相当多的共通之处
overview [ˈəʊvəvjuː]	*n.* 综述；概述
	例 When trying to write a good task one response for IELTS writing, it's essential to write a concise, informative overview. 当你想写出一篇优秀的雅思写作Task 1文章时，写一个简洁且信息完整的概述是非常重要的。
	用 a brief historical overview of transport 运输史的简要概述
orthodox [ˈɔːθədɒks]	*adj.* （观念、方法或行为）传统的，正统的
	例 His methods of teaching were fairly orthodox and many younger students found his classes boring. 他的教学方法非常正统，很多年轻的学生认为他的课很无聊。
	用 orthodox medicine 传统医学
	同 traditional *adj.* 传统的
	反 unorthodox *adj.* 非传统的；非正统的

adjoin [ə'dʒɔɪn]	*v.* 毗邻；连接
	例 The main office building adjoins with the building next door, and connects through a corridor walkway. 主办公楼与隔壁的建筑相邻，并通过走廊过道连接。
	用 an adjoining office 旁边的一间办公室
curve [kɜːv]	*n.* 曲线；弯曲 *v.* 使弯曲；沿曲线运动
	例 The car went around the sharp curve in the road before slowing down. 车辆在经过急转弯之后才减速。
	用 a pattern of straight lines and curves 一幅直线与曲线交织的图案
	考 In order to improve the acoustic properties of the auditorium and to amplify the sound, they are not straight, they are curved. 为了提升礼堂的声学特性并放大声音，它们没有被做成直的，而是被做成曲面的。
innovate ['ɪnəveɪt]	*v.* 创新；改革
	例 It's important to be able to innovate today in the tech industry—things are moving forward very fast and competition is high. 如今在科技领域，创新能力是非常重要的，事物发展迅速，竞争激烈。
	用 innovate to ensure success in a growing market 创新以确保在不断扩大的市场中成功
	扩 innovation *n.* 创新；改革 innovative *adj.* 创新的；革新的 renovate *v.* 革新；更新 renovation *n.* 革新；更新
moderate ['mɒdərət]	*adj.* 温和的；适度的，中等的
	例 He was an easygoing man of very moderate views about everything. 他是个随和的人，对一切都持温和的观点。
	用 moderate views 温和的见解 a moderate approach 温和的方式
coral ['kɒrəl]	*n.* 珊瑚 *adj.* 珊瑚色的
	例 Snorkelers were amazed by the vibrant colours and diverse marine life in the coral reef. 浮潜者为珊瑚礁中鲜艳的色彩和多样的海洋生物所惊叹。
	用 coral reef 珊瑚礁 coral necklace 珊瑚项链
	考 They inhabit the soil, air, rocks and water and are present within every form of life, from seaweed and coral to dogs and humans. 它们住在土壤、空气、岩石和水里，存在于每一种生命形式中，从海草和珊瑚到狗和人类无一例外。

vocation [vəʊˈkeɪʃn]	*n.* 职业；使命感
	例 She struggled for years to find her true vocation in life, before going into teaching. 在从事教学工作前，她努力了多年来找寻自己毕生追求的事业。
	用 find one's true vocation in life 找到毕生追寻的事业
	扩 vocational *adj.* 职业的

recede [rɪˈsiːd]	*v.* 逐渐远离，渐渐退去；逐渐减弱
	例 The flood waters of the river usually recede during the summer months. 这条河的洪水通常在夏季几个月退去。
	用 recede into the distance 在远处渐渐消失
	扩 recession *n.* 衰退

stir [stɜː(r)]	*v./n.* 搅拌，搅和；激发
	例 She used a wooden spoon to stir the soup in the metal pot on the stove. 她用木勺搅拌炉子上金属锅里的汤。
	用 stir the soup for a few seconds 把汤搅动几秒钟

solicitor [səˈlɪsɪtə(r)]	*n.* 初级律师，事务律师；推销员
	例 The solicitor provided legal advice and guidance to clients facing various legal matters. 该律师为面临各种法律问题的客户提供法律意见和指导。
	用 solicitor fee 律师费

remark [rɪˈmɑːk]	*n.* 评论；意见；谈话 *v.* 评论；谈论
	例 She was not happy with his offhand remark about her clothes, as she was very sensitive about her looks. 她对他随意评论自己的穿着感到很不高兴，因为她对自己的外表很敏感。
	用 make a remark 发表评论

laundry [ˈlɔːndri]	*n.* 洗衣店；洗衣房；待洗（或正在洗涤、洗完）的衣物
	例 Of all the domestic chores, she absolutely hated doing the laundry. 在所有家务中，她最讨厌洗衣服。
	用 laundry room 洗衣间

forgive [fəˈgɪv]	*v.* 原谅；免除
	例 He found it very hard to forgive his parents for what they did to him. 他发现很难原谅父母对自己所做的事。
	用 forgive me 请原谅我

explode [ɪk'spləʊd]	*v.* 爆炸，爆发；激增 例 The bomb was defused successfully, so it did not explode, and everyone escaped safely. 炸弹被成功拆除，因此没有发生爆炸，人们安全撤离了。 用 explode the device 引爆这个装置 扩 explosion *n.* 爆炸；爆发
random ['rændəm]	*adj.* 随机的；任意的 例 Police are conducting random breath tests on that bypass after many drunk drivers were found speeding along there. 发现许多醉酒司机在那条路上超速行驶后，警方在那里进行随机呼气测试。 用 be processed in a random order 按随机顺序处理
reinforce [,riːɪn'fɔːs]	*v.* 加强，加固；强化 例 The helmet was reinforced with a special material that made it more durable and resistant to shock on impact. 头盔用一种特殊材料加固，使其更耐用，减少撞击的影响。 用 reinforced steel 强化钢材 reinforce the country's economic decline 加速国家经济的衰退
verbal ['vɜːbl]	*adj.* 口头的；言语的；动词的 例 His verbal communication skills were excellent, but he was weak when it came to reading and writing in English. 他的口头沟通能力很好，但在涉及英语阅读和写作时表现很差。 用 non-verbal communication 非言语交流 verbal agreement 口头协议 扩 verbalise *v.* 描述；用言语表达
impartial [ɪm'pɑːʃl]	*adj.* 公平的，公正的 例 When choosing a career path it is important to seek impartial advice. 在选择职业道路时，获得不带偏见的建议是很重要的。 用 an impartial observer 一位公正的观察者 反 partial *adj.* 不公平的，偏袒的
tenant ['tenənt]	*n.* 房客，租户 例 The landlord welcomed the new tenant to the rental property after signing the contract. 在签订合同后，房东欢迎新房客入住出租的房子。 用 for the benefit of the tenant 为了租户的利益

impulse [ˈɪmpʌls]	*n.* 冲动；心血来潮；刺激；推动力
	例 He bought the bag on an impulse—he is a very impulsive buyer. 他一时冲动买了这个包，他是个很容易冲动的购物者。
	用 resist the impulse to laugh 忍住不笑出来
absorb [əbˈzɔːb]	*v.* 吸收；吸引；使全神贯注 ·
	例 Plants thrive when they absorb plenty of nutrients from the soil. 当植物在土壤中吸收大量养分时，它们就会茁壮生长。
	用 absorb oxygen 吸收氧气 absorb the influx of refugees 接纳涌入的难民
	同 take in 吸入，吸收
	考 Plants absorb CO_2 from the air and transform it into sugars and other carbon-based substances. 植物吸收空气中的二氧化碳并将其转化为糖和其他含碳物质。
commercial [kəˈmɜːʃl]	*adj.* 商业的；商业化的
	例 There were very few commercial flights going to that destination at that time of year. 每年的那个时候，前往那个目的地的商业航班很少。
	用 a centre of industrial and commercial activity 工商业活动中心 the effect of commercial exploitation of forests 对森林进行商业开发所带来的影响
	考 fresh food commercial manager 新鲜食品商业经理
headline [ˈhedlaɪn]	*n.* （报纸的）标题；新闻摘要
	例 The headlines in the news usually tend to be quite dramatic in order to draw the attention of potential readers. 为了吸引潜在读者的注意力，新闻标题通常都很引人注目。
	用 headline news 头条新闻
sense [sens]	*n.* 感觉；观念 *v.* 感觉到；检测出
	例 Sitting in the hot springs gave him an enormous sense of relaxation and well-being. 坐在温泉里带给他极大放松和舒服的感觉。
	用 the five senses 五种感觉 an overwhelming sense of loss 巨大的失落感
	扩 sensible *adj.* 明智的；能感觉到的 sensitive *adj.* 敏感的
	考 Humans start developing a sense of humour as early as six weeks old, when babies begin to laugh and smile in response to stimuli. 人类早在六周大的时候就开始发展出了幽默感，此时的婴儿开始用大笑和微笑回应外界的刺激。

recycle [ˌriːˈsaɪkl]	*v./n.* 回收利用，循环使用 例 If we are going to address environmental concerns it is important that individuals all recycle as much household waste as possible. 如果我们要解决环境问题，重要的是人们要回收尽可能多的家庭垃圾。 用 recycled paper 再生纸
shed [ʃed]	*v.* 去除，摆脱；射出，发出（光） 例 Psychotherapy helped him to shed some of his insecurity. 心理疗法帮助他摆脱了一些不安全感。 用 shed light on 阐明，解释
antenna [ænˈtenə]	*n.* 天线；触角，触须 例 There is an antenna on every roof for receiving television signals. 每个屋顶上都有接收电视信号的天线。 用 radio antennas 收音机天线
compendium [kəmˈpendiəm]	*n.* 纲要；概略；汇编 例 The encyclopedia is a comprehensive compendium of knowledge. 百科全书是一本全面的知识汇编。 用 issue a compendium 发布一份纲要
fundamental [ˌfʌndəˈmentl]	*adj.* 基本的，根本的 *n.* 基本原理；基本原则 例 There was a fundamental difference between the two countries and their values and outlooks. 这两个国家存在根本性的差异，在价值观和世界观上也不相同。 用 fundamental difference 根本区别 fundamental particle 基本粒子 考 A millennium ago, stepwells were fundamental to life in the driest parts of India. 一千年前，在印度最干旱的地区，阶梯井是生活的基本保障。
enlarge [ɪnˈlaːdʒ]	*v.* 扩大；增大；扩展 例 Sometimes an allergic reaction to something causes your glands to enlarge. 有时对某些东西的过敏反应会导致你的腺体增大。 用 enlarge your vocabulary 扩大词汇量
denounce [dɪˈnaʊns]	*v.* 谴责；告发；公然抨击 例 He stood up in disagreement and denounced the new policy. 他站起来反对并谴责了这项新政策。 用 be denounced as spies 被告发是间谍 扩 announce *v.* 声明；宣布 pronounce *v.* 发音

mineral ['mɪnərəl]	*n.* 矿物；矿物质
	例 The country has a big export market in mineral deposits. 该国在矿产方面有很大的出口市场。
	用 mineral extraction 矿物开采 the recommended intake of vitamins and minerals 维生素和矿物质的建议摄入量
	考 Tunnels were also built for mineral extraction. 还修建了用于开采矿产的隧道。
presume [prɪ'zjuːm]	*v.* 假定，假设；推测
	例 I presume that after negotiations they will reach an agreement in the end. 我认为经过谈判他们会最终达成一致。
	用 presume one's innocence 假定某人无罪
	同 assume *v.* 假设，猜想 suppose *v.* 假设，猜想
	扩 resume *v.* 重新开始；恢复 presumably *adv.* 大概，可能
volume ['vɒljuːm]	*n.* 体积；卷；音量
	例 The button on the side of the device is to increase or decrease the audio volume. 设备侧面的按钮可以用来增强或降低音量。
	用 turn the volume up 把音量调大
thrive [θraɪv]	*v.* 繁荣，兴旺；茁壮成长
	例 After a period of slow economic growth in winter, the economy started to thrive in late spring. 在冬季经历了一段增长缓慢的时期后，经济在晚春开始繁荣。
	用 a thriving industry 一个兴盛的行业
botany ['bɒtəni]	*n.* 植物学
	例 I would like to study botany because I've always been interested in how plants and trees grow and how to look after them. 我想学习植物学，因为我一直对植物和树木如何生长以及如何照管它们很感兴趣。
	用 senior lecturer in botany 植物学高级讲师
slash [slæʃ]	*v.* 砍，劈；削减，降低 *n.* 砍，劈；斜杠，斜线号
	例 He used a sharp knife to slash through the thick underbrush in the jungle. 他用一把锋利的刀劈开丛林中茂密的灌木丛。
	用 slash costs 降低成本

conviction [kən'vɪkʃn]	*n.* 定罪；确信，深信
	例 The prosecutor presented strong evidence to secure a conviction in the criminal trial. 检察官出示了强有力的证据，以确保在刑事审判中定罪。
	用 strong moral convictions 坚定的道德信念
	扩 convict *v.* 定罪，宣判
	考 Such conviction was, until recently, reflected in museum displays. 直到最近，这种信念还反映在博物馆的展览中。
boom [buːm]	*n.* 兴旺，繁荣；激增 *v.* 兴旺；快速发展
	例 There was a boom in the amount of births in 1998, then the annual birth rate declined, and continues to do so. 在1998年时出现过新生儿数量的激增，之后年出生率开始持续下降。
	用 a boom in car sales 汽车销售额的剧增 baby boom 婴儿潮 economic boom 经济繁荣
	考 a booming demand 激增的需求
correlation [ˌkɒrə'leɪʃn]	*n.* 相关；关联；相互关系
	例 I believe there is a direct correlation between effort and the results students get in their assignments. 我相信努力与学生在作业中得到的成绩直接相关。
	用 the correlation between smoking and disease 吸烟与疾病的联系
	扩 correlate *v.* 关联，联系
tremendous [trə'mendəs]	*adj.* 极大的，巨大的；极好的
	例 It was a tremendous performance at the gala, which everyone thought was incredibly professional. 晚会上的表演非常精彩，每个人都认为演出非常专业。
	用 a tremendous explosion 一场巨大的爆炸
stereotype ['steriətaɪp]	*n.* 陈腔滥调；模式化形象
	例 There is a rather inaccurate stereotype that all English people are polite. 有一种相当不准确的刻板印象，认为所有英国人都彬彬有礼。
	用 a ridiculous stereotype 荒谬的刻板印象
suspect [sə'spekt] *v.* ['sʌspekt] *n.*	*v.* 怀疑；觉得 *n.* 嫌疑分子，犯罪嫌疑人
	例 I suspect that my keys are in the car, but I haven't checked there yet. 我怀疑钥匙在车里，但我还没有检查过。
	用 a murder suspect 一个谋杀案犯罪嫌疑人

allergy ['ælədʒi]	*n.* 过敏；过敏反应
	例 In springtime it's fairly common that people suffer from pollen allergies, especially if the pollen count is very high. 在春天，人们出现花粉过敏是非常普遍的，尤其是在花粉浓度很高的时候。
	用 an allergy to animal hair 对动物毛发过敏
	扩 allergic *adj.* 过敏的 an allergic reaction 过敏反应
subsidy ['sʌbsədi]	*n.* 补贴；津贴；补助金
	例 During the drought the government gave farmers a subsidy to help them stay in business. 在干旱期间，政府给农民提供补贴，帮助他们维持生计。
	用 agricultural subsidies 农业补贴 reduce the level of subsidy 降低补贴标准
	扩 subsidise *v.* 资助；补助
recession [rɪ'seʃn]	*n.* 衰退；不景气
	例 It's quite normal that every few years the economy may fall into a recession, but we always come out of it in the end. 每隔几年，经济就可能陷入衰退，这是很正常的，但我们最终总会走出来。
	用 in deep recession 正处于严重衰退中 the gradual recession of the floodwater 洪水的渐渐消退
	扩 recede *v.* 后退；减弱；衰退
	考 For example, in one experiment that took place during the peak of a recent economic recession, graduating college seniors were asked to reflect on their job prospects. 例如，在最近经济衰退高峰期进行的一项实验中，要求即将毕业的大学生思考他们的就业前景。

Exercise 06

一、中文释义练习

请选择单词正确的中文释义。

_____	1.	elbow	A. 搅拌	_____	11. headline	A. 回收
_____	2.	compact	B. 紧凑的	_____	12. recycle	B. 矿物
_____	3.	curve	C. 逐渐远离	_____	13. antenna	C. 触角
_____	4.	recede	D. 曲线	_____	14. mineral	D. 标题
_____	5.	stir	E. 肘部	_____	15. botany	E. 植物学
_____	6.	coral	A. 珊瑚	_____	16. conviction	A. 过敏
_____	7.	laundry	B. 口头的	_____	17. slash	B. 砍
_____	8.	random	C. 租户	_____	18. allergy	C. 衰退
_____	9.	verbal	D. 随机的	_____	19. subsidy	D. 补贴
_____	10.	tenant	E. 洗衣店	_____	20. recession	E. 确信

二、英文释义练习

请选择单词正确的英文释义。

_____	1.	overlap	A. to introduce new ideas or ways of doing sth.
_____	2.	orthodox	B. part of one thing covers part of the other
_____	3.	innovate	C. to stop feeling angry with sb. who annoys you
_____	4.	forgive	D. to make a feeling or an idea stronger
_____	5.	reinforce	E. following generally accepted beliefs
_____	6.	impulse	A. a connection between two things
_____	7.	denounce	B. to strongly criticize sb. that you think is wrong
_____	8.	volume	C. a fixed idea that many people have of a person
_____	9.	correlation	D. a sudden strong wish or need to do sth.
_____	10.	stereotype	E. the amount of space that a substance fills

trim [trɪm]	*v.* 修剪，修整；削减，减少 *n.* 修剪；装饰 *adj.* 整齐的，整洁美观的
	例 The barber skillfully trimmed his customer's hair, giving it a neat and stylish appearance. 理发师熟练地修剪顾客的头发，使其看上去整洁而时尚。
	用 the trim and neat gardens 整洁又美观的花园

galaxy ['gæləksi]	*n.* 星系；银河系；显赫的人
	例 Each galaxy in the universe contains millions of stars. 宇宙中的每个星系都包含数百万颗恒星。
	用 a galaxy of Hollywood stars 好莱坞影星的荟萃
	考 An alien civilisation could choose many different ways of sending information across the galaxy, but many of these either require too much energy, or else are severely attenuated while traversing the vast distances across the galaxy. 外星文明可以选择多种不同方式在银河系中传送信息，但这些方式中的许多要么需要太多能量，要么会在穿越银河系广阔空间时衰减严重。

nutrition [nju'trɪʃn]	*n.* 营养；滋养
	例 If you eat plenty of fruit and vegetables you are sure to get a lot of nutrition. 如果你吃大量的水果和蔬菜，你肯定会获取很多营养。
	用 advice on diet and nutrition 有关饮食和营养的建议

evacuate [ɪ'vækjueɪt]	*v.* 疏散，撤离；搬出；排泄
	例 The residents were urged to evacuate the area due to the approaching hurricane. 由于飓风即将来临，居民们被要求紧急撤离该地区。
	用 evacuate nearby buildings 将附近大楼里的居民疏散

notorious [nəʊ'tɔːriəs]	*adj.* 声名狼藉的，臭名昭著的
	例 He was a notorious bad-guy in most of the films that he featured in. 在他主演的大多数电影中，他都是一个臭名昭著的坏人。
	用 a notorious criminal 一个恶名昭彰的罪犯
	扩 notoriety *n.* 恶名；声名狼藉

resident
['rezɪdənt]

n. 居民，住户 *adj.* 居住的；定居的

例 Residents have all complained about the poor conditions of the community gardens.
居民们都抱怨社区花园的条件差。

用 a resident of the United States 一位美国居民

扩 residence *n.* 居住；住宅

insulate
['ɪnsjuleɪt]

v. 使隔热，使隔音，使绝缘；使隔离

例 The new material was ideal for hiking and cold, wet weather and insulated against the wind and rain.
这种新材料非常适合徒步旅行和寒冷潮湿的天气，并且可以阻隔风雨。

用 insulate our house from the noise 使我们的房子隔音

扩 insulation *n.* 隔离；绝缘

summit
['sʌmɪt]

n. 顶点，最高点；峰会

例 After a climb of about three days, the group eventually reached the summit and celebrated the victory by placing a flag in the snow.
经过大约三天的攀登，团队最终到达了山顶，并在雪中放置了一面旗帜以庆祝胜利。

用 the summit of his career 他事业的顶峰

spiral
['spaɪrəl]

adj. 螺旋形的 *n.* 螺旋形 *v.* 螺旋式上升或下降

例 The staircase spiraled upwards, leading to the top of the tower with elegance.
楼梯盘旋而上，优雅地通向塔顶。

用 circle in a slow spiral 缓缓盘旋

考 There are various designs of labyrinth but what they all have in common is a winding spiral path which leads to a central area.
螺旋形迷宫的设计多种多样，但它们的共同点是都有一条蜿蜒的螺旋路径，通向中心区域。

network
['netwɜːk]

n. 网络；人际关系网 *v.* 联网；建立关系

例 She built a strong professional network, connecting with individuals in her industry for mutual support.
她建立了一个强大的专业网络，与她所在行业的人建立联系，相互支持。

用 distribution network 分销网

考 A maze is quite different as it is a kind of puzzle with an intricate network of paths.
矩形迷宫却十分不同，因为它有复杂的路径网络，使人迷惑。

executive [ɪgˈzekjətɪv]	*adj.* 行政的；经营的；执行的 *n.* 行政领导，管理人员
	例 He works as an executive assistant at a top law firm in Shanghai. 他在上海一家顶级律师事务所担任行政助理。
	用 Chief Executive Officer 首席执行官
avenue [ˈævənjuː]	*n.* 大街；林荫大道；途径，方法
	例 The avenue leading to the famous arch is lined with cherry trees. 通往那扇著名拱门的大道两旁种满了樱桃树。
	用 the most expensive apartments on that avenue 那条大街上最昂贵的公寓
contradict [ˌkɒntrəˈdɪkt]	*v.* 矛盾；反驳；否定
	例 His tendency to contradict everything his parents said was very annoying. 他总是反驳父母说的话，这让人非常困扰。
	用 contradict each other 彼此矛盾
	扩 contradiction *n.* 矛盾；否定
	考 The "light screen" hypothesis would initially seem to contradict what is known about chlorophyll. "光屏幕"假说最初似乎与我们所了解的叶绿素是冲突的。
emulate [ˈemjuleɪt]	*v.* 仿效，模仿
	例 Aspiring artists often try to emulate the techniques of famous painters to improve their skills. 有抱负的艺术家经常试着通过模仿著名画家的技巧来提高自己的水平。
	用 emulate her sister's sporting achievements 在运动成绩方面赶上她姐姐
scrutiny [ˈskruːtəni]	*n.* 仔细观察，详细审查
	例 His detailed scientific research study underwent rigorous scrutiny by peers. 他详细的科学研究经历了其他人的严格审查。
	用 under media scrutiny 在媒体的密切关注下
friction [ˈfrɪkʃn]	*n.* 不和，分歧；摩擦；摩擦力
	例 The rough surface created friction, making it challenging to slide the object. 粗糙的表面产生了摩擦，使物体难以滑动。
	用 the friction of braking 因刹车产生的摩擦

plausible
['plɔːzəbl]

adj. 看似可信的，似乎有理的

例 She presented a very plausible explanation for why she had not finished the task on time.
对于为何没有按时完成任务，她给出了一个似乎合理的解释。

用 the only plausible explanation 唯一合理的解释

扩 implausible *adj.* 似乎不合情理的

考 The problem for biologists, psychologists and anthropologists is to sort out which of these two polar explanations is more plausible.
生物学家、心理学家和人类学家所要解决的问题就是找出这两种截然对立的解释哪种更合理。

---

eminent
['emɪnənt]

adj. 杰出的；有名的；明显的

例 She was an eminent scholar in the field of physics—almost everyone looked up to her and read her papers.
她是物理学领域的杰出学者，几乎每个人都尊敬她并研读她的论文。

用 an eminent architect 一位著名的建筑师

考 to attend a series of lectures given by the eminent scientist Michael Faraday
参加著名科学家Michael Faraday的一系列讲座

---

stroll
[strəʊl]

v./n. 散步，闲逛

例 They took a leisurely stroll along the beach, enjoying the soothing sound of the waves.
他们沿着海滩悠闲地散步，享受着海浪舒缓的声音。

用 stroll along the beach 在海滩漫步
stroll around the city 在城市里闲逛

考 The brightest ones will never summit Mount Qomolangma, and the stragglers won't enjoy the lovely stroll in the park they are perhaps more suited to.
那些天资最聪颖者将永远无法登顶珠穆朗玛峰，而那些掉队者也永远无法享受原本也许更适合他们的、公园里的美好漫步。

---

respond
[rɪ'spɒnd]

v. 反应；回答

例 Emails are very convenient for business, as people can respond to questions quickly and efficiently.
电子邮件对商务而言非常便利，因为人们可以快速高效地回答问题。

用 respond to my letter 给我回信

同 react *v.* 反应

扩 response *n.* 反应

notify ['nəʊtɪfaɪ]	*v.* 通报，通知
	例 They said that they would notify me if the application was successful or not. 他们说会通知我申请是否成功。
	用 notify him of our decision 告知他我们的决定

ethical ['eθɪkl]	*adj.* 伦理的；道德的
	例 Some people think that it is not ethical to advertise products to young people. 有些人认为向年轻人推销商品是不道德的。
	用 ethical issues 道德问题

anatomy [ə'nætəmi]	*n.* 解剖；解剖学；剖析
	例 This semester they would be looking at the human anatomy in detail. 这学期他们将细致研究人体解剖学。
	用 a course in anatomy 一门解剖学课程 an anatomy of the current recession 对当前经济衰退的剖析

thorny ['θɔːni]	*adj.* 多刺的；棘手的，麻烦的
	例 The thorny bushes on the trail made the hike more challenging and required careful navigation. 小径上荆棘丛生的灌木丛使徒步旅行更具挑战，需要小心导航。
	用 the thorny issue of immigration policy 移民政策这个棘手的问题 a thorny problem for us to solve 一个需要我们解决的棘手问题

involve [ɪn'vɒlv]	*v.* 包含；涉及
	例 A good team leader always tries to involve all members of the team in the decision-making process. 一个好的团队领导者总会努力让团队中的所有人都参与到决策过程中。
	用 involve an element of risk 有一定风险
	扩 involvement *n.* 参与，加入
	考 We should encourage more young people to become involved in innovation. 我们应当鼓励更多年轻人参与创新。

deviation [ˌdiːvi'eɪʃn]	*n.* 偏离；偏差
	例 He insisted that there must be no deviation from the normal procedure. 他坚持说不能有任何偏离正常程序的地方。
	用 a deviation from the plan 偏离计划

kidney ['kɪdni]	*n.* 肾，肾脏 例 The kidney plays a vital role in filtering waste products from the bloodstream. 肾脏在过滤血液中的垃圾方面起着至关重要的作用。 用 kidney infection 肾感染
stack [stæk]	*n.* 一堆；大量 *v.* 堆叠 例 The librarian organized the books into a neat stack on the shelves. 图书管理员把书整齐地堆放在书架上。 用 a stack of books 一摞书 a stack of unopened mail 一堆没拆的信件
dispense [dɪ'spens]	*v.* 发放，分配；提供，配发 例 He is not yet well enough to dispense with taking that medicine. 他身体还没有好到可以不吃那种药物的程度。 用 dispense advice 给予忠告 dispense with 摒弃；不再需要
utilise ['juːtəlaɪz]	*v.* 利用 例 Hydro-electric dams utilise the power of the sea to generate electricity. 水力发电大坝利用海水的能量来产生电能。 用 utilise a range of techniques 使用各种技术
bond [bɒnd]	*n.* 纽带，联系；债券；契约 *v.* 建立关系或连接 例 The strong bond between the siblings was evident in their close relationship. 兄弟姐妹之间的紧密联系在他们的密切关系中显而易见。 用 a bond of friendship 友谊的纽带
revolve [rɪ'vɒlv]	*v.* 环绕，围绕……旋转 例 Mars takes longer to revolve on its axis than the Earth. 火星绕着轴心转动所花的时间比地球长。 用 revolve around the sun 绕太阳公转
dialect ['daɪəlekt]	*n.* 方言，土话 例 The region's dialect had unique linguistic features, and sounded almost like another language. 该地区的方言具有独特的语言特征，听起来几乎像另一种语言。 用 use the local dialect to communicate messages 用方言来传达信息 扩 diameter *n.* 直径 dialogue *n.* 对话

vulnerable
['vʌlnərəbl]

adj. 易受伤害的；脆弱的

例 He was not a confident young man—whenever he had to speak in front of the class he felt shy and vulnerable.
他不是一个自信的年轻人，当他不得不在全班同学面前讲话时，他感到害羞而脆弱。

用 vulnerable members of our society 我们社会中的弱势群体
be vulnerable to disease 容易患病

扩 vulnerability *n.* 弱点

skyscraper
['skaɪskreɪpə(r)]

n. 摩天大楼

例 The impressive skyscraper towered above the city, a symbol of architectural grandeur.
令人印象深刻的摩天大楼耸立在城市上空，是建筑宏伟的象征。

用 the Skyscraper Index 摩天大楼指数

考 Short regards glass, steel and air-conditioned skyscrapers as symbols of status, rather than practical ways of meeting our requirements.
Short认为，由玻璃、钢铁和空调组成的摩天大楼是社会地位的象征，而不是满足我们需要的实用方式。

hierarchy
['haɪərɑːki]

n. 层级体系；等级制度

例 Some breeds of monkey have a very complex social hierarchy.
一些族群的猴子有非常复杂的社会层级体系。

用 a hierarchy of needs 不同层次的需要

考 In fact, research shows that, when innovating, the best approach is to create an environment devoid of structure and hierarchy and enable everyone involved to engage as one organic group.
实际上，研究显示，在进行创新时，最好的方法就是创造出一个没有任何组织结构和上下级别的环境，让置身其中的每个人都充分参与进来，形成一个有机的群体。

spur
[spɜː(r)]

n./v. 刺激，激励，鼓励

例 The leader's inspiring speech served as a spur for the team to work harder.
领导鼓舞人心的讲话激励着团队更加努力工作。

用 spur economic growth 刺激经济增长

考 These prices, coupled with the increasing demand, spurred the search for new routes to Asia by Europeans eager to take part in the spice trade.
这样的价位，再加上不断上涨的需求，刺激了急于加入香料贸易的欧洲人去寻找通往亚洲的新路线。

exile ['eksaɪl]	*n.* 流放；被流放者，流亡者 *v.* 流放；放逐
	例 The political dissident was forced into exile, living in a foreign country far from home. 这位持不同政见者被迫流亡，居住在远离家乡的国外。
	用 a place of exile 流放地
badge [bædʒ]	*n.* 徽章，奖章；标记，标识
	例 The police officer proudly displayed his badge, a symbol of his authority and commitment to serve and protect. 这位警官自豪地展示了他的徽章，象征着他的权威以及对服务和保护的承诺。
	用 the car's front badge 车头的标志 a police officer's badge 警官的徽章
vertical ['vɜːtɪkl]	*adj.* 垂直的，直立的 *n.* 垂直线，垂直面
	例 The games board consists of vertical and horizontal lines intersecting to make squares. 棋盘由垂直线和水平线组成，它们交叉组成正方形。
	用 the vertical axis of the graph 图表的纵轴
	反 horizontal *adj.* 水平的
	考 Gharib and Graff set themselves the task of raising a 4.5-metre stone column from horizontal to vertical, using no source of energy except the wind. Gharib和Graff尝试只借助风力（除此之外没有其他能源）来把一块水平放置的4.5米长的石柱竖立起来。
maximum ['mæksɪməm]	*n.* 最大值；最大量 *adj.* 最大的；最多的
	例 For maximum benefit certain medicines and vitamins should be taken with food. 为了获得最大效果，一些药物和维生素应随餐服用。
	用 the maximum speed 最快速度 the maximum volume 最大音量
	扩 maximise *v.* 最大化
qualify ['kwɒlɪfaɪ]	*v.* 取得资格；有资格；证明合格
	例 You need to be under thirty years old and have a university degree to qualify for the postgraduate scholarship. 你需要在30岁以下，有大学学位，才能有资格申请研究生奖学金。
	用 be qualified as a doctor 有资格做医生
	扩 qualification *n.* 资格；资质

discharge [dɪs'tʃɑːdʒ] *v.* ['dɪstʃɑːdʒ] *n.*	*v.* 准许离开；释放；排出 *n.* 获准离开，免职；释放；排出
	例 After the operation was a success she was discharged from hospital. 手术获得成功后，她离开了医院。
	用 be discharged from the army following his injury 受伤后他退伍了
finance ['faɪnæns]	*n.* 财政；金融 *v.* 提供资金；资助
	例 Finance for education comes from the tax revenue paid to the government yearly. 教育经费来自政府每年获取的税收收入。
	用 the Minister of Finance 财政部长 a diploma in banking and finance 银行与金融学文凭
	同 fund *v.* 资助 subsidize *v.* 资助
extravagance [ɪk'strævəgəns]	*n.* 奢侈；浪费；过度
	例 Some people think spending money on fancy brands is an unnecessary extravagance. 有人认为把钱花在名牌上是一种不必要的奢侈。
	用 avoid extravagance 避免铺张浪费
	扩 extravagant *adj.* 过度的；奢侈的
adornment [ə'dɔːnmənt]	*n.* 装饰；装饰品
	例 The necklace was of elaborate design and was a beautiful adornment. 这条项链设计精细，是一件精美的饰品。
	用 a building without any adornment 一栋完全未经装修的大楼
	同 decoration *n.* 装饰
	扩 adorn *v.* 装饰
hybrid ['haɪbrɪd]	*n.* 混合物；杂交动（植）物 *adj.* 混合的；杂交的
	例 Hybrid vehicles use a combination of both petrol and electric motors to power them. 混合动力汽车使用汽油和电动发动机的组合来提供动力。
	用 a hybrid of Western pop and traditional folk song 西方流行音乐和传统民歌的融合
	同 mixture *n.* 混合物
	考 The aim of this hybrid science is to create solutions for common geography-based health problems. 这一交叉学科的目的是为普遍存在的基于地理因素的健康问题提供解决方案。

department
[dɪˈpɑːtmənt]

n. 部，部门；系，科，局

例 It was a large company and there were many departments that dealt with different aspects of the business.
这是一家大公司，有许多部门来处理各个方面的业务。

用 the legal department 法律部门

考 different Government departments 不同的政府部门

interfere
[ˌɪntəˈfɪə(r)]

v. 干涉；妨碍；打扰

例 Emotional problems can sometimes interfere with your ability to concentrate on work.
情绪问题有时会影响你专注工作的能力。

用 interfere with your body's ability to process oxygen
干扰你的身体处理氧气的能力

扩 interference *n.* 干涉，干扰

premium
[ˈpriːmiəm]

n. 保险费；附加费 *adj.* 高价的，高品质的

例 He paid a premium price for the high-quality leather jacket, appreciating its durability and style.
他花高价买了这件高品质的皮夹克，因为他很满意衣服的耐用性和款式。

用 a monthly premium 每月的保险费

Exercise 07

一、中文释义练习

请选择单词正确的中文释义。

_____ 1. trim   A. 顶点

_____ 2. galaxy   B. 营养

_____ 3. nutrition   C. 修剪

_____ 4. evacuate   D. 疏散

_____ 5. summit   E. 银河系

_____ 11. stroll   A. 分配

_____ 12. stack   B. 一堆

_____ 13. dispense   C. 散步

_____ 14. exile   D. 流放

_____ 15. revolve   E. 旋转

_____ 6. spiral   A. 大街

_____ 7. executive   B. 杰出的

_____ 8. avenue   C. 螺旋形的

_____ 9. plausible   D. 看似可信的

_____ 10. eminent   E. 行政的

_____ 16. dialect   A. 徽章

_____ 17. badge   B. 方言

_____ 18. qualify   C. 取得资格

_____ 19. adornment   D. 混合的

_____ 20. hybrid   E. 装饰

二、英文释义练习

请选择单词正确的英文释义。

_____ 1. resident   A. to protect sth. with a material that prevents heat

_____ 2. insulate   B. to try to do sth. as well as another person

_____ 3. contradict   C. a person who lives in a particular place

_____ 4. emulate   D. beliefs and principles about what is right and wrong

_____ 5. ethical   E. to say that sth. that sb. else has said is wrong

_____ 6. deviation   A. a system in which people are organized into levels

_____ 7. vulnerable   B. the act of spending more money than you can afford

_____ 8. hierarchy   C. weak and easily hurt physically or emotionally

_____ 9. vertical   D. moving away from what is normal or acceptable

_____ 10. extravagance   E. going straight up or down from a level surface

tortoise
['tɔ:təs]

n. 龟；陆龟

例 The tortoise slowly made its way across the grass, carrying its heavy shell.

乌龟拖着沉重的壳，慢慢地穿过草地。

用 tortoise shell 龟甲

考 If you draw out the family tree of all modern turtles and tortoises, nearly all the branches are aquatic.

如果你画出所有现代海龟与乌龟的家谱图，会发现几乎所有的龟类分支都属于水栖动物。

collapse
[kə'læps]

v. 倒塌；倒下；失败 *n.* 倒塌；崩溃；倒闭

例 The unexpected rainstorm caused a part of the roof to collapse.

突如其来的暴风雨使屋顶的一部分坍塌了。

用 collapsed buildings 坍塌的建筑物

a collapsed investment bank 破产的投资银行

collapse on the sofa and listen to music 倒在沙发上听音乐

考 Only two Japanese pagodas have collapsed in 1,400 years.

在1,400年间，只有两座日本的宝塔倒塌了。

profile
['prəʊfaɪl]

n. 概况；轮廓；外形

例 The newspaper publishes a profile of a leading sportsman every week.

这家报纸每周刊登一篇关于一位优秀运动员的介绍。

用 job profile 工作简介

standard
['stændəd]

n. 标准；水平 *adj.* 标准的；合规的

例 All products sold online must conform to a number of specific standards of quality and safety.

所有在网上售卖的产品必须符合一些特定的质量和安全标准。

用 be up to standard 合格，达到标准

a man of high moral standards 道德水准高的人

扩 standardize *v.* 标准化 standardized *adj.* 标准化的

cognition [kɒɡ'nɪʃn]	*n.* 认知；感知；认识能力 例 His research focused on evidence of cognition in deaf learners. 他的研究重点是耳聋学习者认知能力的证据。 用 processes of perception and cognition 感受和认知的过程 扩 cognitive *adj.* 认知的
warrant ['wɒrənt]	*n.* 正当理由，依据；许可证 *v.* 使有必要；使正当 例 The police issued a search warrant to enter the home of the suspect, to look for evidence. 警方发出了搜查令，进入犯罪嫌疑人的家中寻找证据。 用 arrest warrant 逮捕证
margin ['mɑːdʒɪn]	*n.* 边缘；页边空白；利润 例 The profit margin this year was exceptionally small, largely due to the declining number of customers and the higher costs of production. 今年的利润率非常低，主要是由于客户数量的减少和生产成本的提高。 用 a gross margin of 45% 45%的毛利 扩 marginal *adj.* 边缘的
mercy ['mɜːsi]	*n.* 仁慈；宽容；善行 例 The teacher was far too strict with his punishment, and the boy was upset and begging for mercy. 老师对他的惩罚太严厉了，那个男孩很沮丧，请求原谅。 用 ask for mercy 请求宽恕
premier ['premiə(r)]	*adj.* 首要的，最好的；最早的 *n.* 总理，首相 例 The premier of the movie attracted a large audience to the cinema. 这部电影的首映吸引了大批观众来到电影院。 用 the country's premier opera troupe 这个国家最好的歌剧团
nominate ['nɒmɪneɪt]	*v.* 推荐；提名；任命；指定 例 He was nominated as one of the judges for the singing competition. 他被提名为歌唱比赛的评委之一。 用 be nominated to speak on our behalf 被指派代表我们发言 扩 nomination *n.* 任命；提名
contempt [kən'tempt]	*n.* 轻视，蔑视；忽视 例 The defendant showed contempt for the court during the trial. 被告在审判中对法庭展现出蔑视的态度。 用 look at him with contempt 轻蔑地看着他

conquer ['kɒŋkə(r)]	*v.* 战胜；征服 例 It is important to remain confident and try to be strong and conquer your fears if you want to succeed in an ambitious field. 如果你想在一个竞争激烈的领域获得成功，保持自信、努力变得坚强、战胜恐惧是很重要的。 用 conquered territories 被占领的领土
outdo [ˌaʊt'duː]	*v.* 超过；胜过 例 The determined athlete aimed to outdo her personal best in the upcoming race. 这位意志坚定的运动员决心在即将到来的比赛中超越她的个人最好成绩。 用 outdo each other 胜过对方
suitcase ['suːtkeɪs]	*n.* 手提箱；衣物箱 例 He made great efforts to pack only one suitcase so that he didn't have too much luggage. 他努力只带了一个手提箱，这样就不会有太多的行李。 用 unpack a suitcase 取出手提箱里的东西
reveal [rɪ'viːl]	*v.* 揭示；显示；透露 例 A lot of people I know were incredibly excited when the company revealed the latest edition of their smartphone. 我认识的很多人在该公司发布最新版本的智能手机后感到异常兴奋。 用 reveal a secret 泄露秘密 同 show *v.* 显示
acoustic [ə'kuːstɪk]	*adj.* 声学的；音响的；听觉的 *n.* 音响效果，音质 例 The opera house is a wonderful place to listen to concerts, as the acoustics are second to none. 歌剧院是听音乐会的绝佳地点，因为那里的音响效果首屈一指。 用 acoustic signals 声音信号
overdraw [ˌəʊvə'drɔː]	*v.* 透支（银行账户） 例 You only pay interest if your account is overdrawn. 如果你的银行账户透支了，你只需付利息。 用 overdraw your bank account 透支你的银行账户 扩 withdraw *v.* 撤走；取款

sightseeing ['saɪtsiːɪŋ]	*n.* 观光；游览 例 There are so many places for sightseeing in the country. 这个国家有很多适合观光的地方。 用 sightseeing tour 观光旅行
automobile ['ɔːtəməbiːl]	*n.* 汽车 例 He drove his new automobile with excitement, enjoying the smooth ride. 他兴奋地开着新车，享受着平稳的行驶。 用 automobile industry 汽车工业 考 When primitive automobiles first began to appear in the 1800s, their engines were based on steam power. 当原始的汽车初次出现在19世纪时，它们的引擎是基于蒸汽动力的。
coupon ['kuːpɒn]	*n.* 优惠券；订货单 例 She clipped the coupon and presented it at the store to receive a discount on her purchase. 她剪下优惠券，在商店出示，以获得购物折扣。 用 a money-saving coupon 一张省钱的优惠券
capsule ['kæpsjuːl]	*n.* 胶囊；太空舱；小容器 例 The medicine came in capsule form, which was easy to swallow. 这种药是胶囊形式的，很易于吞咽。 用 space capsule 太空舱
abstract ['æbstrækt] *adj.&n.* [æb'strækt] *v.*	*adj.* 抽象的 *n.* 摘要；抽象；抽象概念 *v.* 写摘要；提取；抽象化 例 I'm not a big fan of abstract works of art; I much prefer more classical realist paintings. 我不太喜欢抽象艺术作品，我更喜欢古典写实主义绘画。 用 abstract knowledge 抽象知识，理论知识 abstract principles such as justice 正义等抽象原则 a modern abstract painting 一幅现代抽象画 反 concrete *adj.* 具体的
consolidation [kən,sɒlɪ'deɪʃn]	*n.* 巩固；合并 例 The company underwent a period of consolidation, merging with a smaller competitor to increase efficiency. 该公司经历了一段整合期，与规模较小的竞争对手合并以提高效率。 用 the consolidation of power 权力的巩固

detach
[dɪ'tætʃ]

v. 拆卸；分离；派遣；超脱

例 She became very emotional about the incident and for a long time she found it very hard to detach herself from it.
她因为这一事件而变得很情绪化，在很长一段时间里，她发现很难将自己从中解脱出来。

用 detach themselves from their problems
让他们从自己的问题中超脱出来

扩 detached *adj.* 分开的；超然的 attach *v.* 贴上；系上

---

trench
[trentʃ]

n. 壕沟，沟渠

例 The soldiers dug deep trenches to provide cover during the intense battle.
士兵们挖了很深的战壕以便在激烈的战斗中提供掩护。

用 fight in the trenches 在战壕里作战

扩 entrench *v.* 使根深蒂固

---

stretch
[stretʃ]

v. 伸展；延伸；延续 *n.* 伸展；一片，一段；一段时间

例 It's important to stretch several times before jogging.
慢跑前做几次拉伸活动是很重要的。

用 stretch the fabric tightly 把布绷紧

同 extend *v.* 延伸，伸展

考 snip out the stretches of the insect's DNA 剪下昆虫的基因片段

---

defect
['diːfekt]

n. 缺点，缺陷，不足

例 If you find that any of our products has a defect you can get a refund.
如果你发现我们的产品有缺陷，你可以得到退款。

用 a speech defect 言语缺陷

---

altitude
['æltɪtjuːd]

n. 海拔高度；高地

例 The climbers started to feel short of breath due to the high altitude of the climb.
由于攀爬的海拔很高，登山者们开始感到呼吸困难。

用 live at high altitudes 生活在高海拔地区

---

sole
[səʊl]

adj. 唯一的；单独的

例 The sole reason for the failure of the business was his laziness in dealing with clients.
生意失败的唯一原因是他在与客户打交道时的懒惰。

用 the sole owner 唯一的拥有者

artery ['ɑːtəri]	*n.* 动脉；干线
	例 The surgeons skillfully repaired the clogged artery in patient's heart. 外科医生熟练地治疗了病人心脏堵塞的动脉。
	用 patients suffering from blocked arteries 患动脉堵塞的病人们
victim ['vɪktɪm]	*n.* 受害人；牺牲者；牺牲品
	例 She had been the victim of discrimination, but the company HR resolved the issue properly. 她曾是歧视的受害者，但公司人力资源部门妥善解决了这个问题。
	用 famine victims 饥荒受害者 victims of crime 犯罪受害者 the innocent victim of an arson attack 纵火案的无辜受害者
publicise ['pʌblɪsaɪz]	*v.* 宣传，宣扬；公布
	例 They worked night and day to publicise their campaign on time. 他们夜以继日地工作，按时宣传他们的活动。
	用 a widely publicised speech 一篇受到广泛报道的讲话
occasion [ə'keɪʒn]	*n.* 时机；场合
	例 The wedding was a very grand occasion which must have cost them a lot of money. 这场婚礼是一个非常盛大的场合，一定花了他们很多钱。
	用 a special occasion 一个特别的场合
	扩 occasional *adj.* 偶尔的；临时的
suspend [sə'spend]	*v.* 延缓，推迟；暂停；悬，挂
	例 Both sides agreed to suspend the meeting until they had further evidence to discuss. 双方都同意暂停会议，直到他们有进一步的证据可以讨论。
	用 suspend judgement 暂不进行判断 suspend production 暂停生产
instance ['ɪnstəns]	*n.* 例子，实例
	例 Although she is usually correct, in this particular instance I think she was mistaken. 虽然她通常是对的，但这次我认为她出错了。
	用 for instance 例如
	扩 distance *n.* 距离 distant *adj.* 遥远的；有距离的
ceremony ['serəməni]	*n.* 典礼，仪式
	例 Everyone is obliged to attend the opening ceremony of the new centre. 每个人都需要参加新中心的启用仪式。
	用 an opening ceremony 开幕仪式 a wedding ceremony 一场婚礼

disparage [dɪ'spærɪdʒ]	*v.* 贬低，诋毁
	例 It is unfair to disparage someone's efforts without understanding the challenges they faced. 不了解别人所面临的挑战就贬低他们的努力是不公平的。
	用 his tendency to disparage literature 他诋毁文学的倾向 an opportunity to disparage his competitors 诋毁竞争对手的机会

amend [ə'mend]	*v.* 修改；改善，改进
	例 The government decided to amend the law to improve data security and privacy in the online domain. 政府决定修改法律，以改善网络领域的数据安全和用户隐私。
	用 the amended version 修订后的版本

territory ['terətri]	*n.* 领土；领域；范围
	例 The country has a huge northern territory which was largely wilderness. 这个国家的北部领土面积很大，那里大部分是荒野。
	用 occupied territories 被占领的土地

enrol [ɪn'rəʊl]	*v.* 登记，注册
	例 He enrolled on the course for the semester beginning September, so he had a couple of months to relax. 他会在九月份开始的这个学期注册入学，因此他还有几个月时间放松。
	用 enrol on a course 注册一门课程
	扩 enrolment *n.* 登记；注册；入学

accelerate [ək'seləreɪt]	*v.* 加速；促进
	例 Constant exposure to the sun's rays can accelerate the ageing process of the skin. 长期暴露在阳光下会加速皮肤的老化过程。
	用 start to accelerate 开始加速
	反 decelerate *v.* 减速
	扩 acceleration *n.* 加速
	考 Discovering the molecules that allow plants to sense temperature has the potential to accelerate the breeding of crops resilient to thermal stress and climate change. 发现能够使植物感知温度的分子有可能加速对于热应力和气候变化有适应性的农作物的培育工作。

interrupt [ˌɪntəˈrʌpt]	*v.* 中断；打断；打扰
	例 Children are usually taught not to interrupt adults when they are speaking. 孩子们通常被教导不要在大人说话时打断他们。
	用 be interrupted by a knock at the door 被敲门声打断
	扩 interruption *n.* 中断；打扰
	考 failed to interrupt her scientific work 没有打断她的科研工作
royal [ˈrɔɪəl]	*adj.* 皇家的，王室的；高贵的 *n.* 王室成员
	例 Historically, royal families often marry people from other foreign royal families. 历史上，王室经常与来自其他国家王室的人通婚。
	用 the royal household 王室
commemoration [kəˌmeməˈreɪʃn]	*n.* 纪念；庆典；纪念会
	例 The monument was erected in commemoration of the victory. 这座纪念碑是为纪念胜利而建立的。
	用 a statue in commemoration of a national hero 一座纪念民族英雄的雕像
access [ˈækses]	*n.* 入口，通道；获得的机会；使用权 *v.* 接近；使用；访问（计算机文件）
	例 Increasingly more people from wider regions of the country have access to quality heath care. 越来越多来自全国更广地区的人能够获得高质量的医疗保健。
	用 the only access to the farmhouse 去农舍的唯一通路 have access to good resources 有机会使用好的资源
	扩 accessible *adj.* 可获得的；可接近的
seize [siːz]	*v.* 抓住；逮捕；攻占，夺取
	例 The dog ran towards the young child and before anyone could do anything, it seized the toy in its jaw and ran off. 那只狗向小孩跑去，大家还没来得及做什么，它就把玩具咬住，跑开了。
	用 seize the precious chance 抓住宝贵的机会
	同 grab *v.* 抓住
acute [əˈkjuːt]	*adj.*（疾病）急性的；严重的；灵敏的
	例 The doctor diagnosed her with acute appendicitis and recommended surgery. 医生诊断她患有急性阑尾炎，建议她进行手术。
	用 acute pain 剧痛 acute sense of smell 灵敏的嗅觉

opportunity [ˌɒpə'tjuːnəti]	*n.* 机会；时机 例 There are plenty of opportunities today for students who have studied computer science and technology. 如今，学习计算机科学和技术的学生有很多机会。 用 no opportunity for further discussion 没有机会进行深入讨论 同 chance *n.* 机会 考 the opportunity of choosing the most appropriate vehicle for each trip 为每次旅行选择最合适的车辆的机会
dean [diːn]	*n.* 院长，教务长 例 The dean of the university addressed the graduating class, congratulating them on their achievements. 大学院长向毕业班致辞，祝贺他们取得的成就。 用 elect him dean 选他为院长
approve [ə'pruːv]	*v.* 批准；赞成；赞赏 例 They were very keen to get married, but her parents did not approve of the arrangement. 他们很想结婚，但是她的父母并不赞成这样的安排。 用 approve of my idea 同意我的想法 反 disapprove *v.* 不同意 扩 approval *n.* 同意，赞成

一、中文释义练习

请选择单词正确的中文释义。

_____ 1. tortoise	A. 边缘
_____ 2. collapse	B. 崩溃
_____ 3. margin	C. 龟
_____ 4. mercy	D. 仁慈
_____ 5. acoustic	E. 声学的

_____ 11. altitude	A. 宣传
_____ 12. publicise	B. 海拔
_____ 13. occasion	C. 修改
_____ 14. amend	D. 领土
_____ 15. territory	E. 时机

_____ 6. overdraw	A. 胶囊
_____ 7. coupon	B. 缺点
_____ 8. capsule	C. 壕沟
_____ 9. trench	D. 优惠券
_____ 10. defect	E. 透支

_____ 16. commemoration	A. 巩固
_____ 17. interrupt	B. 纪念
_____ 18. acute	C. 急性的
_____ 19. dean	D. 教务长
_____ 20. consolidation	E. 中断

二、英文释义练习

请选择单词正确的英文释义。

_____ 1. cognition	A. to do more or better than sb. else
_____ 2. nominate	B. a case used for carrying clothes when travelling
_____ 3. outdo	C. a process by which knowledge is developed in mind
_____ 4. suitcase	D. to formally suggest that sb. should be chosen
_____ 5. sightseeing	E. the activity of visiting interesting places as a tourist

_____ 6. abstract	A. existing in thought without having a physical reality
_____ 7. stretch	B. to make sth. happen faster or earlier than expected
_____ 8. artery	C. to make sth. longer, wider or looser
_____ 9. disparage	D. to suggest that sth. is not important or valuable
_____ 10. accelerate	E. the tubes that carry blood from the heart to other parts

音频

rectify ['rektɪfaɪ]	*v.* 改正；纠正 例 She reviewed the document and attempted to rectify the mistakes in it. 她审阅了文件，并试图修改其中的错误。 用 rectify a fault 改正缺点 扩 correct *v.* 改正，纠正 *adj.* 正确的
meditation [ˌmedɪ'teɪʃn]	*n.* 冥想，沉思 例 At the yoga class they often practised meditation to calm the mind and body. 在瑜伽课上，他们经常练习冥想以使身心平静下来。 用 his meditations on life and art 他对生活和艺术的沉思 考 Labyrinths are thought to encourage a feeling of calm and have been used as a meditation and prayer tool in many cultures over many centuries. 人们认为螺旋形迷宫能够促使人获得平静，几个世纪以来许多文化将其当作冥想和祈祷的辅助工具。
poverty ['pɒvəti]	*n.* 贫穷；贫乏，短缺 例 She worked in a charitable organisation which helped alleviate poverty. 她在一个帮助缓解贫困的慈善组织工作。 用 a poverty of ideas 思想的贫乏
regardless [rɪ'gɑːdləs]	*adv.* 不管；无论如何 例 He was a determined climber and would go out climbing regardless of the weather. 他是一个坚定的登山者，无论天气如何，他都要出去登山。 用 regardless of religion, colour, or creed 不管宗教、肤色或信仰如何
gill [gɪl]	*n.* 鱼鳃；沟壑，溪流 例 The fish's gills allowed it to extract oxygen from the water, enabling it to breathe. 鱼的鳃使它能够从水中吸取氧气，使其能够呼吸。 用 breathe through gills 通过鳃呼吸

compete [kəm'piːt]	*v.* 竞争；比赛；对抗 例 My daughter wants to compete in the athletics competition next season. 我女儿想参加下个季度的田径比赛。 用 competing for the contract 为得到合同而竞争 扩 competitive *adj.* 有竞争力的；竞争激烈的 competition *n.* 竞争；比赛 competent *adj.* 有能力的；能胜任的
perception [pə'sepʃn]	*n.* 知觉；感觉；看法 例 I was shocked to learn of the perception people really have of me. 当我得知人们对我的真实看法时，我很震惊。 用 visual perception 视觉 general public perception 公众的普遍认识 扩 perceive *v.* 感觉到；发觉 考 The perception of smell, therefore, consists not only of the sensation of the odours themselves, but of the experiences and emotions associated with them. 因此，对味觉的感知，不仅包括对气味的感觉本身，还包括与之相关的体验与情感。
mimic ['mɪmɪk]	*v.* 模仿 *n.* 模仿者 例 The AI computer programme is able to mimic the conversation of a real human. 人工智能程序能够模仿真人的对话。 用 mimic her southern accent 模仿她的南方口音 同 imitate *v.* 模仿 扩 mimetic *adj.* 模仿的 考 Another powerful source of information for infants about the effects they can have on the world around them is provided when others mimic them. 另一个婴儿可以获取的、有关他们对周边环境影响的重要途径产生于他人模仿他们之时。
animate ['ænɪmət] *adj.* ['ænɪmeɪt] *v.*	*adj.* 有生命的，有活力的 *v.* 使生气勃勃；使生动；制作动画 例 We appeal to men animated by a spirit of liberty and independence. 我们呼吁那些被自由和独立精神所鼓舞的人。 用 animate the crowd 让人们兴奋 扩 animation *n.* 活力；动画 考 Then we're making an animated diagram to show the geography of the area in prehistoric times. 接下来我们打算用一个动态图表来展示该地区在史前时代的地理位置。

verdict [ˈvɜːdɪkt]	*n.* 结论；裁定
	例 The jury concluded the case with the verdict that the defendant was guilty of the crime, and the judge sentenced him to three years in prison. 陪审团以被告人有罪的决议结案，法官判他三年监禁。
	用 reach a verdict 作出裁定
recommend [ˌrekəˈmend]	*v.* 推荐；介绍；建议
	例 We do not recommend going to the restaurant if you are in a rush since the service is rather slow. 如果你赶时间，我们不建议你去那家餐厅，因为服务相当慢。
	用 be recommended for the post 被推荐到这个岗位 be highly recommended 得到高度赞扬
	扩 recommendation *n.* 推荐；介绍
	考 And which locations would you recommend? 你推荐哪些地点呢？
catalogue [ˈkætəlɒg]	*n.* 目录
	例 The home decoration catalogue had a wide range of furniture of varying styles. 家庭装饰目录上有风格多样的各种家具。
	用 consult the library catalogue 查看图书馆目录
	考 To make it easier to plan motoring holidays, the site catalogued the most popular driving routes in the country, highlighting different routes according to the season and indicating distances and times. 为了让规划驾车度假更加容易，这一网站对国内最受欢迎的驾车路线进行了分类，根据季节标注了不同路线，并标示了距离和时间。
apartment [əˈpɑːtmənt]	*n.* 公寓；房间
	例 They rented an apartment on the seventh floor while waiting to buy their new home. 他们在准备购买新房的同时，在七层租了一套公寓。
	用 her own apartment 她自己的公寓
reject [rɪˈdʒekt]	*v.* 拒绝；排斥；丢弃
	例 Never reject an idea or goal because you think it might be hard work. 永远不要因为你认为一个想法或目标可能很难而拒绝它。
	用 reject an argument 拒绝接受一个观点 reject a suggestion 拒绝接受一项建议
	扩 rejection *n.* 拒绝

odour
['əʊdə(r)]

n. 气味；臭味

例 The men came in from working hard in the fields with the odour of sweat on their bodies.
男人们从地里辛苦劳作回来，身上散发着汗水的味道。

用 the lingering odour of car exhaust 挥之不去的汽车尾气的气味

aerobic
[eə'rəʊbɪk]

adj. 有氧的；需氧的

例 Regular aerobic exercises like jogging and swimming promote cardiovascular health.
定期的有氧运动，如慢跑和游泳，会促进心血管健康。

用 aerobic bacteria 需氧细菌 aerobic exercise 有氧运动

toxic
['tɒksɪk]

adj. 有毒的；中毒的

例 Too much toxic waste is being dumped in the oceans.
太多有毒废物正被倾倒入海洋中。

用 dispose of toxic waste 处理有毒废料

扩 toxin *n.* 毒素；毒质

maternal
[mə'tɜːnl]

adj. 母亲的；母系的

例 Her maternal instincts kicked in when she saw the baby crying.
当她看到婴儿哭泣时，母性本能开始发挥作用。

用 maternal age 育龄 maternal love 母爱

engage
[ɪn'geɪdʒ]

v. 从事，参与；雇用，聘请；吸引

例 Only 20% of people in the country engage in regular physical exercise.
这个国家只有20%的人定期参与体育锻炼。

用 engage in 参加，从事

perpetual
[pə'petʃuəl]

adj. 永久的；无期限的

例 He seems to possess a perpetual enthusiasm for taking up new hobbies and interests.
他似乎对培养新的爱好和兴趣有着永恒的热情。

用 the perpetual noise of traffic 持续不断的交通噪声

考 a perpetual monument 一座永久的丰碑

disclose
[dɪs'kləʊz]

v. 透露，揭露

例 She would not disclose the personal information of her employees to anyone.
她不会向任何人透露雇员的个人信息。

用 refuse to disclose details of the takeover to the press
拒绝向媒体透露公司收购的详细情况

同 reveal *v.* 揭示，揭露

antibiotics [ˌæntibaɪˈɒtɪks]	*n.* 抗生素
	例 It's important to complete your entire course of antibiotics if you want them to be effective. 如果你想让抗生素有效，完成整个疗程是很重要的。
	用 prescribe antibiotics 开抗生素
	考 Farmer ants secrete antibiotics to control other fungi that might act as "weeds", and spread waste to fertilise the crop. 工蚁分泌抗生素以控制其他可能充当"杂草"的真菌，并传播废弃物来为作物施肥。
apportion [əˈpɔːʃn]	*v.* 分配；分派；分摊
	例 They were unhappy with the failure of the product when it hit the market, but they did not apportion blame to anyone on the team. 产品上市时，他们对产品的失败感到不满，但他们没有把责任归咎于团队中的任何人。
	用 be apportioned according to contribution 根据贡献大小进行分配
	扩 proportion *n.* 占比；比例
embassy ['embəsi]	*n.* 大使馆；大使馆全体人员
	例 The embassy will continue discussions with the government until the matter is resolved properly. 大使馆将继续与政府沟通，直到问题妥善解决。
	用 embassy officials 大使馆官员 inform the embassy of the situation 向大使馆报告形势
endeavour [ɪnˈdevə(r)]	*v.* 努力，尽力 *n.* 努力，尝试
	例 Her strong endeavours to improve the company performance were quite successful. 她为改善公司业绩所作的努力相当成功。
	用 make every endeavour to arrive on time 尽全力按时到达
	考 Each definition is slightly different—and tends to reflect the field of endeavour of each pioneer. 每个定义都略有小小的不同，且通常都映射出了每位先锋者所付出努力的领域。
withstand [wɪðˈstænd]	*v.* 抵挡，抵御，经受住
	例 The bridge was made of especially strong steel in order to withstand strong winds. 这座桥用特别坚固的钢建造，以承受强风。
	用 withstand high temperatures 承受高温
	同 resist *v.* 抵抗

gauge [geɪdʒ]	*v.* 测量；估计 *n.* 计量器；尺寸；规格
	例 It is hard to gauge whether he is happy or sad because he displays little emotion. 很难判断他是快乐还是悲伤，因为他没有流露出什么情感。
	用 pressure gauge 压力计
pale [peɪl]	*adj.* 苍白的；浅色的；暗淡的
	例 Her face turned pale when she heard the shocking news, her expression filled with disbelief. 当她听到这个令人震惊的消息时，她的脸变得苍白，表情充满了疑惑。
	用 pale with fear 害怕得脸色苍白 a pale sky 天色昏暗
	考 pale yellow pear-shaped fruits 淡黄色梨形果实
demographic [ˌdemə'ɡræfɪk]	*adj.* 人口的；人口统计的
	例 Currently in Europe they are discussing the implications of the demographic trend towards an ageing population. 目前在欧洲，他们正在讨论人口老龄化趋势的影响。
	用 the demographic trend 人口趋势
countless ['kaʊntləs]	*adj.* 无数的，数不尽的
	例 There are countless romantic stories in the history of all countries and cultures. 在所有国家和文化的历史上，都有无数的浪漫故事。
	用 bring joy to countless people 把快乐带给无数人
infect [ɪn'fekt]	*v.* 使感染，传染
	例 A single mosquito can infect a large number of people with malaria. 一只蚊子就可以让很多人感染疟疾。
	用 eggs infected with salmonella 带沙门氏菌的鸡蛋
	扩 infection *n.* 传染；感染 infectious *adj.* 传染的；感染的
register ['redʒɪstə(r)]	*v.* 登记；注册 *n.* 登记表，注册簿
	例 Please make sure you register for the course before September. 请确保自己在9月份之前注册该课程。
	用 register a company 注册公司 register a trademark 注册商标
	考 This involves the process of receiving and registering information, which is necessary for creating memories of information or events that you experience. 这涉及接收和录入信息的过程，这对于创建你所经历的信息或事件的记忆是必要的。

masterpiece ['mɑːstəpiːs]	*n.* 杰作，代表作 例 Mozart composed so many masterpieces that it's hard to say which is his best. 莫扎特创作了如此多的杰出作品，以至于很难说哪个是他的最佳作品。 用 a masterpiece of simplicity 简洁朴实的典范
accuse [əˈkjuːz]	*v.* 控告，指控；谴责 例 Both sides keep on accusing each other of starting to fight, but to be honest I think they are equally to blame. 双方都指责对方挑起了争斗，但说实话，我认为双方都有责任。 用 be accused of incompetence 被指责无能
lexical ['leksɪkl]	*adj.* 词汇的；词典的 例 He was not strong on grammar or pronunciation, but his lexical resource in English was fantastic. 他在语法和发音方面不擅长，但他在英语词汇方面非常优秀。 用 provide helpful lexical information 提供有用的词汇信息 扩 lexis *n.* 词汇
astronomy [əˈstrɒnəmi]	*n.* 天文学 例 Those that are particularly good at physics sometimes go into the field of astronomy. 那些特别擅长物理的人有时会进入天文学领域。 用 a new era in astronomy 天文学的新纪元 扩 autonomy *n.* 自治；自治权 economy *n.* 经济
arrange [əˈreɪndʒ]	*v.* 安排，筹备；排列，布置 例 He usually arranged important team meetings in the mornings. 他通常在上午安排重要的团队会议。 用 arrange how to get to the airport 安排如何到达机场 扩 arrangement *n.* 安排；约定
implicit [ɪmˈplɪsɪt]	*adj.* 含蓄的；暗示的 例 He did not get straight to the point about whether we would get an extra holiday, but his implicit suggestions seemed to indicate that we would not. 他并没有直接告诉我们是否有额外假期，但他含蓄的建议似乎暗示了我们不会有。 用 implicit criticism 含蓄的批评 反 explicit *adj.* 明确的，清楚的

reciprocal [rɪ'sɪprəkl]	*adj.* 相互的；互惠的 例 They had a reciprocal agreement that both parties adhered to. 他们有一个双方都遵守的互惠协议。 用 a reciprocal trade agreement 一份互利的贸易协议
distract [dɪ'strækt]	*v.* 转移（注意力），使分心 例 He has a problem with his concentration span, and gets distracted very easily with his mobile phone all the time. 他的注意力持续时间存在问题，总是很容易因为手机而分心。 用 distract me from my work 使我不能专心工作 扩 distraction *n.* 注意力分散；分心
exterior [ɪk'stɪəriə(r)]	*adj.* 外部的；表面的 *n.* 外部；表面 例 The exterior of the skyscraper was illuminated by thousands of tiny lights. 摩天大楼的外部被成千上万盏小灯照亮。 用 the exterior of the house 房屋外墙 反 interior *adj.* 内部的；本质的 *n.* 内部；里面 考 The interior has just been repainted, and we're about to start on the exterior of the building—that'll be a big job. 内部刚刚重新喷漆，现在我们正在对外立面进行装修，这可是个大工程。
thrill [θrɪl]	*n.* 兴奋，激动 例 The roller coaster ride provided an exhilarating thrill for the excited students. 过山车为激动的学生们提供了令人兴奋的刺激。 用 the thrill of catching a really big fish 为捉到一条大鱼而兴奋
bud [bʌd]	*n.* 芽，花蕾 *v.* 发芽 例 The tiny bud on the plant indicated that spring was approaching. 植物上的小嫩芽预示着春天快要来临了。 用 taste bud 味蕾 考 Farmers and gardeners have known for hundreds of years how responsive plants are to temperature: warm winters cause many trees and flowers to bud early, something humans have long used to predict weather and harvest times for the coming year. 几百年来，农民和园丁都熟知植物对温度的感应能力：暖冬使许多树木和花朵能够更早发芽，人类长期以来一直以此预测来年的天气和收成。

textile ['tekstaɪl]	*n.* 纺织品；[pl.] 纺织业
	例 The textile industry plays a significant role in the country's economy, employing thousands of workers. 纺织业在该国经济中扮演着重要角色，雇用了数千名工人。
	用 the textile industry 纺织工业 a textile designer 一位纺织品设计师
	考 Organic materials like textiles and hides are relatively rare finds at archaeological sites. 诸如纺织品和兽皮之类的有机材料在考古现场相对罕见。
dull [dʌl]	*adj.* 枯燥的，无聊的；黯淡的；阴沉的
	例 The lecture was so dull that some students struggled to stay awake. 讲座太枯燥了，有些学生难以保持清醒。
	用 a dull grey colour 一种暗灰色
	考 Long periods in the sun or bush fires could transform dull, cloudy lumps into higher quality transparent gum. 长期的日晒或丛林火灾会将灰黑色的树脂块儿变成更高品质的透明树脂。
enthusiasm [ɪn'θjuːziæzəm]	*n.* 热心，热情
	例 He approached the project with great enthusiasm and was determined to make it a success. 他以极大的热情开始这个项目，并决心使其获得成功。
	用 lose her enthusiasm for teaching 失去她对于教书的热忱
	扩 enthusiastic *adj.* 热情的
pulse [pʌls]	*n.* 脉冲；脉搏 *v.* 跳动
	例 The doctor felt his pulse and concluded that his heart rate was indeed very fast. 医生摸了他的脉搏，确定他的心跳确实很快。
	用 an abnormally high pulse rate 异常高的脉率
magnitude ['mægnɪtjuːd]	*n.* 重要性；大小；量级
	例 The magnitude of the earthquake was bigger than any that California had experienced in decades. 这次地震的震级比过去几十年来加利福尼亚州的任何一次地震都高。
	用 realise the magnitude of the problem 意识到这个问题的重要性
argument ['ɑːgjumənt]	*n.* 论证；论据；争吵
	例 He didn't want an argument, so he tried to avoid discussing the serious matter with her. 他并不想进行争论，因此他尽量避免与她讨论严肃的问题。
	用 win an argument 在辩论中胜出

welfare
['welfeə(r)]

n. 幸福，安康；福利

例 The government aimed to improve the welfare of its citizens through various programs.
政府旨在通过各种计划改善公民的福利。

用 child welfare 儿童福利
a social welfare programme 一项社会福利计划

考 The cost is in the collateral damage of the very methods of food production that have made the food cheaper: in the pollution of water, the enervation of soil, the destruction of wildlife, the harm to animal welfare and the threat to human health caused by modern industrial agriculture.
这代价恰恰是使食品变得便宜的生产方式本身所造成的间接伤害，这伤害包括现代工业化农业所造成的水资源污染、土壤贫瘠、野生动植物破坏、对动物权益的损害以及对人类健康的威胁。

Exercise 09

一、中文释义练习

请选择单词正确的中文释义。

_____ 1. rectify   A. 改正   _____ 11. withstand   A. 天文学

_____ 2. gill   B. 贫穷   _____ 12. pale   B. 杰作

_____ 3. poverty   C. 模仿   _____ 13. masterpiece   C. 指控

_____ 4. regardless   D. 不管   _____ 14. accuse   D. 抵挡

_____ 5. mimic   E. 鱼鳃   _____ 15. astronomy   E. 苍白的

_____ 6. catalogue   A. 抗生素   _____ 16. register   A. 含蓄的

_____ 7. toxic   B. 目录   _____ 17. implicit   B. 注册

_____ 8. antibiotics   C. 有毒的   _____ 18. exterior   C. 外部的

_____ 9. disclose   D. 分配   _____ 19. textile   D. 纺织品

_____ 10. apportion   E. 揭露   _____ 20. pulse   E. 脉冲

二、英文释义练习

请选择单词正确的英文释义。

_____ 1. meditation   A. the practice of thinking deeply in silence

_____ 2. perception   B. to be more successful or better than sb. else

_____ 3. compete   C. designed to improve the function of heart and lungs

_____ 4. animate   D. to make sth. more lively or full of energy

_____ 5. aerobic   E. the way you notice things, especially with the senses

_____ 6. perpetual   A. relating to the structure of populations

_____ 7. demographic   B. continuing for a long time without interruption

_____ 8. infect   C. a strong feeling of excitement or pleasure

_____ 9. reciprocal   D. two people or groups who agree to help each other

_____ 10. thrill   E. to make a disease or an illness spread to a person

filter ['fɪltə(r)]	*n.* 过滤器 *v.* 过滤
	例 He used a coffee filter to remove the grounds and enjoy a smooth, flavourful cup of coffee. 他用咖啡过滤器过滤掉咖啡渣，享受一杯丝滑可口的咖啡。
	用 filter paper for the coffee machine 咖啡机滤纸 a filter lane 分流车道
reliance [rɪ'laɪəns]	*n.* 依赖，信赖；信心
	例 Too strong a reliance on a particular market may be dangerous for a company. 过于依赖某一特定市场对公司而言可能是有风险的。
	用 increasing reliance on foreign aid 日益依赖外国援助
	同 dependence *n.* 依靠，依赖
sanitation [ˌsænɪ'teɪʃn]	*n.* 卫生；环境卫生；卫生设备
	例 The Romans were famous for constructing roads, buildings and excellent sanitation systems for cities. 罗马人以修建道路、建筑和完善的城市卫生系统而闻名。
	用 poor sanitation 卫生条件差
	考 Sanitation did not become widespread until the 19th century. 直到19世纪公共卫生才开始普及。
transport ['trænspɔːt] *n.* [træn'spɔːt] *v.*	*n.* 运输，运送；交通工具，运输方式 *v.* 运输，运送；传播
	例 The public transport system in my country has considerably improved over the last decade. 在过去十年中，我们国家的公共交通系统有了很大改善。
	用 air transport 空运 freight transport 货运
outcome ['aʊtkʌm]	*n.* 结果；成果
	例 The investigation had taken months and was nearing its end; everyone was hoping for a positive outcome. 调查用了几个月时间，已经接近尾声：每个人都希望能有一个积极的结果。
	用 the final outcome of the negotiation 谈判的最终结果
	同 result *n.* 结果 consequence *n.* 结果；后果

ornament [ˈɔːnəmənt] *n.* [ˈɔːnəment] *v.*	*n.* 装饰品；装饰；首饰 *v.* 装饰，点缀 例 The Christmas tree sparkled with colourful ornaments, creating a festive atmosphere. 圣诞树上挂满了五颜六色的装饰品，营造出节日的氛围。 用 a glass ornament 玻璃装饰品
memorise [ˈmeməraɪz]	*v.* 记忆；存储 例 It's important to memorise vocabulary in context in order to improve your language use. 为了提高你的语言使用能力，在语境中记忆单词是很重要的。 用 memorise a poem 记住一首诗 扩 memory *n.* 回忆；记忆 memo *n.* 备忘录
junk [dʒʌŋk]	*n.* 垃圾；废旧杂物 例 They cleared out their attic, getting rid of old furniture and other unwanted junk. 他们清理了阁楼，扔掉了旧家具和其他不需要的杂物。 用 a junk shop 一家旧货店 junk food 垃圾食品 考 Concern about space junk goes back to the beginning of the satellite era, but the number of objects in orbit is rising so rapidly that researchers are investigating new ways of attacking the problem. 关于太空垃圾的担忧自卫星时代之始就由来有之，但由于轨道上物体数量的增速如此之快，研究者们正在摸索新的办法来破解这个问题。
internal [ɪnˈtɜːnl]	*adj.* 内部的；国内的 例 The company are encouraging internal applications for the job, rather than employing people from outside of the company. 这家公司鼓励内部申请职位，而不是从公司以外雇人。 用 internal organs 内脏 the internal structure of a building 大楼内部结构 internal divisions within the company 公司内各部门 反 external *adj.* 外部的；表面的 考 the internal thermometer in plant cells 植物细胞内部温度计
tender [ˈtendə(r)]	*adj.* 温柔的，亲切的；嫩的，软的 *v.* 提出，提供；投标 *n.* 投标，投标书 例 The tender, warm touch of a mother usually soothes a crying baby. 母亲轻柔温暖的抚摸通常能安抚哭泣的婴儿。 用 tender words 亲切的话语

inspect [ɪn'spekt]	*v.* 检查；视察；检阅
	例 He got out of the car to inspect the damage after the accident. 事故发生后，他下车检查损坏情况。
	用 inspect the playing field 检查运动场
	扩 inspection *n.* 检查；视察
relief [rɪ'liːf]	*n.* 救济；减轻，解除；轻松，解脱
	例 The cooler weather of autumn gave some relief after the intense heat of summer. 炎热的夏天过后，秋天凉爽的天气使人放松下来。
	用 a sense of relief 解脱感
	扩 relieve *v.* 缓解，解除
diameter [daɪ'æmɪtə(r)]	*n.* 直径
	例 The teapot was about ten centimeters in diameter and about twenty centimetres high. 茶壶大约直径10厘米，高20厘米。
	用 the diameter of a tree trunk 树干的直径
	扩 perimeter *n.* 周长；边界
	考 The diameter of the traps can vary from about 18 mm to 10 cm and the number used can vary from a few to several hundred. 陷阱的直径从18毫米到10厘米不等，数量从几个到几百个不等。
indicate ['ɪndɪkeɪt]	*v.* 表明；指出；暗示
	例 Satellite images indicate the coming of a strong rainstorm in the region. 卫星图像显示该地区即将迎来一场强暴雨。
	用 indicate wind direction 指示风向
	同 imply *v.* 暗示
	考 As work in neurosciences indicates, the acquisition of literacy necessitated a new circuit in our species' brain more than 6,000 years ago. 正如神经科学领域表明的那样，在六千多年前，习得读写能力需要人类大脑构建一个新的回路。
curriculum [kə'rɪkjələm]	*n.* 课程
	例 The new curriculum was much more innovative than the previous one. 新课程比之前的课程更具创新性。
	用 be on the curriculum 被纳入课程内容

privilege ['prɪvəlɪdʒ]	*n.* 特权；优待 *v.* 给予特权 例 She was born with a great privilege—she was from an educated wealthy background—and this gave her a head start in life. 她出身优越，生于受过良好教育的富裕家庭，这让她的人生有了一个很好的开端。 用 have the privilege of working with them again 有幸与他们再度合作
deny [dɪ'naɪ]	*v.* 否定，否认；拒绝 例 He denied the accusations and insisted that he was innocent. 他否认了这些指控，坚称自己是无辜的。 用 deny a claim 否认某种说法
celebrate ['selɪbreɪt]	*v.* 庆祝；赞美；祝贺 例 I enjoy celebrating my birthday over a dinner with friends and family at my favourite restaurant. 我喜欢和朋友家人在我最喜欢的餐厅用餐，来庆祝自己的生日。 用 celebrate his 60th birthday 庆祝他的60岁生日 扩 celebration *n.* 庆祝
opaque [əʊ'peɪk]	*adj.* 不透明的，不透光的；隐晦的 例 The frosted glass windows were opaque, allowing light but maintaining privacy. 磨砂玻璃窗是不透明的，允许光线进入，但保持隐私。 用 opaque glass 不透明的玻璃
inhabit [ɪn'hæbɪt]	*v.* 栖息；居住于；占据 例 Various species of parrot inhabit the tropical rainforests of South America. 各种各样的鹦鹉栖息在南美洲的热带雨林中。 用 some of the rare species that inhabit the area 生活在这个地区的一些罕见物种 扩 inhabitant *n.* 居民；栖息动物 考 They inhabit the soil, air, rocks and water and are present within every form of life, from seaweed and coral to dogs and humans. 它们住在土壤、空气、岩石和水里，也在每一种生命形式身上都存在着，从海草和珊瑚到狗和人类无一例外。
contaminate [kən'tæmɪneɪt]	*v.* 污染；毒害，腐蚀（思想或品德） 例 The waste chemicals contaminated the fresh water supply in the town. 废弃化学药品污染了镇上的淡水供应。 用 contaminated soil 受到污染的土壤

accompany [əˈkʌmpəni]	*v.* 陪伴，伴随；伴奏 例 He always accompanied her home at night when it was late and dark outside. 他总是在天色已晚外面很黑的时候陪她回家。 用 accompany his mother to dinner 陪同他母亲用餐 考 An MRI scanner uses magnetic fields and radio waves to track the changes in oxygenated blood that accompany mental activity. 核磁共振扫描仪利用磁场和无线电波来追踪伴随精神活动的含氧血液的变化。
dopamine [ˈdəʊpəmiːn]	*n.* 多巴胺 例 The brain releases dopamine, a neurotransmitter, when experiencing pleasure or reward. 当经历快乐或奖励时，大脑会释放多巴胺，一种神经递质。 用 dopamine receptor 多巴胺受体 考 the dopamine neurons in the caudate 尾状体内的多巴胺神经元
quality [ˈkwɒləti]	*n.* 质量；品质；特性 *adj.* 优质的；高品质的 例 I have seen the quality of their electronic products improve gradually over time. 我看到他们电子产品的质量随着时间推移而逐渐提高。 用 be of good quality 质量好 goods of a high quality 优质商品 扩 qualify *v.* 获得资格；合格 考 The one factor that was found to affect the child's development was family stress leading to a poor quality of parent–child interaction. 人们发现一个会影响孩子发展的因素就是由于家庭压力所导致的亲子交流质量不佳。
genre [ˈʒɒnrə]	*n.* 类型；种类；体裁；样式 例 Of all the genres of film, horror and fantasy were his least favourite. 在所有类型的电影中，恐怖和幻想类的影片是他最不喜欢的。 用 music genre 音乐类型；音乐风格 考 We have this huge gap in our knowledge about the history and prehistory of storytelling, despite the fact that we know this genre is an incredibly ancient one. 我们在了解有关故事的历史和史前史方面存在巨大差异，尽管我们知道这是一种古老的故事类型。
dispute [dɪˈspjuːt]	*n.* 辩论；争吵；纠纷 *v.* 争论；对……提出质询 例 They agreed to try to settle their dispute by negotiation. 他们同意尽量通过谈判解决他们之间的纠纷。 用 the latest dispute over fishing rights 最近关于捕鱼权的争端

liberty ['lɪbəti]	*n.* 自由 例 After years of living in a small city apartment, he felt an enormous sense of liberty when they moved to the country town. 在城市的小公寓里住了多年后，当他们搬到乡村小镇时，他感到了极大的自由感。 用 the fight for justice and liberty 争取正义和自由的斗争
appointment [ə'pɔɪntmənt]	*n.* 任命；约定 例 The dentist does not open on weekends, so it's best to book an appointment now for a weekday. 牙医诊所周末不营业，因此最好现在就预约工作日。 用 an appointment with my lawyer 与我律师的约定
leap [liːp]	*v.* 跳，跳跃；跳过 *n.* 飞跃；跳跃 例 The hare can leap a distance of around two metres when it is running. 野兔跑起来时能跳跃大约两米的距离。 用 leap into the river 跳入河中
dilemma [dɪ'lemə]	*n.* 困境；进退两难 例 He was in a dilemma as to whether to study his masters in the UK or the USA. 他左右为难，不知道应该在英国还是在美国攻读硕士学位。 用 face a dilemma 面临左右为难的困境 be in a dilemma 处于进退两难的境地
arbitrary ['ɑːbɪtrəri]	*adj.* 专横的，武断的；任意的 例 The decision seemed arbitrary, lacking any clear rationale or reasoning. 这个决定似乎是武断的，缺乏任何明确的逻辑或推理。 用 arbitrary arrests and detention without trial 未经审讯随意逮捕扣押
disappoint [ˌdɪsə'pɔɪnt]	*v.* 使失望 例 It disappointed her greatly when she was not chosen to take part in the competition. 她没有被选去参加比赛，这使她非常失望。 用 disappoint everyone by postponing the visit 由于推迟访问让人们失望 扩 disappointing *adj.* 令人失望的 disappointed *adj.* 失望的 考 They agree it has been disappointing. 他们同意这看起来有些让人沮丧。

accessory [ək'sesəri]	*n.* 配饰；附件 *adj.* 副的；附属的
	例 Some people gain a lot of confidence from purchasing accessories like designer handbags. 有些人从购买名牌手提包等配饰中获得了很多自信。
	用 a range of furnishings and accessories for the home 各种各样的家居装饰物及配件
curtain ['kɜːtn]	*n.* 窗帘，门帘；幕布
	例 She drew the curtains to block out the sunlight and create a cozy ambiance in the room. 她拉上窗帘挡住阳光，在房间里营造一种舒适的氛围。
	用 a pair of curtains 一对窗帘 close the curtains 把窗帘拉上
	考 Then there's the issue of atmosphere—so in the first scene we needed to know how boring life was in the doctor's village in the 1950s, so when the curtain went up on the first scene in the waiting room, there was that long silence before anyone spoke. 然后是关于环境氛围的问题。所以在第一幕，我们需要知道20世纪50年代在医生的村子里生活是多么乏味，因此当大幕拉开时，候诊室里的人们开始说话前有一段长长的寂静。
gorgeous ['gɔːdʒəs]	*adj.* 华丽的，灿烂的；极好的
	例 The landscape views from the hotel window were gorgeous. 从旅馆窗户望出去的风景非常壮丽。
	用 gorgeous mountain scenery 秀丽的山间景色
unleash [ʌn'liːʃ]	*v.* 释放；发泄；使爆发
	例 The unleashed energy of the thunderstorm brought heavy rain and strong winds. 雷暴释放的能量带来了暴雨和强风。
	用 unleash a storm of protest in the press 引发新闻界的抗议浪潮
available [ə'veɪləbl]	*adj.* 可获得的；可找到的；可使用的
	例 The offer at the store is only available for a limited period of one month. 商店的优惠时效有限，只有一个月时间。
	用 available resources 可利用的资源 available facilities 可用的设备
	扩 availability *n.* 可用性；有效 the availability of cheap flights 有廉价机票出售
	考 an inexpensive and readily available coal tar waste product 一种并不昂贵且易于获取的煤焦油废料

reign [reɪn]	*v.* 统治；盛行 *n.* 统治时期；任期 例 Queen Victoria's reign was considered one of the most important in British history. 维多利亚女王的统治被认为是英国历史上最重要的统治时期之一。 用 in/during the reign of Charles II 在查理二世统治期间
comment ['kɒment]	*n.* 评论；意见 *v.* 发表评论；发表意见 例 The ambassador refused to comment to the media about the outcomes of the meeting. 大使拒绝就会议的结果向媒体发表评论。 用 make helpful comments on my work 对我的工作做出有用的评价 同 review *n.* 评论 *v.* 写评论
benevolent [bə'nevələnt]	*adj.* 仁慈的；慈善的；亲切的 例 A benevolent uncle helped to pay for her university studies. 一位仁慈的叔叔帮她支付了大学学费。 用 a benevolent smile 和蔼的笑容 a benevolent attitude 和蔼的态度
screw [skruː]	*n.* 螺丝；螺旋桨 *v.* 用螺钉固定；拧紧 例 The mechanic tightened the screw on the wheel to secure the parts together. 机械师把轮子上的螺丝拧紧，把部件固定在一起。 用 tighten all the screws 把全部螺丝拧紧
coexist [ˌkəʊɪg'zɪst]	*v.* 同时存在，共存 例 The diverse community learned to coexist harmoniously, respecting each other's differences. 这个多元化社区学会了和谐共处，尊重彼此的差异。 用 coexist with other chronic diseases 与其他慢性病同时存在 扩 coexistence *n.* 共存，和平共处
coincide [ˌkəʊɪn'saɪd]	*v.* 一致，符合；同时发生 例 She timed her holiday to coincide with the children's school holidays. 她把自己的假期安排在与孩子们假期一致的时间。 用 coincide with the conference 与大会在同一时间举行 考 What was more, the old ants didn't experience any drop in the levels of either serotonin or dopamine—brain chemicals whose decline often coincides with aging. 此外，年迈的蚂蚁并没有经历血清素或多巴胺水平的任何衰退，这些大脑物质的降低通常伴随着衰老。

fluctuate [ˈflʌktʃueɪt]	*v.* 波动；涨落；动摇
	例 Her moods were unpredictable and often fluctuated between anxiety, depression and excitement. 她的情绪难以预测，经常在焦虑、沮丧和兴奋间波动。
	用 fluctuating prices 波动的价格
	扩 fluctuation *n.* 波动 wild fluctuations in interest rates 利率的疯狂波动

lease [liːs]	*n.* 租约，租契 *v.* 出租，租用
	例 They signed a lease agreement to rent the apartment for a year. 他们签订了租赁协议，租住这套公寓一年。
	用 lease an apartment 租一套公寓

amphibious [æmˈfɪbiəs]	*adj.* 两栖的，水陆两用的
	例 Frogs are amphibious creatures, capable of living both in water and on land. 青蛙是两栖动物，既能在水中生活，也能在陆地上生活。
	用 amphibious vehicles 水陆两用车辆
	考 Sure enough, these amphibious species show up on the triangular graph approximately half way between the "wet cluster" of sea turtles and the "dry cluster" of land tortoises. 当然，这些两栖物种的数据出现在接近三角坐标中间的位置，位于水栖海龟与陆栖乌龟的坐标点之间。

anthropology [ˌænθrəˈpɒlədʒi]	*n.* 人类学
	例 He pursued a degree in anthropology to study the cultural diversity of human societies. 他攻读人类学学位，研究人类社会的文化多样性。
	用 some knowledge of anthropology 一些人类学知识
	扩 anthropologist *n.* 人类学家
	考 DNA teased from these human remains may help answer one of the most puzzling questions in Pacific anthropology: did all Pacific islanders spring from one source or many? 从这些人类遗骸中提取的DNA也许可以帮助解答太平洋人类学中最令人迷惑不解的问题之一：太平洋岛民们到底是来自于同一个源头还是有许多出处？

gender [ˈdʒendə(r)]	*n.* 性别
	例 Most application forms require candidates to state which gender they are. 大多数申请表要求申请人填写自己的性别。
	用 gender discrimination 性别歧视

traverse [trəˈvɜːs]	v. 横穿，穿过
	例 The mountaineers embarked on a challenging journey to traverse the treacherous mountain range. 登山者们踏上了一段充满挑战的旅程，要穿越险峻的山脉。
	用 traverse the narrow pedestrian bridge 走过狭窄的步行桥
	考 Pronghorn, dependent on distance vision and speed to keep safe from predators, traverse high, open shoulders of land, where they can see and run. 叉角羚依靠远视能力和奔跑速度来躲避捕食者，一般穿行于平原的开阔凸起地带，在这样的地方它们才能四下张望和撒蹄狂奔。
lane [leɪn]	n. 小路；车道
	例 The cyclist stayed in the designated bike lane for safety while navigating through traffic. 为安全起见，骑车的人在车流中通行时要使用指定的自行车道。
	用 winding country lanes 蜿蜒的乡间小路 a four-lane highway 一条四车道公路

Exercise 10

一、中文释义练习

请选择单词正确的中文释义。

_____ 1. filter   A. 记忆

_____ 2. transport   B. 运输

_____ 3. memorise   C. 课程

_____ 4. diameter   D. 直径

_____ 5. curriculum   E. 过滤

_____ 6. privilege   A. 特权

_____ 7. deny   B. 自由

_____ 8. dopamine   C. 争论

_____ 9. liberty   D. 多巴胺

_____ 10. dispute   E. 否认

_____ 11. leap   A. 评论

_____ 12. curtain   B. 统治

_____ 13. reign   C. 窗帘

_____ 14. comment   D. 波动

_____ 15. fluctuate   E. 跳跃

_____ 16. coincide   A. 人类学

_____ 17. anthropology   B. 穿过

_____ 18. traverse   C. 车道

_____ 19. gender   D. 一致

_____ 20. lane   E. 性别

二、英文释义练习

请选择单词正确的英文释义。

_____ 1. sanitation   A. things that are considered useless or of little value

_____ 2. ornament   B. to travel or go somewhere with sb.

_____ 3. junk   C. an object used as decoration in a room or garden

_____ 4. inspect   D. the equipment and systems that keep places clean

_____ 5. accompany   E. to look closely to check that everything is as it should be

_____ 6. contaminate   A. to make a substance or place dirty or no longer pure

_____ 7. dilemma   B. able to live both on land and in water

_____ 8. unleash   C. make a difficult choice between things of equal importance

_____ 9. coexist   D. to exist together in the same place or at the same time

_____ 10. amphibious   E. to suddenly let a strong force or emotion be felt

shatter ['ʃætə(r)]	*v.* 破碎，碎裂；破坏，摧毁
	例 The vase slipped from her hands and shattered into pieces on the floor. 花瓶从她手中滑落，掉在地板上摔得粉碎。
	用 the sound of shattering glass 玻璃破碎的声音
	考 One of these young shepherds tossed a rock into an opening on the side of a cliff and was surprised to hear a shattering sound. 其中一位年轻牧羊人把一块石头丢进了悬崖侧面的一个洞口，惊讶地听到了什么东西被打碎的声音。

postpone [pə'spəʊn]	*v.* 延期；延缓
	例 The secretary said that we would have to postpone the company excursion because of the terrible weather. 秘书说，由于恶劣天气，我们将不得不推迟公司出行计划。
	用 postpone the expedition 将探险推迟
	同 delay *v.* 推迟；延期

derive [dɪ'raɪv]	*v.* 源自；起源于
	例 Many English words derive from the Latin and Greek languages. 许多英语单词来源于拉丁语和希腊语。
	用 derive pleasure from helping others 通过帮助他人获得快乐

divorce [dɪ'vɔːs]	*n.* 离婚；分离
	例 They have recently changed the divorce laws to enable couples to have more time to reconsider their possible separation. 他们最近修改了离婚法规，使夫妻有更多时间重新考虑是否分开。
	用 end in divorce 以离婚收场

dominate ['dɒmɪneɪt]	*v.* 统治，支配；占优势
	例 The champion boxer used his superior skills to dominate his opponent in the ring. 拳击冠军利用他高超的技术在拳击场上压制了对手。
	用 dominate the conversation 主导交谈的内容
	扩 dominant *adj.* 主导的，支配的

discount ['dɪskaʊnt]	*n.* 折扣 *v.* 打折；贬损；忽视
	例 The store offers generous discounts on electronic goods at New Year. 这家商店在新年期间对电子产品给出了很大折扣。
	用 get a discount 得到折扣 discount prices 折扣价 a discount shop 一家折扣商店
metaphor ['metəfə(r)]	*n.* 比喻；隐喻
	例 Metaphors are often used in literature and also in everyday sayings. 隐喻经常在文学作品和日常用语中使用。
	用 the writer's striking use of metaphor 这位作家对隐喻的独到运用
accommodation [ə,kɒmə'deɪʃn]	*n.* 住处；住宿
	例 The accomodation situation on the new campus was excellent; they had built new dormitories with improved bathroom facilities. 新校区的住宿条件非常好，他们新建了宿舍，改善了浴室设施。
	用 temporary accommodation 临时的住处
	扩 accommodate *v.* 容纳；使适应；提供住处
helicopter ['helɪkɒptə(r)]	*n.* 直升机
	例 The rescue team arrived quickly in a helicopter to aid the stranded hikers. 救援队乘坐直升机迅速赶到，救助被困的徒步旅行者。
	用 a police helicopter 一架警用直升机 a helicopter pilot 一位直升机驾驶员
admire [əd'maɪə(r)]	*v.* 钦佩；赞美，称赞
	例 I've always admired famous singers who genuinely have creativity and talent; not just those that can look good on stage. 我一直很欣赏那些有创造力和才华的著名歌手，而不是单单喜欢那些在舞台上看起来很好看的人。
	用 admire the way he handled the situation 佩服他处理这种局面的方式
	扩 admiration *n.* 赞美；钦佩
landlord ['lændlɔ:d]	*n.* 房东；地主
	例 The landlord increased the rent by twenty percent, much to the shock of most of the tenants. 房东把租金提高了百分之二十，这让多数房客非常吃惊。
	用 negotiate with the landlord 与房东协商
	类 rent *n.* 租金 tenant *n.* 租户

consult [kən'sʌlt]	*v.* 咨询；商议
	例 You need to consult a professional lawyer about this issue. 关于这个问题你需要咨询专业律师。
	用 consult your doctor 请医生诊治
	扩 consultant *n.* 顾问；咨询师
cell [sel]	*n.* 细胞
	例 The biologist examined the microscopic cell under the microscope, studying its structure and function. 生物学家在显微镜下观察这个微小的细胞，研究它的结构和功能。
	用 blood cells 血细胞 the nucleus of a cell 细胞核
	考 Fortunately, it is now possible to snip out the stretches of the insect's DNA that carry the codes for the interesting compounds and insert them into cell lines that allow larger quantities to be produced. 幸运的是，如今剪下昆虫基因中携带着我们关注的化合物的编码的片段已经成为可能，并且可以将其插入细胞系中以实现更大规模的化合物生产。
affect [ə'fekt]	*v.* 影响；使感染；深深打动
	例 Climate and weather conditions affect almost every aspect of our lives. 气候和天气状况几乎影响着我们生活的各个方面。
	用 affect my decision 影响我的决定
	同 influence *v./n.* 影响
	扩 affection *n.* 感情；喜爱
timetable ['taɪmteɪbl]	*n.* 时间表；时刻表；课程表
	例 The timetable for the forthcoming semester will be published this week. 下一学期的课程表将于本周公布。
	用 a train timetable 火车时刻表
	同 schedule *n.* 时间表；时刻表；课程表
decipher [dɪ'saɪfə(r)]	*v.* 破译；辨认
	例 The archaeologist studied the ancient hieroglyphics, trying to decipher their meaning. 考古学家研究了古代的象形文字，试图破译它们的含义。
	用 decipher his handwriting 辨认他的字迹 decipher a code 破译密码

bilingual [ˌbaɪˈlɪŋgwəl]	*adj.* 双语的；使用双语的
	例 She grew up to be bilingual by virtue of living overseas for so long. 由于在海外生活了很长时间，她长大后会说两种语言。
	用 bilingual education 双语教育
	类 corpus *n.* 语料库 dialect *n.* 方言 phonetic *adj.* 语音的 syntax *n.* 句法 semantics *n.* 语义学
	考 According to the latest figures, the majority of the world's population is bilingual or multilingual, having grown up speaking two or more languages. 根据最新数据，世界人口的大多数都是双语或多语使用者，他们说着两种或更多种语言长大。
bow [baʊ]	*v./n.* 鞠躬，点头
	例 The audience applauded enthusiastically, and she came back on stage to take another bow. 观众热烈地鼓掌，她又回到舞台上再次向观众鞠躬致谢。
	用 bow to the assembled crowd 向集结的人群鞠躬
accumulate [əˈkjuːmjəleɪt]	*v.* 累积；积聚
	例 In her years working in the Middle East she accumulated a vast amount of intercultural experience. 在中东工作的日子里，她积累了大量的跨文化经验。
	用 accumulate a lot of books 收集了很多书
	扩 accumulation *n.* 积累
	考 accumulate intense radioactive sources 积累强放射源
menace [ˈmenəs]	*n.* 威胁，危险；烦人的人（或事物）*v.* 威胁，威吓
	例 His dog barked every night and was a menace to the neighbourhood. 他的狗每天晚上都叫，对邻居们是一种扰乱。
	用 a menace to the public 对公众的一个威胁
evolution [ˌiːvəˈluːʃn]	*n.* 进化；进化论；进展
	例 Charles Darwin is famous for the theory of evolution of the species. 查尔斯·达尔文以物种进化论而闻名。
	用 the evolution of the human species 人类的进化
	扩 evolve *v.* 演化；进化
	考 We want to know whether life evolves naturally if given the right conditions. 我们想知道如果获得适合的环境，生命是否会自然进化。

byproduct ['baɪprɒdʌkt]	*n.* 副产品 例 A fruit is actually a byproduct of a plant, containing the seeds. 水果实际上是植物的副产品，含有种子。 用 a byproduct of my research 我所做的研究的附属品 考 an almost unlimited byproduct of London's gas street lighting 伦敦煤气路灯所产生的几乎无穷无尽的副产品
manipulate [məˈnɪpjuleɪt]	*v.* 操纵；操作 例 She was never direct, but usually found ways to manipulate people in order to get what she wanted. 她从不直截了当，经常想方设法操控他人以得到想要的东西。 用 manipulate a computer 操作电脑 扩 manipulation *n.* 操作；操纵
dwell [dwel]	*v.* 居住；存在于 例 The small indigenous community dwelt near the banks of the river for easy access to fish and resources. 这个小型原住民社区位于河岸附近，方便获取鱼类和资源。 用 dwell in the caves 居住在洞穴中 扩 dwelling *n.* 住处，处所 dweller *n.* 居民，居住者
thesis [ˈθiːsɪs]	*n.* 论文；论点 例 His PhD thesis required intense research and took almost two years to complete. 他的博士论文需要进行大量研究，花了近两年时间才完成。 用 a thesis on industrial robots 一篇研究工业机器人的论文
exemplify [ɪgˈzemplɪfaɪ]	*v.* 例证；示例 例 He works hard in every game and he exemplifies what a great player should be like. 他在每一场比赛中都很努力，他是一个伟大球员的典范。 用 exemplify the use of the word 举例说明这个词的用法 扩 example *n.* 例子，范例
diagram ['daɪəgræm]	*n.* 图表；图解 例 The instructions featured a clear diagram of how the machine works. 说明书上有一张清晰的图表，描述了机器的工作原理。 用 process diagram 流程图 考 The diagram below shows the process for recycling plastic bottles. 下图显示了回收塑料瓶的过程。

remedy
['remədi]

n. 解决方法，纠正方法；疗法

例 Natural remedies are always better for the body than chemical medicines.
自然疗法总是比化学药物对身体更好些。

用 a number of possible remedies to this problem 解决问题的可能方法

infant
['ɪnfənt]

n. 婴儿，幼儿 *adj.* 供婴幼儿用的；初期的

例 The nurse carefully cradled the newborn infant in her arms.
护士小心翼翼地把新生儿抱在怀里。

用 a nursery for infants under two 两岁以下婴幼儿的托儿所

考 In order to get a reward, the infants had to adjust the rule they'd learned; only the bilingual babies were able to successfully learn the new rule.
为了获得奖赏，婴儿需要调整他们学到的规则；只有双语婴儿能够成功学习新的规则。

segment
['segmənt]

n. 一段，部分

例 The pie chart is divided into six segments, each showing the percentage of electricity consumed by different household devices.
这个饼状图被分为六个部分，每一部分说明了不同家用设施所消耗电量的比例。

用 a small segment of the painting 这幅画的一小部分

predator
['predətə(r)]

n. 捕食者；食肉动物；掠夺者

例 Even a predator as powerful as a tiger is scared of getting into fights with other animals.
即使像老虎这样强大的捕食者也害怕与其他动物争斗。

用 the relationship between predator and prey
捕食性动物与猎物之间的关系

考 They do not suffer from the threat or stress of predators, or the irritation and pain of parasites or injuries.
它们不需要承受来自捕食者的威胁和压力，也没有寄生虫或伤病带来的刺激和痛苦。

compensate
['kɒmpenseɪt]

v. 补偿，赔偿

例 He worked incredibly long hours and his job was very stressful, but the high salary compensated for this.
他的工作时间非常长，压力很大，但高薪弥补了这些。

用 compensate victims for their direct losses 补偿受害人的直接损失

同 make up for 补偿

扩 compensation *n.* 补偿

intake [ˈɪnteɪk]	*n.* 摄取量，吸入量 例 To get your recommended daily intake of vitamins, dietitians suggest you eat five portions of fruit and vegetables per day. 为了获取建议的每日维生素摄入量，营养师建议你每天吃五份水果和蔬菜。 用 reduce your daily intake of salt 减少每天的食盐摄入量 考 This is a disease where bones show reduced density, usually caused by insufficient exercise, reduced calcium intake or food starvation. 此病会导致骨密度降低，原因通常是运动量不足、钙质摄入减少或食物匮乏。
fame [feɪm]	*n.* 名声，名望 例 She shot to fame very quickly after appearing in the blockbuster movie—mainly for her amazing acting skills and incredible natural beauty. 她在这部轰动一时的电影中一举成名，主要是因为她惊人的演技和令人难以置信的自然美。 用 rise to fame overnight 一夜之间成名 同 reputation *n.* 名声，名誉 考 achieve instant fame 一举成名
abide [əˈbaɪd]	*v.* 遵守；忍受 例 We must all strictly abide by the new rules and regulations. 我们都必须严格遵守新的规章制度。 用 abide by 遵守；接受
circuit [ˈsɜːkɪt]	*n.* 电路，回路 例 The electric current flowed through the circuit, powering the electronic devices connected to it. 电流流经电路，为与其相连的电子设备供电。 用 an electrical circuit 电路
unwind [ˌʌnˈwaɪnd]	*v.* 放松；解开；展开 例 After a very long day at work, and a tiring commute, he liked to sit down and unwind at home before dinner. 在一天漫长的工作和疲惫的通勤后，他喜欢在晚饭前坐在家里放松一下。 用 unwind his scarf from his neck 从脖子上解下围巾 同 relax *v.* 放松，轻松

primitive ['prɪmətɪv]	*adj.* 原始的，远古的；简陋的
	例 The accomodation at the mountain village was quite primitive and basic, but the place had a unique charm. 山上村庄中的住宿条件非常原始和简单，但那里有其独一无二的魅力。
	用 primitive tribe 原始部落 primitive instinct 原始本能
dose [dəʊs]	*n.* （药的）一剂，一服 *v.* 给……服药
	例 She was given a low dose of painkillers to manage her arthritis. 她使用低剂量的止痛药来治疗关节炎。
	用 a high dose 大剂量 a low dose 小剂量
compass ['kʌmpəs]	*n.* 指南针，罗盘；圆规
	例 The compass was a key invention in the days of early international shipping, and solved many navigation issues sailors used to encounter. 指南针是早期国际航运业的一项重要发明，解决了水手在航海中会遇到的许多问题。
	用 a pair of compasses 一副圆规
dimension [daɪ'menʃn]	*n.* 大小，尺寸；方面；维度
	例 He measured the room to work out the dimensions of the new carpet. 他测量了房间，以计算出新地毯的尺寸。
	用 the dimensions of the kitchen 厨房的大小 a problem of considerable dimensions 一个涉及面相当广的问题
	考 Rubin and colleagues did not assign greater weight to any one dimension in determining playfulness; however, other researchers have suggested that process orientation and a lack of obvious functional purpose may be the most important aspects of play. Rubin及其同事并没有给予有关决定游戏性的任何一个维度更多重视；但是其他要求人员认为过程导向和缺乏明显的功能性目的或许是游戏最重要的方面。
alleviate [ə'liːvieɪt]	*v.* 减轻，缓和
	例 The medicine could not fully prevent the pain she was experiencing, but it alleviated it somewhat. 这种药物并不能完全解除她正在经历的痛苦，但可以在一定程度上缓解痛苦。
	用 alleviate the problem 缓解这一问题
	考 What can we do to alleviate it before it comes to that? 在事情变成那样之前，我们能做什么来缓和这种状况？

conference ['kɒnfərəns]	*n.* （大型正式）会议；体育协会
	例 The conference was held in the hotel just opposite Central Park. 会议在中央公园对面的酒店举行。
	用 a conference room 一间会议室

freight [freɪt]	*n.* 货运；货物
	例 A freight train can carry hundreds of tonnes of cargo in one journey. 货运火车可以一次行程中运载数百吨货物。
	用 a freight business 一家货运公司 passenger and freight transportation services 客运及货运服务

identical [aɪ'dentɪkl]	*adj.* 同一的；相同的
	例 The twins were almost identical and you couldn't tell the difference between them unless you looked very closely. 这对双胞胎几乎一模一样，除非你看得非常仔细，否则你无法分辨出他们的区别。
	用 a row of identical houses 完全一样的一排房子 be identical with 与……一致
	考 almost identical to each other 彼此几乎一模一样

penetrate ['penətreɪt]	*v.* 渗透；穿透；洞察
	例 The wood was so hard that the nail could not penetrate it easily. 木头很坚硬，钉子无法轻易穿透。
	用 penetrate deep into enemy lines 深入敌军防线
	扩 penetration *n.* 渗透；穿透

hydrogen ['haɪdrədʒən]	*n.* 氢；氢气
	例 Hydrogen is a colourless, odourless gas which is highly flammable. 氢气是一种无色、无味的气体，非常易燃。
	用 very little hydrogen and helium 非常少的氢和氦

iron ['aɪən]	*n.* 铁；熨斗；铁器 *v.* 熨，烫 *adj.* 坚强的
	例 She used the electric iron to smooth out the wrinkles in her clothes. 她用电熨斗把衣服上的褶皱熨平。
	用 an iron and steel works 一家钢铁厂

manual ['mænjuəl]	*n.* 说明书，册子，指南 *adj.* 体力的；手工的
	例 Making small, delicate models requires a high degree of manual skill. 制作小巧精致的模型需要高超的手工技巧。
	用 manual and non-manual workers 体力劳动者和非体力劳动者

outbreak
['aʊtbreɪk]

n. 爆发，突然发生

例 Health officials quickly responded to the outbreak of the infectious disease.

卫生官员对这种传染病的爆发做出了迅速反应。

用 the outbreak of war 战争的爆发

考 They leave vigorous trees that have stayed healthy enough to survive the outbreak.

这种做法留下的是生命力旺盛的树木，它们足够健康，能抵御灾病而存活。

Exercise 11

一、中文释义练习

请选择单词正确的中文释义。

_____	1. derive	A. 源自	
_____	2. divorce	B. 离婚	
_____	3. metaphor	C. 隐喻	
_____	4. accommodation	D. 住处	
_____	5. helicopter	E. 直升机	

_____	11. dwell	A. 居住	
_____	12. intake	B. 忍受	
_____	13. fame	C. 电路	
_____	14. abide	D. 名声	
_____	15. circuit	E. 摄取量	

_____	6. landlord	A. 房东	
_____	7. timetable	B. 时间表	
_____	8. bow	C. 鞠躬	
_____	9. byproduct	D. 副产品	
_____	10. manipulate	E. 操纵	

_____	16. primitive	A. 铁	
_____	17. identical	B. 相同的	
_____	18. alleviate	C. 原始的	
_____	19. iron	D. 减轻	
_____	20. manual	E. 说明书	

二、英文释义练习

请选择单词正确的英文释义。

_____	1. postpone	A. to arrange for an event to happen at a later time
_____	2. discount	B. to go to sb. for information or advice
_____	3. consult	C. an amount of money that is taken off the usual cost
_____	4. decipher	D. to gradually get more and more of sth. over time
_____	5. accumulate	E. to find the meaning of sth. that is difficult to read

_____	6. predator	A. an instrument for finding direction
_____	7. compensate	B. to undo sth. that has been wrapped into a ball
_____	8. unwind	C. to provide sth. good to reduce the bad effects
_____	9. compass	D. getting into or passing through a physical object
_____	10. penetrate	E. an animal that kills and eats other animals

suppress [sə'pres]	v. 抑制；镇压
	例 He was so angry at the changes that had occurred at his company, but he tried his best to suppress his feelings, and get on with his work. 他对公司发生的变化感到非常生气，但他尽力抑制自己的情绪，继续工作。
	用 drugs that suppress the appetite 抑制食欲的药
	扩 suppression n. 压制；禁止；镇压
excavate ['ekskəveɪt]	v. 发掘，挖掘；开凿
	例 The archaeologists carefully excavated the ancient ruins, uncovering artifacts from centuries ago. 考古学家仔细地挖掘了古代遗址，发现了几个世纪前的文物。
	用 pottery and weapons excavated from the burial site 从墓地中挖掘出的陶器和兵器
	扩 excavation n. 挖掘
	考 Excavated vessels also provide some clues about ancient shipbuilding techniques. 挖掘出来的船只也向公众提供了一些古代造船技术的线索。
pine [paɪn]	n. 松树；松木
	例 The fresh scent of pine filled the air as they walked through the dense forest. 他们穿过茂密的森林时，空气中弥漫着松树的清香。
	用 pine forests 松树林
surpass [sə'pɑːs]	v. 超越；胜过，优于
	例 She excelled in school and her progress surpassed the expectations of the teachers. 她在学校表现优异，她的进步超出了老师们的预期。
	用 surpass the world record 刷新世界纪录
	考 surpass the available supply 超出了可获得的供给量

debris ['debriː]	*n.* 残骸；碎片；散落的垃圾
	例 After the storm, the streets were filled with debris from fallen trees and scattered branches. 暴风雨过后，街道上到处都是倒下的树木和散落的树枝。
	用 clear away leaves and other garden debris 清除树叶和其他庭院垃圾 space debris 太空垃圾 debris flow 泥石流
	考 Satellites, rocket shards and collision debris are creating major traffic risks in orbit around the planet. 卫星、火箭碎片和撞击残骸正在围绕地球运行的轨道上制造巨大的交通隐患。
execution [ˌeksɪˈkjuːʃn]	*n.* 执行；实行；完成
	例 His original idea was good, but his execution of the final project was terrible. 他最初的想法很好，但对最终项目的执行却很糟糕。
	用 fail in the execution of his duty 未能履行他的职责
guarantee [ˌgærənˈtiː]	*n./v.* 保证；担保
	例 We cannot guarantee that we will continue to employ him after his contract ends. 我们不能保证在合同期满后还会继续雇佣他。
	用 give a guarantee of good behaviour 保证行为端正
prone [prəʊn]	*adj.* 有……倾向的；易于……的
	例 Some types of fish are prone to skin disease so they must be kept in a special aquarium. 有些鱼类容易患皮肤病，所以必须把它们养在专门的鱼缸里。
	用 prone to injury 容易受伤 prone to error 容易出错
decorate ['dekəreɪt]	*v.* 装饰；布置
	例 The task of decorating the new house was something she found exciting. 她发现装饰新房子的任务非常令人兴奋。
	用 decorate the room with flowers and balloons 用花和气球装饰房间
	扩 decoration *n.* 装饰
	考 We've got some people to decorate his kitchen, but if you could do some weeding in his garden, that would be wonderful. 我们已经找了人来装饰他的厨房。但如果你能给他的花园除草，那就太好了。

repetition [ˌrepəˈtɪʃn]	*n.* 重复，重说，重做 例 It's important to avoid repetition when you are in a job interview and try to be concise and to the point at all times. 在求职面试中避免重复是很重要的，并且在任何时候都应表达简洁，直击要点。 用 learning by repetition 通过重复进行学习 扩 repeat *v.* 重复
psychic [ˈsaɪkɪk]	*adj.* 精神的；心灵的；超自然的 例 There are people who believe that we have psychic abilities that enable us to foresee the future, or read other people's minds. 有些人相信我们有预知未来或读懂他人心思的超自然能力。 用 psychic phenomena 超自然现象
interpret [ɪnˈtɜːprət]	*v.* 解释，说明；口译 例 Some people interpret dreams as having significant meanings to our lives. 有些人认为梦对我们的生活有重要的意义。 用 interpret the poem 诠释诗的含义 扩 interpretation *n.* 解释；说明
tutor [ˈtjuːtə(r)]	*n.* 导师；助教；家庭教师 *v.* 辅导，指导 例 I was not very good at mathematics in school, so I hired a private tutor who helped me a lot with my studies. 我在学校时数学不是很好，所以我请了一个家教，他在学习上帮助了我很多。 用 my personal tutor at university 我大学时的个人指导教师
wrinkle [ˈrɪŋkl]	*n.* 皱纹 *v.* 起皱纹 例 She was overly concerned about her looks and was constantly studying the wrinkles at the sides of her eyes. 她过于在意自己的外表，不断研究着自己眼角的皱纹。 用 begin to wrinkle 开始起皱纹
paraphrase [ˈpærəfreɪz]	*n./v.* 释义；解释；同义替换 例 She gave the class a quick paraphrase of the article. 她给全班同学简要地转述了这篇文章。 用 paraphrase the question before you answer it 先解释一下问题再回答

slip [slɪp]	*v.* 滑倒；溜走，滑落 *n.* 滑，滑倒；滑动
	例 She lost her balance and almost slipped on the wet floor. 她失去了平衡，几乎滑倒在湿地板上。
	用 slip out of my hand 从我手里滑掉了

hook [hʊk]	*n.* 钩，挂钩 *v.* 钩住；把……连接到
	例 He used a grappling hook to climb up the steep cliff. 他用抓钩爬上了陡峭的悬崖。
	用 fish hook 鱼钩 picture hook 挂画钩
	考 They would put the Desolenator on their roof and hook it up to their municipal supply and they would get very reliable drinking water on a daily basis. 他们会把Desolenator放在屋顶上，并把它与市政供水系统连接起来，这样他们就能每天得到非常可靠的饮用水。

subject ['sʌbdʒekt] *n.&adj.* [səb'dʒekt] *v.*	*n.* 主题；科目 *adj.* 易受……的 *v.* 使服从
	例 Chemistry is my favorite subject, but I like to learn about other aspects of science as well. 化学是我最喜欢的学科，但是我也喜欢学习科学的其他课程。
	用 books on many different subjects 题材广泛的各种书籍
	考 Some people say History is one of the most important school subjects. 有人说历史是学校最重要的科目之一。

ambition [æm'bɪʃn]	*n.* 野心，雄心；抱负，志向
	例 This basketball team always plays with such ambition and drive. 这支篮球队总是充满雄心和动力。
	用 sporting ambitions 运动追求
	扩 ambitious *adj.* 有野心的；有雄心壮志的

protrude [prə'truːd]	*v.* 伸出；突出
	例 The sharp rocks protruded from the ground, posing a risk to hikers. 尖锐的岩石从地面突出，对徒步旅行者构成危险。
	用 a huge round mass of smooth rock protruding from the water 从水中突出来的一块光滑的圆形巨石

seal [siːl]	*n.* 密封；盖章；海豹 *v.* 密封；盖章
	例 He gave the plans his seal of approval, and they began to work on the product launch. 他批准了这些计划，然后他们就开始着手产品发布工作。
	用 seal the envelope 封上信封
	考 a sealed box 一个密封的盒子

layer [ˈleɪə(r)]	*n.* 层；层次
	例 Everything in the abandoned house was covered in a thick layer of dust. 这所废弃房子里的一切都盖上了一层厚厚的灰尘。
	用 a thin layer of dust 一层薄薄的灰
	考 The wall of the fruit has three layers: a waterproof outer layer, a fibrous middle layer and a hard, inner layer. 这种果实的外壁分为三层：不透水的外层、纤维状的中层、坚硬的内层。
frustrate [frʌˈstreɪt]	*v.* 挫败；失败；受挫
	例 She got very frustrated when she could not solve the maths sum. 当解不出这道数学题时，她感到很受挫。
	用 be frustrated by the result 对结果感到挫败
	扩 frustration *n.* 挫败
fraud [frɔːd]	*n.* 欺诈，骗局，诡计
	例 The company uncovered a fraud scheme within its financial department. 该公司揭露了财务部门内部的欺诈计划。
	用 property that has been obtained by fraud 欺诈所得的财产
resist [rɪˈzɪst]	*v.* 抵抗；忍耐
	例 She was trying to keep to her strict diet, but whenever she saw a cake she couldn't resist it. 她试图严格控制饮食，但每当看到蛋糕，她就无法抗拒。
	用 resist infection 抗感染
	扩 resistant *adj.* 有抵抗力的；抵抗的 resistance *n.* 抵抗；对抗
	考 Clasen believes that scary stories teach us what it feels like to be afraid without having to experience real danger, and so build up resistance to negative emotions. Clasen相信恐怖故事教会我们如何在没有经历真实危险的情况下感受恐惧，从而产生对负面情绪的抵御。
tariff [ˈtærɪf]	*n.* 关税；关税表；收费表
	例 They increased the import tariffs, which as a result caused a number of problems with their trading relationship. 他们提高了进口关税，结果造成了与贸易关系有关的一系列问题。
	用 eliminate tariffs on items such as electronics 取消电子产品等的关税

cultivate ['kʌltɪveɪt]	*v.* 培养，栽培；耕作
	例 It's important that teachers learn to cultivate a sense of moral behaviour in young students in order that they can become good members of society. 教师学会培养年轻学生的道德行为意识非常重要，这是为了他们可以成为好的社会成员。
	用 cultivate rice and beans 种植稻子和豆类
	扩 cultivation *n.* 耕作；培养
	考 The ants therefore cultivate these fungi in their nests, bringing them leaves to feed on, and then use them as a source of food. 因此蚂蚁在自己的巢穴中培育这些真菌，带来树叶供养它们，之后将其作为食物的来源。
dismiss [dɪs'mɪs]	*v.* 解雇；解散；不予理会；驳回
	例 He had terrible annual performance reports, so the manager dismissed him. 他的年度业绩报告很糟糕，所以经理解雇了他。
	用 dismiss rumours 否认传言
combustion [kəm'bʌstʃən]	*n.* 燃烧；氧化
	例 The engine roared to life, igniting the combustion process and propelling the vehicle forward. 发动机轰鸣起来，激发了燃烧进程，推动着汽车前进。
	用 the combustion of fossil fuels 燃烧矿物燃料 a large combustion plant 大型燃烧设备
	考 the convenience of an internal combustion engine 内燃机的便利性
stroke [strəʊk]	*n.* 划；击，打；中风；笔画 *v.* 轻抚，轻触；击球
	例 Some Chinese characters are complicated to learn as they consist of many strokes. 有些汉字学起来是很复杂的，因为它们由许多笔画组成。
	用 take a few more strokes to reach the bank 多划几下游到岸边
	考 Doctors can use it to predict when a patient is most likely to have a heart attack or stroke. 医生可以利用它来预测病人何时最有可能心脏病发作或中风。
vaccine ['væksiːn]	*n.* 疫苗
	例 The vaccine proved to be very effective, and after a number of years the entire population was immunised. 疫苗被证明非常有效，几年后整个人群都具备了免疫能力。
	用 an effective vaccine against malaria 一种有效预防疟疾的疫苗

relic ['relɪk]	*n.* 遗迹；遗物；废墟 例 The museum boasts a collection of over ten thousand ancient relics. 这个博物馆以收藏一万多件古代文物而自豪。 用 a museum of war relics 一座战争遗迹博物馆 考 historical relics 历史遗迹
decode [diːˈkəʊd]	*v.* 解码；破译；转换 例 During the first world war teams of experts decoded enemy messages. 第一次世界大战期间，专家团队破译了敌人的信息。 用 decoding equipment 译码设备
beneath [bɪˈniːθ]	*prep.* 在下面 *adv.* 在下面，在底下 例 The hidden treasure lay buried beneath the ancient ruins. 隐藏的宝藏被埋在古代遗迹的下面。 用 beneath a pile of leaves 在一堆树叶下面 同 underneath *prep.* 在下面 *adv.* 在下面
adjacent [əˈdʒeɪsnt]	*adj.* 邻近的，毗连的 例 The two houses were located adjacent to each other, sharing a common wall. 这两座房子彼此相邻，共用同一堵墙。 用 an adjacent room 一间相邻的房间 考 These are located adjacent to the airport medical centre on the first floor. 它们位于一楼的机场医疗中心附近。
contemporary [kənˈtemprəri]	*adj.* 同时期的；当代的 *n.* 同代人；同辈人 例 She didn't like classical or ancient art very much; she was keen on contemporary works. 她不太喜欢古典艺术或者古代艺术，她非常热衷于当代作品。 用 life in contemporary Britain 当代英国的生活 考 A majority of the contemporary definitions of play focus on several key criteria. 当前多数有关游戏的定义都集中在一些核心标准上。
souvenir [ˌsuːvəˈnɪə(r)]	*n.* 纪念品；纪念物 例 The souvenir market in Xi'an is a fascinating place for tourists to visit. 西安的纪念品市场是一个非常吸引游客参观的地方。 用 a souvenir shop 一家纪念品商店

specific [spə'sɪfɪk]	*adj.* 特定的；明确的；详细的
	例 The information in the scientific report needs to be detailed and highly specific. 科学报告中的信息需要详尽且高度具体。
	用 a specific age group 一个特定的年龄组
	考 He worked for the benefit of specific groups of people. 他为特定群体的利益而工作。

replace [rɪ'pleɪs]	*v.* 代替；替换
	例 The company were forced to replace over 100,000 cellphones of that particular model, due to faulty screens. 由于屏幕故障，公司被迫更换了10万多台相应型号的手机。
	用 replace all existing models 取代所有现有的型号
	考 Extinct species are being replaced by new species. 灭绝的物种正被新的物种代替。

encompass [ɪn'kʌmpəs]	*v.* 包含；包围，围绕
	例 The new job encompasses a wide range of responsibilities. 这项新的工作包含的职责范围很广。
	用 encompass the castle 在城堡周围
	同 contain *v.* 包含；容纳

pasture ['pɑːstʃə(r)]	*n.* 牧场，牧草地 *v.* 放牧；吃草
	例 The cows grazed peacefully in the lush green pasture. 牛在郁郁葱葱的草地上安静地吃草。
	用 an area of rich pasture 一片富饶的牧场 high mountain pastures 高山牧场

ailment ['eɪlmənt]	*n.* 疾病，小病
	例 He sought medical advice for his persistent ailment, hoping for a diagnosis and treatment. 他为自己的长期疾病寻求医疗建议，希望得到诊断和治疗。
	用 the treatment of common ailments 治疗平常小病
	考 the soothing and curing of our ailments 减轻和治愈疾病

extract [ɪk'strækt] *v.* ['ekstrækt] *n.*	*v.* 提取；选取；摘录 *n.* 摘录；提取物
	例 They extract the minerals from underground mines and open pits. 他们从地下矿井和露天矿井中提取矿物。
	用 natural plant extracts 天然植物提取物
	扩 extraction *n.* 取出；提取物

convert [kən'vɜːt]	*v.* 转变；转换；变换 例 They decided to convert their spare bedroom into a study room. 他们决定把闲置的卧室改成一间书房。 用 convert my dollars into euros 将我的美元兑换成欧元 考 The warm water flows into a small boiler (heated by a solar-powered battery) where it is converted to steam. 温暖的水流入一个小锅炉（靠太阳能电池加热），在锅炉里被加热成蒸汽。
keen [kiːn]	*adj.* 喜爱的，着迷的；热情的；灵敏的 例 She had a keen eye for detail, easily spotting even the smallest imperfections. 她对细节有敏锐的双眼，能轻易发现即使最小的瑕疵。 用 very keen to help 很愿意帮忙 a keen sportsman 一个热爱运动的人
abundance [ə'bʌndəns]	*n.* 充裕，丰富；大量 例 The harvest was plentiful and the entire village enjoyed an abundance of crops that year. 那年收成很好，全村的庄稼都收获颇丰。 用 an abundance of wildlife 大量野生动植物 扩 abundant *adj.* 大量的；充足的
deteriorate [dɪ'tɪəriəreɪt]	*v.* 恶化；变坏 例 As the illness got worse we could see her health deteriorate week by week. 随着病情恶化，我们可以看到她的健康状况一周比一周差。 用 deteriorating weather conditions 不断恶化的天气状况
mastery ['mɑːstəri]	*n.* 掌握；精通 例 He had spent years gaining mastery of the art of calligraphy. 他花了多年时间，达到对书法艺术的精通。 用 have mastery of several languages 精通数门语言
spotlight ['spɒtlaɪt]	*n.* 聚光灯；注意的中心 *v.* 用聚光灯照；使备受关注 例 A sharp, bright spotlight beamed down onto the actor on stage. 明亮的聚光灯照射在舞台上的演员身上。 用 under the spotlight 作为焦点问题；备受瞩目
ambience ['æmbiəns]	*n.* 气氛，布景；周围环境 例 The calm, peaceful ambience at the temple was very relaxing. 寺庙里宁静祥和的氛围令人非常放松。 用 the relaxed ambience of the city 这座城市轻松的氛围

Exercise 12

一、中文释义练习

请选择单词正确的中文释义。

_____ 1. pine   A. 松树
_____ 2. surpass   B. 导师
_____ 3. debris   C. 残骸
_____ 4. repetition   D. 超越
_____ 5. tutor   E. 重复

_____ 6. wrinkle   A. 挫败
_____ 7. hook   B. 钩
_____ 8. protrude   C. 伸出
_____ 9. seal   D. 皱纹
_____ 10. frustrate   E. 密封

_____ 11. combustion   A. 纪念品
_____ 12. relic   B. 燃烧
_____ 13. decode   C. 邻近的
_____ 14. adjacent   D. 解码
_____ 15. souvenir   E. 遗迹

_____ 16. specific   A. 丰富
_____ 17. replace   B. 代替
_____ 18. ailment   C. 特定的
_____ 19. abundance   D. 恶化
_____ 20. deteriorate   E. 疾病

二、英文释义练习

请选择单词正确的英文释义。

_____ 1. excavate   A. to prevent sth. from happening or succeeding
_____ 2. interpret   B. to explain the meaning of sth. clearly
_____ 3. layer   C. a tax that is paid on goods coming into a country
_____ 4. frustrate   D. a quantity or thickness of sth. that lies over a surface
_____ 5. tariff   E. to dig in the ground to look for old objects

_____ 6. vaccine   A. to change or make sth. change from one to another
_____ 7. contemporary   B. belonging to the present time or the same time
_____ 8. encompass   C. a substance put into the blood to protect the body
_____ 9. convert   D. to include a large number or range of things
_____ 10. ambience   E. the character and atmosphere of a place

delicate ['delɪkət]	*adj.* 精美的；精密的；易碎的；纤弱的
	例 Paper cuts are a delicate form of decoration popular in China. 剪纸是一种精美的装饰形式，在中国很流行。
	用 the delicate mechanisms of a clock 钟表的精密装置

pitfall ['pɪtfɔːl]	*n.* 陷阱，圈套；缺陷
	例 One of the major pitfalls of the whole project was the lack of a good marketing strategy. 整个项目的主要缺陷之一是缺少优秀的营销策略。
	用 the potential pitfalls of buying a house 购买房屋可能遇到的圈套

beforehand [bɪ'fɔːhænd]	*adv.* 事先；预先
	例 If you want to make good Chinese food at home, you need to find a decent recipe book and get the right ingredients beforehand. 如果你想在家里做出美味的中餐，那么你需要一本不错的食谱并提前准备好需要的食材。
	用 two weeks beforehand 提前两周
	同 in advance 提前，事先

intend [ɪn'tend]	*v.* 打算；想要
	例 He did not intend to be rude, but sometimes he just said the wrong thing. 他并不是有意无礼，但有时候他会说错话。
	用 intend to do 想要做某事
	扩 intention *n.* 目的；意义 intentional *adj.* 故意的；有目的的

extrovert ['ekstrəvɜːt]	*n.* 性格外向者 *adj.* 外向的，活泼的
	例 Unlike her introverted sister, she was an outgoing and sociable extrovert. 与内向的姐姐不同，她是一个开朗、乐于交际、性格外向的人。
	用 his extrovert personality 他外向的个性
	反 introvert *n.* 性格内向者 *adj.* 内向的
	考 Now my extrovert behaviour is spontaneous. 现在我外向的行为是自发的。

census ['sensəs]	*n.* 人口普查，人口调查；统计，调查
	例 The census results showed that there was a declining birth rate. 人口普查结果显示出生率正在下降。
	用 the latest census 最新的人口普查

bind [baɪnd]	*v.* 捆绑，系；（使）黏合；使结合
	例 He used a strong adhesive to bind the broken pieces of the vase back together. 他用强力黏合剂把花瓶的碎片重新粘在一起。
	用 bind up his wounds 把他的伤口包扎好
	考 In their active state, phytochrome molecules bind themselves to DNA to restrict plant growth. 植物色素分子在其活跃状态下会与DNA结合，从而限制植物的生长。

emission [ɪ'mɪʃn]	*n.* 发射，散发；排放；喷射
	例 There are a number of new technologies designed to reduce emissions from motor vehicles. 有许多新技术旨在减少机动车的废气排放。
	用 the emission of carbon dioxide into the atmosphere 向大气中排放二氧化碳
	扩 emit *v.* 发出，散发

sacrifice ['sækrɪfaɪs]	*n.* 牺牲；供奉 *v.* 牺牲；奉献
	例 Sometimes you have to sacrifice your time and energy if you want a successful career. 如果你想事业成功，有时候你不得不牺牲自己的时间和精力。
	用 no sacrifice of quality 没有牺牲质量
	考 If successfully implemented, proponents claim, vertical farms offer the promise of urban renewal, sustainable production of a safe and varied food supply (through year-round production of all crops), and the eventual repair of ecosystems that have been sacrificed for horizontal farming. 支持者们称，如果成功实施，垂直农场会带来城市复苏的希望，持续提供安全多样的食物供应（通过整年生产所有谷物），并且最终修复由于水平农业而造成损害的生态系统。

inhibit [ɪn'hɪbɪt]	*v.* 禁止；抑制
	例 A lack of oxygen may inhibit brain development in young children. 缺氧可能会抑制幼儿的大脑发育。
	用 inhibit plant growth 抑制植物生长
	扩 inhibition *n.* 抑制；压抑

smooth [smuːð]	*adj.* 顺利的；光滑的；平稳的 *v.* 抚平，弄平滑
	例 When the lake freezes in winter it becomes as smooth as glass. 当湖面在冬天结冰时，它变得像玻璃一般光滑。
	用 make a smooth landing 平稳降落 a lotion to make your skin feel soft and smooth 能使皮肤柔软光滑的护肤液
	反 rough *adj.* 粗糙的；不平的
exhale [eks'heɪl]	*v.* 呼气；散发出
	例 After holding her breath underwater, she finally surfaced and exhaled deeply. 在水下屏住呼吸之后，她终于浮出水面，深呼一口气。
	用 hold your breath for a moment and exhale 屏息一会儿然后呼气
	反 inhale *v.* 吸入，吸气
holistic [hə'lɪstɪk]	*adj.* 整体的；全盘的
	例 Chinese medicine takes a holistic approach to disease where the whole mind and body is treated. 中医采取整体性的方法来治疗疾病，使身心都能够被治愈。
	用 holistic medicine 整体医学
	反 partial *adj.* 部分的
focus ['fəʊkəs]	*n.* 焦点；中心 *v.* 集中，关注；聚焦
	例 The main focus of his presentation was the revenue in the past quarter, but he also touched upon plans for the coming financial year. 他的演讲主要聚焦于上个季度的收入，但他也谈到了下个财年的计划。
	用 focus on 集中于；聚焦于
	同 concentrate *v.* 聚焦
	考 focus on the power of suggestion 关注暗示的力量
hypnosis [hɪp'nəʊsɪs]	*n.* 催眠；催眠状态
	例 Hypnosis can be a good way to help you give up smoking or increase your positivity. 催眠可以帮助你戒烟或提高你的积极性。
	用 under hypnosis 在催眠状态下
	考 Lozanov experimented with teaching by direct suggestion during sleep, hypnosis and trance states, but found such procedures unnecessary. Lozanov试验过在睡眠状态下、催眠状态下或精神恍惚之际给出直接暗示的教学法，结果发现这些过程都是没有必要的。

tempt [tempt]	*v.* 引诱，诱惑 例 The aroma of freshly baked cookies tempted him to enter the cake shop. 刚烤好的饼干的香味诱使他走进蛋糕店。 用 tempt thieves by leaving valuables clearly visible 把贵重物品放在显眼处招来小偷 扩 temptation *n.* 引诱，诱惑
painstaking ['peɪnzteɪkɪŋ]	*adj.* 艰苦的；勤勉的 例 It took months of painstaking effort to complete the research. 完成这项研究花费了几个月艰苦卓绝的努力。 用 painstaking research 细心的研究 painstaking effort 艰苦的努力
document ['dɒkjumənt] *n.* ['dɒkjument] *v.*	*n.* 文件；文档 *v.* 记录，记载 例 It's wise to keep all of your important documents in a safe or filing cabinet. 把你所有的重要文件都放在保险箱或文件柜里是明智的。 用 legal documents 法律文件 扩 documentary *n.* 纪录片 *adj.* 记录的
erode [ɪˈrəʊd]	*v.* 腐蚀，侵蚀；削弱，损害 例 The sea washed against the rocks of the cliff and gradually eroded them until they were smooth stones. 海水冲刷着悬崖上的岩石，渐渐地把它们侵蚀成光滑的石头。 用 erode his authority 削弱他的权威 扩 erosion *n.* 侵蚀；腐蚀
worthwhile [ˌwɜːθˈwaɪl]	*adj.* 值得的；重要的；有价值的 例 It's a worthwhile investment to consider saving money in a special savings account. 考虑将钱存入一个特殊的储蓄账户是一项值得做的投资。 用 a worthwhile cause 一项有意义的事业 考 The reduction in bullying—and the consequent improvement in pupil happiness—is surely a worthwhile objective. 霸凌行为的减少以及随之而来的儿童幸福感提升必然是一个值得追求的目标。
contain [kənˈteɪn]	*v.* 包含；容纳 例 This dessert contains nuts, so some people might be allergic to it. 这种甜点含有坚果，因此有些人可能对它过敏。 用 contain one or two inaccuracies 有一两处不准确 扩 container *n.* 容器

precede [prɪˈsiːd]	*v.* 领先，在前面 例 Those types of clouds usually precede the arrival of low pressure weather systems. 这种类型的云通常在低气压天气到来之前出现。 用 the years preceding the war 战前的几年
waist [weɪst]	*n.* 腰；（衣服的）腰部 例 She tightened the belt around her waist, ensuring a secure and comfortable fit. 她系紧腰间的腰带，确保其安全舒适。 用 a jacket with a high waist 一件高腰身的上衣 a skirt with an elasticated waist 一条腰部有松紧带的裙子
trait [treɪt]	*n.* 特性；特点；品质 例 His most outstanding character trait was his incredible, sharp sense of humour and ability to tell jokes. 他最突出的性格特点是难以置信的敏锐的幽默感和讲笑话的能力。 用 personality traits 个性特点 考 Humans are also highly social, a trait that has been connected to healthier aging. 人类也是高度社会化的，这种特质与更健康的衰老过程有关。
eliminate [ɪˈlɪmɪneɪt]	*v.* 消除；排除 例 The policy was aimed at eliminating the problem of inflation through a series of fiscal measures. 这项政策旨在通过一系列财政措施消除通货膨胀问题。 用 eliminate toxins from the body 排除体内毒素 扩 elimination *n.* 排除，除去 考 If the individual knows that he or she can control the noise, this seems to eliminate both its negative effects at the time and its after-effects. 如果这个人知道自己可以控制噪音，或者这就可以消除当时的负面影响和后续影响。
sheer [ʃɪə(r)]	*adj.* 程度深的，数量大的；纯粹的，完全的；陡峭的 例 The sheer cliffs stood tall, offering an awe-inspiring view of the deep valley below. 陡峭的悬崖高耸着，下面的深谷令人敬畏。 用 sheer size of the cathedral 大教堂的宏大规模 考 The sheer scale of manufacture is so huge, and that is the issue. 制造业的规模如此之大，这就是问题所在。

limb [lɪm]	*n.* 肢，臂，腿；树枝
	例 The athlete stretched her leg muscles, feeling the tension release from every limb. 运动员伸展腿部肌肉，感觉每条腿的紧绷感都得以释放。
	用 an artificial limb 假肢
	考 Experiments showed that, in fact, facial vision is nothing to do with touch or the front of the face, although the sensation may be referred to the front of the face, like the referred pain in a phantom limb. 实验表明面感视觉实际上与"感"和"面"没有任何关系，尽管这种感觉可能被认为源自面部正前方，正如幻肢中的牵涉性痛感一样。
bulb [bʌlb]	*n.* 电灯泡；球状物
	例 She planted flower bulbs in the garden, eagerly waiting for them to sprout and blossom. 她在花园里种了一些球茎花卉，热切地等待着它们发芽开花。
	用 a room lit by bare bulbs 一间只有光秃秃的电灯泡照明的屋子
	考 Our brains run at slow biochemical processing speeds on the power of a light bulb, and their size is restricted by the dimensions of the human birth canal. 我们的大脑以一种低生物化学处理速度、用相当于一个灯泡的耗能运行着，而其尺寸也被人类生育通道的尺寸所限制着。
surface ['sɜːfɪs]	*n.* 表面；表层；外观
	例 I've always been into the kind of marine life that lives just below the surface of lagoons. 我一直很喜欢那种生活在泻湖表面下的海洋生物。
	用 an uneven road surface 凹凸不平的路面
	考 Water enters through a pipe, and flows as a thin film between a sheet of double glazing and the surface of a solar panel, where it is heated by the sun. 水通过管道流入，在双层玻璃片和太阳能电池板面之间形成的薄膜状空间里流动，此时的水由太阳能加热。
refrain [rɪ'freɪn]	*v.* 克制，避免 *n.* 叠句；副歌
	例 The catchy chorus made everyone hum and sing along to the refrain. 朗朗上口的合唱让每个人都跟着副歌哼唱起来。
	用 refrain from smoking 不要吸烟

curb [kɜːb]	*v./n.* 控制，抑制
	例 The city implemented measures to curb excessive water usage during the drought. 该市在干旱期间采取措施控制过度用水。
	用 curbed one's temper 控制脾气
	考 In the short term it might curb the growth in road transport through the better loading ratio of goods vehicles and occupancy rates of passenger vehicles expected as a result of the increase in the price of transport. 运输价格上涨预计会带来货运车辆更好的荷载比例以及客运车辆更合理的载客率，短期内这或许可以控制公路运输的增长。
flaw [flɔː]	*n.* 瑕疵，缺点；裂缝
	例 The only flaw in the design was that the handle of the new device was in an awkward position. 设计上的唯一缺陷是新设备的手柄处于一个尴尬的位置。
	用 a number of crucial flaws 很多关键性的问题
	同 defect *n.* 缺点 fault *n.* 过错，过失
investigate [ɪnˈvestɪɡeɪt]	*v.* 调查；研究
	例 The detectives were sent to the scene to investigate the crime. 侦探被派到犯罪现场调查这起案件。
	用 investigate the effects of diet on fighting cancer 研究饮食的抗癌作用
colony [ˈkɒləni]	*n.* 殖民地；（动植物）群体，群落
	例 Algeria was formerly a French colony before independence was declared in 1959. 阿尔及利亚在1959年宣布独立前曾是法国的殖民地。
	用 former British colonies 前英国殖民地
	扩 colonial *adj.* 殖民地的
	考 Giraldo watched how well the ants took care of the young of the colony. Giraldo观察了蚂蚁如何照料种群中的幼蚁。
immune [ɪˈmjuːn]	*adj.* 免疫的；免于……的
	例 After you develop antibodies you are usually immune to a virus for some time. 当你产生抗体后，你通常在一段时间内对病毒有免疫力。
	用 become immune to criticism 不在乎批评
	考 become immune to a variety of insecticides 对各种杀虫剂免疫

comprise [kəm'praɪz]	*v.* 包含；组成，构成
	例 Women comprise 60% to 65% of the workforce in our company these days.
	目前我们公司60%到65%的员工都是女性。
	用 comprise a large proportion of those living in poverty
	占了贫困人口中的很大比例

immediate [ɪ'miːdiət]	*adj.* 立即的；直接的
	例 The injection brought him immediate pain relief after the injury.
	在受伤之后，通过注射，他的疼痛很快缓解了。
	用 an immediate reaction 即时的反应
	an immediate effect 即刻产生的效果
	考 Bakelite was immediately welcomed as a practical and versatile material.
	人造树胶很快作为一种实用而万能的材料而受人欢迎。

relative ['relətɪv]	*adj.* 相对的；比较而言的；有关系的 *n.* 亲属；相关物
	例 I'm a relative newcomer to this city so I am not very familiar with how to get around.
	对这座城市而言，我是相对新来的人，因此我不太了解如何去各种地方走走。
	用 the position of the sun relative to the earth 太阳与地球的相对位置
	扩 relate *v.* 与……有联系 relation *n.* 关系，联系
	relationship *n.* 关系，关联

substance ['sʌbstəns]	*n.* 物质；实质；资产
	例 He enjoyed playing with his home chemistry set—it was full of chemical substances to do experiments with.
	他喜欢摆弄自己的家用化学用具，里面装满了可以用来做实验的化学物质。
	用 illegal substances 非法物品
	扩 substantial *adj.* 大量的；重要的

pile [paɪl]	*n.* 一堆，一叠；大量 *v.* 堆放；蜂拥，拥挤
	例 The children gleefully jumped into the leaf pile, scattering them everywhere.
	孩子们兴高采烈地跳进树叶堆里，使树叶散得到处都是。
	用 a pile of sand 一堆沙

analysis [ə'næləsɪs]	*n.* 分析
	例 His analysis of the situation was very insightful and informative.
	他对形势的分析非常有见地，且信息丰富。
	用 statistical analysis 统计分析

legitimate [lɪ'dʒɪtɪmət]	*adj.* 合法的；正当的，合理的
	例 Most scientists believe it is legitimate to use animals in medical research. 大多数科学家认为在医学研究中使用动物是合法的。
	用 a legitimate grievance 合乎情理的抱怨
alloy ['ælɔɪ] *n.* [ə'lɔɪ] *v.*	*n.* 合金 *v.* 把……铸成合金
	例 The new alloy material offered greater strength and durability for the construction industry. 这种新的合金材料为建筑行业提供了更高的强度和耐久性。
	用 an alloy of copper and zinc 铜和锌的合金
conspicuous [kən'spɪkjuəs]	*adj.* 显眼的；显而易见的
	例 Her blonde hair was very conspicuous because everyone else had natural black hair. 她的金发非常显眼，因为其他人都是天然的黑发。
	用 a conspicuous success 非常成功
	同 obvious *adj.* 明显的 evident *adj.* 明显的 distinct *adj.* 明显的；不同的；清楚的
	反 inconspicuous *adj.* 不明显的
	考 Schimmelpennink designed conspicuous, sturdy white bikes locked in special racks which could be opened with the chip card—the plan started with 250 bikes, distributed over five stations. Schimmelpennink设计了醒目坚固的白色自行车，锁在特殊的车架上，用芯片卡可以开锁，计划开始时共有250辆自行车，分别布置在五个站点。
concession [kən'seʃn]	*n.* 让步，妥协；许可，承认
	例 She did not want to compromise with him, but finally, after a short discussion, she made a concession. 她不想与他妥协，但最终，经过短暂讨论后，她做出了让步。
	用 an important concession 一次重要的让步
auditory ['ɔːdətri]	*adj.* 听觉的，听力的
	例 He overcame his auditory difficulties after seeing several specialist therapists. 在看了几位专家医生后，他克服了听觉上的问题。
	用 auditory stimuli 听觉刺激 auditory input 听觉输入
	考 hearing impairment or other auditory function deficit in young children 幼儿的听力障碍或其他听觉功能缺陷

remnant ['remnənt]	n. 残余部分，残迹 例 The ancient ruins were the now only remnants of a once-thriving and grand civilization. 古代的废墟是曾经繁荣昌盛的文明现存的唯一遗迹。 用 remnants of a huge forest 大森林剩下的一部分
convention [kən'venʃn]	n. 大会，集会；惯例，习俗 例 The national animated film convention is due to take place in southern China in the autumn of this year. 全国动画电影大会将于今年秋天在中国南方举行。 用 hold a convention 召开大会 扩 conventional adj. 传统的；常用的
framework ['freɪmwɜːk]	n. 框架；结构 例 The new framework for the proposed tax agreement should be passed by the end of the next government meeting. 税收协议的新框架会在下次政府会议结束时通过。 用 a framework for further research 进一步研究的框架 the basic framework of society 社会的基本结构 考 One of the virtues of this rich, lucid and arresting book is that it places the current cult of happiness in a well-defined historical framework. 这本内容丰富、逻辑清晰且吸引人的书的优点之一是它将当前对幸福的追求放在一个被界定清晰的历史框架中。
manuscript ['mænjuskrɪpt]	n. 手稿，原稿；手写本 例 The author meticulously edited her manuscript before submitting it to the publisher. 作者在把手稿交给出版商之前，对其进行了认真仔细的编辑。 用 an unpublished manuscript 一份未经发表的手稿 扩 transcript n. 文字记录；转录本 考 However, if *Mona Lisa* was a famous novel, few people would bother to go to a museum to read the writer's actual manuscript rather than a printed reproduction. 然而，如果《蒙娜丽莎》是一部著名的小说，那么没有多少人会费力去博物馆阅读作者真正的手稿，而是更倾向于阅读印刷的复制品。

Exercise 13

一、中文释义练习

一、中文释义练习

请选择单词正确的中文释义。

_____ 1. pitfall	A. 外向的	_____ 11. bulb	A. 立即的
_____ 2. extrovert	B. 整体的	_____ 12. investigate	B. 电灯泡
_____ 3. exhale	C. 呼气	_____ 13. colony	C. 调查
_____ 4. inhibit	D. 禁止	_____ 14. immediate	D. 合法的
_____ 5. holistic	E. 陷阱	_____ 15. legitimate	E. 种群
_____ 6. tempt	A. 值得的	_____ 16. alloy	A. 显著的
_____ 7. erode	B. 肢	_____ 17. pile	B. 物质
_____ 8. worthwhile	C. 腐蚀	_____ 18. substance	C. 听觉的
_____ 9. waist	D. 引诱	_____ 19. conspicuous	D. 一堆
_____ 10. limb	E. 腰	_____ 20. auditory	E. 合金

二、英文释义练习

请选择单词正确的英文释义。

_____ 1. census	A. an unconscious state one can be influenced
_____ 2. sacrifice	B. needing a lot of care, effort and attention to detail
_____ 3. hypnosis	C. giving up sth. important to get sth. more important
_____ 4. painstaking	D. to remove or get rid of sth.
_____ 5. eliminate	E. the process of officially counting a country's population
_____ 6. curb	A. something you allow to make a situation less difficult
_____ 7. immune	B. a copy of a book before it has been printed
_____ 8. relative	C. considered or judged by being compared with sth. else
_____ 9. concession	D. cannot be affected by a particular disease or illness
_____ 10. manuscript	E. to control or limit sth., especially sth. bad

furniture [ˈfɜːnɪtʃə(r)]	*n.* 家具
	例 A thick layer of dust lay on the furniture in the old house. 旧房子里的家具上积了一层厚厚的灰尘。
	用 a piece of furniture 一件家具 buy some new furniture 买一些新家具

geology [dʒiˈɒlədʒi]	*n.* 地质学；地质状况
	例 As a professor of geology he was particularly interested in rock formations, fossils and prehistoric history. 作为一名地质学教授，他对岩层、化石和史前历史很感兴趣。
	用 the geology of the British Isles 不列颠群岛的地质
	扩 geological *adj.* 地质的 a geological survey 一次地质勘察

accredit [əˈkredɪt]	*v.* 把……归于，归因于；委派；正式认可
	例 During the ceremony, the dean will accredit students who met the graduation requirements. 在典礼上，院长将授予符合毕业要求的学生毕业资格。
	用 accredited medical schools in the U.S. 在美国经认可的医学院

recipe [ˈresəpi]	*n.* 食谱；处方
	例 When you are making a dish for the very first time it's important to strictly follow the recipe. 当你第一次做一道菜时，严格按照食谱操作非常重要。
	用 a recipe book 一本烹饪书 a recipe for chicken soup 鸡汤的做法

reproduce [ˌriːprəˈdjuːs]	*v.* 复制；再生；繁殖
	例 His paintings became so famous that his works are often seen reproduced on posters, prints, postcards and in books all over the world. 他的画非常有名，他的作品经常被复制，出现在世界各地的海报、印刷品、明信片和书籍上。
	用 reproduce by laying eggs on land 通过在陆地产卵来繁殖
	扩 produce *v.* 生产；产生 *n.* 产品 product *n.* 产品 production *n.* 生产；产量 productive *adj.* 富有成效的；多产的 productivity *n.* 生产率；生产力

criterion [kraɪˈtɪəriən]	*n.* 标准；准则；规范
	例 Academic achievement is not the sole criterion for admission into college.
	学习成绩并不是进入大学的唯一标准。
	用 the main criterion 主要标准

mainspring [ˈmeɪnsprɪŋ]	*n.* 主要动力；主要原因
	例 The export market is the mainspring of the country's economy.
	出口市场是该国经济的主要来源。
	用 the mainspring of my life 我生活的动力

condense [kənˈdens]	*v.* （使）浓缩，压缩；精简
	例 We have learned how to condense long sentences into short, informative phrases.
	我们已经学会了如何把长句子压缩成简短的、信息充分的短语。
	用 condense the soup 把汤熬浓
	扩 dense *adj.* 密集的；浓密的 density *n.* 密度

peril [ˈperəl]	*n.* 极大危险，危难
	例 The hiker found himself in great peril as a sudden storm descended upon the mountain.
	山里突然出现了暴风雨，徒步旅行者发现自己处于极大的危险中。
	用 a warning about the perils of drug abuse 对吸毒危害的警告
	扩 imperil *v.* 危及；使陷入危险

quota [ˈkwəʊtə]	*n.* 定额；限额；配额
	例 Due to a very heavy workload, he almost never takes his full quota of holidays.
	由于工作量很大，他几乎从不把假期休满。
	用 introduce a strict import quota on grain 严格限制谷物进口量

transform [trænsˈfɔːm]	*v.* 使改变，使变形，使转化
	例 A good job in a career you enjoy can totally transform your life.
	职业生涯中，有一份自己喜欢的好工作可以完全改变你的人生。
	用 transform food into energy 将食物转化成能量
	扩 transformation *n.* 变化
	考 Psychologists have long held that a person's character cannot undergo a transformation in any meaningful way and that the key traits of personality are determined at a very young age.
	心理学家一直认为一个人的性格无法以任何有益的方式发生改变，并且性格中的主要特质是在很年幼的时候决定的。

discover [dɪ'skʌvə(r)]	*v.* 发现；发觉
	例 Scientists are constantly discovering new things about outer space. 科学家们不断发现有关太空的新事物。
	用 discover a cure for the disease 发现治疗疾病的方法
	扩 discovery *n.* 发现，探索
	考 It is even possible that the older civilisation may pass on the benefits of their experience in dealing with threats to survival such as nuclear war and global pollution, and other threats that we haven't yet discovered. 更为古老的文明甚至有可能会带给我们一些他们应对生存危机的经验，例如核战争、全球污染以及其他我们尚未发现的威胁。
dissolve [dɪ'zɒlv]	*v.* 溶解；分解；消失
	例 Both salt and sugar dissolve quickly and easily in warm water. 盐和糖在温水中都容易迅速溶解。
	用 dissolve in water 溶于水
intermediate [ˌɪntə'miːdiət]	*adj.* 中间的；中级的 *n.* 中级水平者，中级学生
	例 The school usually caters for intermediate learners of languages. 这所学校一般招收中级水平的语言学习者。
	用 an intermediate coursebook 中级课本
opponent [ə'pəʊnənt]	*n.* 对手；反对者
	例 When you're playing chess it's important to consider the strategy of the opponent. 下棋时，考虑对手的策略是很重要的。
	用 a formidable opponent 一个强大的对手
	扩 oppose *v.* 反对；抗争 opposite *adj.* 相反的
neglect [nɪ'glekt]	*v./n.* 忽视，忽略
	例 If you neglect to perform your duties you will end up losing your job and your reputation. 如果你不履行你的职责，你最终将失去自己的工作和声誉。
	用 a neglected aspect of the city's history 这座城市历史中一个被忽视的方面
	同 omit *v.* 忽略
	考 Well, currently teamwork is in fashion in the workplace and in my opinion the importance of the individual is generally neglected. 如今所有工作场所都提倡团队合作，我觉得个体的重要性普遍被忽视了。

hint
[hɪnt]

n. 暗示；线索；建议

例 He faced his illness bravely without a single hint of self-pity.
他勇敢面对自己的疾病，丝毫没有一丝自我怜悯。

用 some helpful hints to make your journey easier
一些使你的旅途更舒适的建议

同 sign *n.* 迹象 suggestion *n.* 暗示

bypass
['baɪpɑːs]

n. 旁路，支路 *v.* 绕过，避开；忽视，不顾

例 When you are taking that country road, instead of driving down the highway, you bypass a small town to the east of the river.
如果你走那条乡间小路，而不是沿着高速公路行驶，你会绕过一个小镇到达河的东边。

用 heart bypass surgery 心脏搭桥手术

unify
['juːnɪfaɪ]

v. 联合；统一；使成一体

例 Music serves to unify people and create a common sense of identity and purpose.
音乐可以使人们团结一致，创造一种共有的认同和目标。

用 a unified transport system 统一的运输体系

扩 union *n.* 联盟；工会 unique *adj.* 独一无二的

peculiar
[pɪˈkjuːliə(r)]

adj. 特殊的；独特的；奇怪的

例 There was a peculiar smell in the air after the firework display.
烟花表演结束后，空气中有一种奇怪的味道。

用 a peculiar smell 一种奇怪的气味
a species of bird peculiar to Asia 亚洲独有的一种鸟类

navigate
['nævɪɡeɪt]

v. 导航；航行；找到正确方法

例 I am a great driver but I am not good at using maps and navigating in new places.
我是一个很棒的司机，但在陌生的地方我不擅长使用地图和导航。

用 navigate by the stars 根据星星确定航向

扩 navigation *n.* 航行；航海；导航

考 navigate through a maze 在迷宫中穿行

convey
[kənˈveɪ]

v. 传达，表达；运输，运送

例 His speech was eloquent and conveyed accurately the challenges that the company was facing.
他的演讲非常有说服力，准确地传达了公司面临的挑战。

用 convey my apologies to him 向他转达我的歉意

respectively [rɪ'spektɪvli]	*adv.* 分别地；各自地
	例 The two criminals received sentences of one year and eighteen months, respectively. 这两名罪犯分别被判处一年和十八个月刑期。
	用 four and nine years old respectively 分别是4岁和9岁
viable ['vaɪəbl]	*adj.* 可行的
	例 The only viable solution to the problem is to reduce costs by hiring less people and attempt to put more effort into advertising. 解决问题唯一可行的方法是通过少雇人来降低成本，并努力在广告推广上投入更多精力。
	用 to be commercially viable 在商业上可行
sufficient [sə'fɪʃnt]	*adj.* 足够的；充分的
	例 The business had not been a great success, and by the end of the quarter they did not have sufficient funds to pay the rent. 业务经营并不成功，到季度末，他们没有足够的资金支付房租。
	用 sufficient time 足够的时间
	反 insufficient *adj.* 不足的；不够的
	扩 sufficiently *adv.* 充足地
	考 The simple detection of a radio signal will be sufficient to answer this most basic of all questions. 对无线电信号的简单探察就足以回答这个最基本的问题。
silicon ['sɪlɪkən]	*n.* 硅
	例 Silicon is a commonly used material in the production of computer chips and electronic devices. 硅是生产计算机芯片和电子设备的常用材料。
	用 a piece of silicon 一块硅片
	考 But are we ready for ethical silicon police limiting our options? 但是我们做好了准备去接受限制我们选择的硅基道德警察吗？
elastic [ɪ'læstɪk]	*adj.* 有弹性的；灵活的
	例 The elastic band will snap if you stretch it too far and too hard. 如果你把橡皮筋拉得太长太紧，它就会绷断。
	用 an elastic rope 一条有弹性的绳子
refresh [rɪ'freʃ]	*v.* 使恢复精神，使消除疲劳；使想起；翻新；刷新
	例 Before going into the exam room, he took one last look at his revision notes to refresh his memory. 在进入考场前，他最后看了一眼复习笔记，以唤起记忆。
	用 feel calm and refreshed 感到心情平静，精神振作

align [ə'laɪn]	v. 与……结盟；使对齐；使一致
	例 We must align the company operations and product development to the new policies the CEO announced. 我们必须使公司的运营和产品开发与CEO宣布的新政策保持一致。
	用 be aligned with 与……对准，与……一致

eloquently ['eləkwəntli]	adv. 雄辩地；有口才地；有表现力地
	例 He delivered the speech to the attentive audience confidently and eloquently. 他自信又有感染力地向参会听众发表了演说。
	用 speak eloquently on the subject 对这个话题滔滔不绝
	扩 eloquent adj. 雄辩的；有说服力的 an eloquent speech 雄辩的演讲

stream [striːm]	n. 溪流；流动；潮流
	例 The holiday resort in the mountains was an idyllic place of flowing streams and beautiful trees and flowers. 山上的度假胜地是一个田园诗般的地方，那里有溪流、美丽的树木和鲜花。
	用 mountain streams 山间溪流 a constant stream of enquiries 接连不断的询问
	考 Clothes were washed without soap in streams. 人们在溪流中洗衣服，并且不使用肥皂。

distort [dɪ'stɔːt]	v. 扭曲；曲解；变形
	例 We have to be careful with social media, because some people intentionally distort information to cause trouble. 我们需要小心使用社交媒体，因为有些人会故意歪曲信息来制造麻烦。
	用 distort his voice 使他声音失真

liable ['laɪəbl]	adj. 有责任的；有义务的
	例 You are liable for damages if you break anything in this store. 如果你打碎了这家商店里的任何东西，你要负赔偿责任。
	用 be liable for any damage caused 对造成的任何损失负责

deem [diːm]	v. 认为，相信
	例 After failing the alcohol test, and his failure to cooperate with the police, he was deemed unfit to drive. 他没有通过酒精测试，也没有配合警方，因此被认为不适合开车。
	用 deem it advisable to buy property now 认为现在购置房产是明智的

landmark ['lændmɑːk]	*n.* 地标；里程碑；纪念碑
	例 The building was not his favourite in the city, but it was certainly an important historical landmark. 这座建筑并不是这座城市中他最喜欢的，但这里确实是一个重要的历史地标。
	用 a landmark decision 具有里程碑意义的决策
	同 milestone *n.* 里程碑　monument *n.* 丰碑；遗址
spectrum ['spektrəm]	*n.* 光谱；频谱；范围
	例 The different modules in her course covered a whole spectrum of issues in psychology. 她课程中的不同模块涵盖了心理学各个领域的话题。
	用 at opposite ends of the spectrum 位于光谱的两端
	考 Autism spectrum disorders often result in major difficulties in comprehending verbal information and speech processing. 自闭症谱系障碍常常导致理解语言信息和文本处理方面的巨大困难。
seminar ['semɪnɑː(r)]	*n.* 讨论会，研讨班
	例 The seminar was a valuable exercise in information sharing. 讨论会是分享信息的重要活动。
	用 a seminar room 研讨室 a one-day management seminar 为期一天的管理研讨会
label ['leɪbl]	*n.* 标签；商标，品牌 *v.* 贴标签于
	例 She carefully labeled each jar to indicate its contents and expiration date. 她仔细地在每个罐子上贴上标签，标明里面的物品和保质期。
	用 price labels 价格标签
insomnia [ɪn'sɒmniə]	*n.* 失眠
	例 She struggled with insomnia, and couldn't get to sleep most nights, or woke up and found it hard to get back to sleep again. 她受失眠的困扰，大多数晚上睡不着，或者醒来后发现很难再入睡。
	用 suffer from insomnia 失眠
dwindle ['dwɪndl]	*v.* 减少；变小
	例 The numbers of marine species are dwindling due to environmental pollution in the oceans. 由于海洋环境污染，海洋物种的数量正在减少。
	用 dwindle from 50 to 40 从50减少到40

womb
[wuːm]

n. 子宫

例 The baby grew and developed inside the protective environment of the mother's womb.
婴儿在母亲子宫的保护性环境中生长发育。

用 the development of the fetus in the womb 胎儿在子宫里的发育

考 Most babies start developing their hearing while still in the womb, prompting some hopeful parents to play classical music to their pregnant bellies.
多数婴儿在母亲的子宫中就开始发展听力了，这促使一些满怀希望的家长为自己未出生的孩子播放古典音乐。

specification
[ˌspesɪfɪ'keɪʃn]

n. 规格；说明书；详述

例 The job specification was highly detailed and listed all the skills and qualifications the company was looking for in an employee.
这份工作要求非常详细，列出了公司需要雇员具备的所有技能和资质。

用 the technical specifications of the new model 新型号的技术规格

考 the technical specifications of different engine types
不同发动机类型的技术参数

optimal
['ɒptɪməl]

adj. 最佳的；最理想的

例 After years working on the product they believed they have come up with the optimal solution.
经过多年的产品研究，他们相信自己已经找到了最佳方案。

用 the optimal solution 最佳解决方案

扩 optimistic adj. 乐观的 optimum adj. 最适合的

考 Researcher Joan Goodman (1994) suggested that hybrid forms of work and play are not a detriment to learning; rather, they can provide optimal contexts for learning.
研究者Joan Goodman在1994年表明工作和游戏结合的形式不会对学习有害；相反，这会为学习提供最佳环境。

disseminate
[dɪ'semɪneɪt]

v. 传播，散布

例 One of the key functions of marketing is to disseminate information about a product to a wide audience.
营销的关键功能之一是将产品的信息传播给广大的受众。

用 be widely disseminated 广为传播

考 need to be disseminated and implemented effectively
需要有效地传播和实施

distinguish [dɪ'stɪŋgwɪʃ]	*v.* 区分；辨别；使著名
	例 The difference between a rabbit and a hare is not obvious, but they can be distinguished because the hare usually has bigger ears. 家兔和野兔之间的差别并不明显，但是它们能够被区分开来，因为野兔通常有更大的耳朵。
	用 distinguish between right and wrong 分辨是非
	同 differentiate *v.* 区分，辨别
	扩 distinguishable *adj.* 可辨别的
	考 Two things distinguish food production from all other productive activities. 两个因素将粮食生产与所有其他生产活动区分开来。
purchase ['pɜːtʃəs]	*v./n.* 购买，采购
	例 She was completely obsessed with online shopping—she purchased almost all of her clothes, accessories and food through apps on her phone. 她完全沉迷于网络购物，几乎通过手机应用程序购买自己所有的衣服、饰品和食品。
	用 make a purchase 采购
	扩 purchaser *n.* 购买者
	考 Native people in the desert regions of the American Southwest have followed similar strategies, encouraging tourists to visit their pueblos and reservations to purchase high-quality handicrafts and artwork. 美国西南部沙漠地区的当地人沿用了类似的策略，鼓励游客去印第安人村庄和保留区购买高质量的手工艺品和艺术品。
exhibit [ɪg'zɪbɪt]	*v.* 展览；显示，表现出 *n.* 展品；证物
	例 The latest collection of exhibits at the National Museum were fascinating to him. 国家博物馆最新收藏的展品使他着迷。
	用 exhibit regularly in local art galleries 经常在当地画廊办画展
	扩 exhibition *n.* 展览；展览品
interact [ˌɪntər'ækt]	*v.* 交流，互动；互相影响，互相作用
	例 He was not confident about interacting with people from different cultural backgrounds. 他对与来自不同文化背景的人交流感到不自信。
	用 interact with each child 和每个孩子沟通
	扩 interaction *n.* 互相作用，互相影响 interactive *adj.* 交互的，相互作用的

configuration [kənˌfɪɡəˈreɪʃn]	*n.* 配置；布局，构造 例 The IT specialist adjusted the network configuration to enhance security. 信息技术工程师调整了网络配置以增强安全性。 用 an ancient configuration of giant stones 一座古代巨石阵列 扩 configure *v.* 安装；配置 考 The four-year pilot study included 380 families who were about to have their first child and who represented a cross-section of socio-economic status, age and family configurations. 该试点研究项目为期四年，包含了380个即将迎来第一个孩子的家庭，涵盖了不同的社会经济地位、年龄段和家庭构成。
discrepancy [dɪˈskrepənsi]	*n.* 差异，不符 例 The auditor identified a discrepancy in the financial records and pursued the issue with her boss. 审计员在财务记录中发现了一处不符之处，并向她的老板追究这个问题。 用 measurement discrepancy 测量偏差

Exercise 14

一、中文释义练习

请选择单词正确的中文释义。

_____ 1. furniture   A. 浓缩

_____ 2. accredit   B. 归因于

_____ 3. condense   C. 溶解

_____ 4. transform   D. 改变

_____ 5. dissolve   E. 家具

_____ 6. opponent   A. 对手

_____ 7. neglect   B. 导航

_____ 8. bypass   C. 忽视

_____ 9. navigate   D. 硅

_____ 10. silicon   E. 绕过

_____ 11. align   A. 结盟

_____ 12. stream   B. 里程碑

_____ 13. liable   C. 溪流

_____ 14. landmark   D. 标签

_____ 15. label   E. 有责任的

_____ 16. insomnia   A. 子宫

_____ 17. womb   B. 失眠

_____ 18. purchase   C. 互动

_____ 19. exhibit   D. 展览

_____ 20. interact   E. 购买

二、英文释义练习

请选择单词正确的英文释义。

_____ 1. reproduce   A. located between two places, things or states

_____ 2. quota   B. that can be done or will be successful

_____ 3. intermediate   C. something that suggests what will happen in the future

_____ 4. hint   D. the limited number that is officially allowed

_____ 5. viable   E. to make a copy of a picture or a piece of text

_____ 6. elastic   A. material that can stretch and return to its original size

_____ 7. distort   B. to become gradually less or smaller

_____ 8. spectrum   C. a band of coloured lights in order of their wavelengths

_____ 9. dwindle   D. to spread information so that it reaches many people

_____ 10. disseminate   E. to change the shape, appearance or sound of sth.

blade
[bleɪd]

n. 刀片，刀刃；叶片

例 The sharp blade of the knife made slicing through vegetables effortless.
这把刀的刀刃锋利，切蔬菜毫不费力。

用 the blades of a propeller 螺旋桨叶

routine
[ruːˈtiːn]

n. 常规，惯例；程序 *adj.* 常规的，例行的；平常的

例 Before joining the company officially, you will need to have a routine medical examination.
在正式加入公司之前，你需要做一次常规体检。

用 a part of the daily routine 日常生活的一部分

考 If routine cognitive tasks are taken over by AI, how do professions develop their future experts?
如果常规的认知任务都被AI接手了，那么各行各业该如何培养它们领域中那些未来的专家呢？

commiserate
[kəˈmɪzəreɪt]

v. 同情，怜悯

例 Friends gathered to commiserate with her after her team's loss in the championship.
她的队伍在比赛中失利后，朋友们聚在一起对她表示同情。

用 commiserate with the losers on their defeat 对失败的一方表示同情

扩 commiseration *n.* 同情，怜悯

propose
[prəˈpəʊz]

v. 建议；提出；计划；求婚

例 She proposed a solution to the problem that nobody had thought of.
她提出了一个没有人想到过的针对这一问题的解决方法。

用 propose changes to the voting system 提议修改表决制度

扩 proposal *n.* 提议

crack
[kræk]

v. 破裂，裂开；砸开；崩溃 *n.* 裂缝，裂纹；爆裂声

例 The loud bang and crack of thunder signaled the arrival of a storm.
巨大的爆裂声和霹雳声预示着暴风雨的到来。

用 crack a nut 把坚果砸开
crack a bone in his arm 他的手臂有一处骨裂

amusement [ə'mjuːzmənt]	*n.* 消遣；娱乐；乐趣
	例 The children got great amusement from performing in the school play. 孩子们在学校演出中获得了极大乐趣。
	用 to my amusement 让我感到好笑的是
	同 entertainment *n.* 消遣，娱乐

beam [biːm]	*n.* 梁，横梁；光线，光柱 *v.* 照射；笑容满面
	例 The sunlight streamed through the window, casting a warm beam of light in the room. 阳光从窗户射进来，在房间里投下一束温暖的光。
	用 the beam of a torch 手电筒的光柱

pension ['penʃn]	*n.* 退休金，抚恤金；津贴
	例 The usual age in Europe when one can start drawing a pension is 65 years. 在欧洲，人们通常开始领取养老金的年龄是65岁。
	用 disability pension 残疾抚恤金

boast [bəʊst]	*v./n.* 吹嘘，夸耀
	例 A lot of proud parents can't help but boast about their child's achievements. 许多骄傲的父母都忍不住夸耀他们孩子的成就。
	用 boast about how wonderful her children are 夸耀她的孩子们多么出色

hemisphere ['hemɪsfɪə(r)]	*n.* （地球的）半球；脑半球
	例 The Northern Hemisphere is the part of the world north of the equator, and the Southern Hemisphere is south of the equator. 北半球是地球赤道以北的部分，南半球是赤道以南的部分。
	用 the Northern Hemisphere 北半球

protein ['prəʊtiːn]	*n.* 蛋白质
	例 Chicken and red meats are rich in protein, an essential ingredient in the diet of anyone wanting to do strength training. 鸡肉和红肉富含蛋白质，这是任何想进行力量训练的人饮食中的基本成分。
	用 essential proteins and vitamins 必不可少的蛋白质和维生素 protein deficiency 蛋白质缺乏
	类 vitamin *n.* 维生素 fat *n.* 脂肪 nutrition *n.* 营养

scrape [skreɪp]	v. 刮除；刮擦；擦伤 n. 擦伤，擦痕 例 She accidentally scraped her knee while running, causing a minor injury. 她跑步时不小心擦伤了膝盖，造成了轻伤。 用 scrape the mud off the boots 刮掉靴子上的泥
survey ['sɜːveɪ] n. [sə'veɪ] v.	n. 民意调查；测量，勘测；概述 v. 做民意调查；审视，检查；测量，勘测 例 According to a recent survey, more women than men in Norway are now spending time engaging in adventure sports. 根据一项近期的调查，在挪威，如今花时间从事冒险运动的女性比男性多。 用 conduct / carry out a survey 进行调查 a comprehensive survey of modern music 现代音乐概述 考 We now have the results of the survey carried out last month about traffic and road transport in the town. 我们现在有了上个月所做的关于城镇交通和道路运输调查的结果。
unanimous [juˈnænɪməs]	adj. 全体同意的；意见一致的 例 The jury reached a unanimous verdict, concluding the trial with a definitive decision. 陪审团达成了一致裁决，以明确的决定结束了审判。 用 be unanimous in the condemnation of the proposals 一致谴责这些提议
expire [ɪkˈspaɪə(r)]	v. 到期；终止；去世，故去 例 A driving licence usually expires after ten years, and then you have to renew it. 驾驶执照通常在10年后到期，之后需要更新执照。 用 expire at the end of February 二月底到期 扩 expiration n. 到期；终止；呼气
engender [ɪnˈdʒendə(r)]	v. 产生；引起 例 The issue continued to engender controversy so they tried to avoid talking about it as much as possible when the family got together each holiday. 这个问题一直在引起争议，所以每当节日全家人聚在一起时，他们都尽量避免谈论这个问题。 用 engender a sense of achievement 产生成就感

glimpse [glɪmps]	*n.* 一瞥，一看 *v.* 瞥见
	例 They caught a glimpse of the tiger as the car drove through the safari park. 当汽车驶过野生动物园时，他们瞥见了那只老虎。
	用 get my first glimpse of the island 第一次看到这座岛
	考 These giant carvings are a fascinating glimpse into the minds of their creators and how they viewed the landscape in which they lived. 这些巨大的雕刻画像带给我们惊鸿一瞥，让我们得以一窥其创作者的想法和他们当时如何看待自己所生活其中的风景。
species ['spiːʃiːz]	*n.* 物种；种类
	例 There are over forty species of whales, which include some of the largest creatures on earth. 有四十多种鲸鱼，其中包括一些地球上最大的生物。
	用 a conservation area for endangered species 濒危物种保护区
ancestor ['ænsestə(r)]	*n.* 祖先
	例 Every year they take part in a ceremony in reverence to their ancestors. 他们每年都参加祭拜祖先的仪式。
	用 a reptile that was the common ancestor of lizards and turtles 作为蜥蜴和龟的共同原种的一种爬行动物
	考 our ancient ancestors 我们古老的祖先们
descend [dɪ'send]	*v.* 下来，下降；遗传
	例 He slowly descended the stairs into the basement of the building, looking for the underground car park. 他慢慢地走下楼梯，进入大楼的地下室，寻找地下停车场。
	用 begin to descend 开始降落
	反 ascend *v.* 上升
	扩 descendant *n.* 后代；后裔
impression [ɪm'preʃn]	*n.* 印象；效果，影响
	例 My first impression of him was very favourable, as he was positive, friendly and confident. 我对他的第一印象非常好，因为他积极、友善、自信。
	用 a general impression 总的印象
committee [kə'mɪti]	*n.* 委员会；组委会
	例 The committee met to vote to elect a new chairman of the club. 组委会开会投票选举俱乐部的新主席。
	用 a member of the committee 委员会的委员

allure
[əˈlʊə(r)]

n. 吸引力，魅力

例 The charming coastal town had a certain allure for tourists who enjoyed peaceful locations.
这个迷人的海滨小镇对喜欢宁静环境的游客有一定的吸引力。

用 the allure of the big city 大城市的吸引力

ingredient
[ɪnˈɡriːdiənt]

n. 原料；要素；组成部分

例 Coconut milk is a key ingredient in a lot of Thai curries.
椰奶是很多泰国咖喱的关键原料。

用 contain only natural ingredients 只含天然成分

同 component *n.* 组成部分；要素 element *n.* 元素；要素

mechanism
[ˈmekənɪzəm]

n. 机制；机械装置，机件

例 These automatic cameras have a special auto-focus mechanism.
这些自动摄像机有一种特殊的自动对焦机制。

用 a delicate watch mechanism 精致的手表机件

扩 mechanical *adj.* 机械的

考 keep the cognitive mechanism sharp 保持认知机制灵敏

authority
[ɔːˈθɒrəti]

n. 权威；权力；当局

例 The new boss spoke with authority about the changes he wanted to make to the business.
新老板以富有权威的口吻谈论了他想对业务进行的变革。

用 have the authority to sign cheques 有权签支票

obesity
[əʊˈbiːsəti]

n. 过度肥胖；肥胖症

例 The rising rate of obesity in the country is a concerning health issue.
这个国家肥胖率的上升是一个令人担忧的健康问题。

用 a direct link between obesity and mortality
肥胖和死亡率之间的直接关系

考 And research has found that access to even the most basic green spaces can provide a better quality of life for dementia sufferers and help people avoid obesity.
研究还发现：哪怕是接触到最简单的绿色空间，也能为精神疾病类患者提供更好的生活质量，并且帮助人们避免肥胖。

distil
[dɪˈstɪl]

v. 蒸馏；提取，提炼

例 Water can be purified by distilling it through a careful process.
水可以通过精心的蒸馏过程得到净化。

用 distilled water 蒸馏水
distil fresh water from sea water 从海水中提取淡水

invert [ɪnˈvɜːt]	*v.* （使）倒转，颠倒，倒置 例 When you change the soil in a plant, you should invert the pot and tip the old soil out. 当你为植物换土时，你应该把花盆倒过来，把之前的土倒出。 用 a black inverted triangle 一个黑色的倒三角 扩 convert *v.* 转变；转化
apply [əˈplaɪ]	*v.* 申请；应用，使用 例 She was nervous because the deadline was approaching for her to apply for the job. 她很紧张，因为申请这份工作的截止日期快到了。 用 apply for jobs 找工作 扩 application *n.* 申请；应用
rent [rent]	*v.* 出租；租用 *n.* 租金 例 The majority of students live in dormitories but some rent apartment rooms in the city. 大多数学生住在宿舍里，但也有一些人在市里租住公寓。 用 put the rent up 提高房租 a month's rent in advance 预付的月租金
generous [ˈdʒenərəs]	*adj.* 慷慨的，大方的 例 The generous old woman decided to donate twenty five dollars to our organization even though we only asked for ten. 那位慷慨的年长女性决定向我们的组织捐赠25美元，尽管我们只要求10美元。 用 a generous benefactor 一个慷慨的捐助者 扩 generosity *n.* 慷慨，大方
metabolic [ˌmetəˈbɒlɪk]	*adj.* 新陈代谢的 例 Certain foods contain vitamins which increase the metabolic rate of digestion in the body. 某些食物含有维生素，可以提高人体消化的代谢率。 用 a low metabolic rate 低新陈代谢率 扩 metabolism *n.* 新陈代谢
tedious [ˈtiːdiəs]	*adj.* 冗长的，单调乏味的 例 The repetitive task became increasingly tedious after doing it for hours. 重复的工作做了几个小时后变得越来越乏味。 用 a tedious journey 一次单调乏味的旅行

budget [ˈbʌdʒɪt]	*n.* 预算；政府年度预算
	例 The budget for the new project is quite small, so we must be very careful how we allocate the funds. 这个新项目的预算很少，所以我们在分配资金时必须非常谨慎。
	用 education budget 教育预算
worship [ˈwɜːʃɪp]	*n.* 崇拜；礼拜；尊敬 *v.* 崇拜；做礼拜
	例 We are in an era where people are worshipping physical and mental fitness. 我们处在一个人们崇尚身体和心理健康的时代。
	用 ancestor worship 祖先崇拜
	考 During their heyday, they were places of gathering, of leisure and relaxation and of worship for villagers of all but the lowest classes. 在全盛时期，这里是除最底层之外的村民们进行集会、休闲、放松和礼拜的地方。
patent [ˈpeɪtnt]	*n.* 专利；专利权 *adj.* 受专利保护的；明显的 *v.* 取得专利权
	例 To patent a new invention can be a long and complicated process. 申请一项新发明专利会经过一个漫长而复杂的过程。
	用 apply for a patent on an invention 申请发明专利权
	考 Realizing the importance of this breakthrough, he lost no time in patenting it. 意识到这一突破的重要性，他立即为其申请了专利。
rationale [ˌræʃəˈnɑːl]	*n.* 基本原理；根本原因
	例 His rationale behind the changes was to reduce the amount of working hours, but improve efficiency. 他做出这些改变背后的理念是减少工作时间，但提升工作效率。
	用 the rationale behind these new exams 这些新测试的理论依据
hamper [ˈhæmpə(r)]	*v.* 阻碍，妨碍
	例 The heavy rain hampered their progress, making the hike more challenging than anticipated. 大雨阻碍了他们的前行，使徒步旅行比预期中更具挑战性。
	用 hamper rescue operations 阻碍救助行动
timid [ˈtɪmɪd]	*adj.* 羞怯的，胆小的
	例 The timid kitten cautiously crossed the path and peered into the garden. 胆怯的小猫小心翼翼地穿过小路，向花园里张望。
	用 a timid child 一个害羞的孩子

psychiatric [ˌsaɪki'ætrɪk]	*adj.* 精神病学的；精神疾病的 例 The patient received psychiatric treatment to address their mental health challenges. 病人接受了精神治疗，以解决他们的心理健康问题。 用 psychiatric treatment 精神病治疗 seek psychiatric help 寻求精神治疗方面的帮助 扩 psychiatrist *n.* 精神病学家；精神病医生
refuge ['refjuːdʒ]	*n.* 避难；避难所；庇护 例 They sought refuge from the storm behind a large oak tree. 他们在一颗巨大的橡树后面躲避暴风雨。 用 a place of refuge 避难所 a wetland refuge for birds 湿地鸟类保护区
evaporate [ɪ'væpəreɪt]	*v.* （使）蒸发，挥发；消失 例 The water evaporated quickly in the midday heat of summer. 在夏天正午的酷热天气中，水蒸发得很快。 用 make the water evaporate 使水蒸发 evaporate the earth's moisture 使地球上的水分蒸发 扩 vapor *n.* 水汽；水蒸气 考 In a related development, the sharp distinction between museum and heritage sites on the one hand, and theme parks on the other, is gradually evaporating. 在类似的发展中，博物馆与历史遗址和主题公园之间的清晰划分在逐渐消失。
conservation [ˌkɒnsə'veɪʃn]	*n.* 保存，保持；保护 例 The lake was recently designated as a national conservation area. 这个湖最近被指定为国家自然保护区。 用 wildlife conservation 野生动物保护 energy conservation 能源节约 考 This can make a real difference to conservation efforts and to the reduction of human-animal conflicts, and can provide a knowledge base for helping with the increasing threats of habitat destruction and other problems. 这会非常有助于动物保护及减少人类与动物的冲突，并且可以提供一个知识库以利于缓解不断增加的栖息地破坏等问题。
inform [ɪn'fɔːm]	*v.* 通知；告诉 例 It is advisable to inform your teacher twenty-four hours in advance if you are unable to attend class. 如果你无法上课，最好提前24小时告知你的老师。 用 inform sb. of sth. 通知某人某事 扩 information *n.* 信息，消息

inscribe [ɪnˈskraɪb]	*v.* 题写；铭记；雕刻
	例 The artist carefully inscribed her signature on the corner of the painting, marking it as her creation. 这位艺术家在画的一角仔细地签上名字，表明这是她的作品。
	用 inscribe his name on the trophy 把他的名字刻在奖杯上
	扩 prescribe *v.* 开处方；规定 describe *v.* 描写
fusion [ˈfjuːʒn]	*n.* 融合，结合；核聚变；融合物
	例 The chef combined different culinary styles, creating a unique fusion of flavours. 厨师将不同的烹饪风格结合在一起，创造出独特的风味融合。
	用 the fusion of copper and zinc to produce brass 铜与锌熔合成黄铜
	考 But the true originality of Leonardo's vision was its fusion of architecture and engineering. 但是列奥纳多设计中真正的创意之处在于它将建筑学与工程学的融合。
federation [ˌfedəˈreɪʃn]	*n.* 联邦政府，联邦；联合会
	例 The World Chess Federation is a serious international organization of highly professional chess players from all over the world. 世界象棋联合会是一个重要的国际组织，由来自全世界高度职业的棋手们组成。
	用 the International Tennis Federation 国际网球联合会
patriotic [ˌpeɪtriˈɒtɪk]	*adj.* 爱国的
	例 He really loves his country and is noted for being very patriotic in his speeches. 他非常热爱自己的国家，并因其爱国的演讲而为人所知。
	用 patriotic songs 爱国歌曲
ally [ˈælaɪ]	*n.* 同盟国；盟友，支持者 *v.* 与……结盟
	例 He will have no choice but to ally himself with the new movement. 他将别无选择，只能与这个新运动结盟。
	用 a close ally 一个亲密盟友
	考 Soil is also an ally against climate change: as microorganisms within soil digest dead animals and plants, they lock in their carbon content, holding three times the amount of carbon as does the entire atmosphere. 土壤同样可以帮助我们对抗气候变化：由于土壤中的微生物消化死去的动物和植物，它们可以留住动植物的碳成分，保存相当于整个大气层三倍的碳含量。

Exercise 15

一、中文释义练习

请选择单词正确的中文释义。

_____ 1. blade	A. 一瞥
_____ 2. amusement	B. 光线
_____ 3. beam	C. 半球
_____ 4. hemisphere	D. 刀片
_____ 5. glimpse	E. 娱乐

_____ 11. distil	A. 预算
_____ 12. metabolic	B. 单调乏味的
_____ 13. tedious	C. 崇拜
_____ 14. budget	D. 蒸馏
_____ 15. worship	E. 新陈代谢的

_____ 6. species	A. 物种
_____ 7. ancestor	B. 祖先
_____ 8. mechanism	C. 权威
_____ 9. authority	D. 机制
_____ 10. obesity	E. 肥胖

_____ 16. patent	A. 精神病的
_____ 17. psychiatric	B. 通知
_____ 18. timid	C. 专利
_____ 19. fusion	D. 融合
_____ 20. inform	E. 羞怯的

二、英文释义练习

请选择单词正确的英文释义。

_____ 1. scrape	A. to make a feeling or situation exist
_____ 2. protein	B. remove sth. by pulling a sharp object over the surface
_____ 3. unanimous	C. a natural substance in meat, eggs or fish
_____ 4. engender	D. the things that are used to make something
_____ 5. ingredient	E. agreed or shared by everyone in a group

_____ 6. generous	A. the principles or reasons which explain an action
_____ 7. rationale	B. giving or willing to give freely; given freely
_____ 8. conservation	C. saving and protecting the environment
_____ 9. inscribe	D. a liquid changes into a gas, especially steam
_____ 10. evaporate	E. to write or cut words or your name onto sth.

Word List **16**

manufacture [ˌmænjuˈfæktʃə(r)]	*v./n.* 大量生产，成批制造 例 To manufacture high quality solar panels, you need a lot of silicon and the right technical equipment. 要制造高质量的太阳能板，你需要大量的硅和合适的技术设备。 用 manufactured goods 工业品
constant [ˈkɒnstənt]	*adj.* 不变的；恒定的；经常的 例 The problem with being famous is the constant attention you get from the media. 出名带来的问题在于媒体对你的持续关注。 用 constant interruptions 无休止的干扰
version [ˈvɜːʃn]	*n.* 版本；（从不同角度的）说法，描述 例 He downloaded the latest version of the anti-virus software to install on his new laptop. 他下载了最新版本的杀毒软件，安装在自己的新笔记本电脑上。 用 the luxury version 豪华型 two versions of the game 游戏的两种类型
proclaim [prəˈkleɪm]	*v.* 宣告，声明 例 In a ceremony today the minister proclaimed the new building officially open. 在今天的仪式上，部长宣布新大楼正式开放。 用 proclaim a state of emergency 宣布紧急状态 同 declare *v.* 宣告；声明
prompt [prɒmpt]	*adj.* 迅速的；立刻的 *v.* 促进；导致 例 He was very prompt in responding to her emergency call. 他迅速接通了她的紧急呼叫。 用 prompt treatment 立即治疗 同 immediate *adj.* 立即的 考 Luckily, Perkin's scientific training and nature prompted him to investigate the substance further. 幸运的是，Perkin的科学训练和素养促使他进一步研究这种物质。

ascertain [ˌæsə'teɪn]	v. 确定；查明 例 The detectives were called to ascertain exactly how the crime was committed. 侦探们被召去查明这起犯罪是如何发生的。 用 ascertain the facts 查明事实真相
entail [ɪn'teɪl]	v. 使必要，需要 例 The project would entail significant effort and coordination among team members. 该项目需要团队成员之间的重大努力和协调。 用 a situation which entails considerable risks 必然会有很多风险的局面
classify ['klæsɪfaɪ]	v. 分类；分等 例 When you study chemistry you usually learn about elements and how they are classified into metals and non-metals. 学习化学时，你通常会学习元素以及它们是如何被划分为金属和非金属的。 用 classify the headaches into certain types 将头痛分为几个类型 扩 classification n. 分类；类别 考 a reference to classifying diseases on the basis of how far they extend geographically 提到根据疾病在地理上的分布对其进行分类
establish [ɪ'stæblɪʃ]	v. 建立，创立 例 The two nations agreed to establish strong diplomatic relations. 两国同意建立坚实稳定的外交关系。 用 establish a free trade zone 设立自由贸易区 扩 establishment n. 建立；建设
represent [ˌreprɪ'zent]	v. 代表；表现 例 Women now represent at least 50% of the workforce in our company. 我们公司目前至少有一半员工是女性。 用 represent the interests of women artists 代表女性艺术家的利益 represent 20% of the annual revenue 占年收入的20% 扩 representative n. 代表 考 Recent urban developments represent massive environmental changes. 最近的城市发展代表着巨大的环境变化。

emphasis ['emfəsɪs]	*n.* 重点；强调 例 Teachers have expressed concern about the heavy emphasis on exams and testing. 教师们表达了对过度强调考试和测验的担忧。 用 place emphasis on sth. 强调某事 同 stress *n.* 重点 *v.* 强调 扩 emphasise *v.* 强调；加强
principal ['prɪnsəpl]	*adj.* 主要的，最重要的 *n.* 大学校长；本金，资本 例 The country's principal exports are oil and carbonates, which contribute to about 40% of their GDP. 该国主要出口石油和碳酸盐，二者贡献了大约40%的国内生产总值。 用 the principal reason 主要原因 考 make the mistake of focusing only on the principal consumer trends 犯了只关注主要消费者动向的错误
placebo [plə'siːbəʊ]	*n.* 安慰剂 例 To test the efficacy of a drug, placebos are often given to part of the control group. 为了测试一种药物的功效，安慰剂通常会给部分对照组服用。 用 the placebo effect 安慰剂效应
rage [reɪdʒ]	*n.* 愤怒 *v.* 发怒；迅速蔓延，快速扩散 例 She had a terrible temper and was swift to fly into a rage when someone disagreed with her. 她的脾气很差，当有人不同意她的观点时，她就会勃然大怒。 用 speechless with rage 气愤得说不出话 扩 outrage *v.* 使气愤 outrageous *adj.* 粗暴的，无礼的
concur [kən'kɜː(r)]	*v.* 同意，赞同，意见一致 例 Some experts concur that plastic pollution in the oceans is a significant global issue. 一些专家一致认为，海洋中的塑料污染是一个重大的全球性问题。 用 concur with each other in this view 在这个观点上取得一致意见
alley ['æli]	*n.* 小巷，胡同 例 They strolled down the narrow alley, exploring the hidden gems of the city. 他们沿着狭窄的小巷漫步，探索这座城市隐藏的瑰宝。 用 a dark, narrow alley 一条黑暗的狭窄小巷

underpin [ˌʌndəˈpɪn]	*v.* 巩固；加固；构成……的基础；支撑
	例 The qualities of objectivity and truth-seeking underpin good journalism. 客观和求真的品质构成了高质量新闻的基础。
	用 be underpinned by extensive research 以广泛的研究为基础
	考 Now, finally I want to consider the psychology underpinning the traditional holiday hotel industry. 最后我们来探讨一下传统度假酒店行业运营背后的心理学。
subliminal [ˌsʌbˈlɪmɪnl]	*adj.* 潜意识的
	例 The advertisement contained subliminal messages that influenced viewers' purchasing decisions. 广告里包含了影响观众购买决策的潜意识信息。
	用 subliminal advertising 隐性广告 subliminal influence on our senses and moods 对我们的感觉和情绪有潜意识的影响
contribute [kənˈtrɪbjuːt]	*v.* 捐赠，捐助；（为……）做贡献，有助于
	例 He donated fifty dollars to the upkeep of the cathedral as he believed everyone should contribute a little. 他为维修大教堂捐了50美金，因为他认为每个人都应该有些贡献。
	用 contribute to the discussion 对讨论有贡献
	扩 contribution *n.* 贡献
steep [stiːp]	*adj.* 陡峭的；急剧的，大幅度的
	例 The hiker faced a steep ascent, requiring determination and physical exertion to reach the summit. 徒步旅行者面临着陡峭的上坡，需要决心和体力才能到达山顶。
	用 a steep flight of stairs 一段很陡的楼梯 a steep descent 陡直的下降
	考 This small volcanic island is mountainous, with steep rocky slopes and deep, wooded ravines, rising to 1,487 metres at its highest peak. 这个小火山岛地形多山，有陡峭的岩石斜坡和树木繁茂的深谷，最高可达1,487米。
diverge [daɪˈvɜːdʒ]	*v.* 分开；有分歧；偏离
	例 The two friends' paths diverged as they pursued different careers. 这两个朋友在追求不同的职业时走上了不同的道路。
	用 diverge from a single ancestor 从同一原种进化而来

reptile
['reptaɪl']

n. 爬行动物

例 Known as the world's largest reptile, salt-water crocodiles often reach six metres long.
咸水鳄鱼是世界上最大的爬行动物，身长通常可达六米。

用 the most developed of any reptile 所有爬行动物中最发达的

类 mammal *n.* 哺乳动物 vertebrate *n.* 脊椎动物 primate *n.* 灵长类动物

考 Last week, we started looking at reptiles, including crocodiles and snakes.
上周，我们研究了包括鳄鱼和蛇在内的爬行动物。

---

neuron
['njʊərɒn]

n. 神经元；神经单位

例 I don't know much about the science of the brain, but I do know that the brain is full of neurons that are fundamental components of our nervous systems.
我对大脑科学了解不多，但我知道大脑中有大量神经元，它们是我们神经系统的基本组成部分。

用 be transferred along each neuron 沿着神经元传递

---

thermal
['θɜːml]

adj. 热的；热量的

例 In winter he always wore thermal underclothes to keep warm.
冬天他总是穿着保暖内衣来保暖。

用 thermal energy 热能 thermal underwear 保暖内衣裤

---

oppose
[ə'pəʊz]

v. 反对；对抗

例 Our company opposes racism and discrimination of all forms.
我们公司反对一切形式的种族主义和歧视。

用 oppose changing the law 反对改变这项法规

---

fluent
['fluːənt]

adj. 流畅的；流利的

例 She is highly fluent in Japanese, but her spoken English language skills are less impressive.
她的日语非常流利，但她的英语口语能力却并不令人印象深刻。

用 a fluent speaker 一个讲话流利的人

扩 fluency *n.* 流利；流利度

---

clue
[kluː]

n. 线索，提示

例 He was frustrated because he simply couldn't solve the final clue to the crossword puzzle.
他很沮丧，因为他根本无法解开填字游戏的最后一条线索。

用 the vital clue to the killer's identity 关于杀手身份的重大线索

intern [ɪn'tɜːn]	v. 拘留，扣押 n. 实习生；实习医生 例 The ambitious young intern eagerly learned from experienced professionals. 这位雄心勃勃的年轻实习生热切地向经验丰富的专业人士学习。 用 a medical intern 一位实习医生
balcony ['bælkəni]	n. 阳台；包厢 例 My grandmother always uses her balcony for hanging up clothes to dry and planting flowers. 我的祖母总是用她的阳台晾晒衣服和种植花草。 用 go out to the balcony 出去到阳台上 类 kitchen n. 厨房 bedroom n. 卧室 dining room 餐厅 living room 客厅
stem [stem]	n. 干；茎 v. 阻止，遏制；起源于 例 Many of her emotional problems stem from her tough childhood experiences. 她的许多情感问题源于艰难的童年经历。 用 stem from 来源于；由于
exotic [ɪg'zɒtɪk]	adj. 异国的；外来的 例 Exotic foods from a variety of countries are now available in most supermarkets. 现在多数超市里都能买到来自不同国家的进口食品。 用 brightly-coloured exotic plants 色彩鲜艳的异国植物
surge [sɜːdʒ]	v. 急剧上升；汹涌 n. 激增；（情感的）涌起，翻涌；汹涌 例 She felt a surge of relief and happiness when they announced she had won the contest. 当他们宣布她赢得比赛时，她感到非常放松和快乐。 用 surge into their homes 涌进他们的房子
account [ə'kaʊnt]	n. 账户；解释；理由 v. 解释；导致 例 The evidence they discovered last week doesn't account for all the cases. 他们上周发现的证据无法解释这些情况。 用 open an account 开账户 bank account 银行账户 account for 占……比例；解释
pedal ['pedl]	n. （自行车的）踏板 v. 骑自行车前进；踩踏板 例 He pressed down on the pedal hard and the car accelerated rapidly. 他用力踩下踏板，汽车迅速加速。 用 press her foot down sharply on the brake pedal 猛踩刹车踏板

tuition [tjuˈɪʃn]	*n.* 学费；讲授，指导
	例 The students at that school get very personalised expert tuition in small groups. 那所学校的学生以小组形式接受非常个性化的专家指导。
	用 receive private tuition in French 由私人教授法语

inclination [ˌɪnklɪˈneɪʃn]	*n.* 倾向；斜坡
	例 She hated doing housework and had no inclination to tidy up. 她讨厌做家务，并且不愿意进行整理。
	用 the inclination to help them 愿意帮助他们

capture [ˈkæptʃə(r)]	*v.* 抓住；获得；捕获 *n.* 捕获；战利品
	例 The advertisement will certainly capture the attention of the TV audiences. 这则广告一定会引起电视观众的注意。
	用 capture the historian's attention 吸引历史学家的注意

export [ˈekspɔːt] *n.* [ɪkˈspɔːt] *v.*	*n./v.* 输出；出口
	例 They have imposed a number of export constraints on products in recent years. 近年来，他们对产品实施了一些出口限制。
	用 export sugar and fruit 出口糖和水果
	反 import *n./v.* 输入；进口

vessel [ˈvesl]	*n.* 船，舰；血管；容器
	例 Container ships are huge vessels that travel thousands of miles across the ocean to transport goods from one place to another. 集装箱船是一种巨大的船只，它在海洋上行驶数千英里，将货物从一个地方运到另一个地方。
	用 a fishing vessel 一艘渔船

marvel [ˈmɑːvl]	*n.* 令人惊异的人（或事），奇迹
	例 When the tallest building in the world was constructed, it was referred to as an architectural marvel. 当世界上最高的建筑建成时，被称为建筑奇迹。
	用 a symbol of the marvels of creation 造物杰作的象征

calendar [ˈkælɪndə(r)]	*n.* 日历；历法；日程表
	例 The current calendar used by most of the world dates back to the time of the Roman Empire. 目前世界上大多数国家使用的历法可以追溯到罗马帝国时代。
	用 in the last calendar year 在上一个日历年度

module
['mɒdjuːl]

n. 模块；组件

例 His university course consisted of three different modules per year, with two main assignments per module.
他每年的大学课程包括三个不同的模块，每个模块有两项主要作业。

用 core modules 核心模块

severe
[sɪ'vɪə(r)]

adj. 严重的；严厉的；剧烈的

例 The roads had become blocked by the severe snowstorm.
道路被严重的暴风雪堵塞了。

用 a severe winter 严冬
a severe shortage of qualified staff 严重缺少合格员工

扩 severity n. 严重性

考 Massive floods, long droughts, hurricanes and severe monsoons take their toll each year, destroying millions of tons of valuable crops.
大洪水、长期干旱、飓风和严重的季风每年都会发生，使数百万吨有价值的农作物遭受破坏。

engross
[ɪn'grəʊs]

v. 使全神贯注；吸引

例 The captivating novel engrossed her so much that she lost track of time.
这本引人入胜的小说使她全神贯注，以至于忘记了时间。

用 an engrossing problem 引人关注的问题

考 More than most other hobbies, collecting can be totally engrossing, and can give a strong sense of personal fulfilment.
不像其他大多数爱好，收藏可以使人全情投入，并带来非常强的个人满足感。

molecule
['mɒlɪkjuːl]

n. 分子；微粒

例 Water molecules are made up of a special combination of hydrogen and oxygen.
水分子由氢元素和氧元素特殊的结合而构成。

用 the chemical structure of this particular molecule
这种特殊分子的化学结构

扩 molecular adj. 分子的 molecular structure 分子结构

考 Summer leaves are green because they are full of chlorophyll, the molecule that captures sunlight and converts that energy into new building materials for the tree.
夏天的树叶是绿色的，因为它们充满叶绿素，这些分子可以获取阳光并将这种能量转化为树木新的生长材料。

rhythm ['rɪðəm]	*n.* 节奏；韵律
	例 She was excellent at dancing mainly because she had a great sense of rhythm. 她擅长跳舞，主要因为她有很强的节奏感。
	用 the rhythm of the seasons 四季的更迭
	考 Firstly it is used as a cue for the timing of daily and seasonal rhythms in both plants and animals, and secondly it is used to assist growth in plants. 首先它被作为记录植物和动物每日和每季度节律的线索，其次它被用于辅助植物生长。
tangible ['tændʒəbl]	*adj.* 有形的；可触摸的
	例 The new policy creates tangible benefits for the unemployed in the community. 新政策为社区失业者带来了实际的好处。
	用 tangible assets 有形资产
	反 intangible *adj.* 无形的
device [dɪ'vaɪs]	*n.* 装置，设备；策略，方法
	例 Today people are using computers less and less and doing more on tablets and other mobile devices. 如今人们越来越少地使用电脑，而更多使用平板电脑和其他移动设备。
	用 a water-saving device 节水装置
	考 Two decades later Janssen developed that basic idea he saw in Southeast Asia into a portable device that uses the power from the sun to purify water. 20年后，Janssen把他在东南亚形成的基本想法运用于一种利用太阳能净化水质的便携式设备。
narrative ['nærətɪv]	*n.* 叙述，叙事
	例 The novel contains a lot more narrative than dialogue. 这本小说中包含的叙事比对话多得多。
	用 narrative fiction 叙事小说 a narrative of their journey up the Amazon 关于他们沿亚马孙河而上的旅程的描述
band [bænd]	*n.* 乐队；带状物，条纹
	例 The band performed their new song, captivating the audience with their musical talent. 乐队演奏了他们的新歌，以其音乐才能吸引了听众。
	用 a rock band 摇滚乐队

Exercise 16

一、中文释义练习

请选择单词正确的中文释义。

_____ 1. version   A. 版本

_____ 2. proclaim   B. 建立

_____ 3. entail   C. 宣告

_____ 4. establish   D. 强调

_____ 5. emphasis   E. 使必要

_____ 6. represent   A. 代表

_____ 7. placebo   B. 流畅的

_____ 8. rage   C. 愤怒

_____ 9. steep   D. 安慰剂

_____ 10. fluent   E. 陡峭的

_____ 11. clue   A. 实习生

_____ 12. intern   B. 异国的

_____ 13. stem   C. 起源于

_____ 14. exotic   D. 脚踏板

_____ 15. pedal   E. 线索

_____ 16. vessel   A. 模块

_____ 17. marvel   B. 血管

_____ 18. module   C. 分子

_____ 19. tangible   D. 有形的

_____ 20. molecule   E. 奇迹

二、英文释义练习

请选择单词正确的英文释义。

_____ 1. manufacture   A. affecting your mind even if you are not aware of it

_____ 2. classify   B. to make goods in large quantities, using machinery

_____ 3. underpin   C. to support or form the basis of an argument or a claim

_____ 4. subliminal   D. any animal that has cold blood and lays eggs

_____ 5. reptile   E. to decide which type or group sb./sth. belongs to

_____ 6. diverge   A. a feeling that makes you want to do sth.

_____ 7. balcony   B. a platform built on upstairs outside wall of a building

_____ 8. inclination   C. a description of events, especially in a novel story

_____ 9. rhythm   D. a strong regular repeated pattern of sounds

_____ 10. narrative   E. to separate and go in different directions

detrimental
[ˌdetrɪ'mentl]

adj. 不利的；有害的

例 The dumping of plastic in the oceans has a detrimental effect on marine life.
向海洋中倾倒塑料会对海洋生物产生有害影响。

用 the sun's detrimental effect on skin 日光对皮肤的有害影响

同 damaging *adj.* 有危害的

反 beneficial *adj.* 有益的，有好处的

考 the detrimental effects of noise in classroom situations
噪声对课堂的不利影响

induce
[ɪn'djuːs]

v. 诱导；引起；劝说

例 The wonderful natural beauty of the area induces many travellers to go there.
这个地区美丽的自然风光吸引了很多旅行者。

用 induce me to take the job 劝我接受这份工作
drugs which induce sleep 使人昏昏欲睡的药物

draft
[drɑːft]

n. 草稿，草案 *v.* 起草，草拟

例 He carefully revised his first draft, making necessary corrections and improvements.
他仔细修改了初稿，做了必要的修改和完善。

用 a rough draft of the letter 这封信的草稿

考 draft your proposal 起草建议书

telescope
['telɪskəʊp]

n. 望远镜

例 He peered through the telescope to observe the stars in the night sky.
他透过望远镜观察夜空中的星星。

用 look at the stars through a telescope 用望远镜观察星星

扩 microscope *n.* 显微镜

dismal
['dɪzməl]

adj. 忧郁的，阴沉的；糟糕的

例 The dark and rainy weather created a dismal and depressing atmosphere.
阴暗多雨的天气营造出一种阴沉压抑的气氛。

用 their dismal record in the Olympics 他们在奥运会上的惨淡纪录

coordinate
[kəʊ'ɔːdɪneɪt] *v.*
[kəʊ'ɔːdɪnət] *n.*

v. 使协调；使相配合 *n.* 坐标

例 It's sometimes quite difficult to coordinate a large group of people on a company excursion.

有时协调很多人参加公司远足活动是很困难的。

用 coordinate the work of the team 协调这个团队的工作

扩 coordination *n.* 协调

steer
[stɪə(r)]

v. 驾驶，掌舵；操控，引导

例 She steered the boat slowly towards the busy port.

她驾驶着船缓慢地驶向繁忙的港口。

用 steer a course between the island 在岛屿之间穿行

考 And satellite operators can't steer away from every potential crash, because each move consumes time and fuel that could otherwise be used for the spacecraft's main job.

人造卫星的操控者无法操纵卫星躲闪开每一次潜在的撞击，因为每一次移动都要消耗时间和燃料，而这些原本都是要用在这架飞行器的主要工作上的。

seek
[siːk]

v. 寻求；寻找

例 They reached the top of the mountain after a very long hike, and started to seek shelter from the bitter winds.

经过长途跋涉，他们到达了山顶，开始寻找避风的地方。

用 seek funding for a project 为项目筹募资金

同 search for 搜索

bounce
[baʊns]

v. 弹起，反弹 *n.* 弹跳；弹性，弹力

例 The children loved bouncing on the trampoline in the backyard.

孩子们喜欢在后院的蹦床上蹦蹦跳跳。

用 bounce the ball against the wall 对着墙打球

decay
[dɪ'keɪ]

v./n. 衰退；腐烂

例 Without proper care, fruits and vegetables will quickly decay and become inedible.

缺少适当的护理，水果和蔬菜会很快腐烂，变得不可食用。

用 tooth decay 蛀牙 the decay of the old industries 旧工业的衰败

考 In the wild, when plants grow they remove nutrients from the soil, but then when the plants die and decay these nutrients are returned directly to the soil.

自然环境下，植物生长时会带走土壤中的营养物质，但随着植物衰退腐烂，这些营养物质会直接返还到土壤中。

reverse [rɪˈvɜːs]	*v.* 反转，倒转；改变 *n.* 逆向；相反 *adj.* 相反的
	例 It would be a struggle to reverse the damage caused by the failure of the project. 扭转项目失败所造成的损害将是非常困难的。
	用 reverse the order 将顺序颠倒
	扩 revert *v.* 倒转；还原 reversible *adj.* 可逆转的，可倒转的 irreversible *adj.* 不可逆转的，不可扭转的
	考 reverse the traffic growth trend 扭转交通增长的趋势
lobe [ləʊb]	*n.*（脑、肺等的）叶
	例 There have been extensive scientific studies into how the brain's frontal lobe affects intelligence and decision-making. 关于大脑额叶如何影响智力和决策，已经有了非常广泛的科学研究。
	用 damage to the temporal lobe of the brain 对大脑颞叶的损伤
	类 frontal lobe 大脑额叶 temporal lobe 大脑颞叶 occipital lobe 大脑枕叶 parietal lobe 大脑顶叶
indigenous [ɪnˈdɪdʒənəs]	*adj.* 本土的，当地的
	例 The indigenous people have lived in harmony with nature for centuries, respecting their ancestral lands. 几个世纪以来，当地人与自然和谐相处，尊重他们祖先的土地。
	用 the indigenous languages of the area 该地区的本地语言
	考 A team made up of more than 30 psychological scientists, anthropologists, and biologists then played these recordings to listeners from 24 diverse societies, from indigenous tribes in New Guinea to city-dwellers in India and Europe. 由30多位心理科学家、人类学家和生物学家组成的团队继而将这些录音播放给了来自24个不同社会——从新几内亚的原住民部落到印度和欧洲的城市居民——的听众。
scheme [skiːm]	*n.* 计划，方案；阴谋 *v.* 密谋，策划
	例 The new employment scheme for graduates helps to find internships in companies related to their studies. 新的就业计划帮助毕业生在与其专业相关的公司寻求实习机会。
	用 a training scheme 培训方案
sequence [ˈsiːkwəns]	*n.* 顺序；一系列，一连串 *v.* 按顺序排列
	例 It's important that your essay outline follows a clear and logical sequence. 你的文章大纲遵循清晰有逻辑的顺序是很重要的。
	用 in a particular sequence 按照一定次序

template ['templeɪt]	*n.* 模板；样板 例 In our DNA we all carry a genetic template for the next generation. 在我们的DNA中，我们都携带着给下一代的基因模板。 用 provide a template 提供模板 考 Reliance on a template like this offers the huge advantage of built-in consistency. 依托于这样的一个模板能够产生内部一致的明显优势。
archive ['ɑːkaɪv]	*n.* 档案馆；档案文件 *v.* 存档 例 The archive offers a central facility for categorising and organising data. 档案馆提供了对数据进行分类和组织的服务中心。 用 archive material 档案资料
edible ['edəbl]	*adj.* 可食用的 例 Some mushrooms are edible and others are inedible and poisonous to humans. 有些蘑菇是可食用的，有些蘑菇是不可食用、对人类有毒的。 用 edible fungi 可食用的菌类 反 inedible *adj.* 不可食用的
tram [træm]	*n.* 有轨电车；煤车，矿车 例 The tram smoothly glided along the tracks, transporting passengers through the city streets. 有轨电车平稳地沿着轨道行驶，载着乘客穿过城市街道。 用 a tram route 有轨电车路线 考 This begins with a leisurely ride along the promenade in Douglas in a horse-drawn tram. 当天早上，我们可以沿着道格拉斯的散步长廊乘坐马拉车，打发一段悠闲的时光。
remuneration [rɪ,mjuːnə'reɪʃn]	*n.* 薪水，报酬 例 He received a generous remuneration for his hard work and dedication to the company. 由于辛勤工作和对公司的奉献，他得到了丰厚的报酬。 用 a generous remuneration 一份很不错的薪水 考 Problems of recruitment, remuneration and independence could also arise and this structure would not be appropriate for all companies. （如果采用这个办法，）可能还要面临招聘、薪酬和独立性等相关问题，且这个结构未必适用于所有公司。

dismantle
[dɪsˈmæntl]

v. 拆除；取消；解散

例 It was quite easy to assemble the piece of furniture, but dismantling it was tough.
组装那件家具很容易，但拆卸起来却很困难。

用 dismantle the engine in order to repair it 把发动机拆开来修理

empirical
[ɪmˈpɪrɪkl]

adj. 以实验（或经验）为依据的；经验主义的

例 The scientist conducted extensive experiments to gather empirical evidence for her research.
这位科学家进行了大量实验，为她的研究收集实证证据。

用 empirical research 基于实验的研究

考 limited empirical evidence 有限的实验数据

reclaim
[rɪˈkleɪm]

v. 收回，取回；利用，改造

例 The tax is quite high in Sweden, but at the end of the financial year you can reclaim a certain percentage from the bureau.
瑞典的税收相当高，但在财政年结束时，你可以从财政部门收回一定的比例。

用 reclaimed marshland 被开发的沼泽地

junction
[ˈdʒʌŋkʃn]

n. 连接；交叉点；连接点

例 When you get to the next junction, don't take the first left, but take the second left to the north onto the expressway.
当你到达下一个路口时，不要在第一个路口左转，而是在第二个路口左转，向北进入高速公路。

用 a telephone junction box 电话分线盒

ultimate
[ˈʌltɪmət]

adj. 最终的；极限的；根本的

例 Although they are allowed to give their opinions, the ultimate decision lies with their manager.
尽管他们可以发表自己的意见，但最终决定权在经理手中。

用 our ultimate target 我们的最终目标

考 the ultimate goal 最终目标

pedestrian
[pəˈdestriən]

n. 行人；步行者 *adj.* 行人的，行人使用的

例 The pedestrian street near my office is a pleasant place for a quiet stroll during lunch hour.
我办公室附近的步行街是午餐时间安静散步的好地方。

用 pedestrian areas 步行区

考 pedestrian crossing 人行横道

enrich [ɪn'rɪtʃ]	*v.* 使充实；使富裕；使（土壤）肥沃 例 Farmers often add fertiliser to enrich the soil so crops grow better. 农民们经常施肥使土壤肥沃，以便让作物更好地生长。 用 enrich all our lives 丰富我们的整个生活
feat [fiːt]	*n.* 功绩，壮举；武艺，技艺 例 Climbing Mount Qomolangma is considered a remarkable feat of human endurance. 攀登珠穆朗玛峰被认为是人类耐力的非凡壮举。 用 a brilliant feat of engineering 工程领域的光辉业绩
disorder [dɪs'ɔːdə(r)]	*n.* 混乱；骚乱，动乱；紊乱，疾病 例 When the teacher was away the class fell into total disorder as the children misbehaved. 由于孩子们的调皮行为，老师不在的时候，班里陷入了完全的混乱。 用 mental disorder 心理问题；精神错乱 psychiatric disorder 精神疾病 考 This makes it too common to be considered a mental disorder. 这使它过于普通，以至于不会被当作一种心理问题
submit [səb'mɪt]	*v.* 提交；主张；屈服，投降 例 I am in a real hurry this week because I have three assignments to submit to the tutor and I'm still a little behind on them. 我这周真的很忙，因为我需要提交三个作业给导师，而且我目前还没有完成。 用 submit an application 提交申请书
advocate ['ædvəkeɪt] *v.* ['ædvəkət] *n.*	*v.* 提倡，主张 *n.* 提倡者；支持者 例 Some famous people are advocates of environmental causes like wildlife preservation. 一些有名的人是野生动物保护等环境事业的倡导者。 用 advocate rewarding your child for good behaviour 主张对孩子的优异表现加以奖励 同 support *v.* 支持 反 oppose *v.* 反对
patronage ['pætrənɪdʒ]	*n.* 赞助，资助 例 The artist was grateful for the generous patronage of art enthusiasts. 这位艺术家很感激艺术爱好者的慷慨赞助。 用 government patronage of the arts 政府对艺术的资助

sophisticated [sə'fɪstɪkeɪtɪd]	*adj.* 复杂的；精致的；水平高的；老练的 例 She had quite sophisticated taste in fine French foods and classical music. 她对精致的法国餐食和古典音乐有相当的鉴赏力。 用 the sophisticated pleasures of city life 城市生活中各式各样的快乐 考 Shipbuilding today is based on science and ships are built using computers and sophisticated tools. 科学技术是现代造船业的基础，人们会使用电脑科技以及多种复杂的工具来建造船只。
roam [rəʊm]	*v.* 漫步，闲逛 例 They loved to roam freely in the vast wilderness, exploring nature's wonders. 他们喜欢在广阔的荒野中自由漫步，探索大自然奇观。 用 roam the countryside 在乡间漫步 考 roam around the whole area 在整个地区漫游
expenditure [ɪk'spendɪtʃə(r)]	*n.* 支出，花费；经费 例 She was happy about the idea of going to university in New Zealand, although the expenditure was a huge burden on her family. 去新西兰读书的计划令她非常开心，尽管这份支出对其家庭而言是很大的负担。 用 a reduction in public expenditure 削减公共开支 plans to increase expenditure on health care 增加医疗保健开支的计划
restore [rɪ'stɔː(r)]	*v.* 恢复；修复；还原 例 Construction teams worked to restore the damage caused by the hurricane. 施工队努力修复飓风造成的破坏。 用 restore public confidence in the economy 恢复公众对经济的信心 考 restore the stepwells throughout the state 修复全州的阶梯井
witness ['wɪtnəs]	*n.* 证人；目击者 *v.* 目击，见证；作证 例 He witnessed the signing of the will in the lawyer's office. 他在律师事务所见证了遗嘱的签署。 用 a defence witness 被告的证人 a prosecution witness 控方的证人
stubborn ['stʌbən]	*adj.* 固执的 例 However much his mother pushed him, the stubborn child refused to eat his vegetables. 不管妈妈怎么催他，这个倔强的孩子都不肯吃蔬菜。 用 a stubborn resistance to change 顽固抵制变革

facility [fə'sɪləti]	*n.* 设施，设备；才能 例 The new medical facility is dedicated to infectious disease research. 新的医疗设施专门用于传染病研究。 用 conference facilities 会议设施
format ['fɔːmæt]	*n.* 格式；版式 *v.* 使格式化 例 The format of the new magazine is very attractive; it's clear it was done by a professional designer. 新杂志的样式很吸引人，很明显这是由专业设计师设计的。 用 the format of the quiz 测验的形式 考 the typical format of a maths lesson 一堂数学课的典型结构
endure [ɪn'djʊə(r)]	*v.* 忍受，忍耐；持久，持续 例 Despite the challenges, she continued to endure and persevere with determination. 尽管面临种种挑战，她仍然坚定地继续坚持。 用 have to endure a long wait 需要忍受长久的等待 扩 endurance *n.* 忍耐力；耐久性
manoeuvre [mə'nuːvə(r)]	*v.* 操控；移动 *n.* 策略，手段 例 The traffic jam was so bad, so he had to manoeuvre the car, turn around and head back down the highway and find another route to the airport. 交通堵塞太严重了，他只好驾驶车辆掉头沿着高速公路开回去，另找一条路去机场。 用 manoeuvre the car carefully into the garage 小心地将车开进车库
bilateral [ˌbaɪ'lætərəl]	*adj.* 双边的；两边的 例 The two countries are currently working on a bilateral agreement to recognize each other's vaccines. 两国目前正在协商一项双边协议，以互认彼此的疫苗。 用 bilateral relations 双边关系 bilateral agreements 双边协议
enhance [ɪn'hɑːns]	*v.* 提高；加强；增加 例 He believes that good lighting will enhance the atmosphere of the room. 他相信好的照明会改善房间的氛围。 用 an opportunity to enhance the reputation of the company 提高公司声誉的机会 扩 enhancement *n.* 增强；增加 考 enhance employee motivation and retention 提升员工积极性和员工保留率

sediment ['sedɪmənt]	*n.* 沉积；沉淀物 例 When the water level went down in summer you could see the muddy brown sediment at the bottom of the canal. 当夏季水位下降时，你可以在运河底部看到泥泞的棕色沉积物。 用 ocean sediments 海洋沉积物
shrink [ʃrɪŋk]	*v.* 收缩；缩小 例 If you put a cashmere sweater in the washing machine on a high temperature, it will shrink. 如果你把羊绒毛衣放在洗衣机里高温洗涤，它就会缩水。 用 shrank in the wash 缩水了 shrink the world 使世界变小 同 condense *v.* 压缩；精简
perfume ['pɜːfjuːm]	*n.* 香水；香味 *v.* 散发香气 例 I don't really like strong-smelling perfume—I prefer the more subtle fragrances. 我不太喜欢味道浓的香水，我更喜欢淡淡的香味。 用 a bottle of expensive perfume 一瓶昂贵的香水
stationary ['steɪʃənri]	*adj.* 固定的；静止的 例 You should not get up from your seat until the train has come to a halt and is completely stationary. 在火车完全停稳之前，你不能从自己的座位上站起来。 用 a stationary population 稳定的人口 a stationary exercise bike 固定式健身自行车 同 static *adj.* 静止的 反 mobile *adj.* 运动的
encounter [ɪn'kaʊntə(r)]	*v.* 遭遇；遇到 例 Many airline pilots claim to have encountered UFOs and other strange flying objects in the sky. 许多飞行员都声称在空中遇到过不明飞行物以及其他奇怪的飞行物体。 用 encounter stress 面临压力
portfolio [pɔːt'fəʊliəʊ]	*n.* 公文包；作品集；投资组合 例 The investor carefully managed her diverse portfolio, aiming for long-term growth and stability. 投资者谨慎地管理着她的多元投资组合，目标是实现长期增长和稳定性。 用 an investment portfolio 投资组合

Exercise 17

一、中文释义练习

一、中文释义练习

请选择单词正确的中文释义。

_____	1.	telescope	A. 望远镜	_____	11.	pedestrian	A. 漫步
_____	2.	steer	B. 叶	_____	12.	advocate	B. 恢复
_____	3.	decay	C. 衰退	_____	13.	sophisticated	C. 复杂的
_____	4.	reverse	D. 驾驶	_____	14.	roam	D. 行人
_____	5.	lobe	E. 反转	_____	15.	restore	E. 提倡

_____	6.	template	A. 最终的	_____	16.	facility	A. 沉积
_____	7.	archive	B. 拆除	_____	17.	bilateral	B. 设施
_____	8.	edible	C. 模板	_____	18.	sediment	C. 遭遇
_____	9.	dismantle	D. 可食用的	_____	19.	shrink	D. 双边的
_____	10.	ultimate	E. 档案馆	_____	20.	encounter	E. 收缩

二、英文释义练习

请选择单词正确的英文释义。

_____	1.	draft	A. set of events or actions which have a particular order
_____	2.	coordinate	B. organize people involved so that an activity works well
_____	3.	indigenous	C. based on experiments rather than theories
_____	4.	sequence	D. a rough written version of sth. that is not its final form
_____	5.	empirical	E. belonging to a place, not coming from other places

_____	6.	enrich	A. to give a document or proposal to sb. in authority
_____	7.	submit	B. a person who sees sth. happen and can describe it
_____	8.	witness	C. a liquid that you put on your skin to smell nice
_____	9.	endure	D. to improve the quality of sth., often by adding sth. to it
_____	10.	perfume	E. to experience sth. unpleasant without complaining

disdain [dɪs'deɪn]	*n./v.* 鄙视，蔑视
	例 She looked at him with disdain, unable to hide her contempt and disapproval. 她轻蔑地望着他，无法掩饰自己的蔑视和不认同。
	用 a disdain for the law 对法律的藐视
recap ['riːkæp]	*v.* 重述；概括
	例 The team leader gave everyone a quick recap of the plan before they went into the meeting. 在开会之前，组长给大家快速概括了一下计划。
	用 recap on what we've decided so far 概括一下到目前为止我们所作的决定
restrain [rɪ'streɪn]	*v.* 制止，阻止；克制，抑制
	例 The police officer had to restrain the agitated suspect to maintain order and ensure everyone's safety. 为了维持秩序，确保每个人的安全，警察不得不制服激动的犯罪嫌疑人。
	用 restrain his anger 压制住怒气
annoy [ə'nɔɪ]	*v.* 使恼怒，使烦恼；打扰
	例 The constant noise from construction work began to annoy the residents. 建筑工程持续不断的噪音开始惹恼居民。
	用 make a note of the things that annoy you 把让你心烦的事记下来
scope [skəʊp]	*n.* 范围，领域；机会
	例 After months they still had not solved the crime, so the police decided to widen the scope of the investigation. 几个月之后他们依然没有破案，因此警察决定扩大搜查范围。
	用 beyond the scope of our investigation 超出我们的调查范围
	同 field *n.* 领域
	扩 microscope *n.* 显微镜 telescope *n.* 望远镜

compromise ['kɒmprəmaɪz]	*n./v.* 妥协；折中
	例 I don't always share the same views as my team members, but we always find a way to reach a compromise. 我与团队成员并不总是观点一致，但是我们会找到方法达成妥协。
	用 a compromise solution 一个折中方案
	同 concede *v.* 承认；让步
enervation [ˌenə'veɪʃn]	*n.* 衰弱；虚弱；削弱
	例 He felt a sense of enervation and frustration after failing the exam. 没有通过考试使他感到非常疲惫和挫败。
	用 either enervation or enjoyment 沮丧或者快乐
	考 the enervation of soil 土壤的退化
neutron ['njuːtrɒn]	*n.* 中子
	例 We learned in physics that a neutron decays into a proton. 我们在物理学中学过中子会衰变为质子。
	用 be made up of neutrons and protons 由中子和质子组成
	考 the discovery of the neutron 中子的发现
parallel ['pærəlel]	*n.* 相似的人（或物） *v.* 与……相似；与……同时发生 *adj.* 平行的；类似的
	例 In the poem he drew an interesting parallel between emotions and the ocean waves. 在这首诗中，他把情感和海浪进行了有趣的对比。
	用 parallel lines 平行线
	扩 paralleled *adj.* 平行的；相同的 unparalleled *adj.* 不可比拟的；空前的
phenomenon [fə'nɒmɪnən]	*n.* 现象；杰出人才
	例 The Northern Lights that appear in the sky at certain times of year around Alaska, are a fascinating and beautiful phenomenon. 北极光会在每年的特定时间出现在阿拉斯加地区的上空，这是一种迷人而美丽的现象。
	用 scientific explanations of natural phenomena 自然现象的科学解释
audit ['ɔːdɪt]	*n./v.* 审计；查账；审查
	例 The accountants were preparing for the annual external audit of the company accounts. 会计师们正在为公司账目的年度外部审计做准备。
	用 an annual audit 年度审计 a tax audit 税项审计

complex ['kɒmpleks]	*adj.* 复杂的；合成的；复合的 例 A good logical and mathematical knowledge is key to solving complex equations. 优秀的逻辑和数学知识是解决复杂方程的关键。 用 complex machinery 结构复杂的机器 the complex structure of the human brain 错综复杂的人脑构造 考 Their story, though not as spectacular to the eye, will surely turn out to be as subtle and as complex. 也许表面看来它们的故事没有那么辉煌多彩，但一旦公之于众必定也是同样的精妙而复杂。
tranquil ['træŋkwɪl]	*adj.* 平静的；安静的；稳定的 例 The lakeside resort was a tranquil place to enjoy the holiday away from the city. 湖边的度假村是一个远离城市、安静度假的地方。 用 a tranquil scene 一副静谧的景象
abound [ə'baʊnd]	*v.* 大量存在；富于 例 The forest abounds with a diverse range of plant and animal species. 森林里有大量的、各种各样的动植物。 用 abound with fish 盛产鱼类
prodigious [prə'dɪdʒəs]	*adj.* 巨大的，庞大的 例 The young pianist displayed prodigious talent, captivating the audience with her virtuoso performance. 这位年轻钢琴家表现出了惊人的才能，以精湛的演奏令观众着迷。 用 a prodigious achievement 一项惊人的成就 考 these prodigious accomplishments 这些伟大的成就
verify ['verɪfaɪ]	*v.* 核实；查证 例 On most apps you need to have a message sent to your phone number so that they can verify your user status for security. 在大多数应用中，出于安全考虑，你的手机号码需要收到一条信息，这样才能验证你的用户状态。 用 verify that there is sufficient memory available 核实有足够的存储空间 同 confirm *v.* 证实 扩 verification *n.* 证明，证实

cable ['keɪbl]	*n.* 电缆；缆绳
	例 Wireless technology is a real innovation—you no longer have to worry about so many wires and cables running across your desk at work. 无线技术是一项真正的创新，你再也不用担心办公桌上有那么多电线和电缆了。
	用 overhead cables 高架电缆 underground cables 地下电缆
	考 Each turbine will be mounted on a tower which will connect to the national power supply grid via underwater cables. 每个涡轮被安装在塔上，这里通过水下电缆与国家电网连接。

transplant [træns'plɑːnt] *v.* ['trænsplɑːnt] *n.*	*v./n.* 移植；迁移
	例 After the liver transplant he made a relatively steady recovery. 肝脏移植完成后，他恢复得相对稳定。
	用 a heart transplant operation 心脏移植手术

pitch [pɪtʃ]	*n.* 体育场；音高；推销语 *v.* 投，掷，扔；推销
	例 The salesperson delivered a compelling pitch to potential customers. 销售人员向潜在客户进行了令人信服的推销。
	用 a rugby pitch 橄榄球场

glacier ['glæsiə(r)]	*n.* 冰河，冰川
	例 The massive glacier slowly advanced, carving the landscape with its icy presence. 巨大的冰川缓慢前进，以其冰冷的存在雕刻着景观。
	用 upper surface of glacier 冰川表面上层
	考 The slow but steady movement of glaciers tends to destroy anything at their bases, so the team focused on stationary patches of ice, mostly above 1,400 metres. 缓慢而稳定的冰川移动往往会破坏其底部的所有东西，因此科考团队主要专注于海拔1,400米以上的静止冰块。

longevity [lɒn'dʒevəti]	*n.* 长寿；寿命
	例 Ancient priests used to believe that consuming heavy metals induced longevity. 古代的祭司们曾经认为，食用重金属可以长寿。
	用 the longevity of the company 公司的悠久历史

bargain ['bɑːgən]	*n.* 便宜货；协议，交易 *v.* 讨价还价，谈判
	例 They negotiated a bargain price for the antique at the flea market. 他们在跳蚤市场上把那件古董谈到了便宜的价钱。
	用 keep your side of the bargain 遵守你方协议

vain
[veɪn]

adj. 虚荣的，自负的；徒劳的

例 He was vain about his appearance, spending hours in front of the mirror.
他对自己的外表很在意，经常花好几个小时对着镜子。

用 in a vain attempt to finish on schedule 徒劳地试图按期完成工作

---

prejudice
['predʒədɪs]

n. 偏见

例 There are big trends in the world today focused on trying to promote equality and tolerance and reduce racial prejudice.
如今全球的大趋势是推崇平等与宽容，减少种族歧视。

用 a victim of racial prejudice 种族偏见的受害者

同 bias n. 偏见

---

region
['riːdʒən]

n. 地区；范围

例 The region attracts a lot of tourists who come to see the famous mountains.
这个地区吸引了大量前来参观有名山脉的游客。

用 one of the most densely populated regions of North America
北美人口最稠密的地区之一

pains in the abdominal region 腹部的疼痛

扩 regional adj. 地区的；当地的

---

aggressive
[ə'gresɪv]

adj. 侵略性的；有进取心的

例 Tigers are incredibly cute animals when they are young, but they can also be highly aggressive, especially when they're hungry or provoked.
老虎小的时候是非常可爱的动物，但它们也有很强的攻击性，尤其是当它们饿了或被激怒时。

用 an aggressive advertising campaign 一场声势浩大的广告宣传活动

---

liver
['lɪvə(r)]

n. 肝脏

例 The liver plays a crucial role in detoxifying the body and metabolizing nutrients.
肝脏在身体排毒和代谢营养物质方面起着重要作用。

用 liver cancer 肝癌

---

grind
[graɪnd]

v. 磨碎，碾碎；摩擦

例 He used a mortar and pestle to grind the spices into a fine powder.
他用研钵和杵把香料磨成细细的粉末。

用 to grind coffee 将咖啡磨粉

考 break up and grind into powder 打碎磨成粉末

aesthetic [iːs'θetɪk]	*adj.* 美的；美学的；审美的
	例 It is a place of incredible aesthetic beauty, with rolling hills, picturesque views and incredible tourist attractions. 这是一个有着令人难以置信的美感的地方，有起伏的山丘、如画般的景色和令人惊叹的旅游景点。
	用 an aesthetic appreciation of the landscape 用审美的眼光欣赏风景
	扩 aesthetics *n.* 美学
signify ['sɪɡnɪfaɪ]	*v.* 表示；意味；预示
	例 The decision to employ more technical staff in the department signified a fundamental change in their priorities. 在这个部门招聘更多技术人员的决定意味着他们的工作优先级发生了根本变化。
	用 signify a radical change 意味着巨大改变
	同 mean *v.* 意味着；意思是
spectacular [spek'tækjələ(r)]	*adj.* 壮观的，惊人的
	例 The views of the landscape from the hotel windows were spectacular. 从酒店窗户看到的景色非常壮观。
	用 spectacular scenery 壮丽的景色
	扩 spectacle *n.* 景象；奇观；[pl.]眼镜
	考 The energy use and carbon emissions this generates is spectacular and largely unnecessary. 这产生的能源使用和碳排放量非常巨大，并且很大程度上并无必要。
resemble [rɪ'zembl]	*v.* 类似；像
	例 She resembles her father, facially, but in other respects she's not like him at all. 她在外貌方面很像她的父亲，但在其他方面却一点也不像。
	用 closely resembles her sister 和她姐姐很像
	扩 assemble *v.* 集合
	考 With its five distinct volcanoes, the island resembles a lunar landscape. 这座岛屿拥有五座独特的火山，看上去像是月球的景色。
antique [æn'tiːk]	*adj.* 古老的，古董的 *n.* 古物，古董
	例 The antique shop displayed a wide selection of vintage items at quite high prices. 这家古董店以相当高的价格陈列着各种各样的古董。
	用 a genuine antique 一件真古董

entwine [ɪn'twaɪn]	*v.* 盘绕，缠绕；密切相关
	例 Some creeping plants entwine themselves around sticks as they grow. 一些蔓生类植物在生长过程中会缠绕在杆子上。
	用 became entwined with management 与管理交织在一起
	考 The history of human civilization is entwined with the history of the ways we have learned to manipulate water resources. 人类文明的历史是与我们学习用何种方式使用水资源的历史交织在一起的。
retire [rɪ'taɪə(r)]	*v.* 退休；退出；撤退
	例 He had worked hard since he was about 20 years old and was lucky enough to be able to retire young and relax for the rest of his life. 他从大约20岁起就一直努力工作，幸运的是，他能够早早退休，轻松地度过余生。
	用 retire as editor of the magazine 从杂志编辑的职位退休
scarce [skeəs]	*adj.* 缺乏的，不足的 *adv.* 仅仅；几乎不
	例 Food was scarce in the country and they had begun to experience a terrible famine. 这个国家食物匮乏，他们开始经历一场可怕的饥荒。
	用 scarce resources 稀缺资源
submerge [səb'mɜːdʒ]	*v.* 淹没；浸入；潜入水中
	例 The towns were almost submerged in water when the dam broke. 水坝决堤时，城镇几乎被水淹没了。
	用 be submerged by floodwater 洪水淹没
implication [ˌɪmplɪ'keɪʃn]	*n.* 含义；暗示；影响
	例 The implications of the new tax reforms are most concerning for middle-class, middle-income wage earners. 新税收改革的影响与中产阶级、中等收入的人群最为相关。
	用 consider the wider implications of their actions 考虑他们的行动带来的更广泛影响
	扩 implicate *v.* 暗示
	考 International bodies like the United Nations and the European Union have begun to develop policies concerned with children's right to play, and to consider implications for leisure facilities and educational programmes. 联合国和欧盟等国际机构已经开始制定与儿童游戏权利相关的政策，并开始考虑娱乐设施和教育项目的意义。

complementary [ˌkɒmplɪ'mentri]	*adj.* 补足的；互补的
	例 The living room was painted in two strong complementary colours. 客厅被刷成两种高度互补的颜色。
	用 two complementary strategies 两种相辅相成的策略
	考 This option would not be accompanied by complementary measures in the other modes of transport. 不会对其他运输方式采取任何补充措施。

handicap ['hændikæp]	*n.* 障碍；不利条件 *v.* 妨碍，阻碍
	例 Not being able to speak English today is a real handicap if you want to work internationally. 如果你想在国际上工作，如今不会说英语是一个真正的障碍。
	用 visual handicap 视力缺陷
	同 disability *n.* 缺陷 obstacle *n.* 障碍

bacteria [bæk'tɪəriə]	*n.* 细菌
	例 If you get bacteria in a wound it can cause an infection and inflammation. 如果伤口上有细菌，会引起感染和炎症。
	用 avoid contamination with bacteria 避免细菌感染

statement ['steɪtmənt]	*n.* 声明；陈述
	例 The foreign secretary gave an official statement about the new policy on television last night. 外交大臣昨晚在电视上就这项新政策发表了正式声明。
	用 make a statement to the press 向新闻界发表一份声明
	扩 state *n.* 状态；州 *v.* 陈述；声明

expel [ɪk'spel]	*v.* 开除；驱逐；排出
	例 The school decided to expel the student for repeated disciplinary issues. 由于屡次违规行为，学校决定开除这名学生。
	用 be expelled from school at 15 在15岁时被学校开除
	考 By 1658, they had permanently expelled the Portuguese from the island, thereby gaining control of the lucrative cinnamon trade. 到1658年，他们已经永久性地将葡萄牙人从岛上驱逐了出去，由此赢得了对这门一本万利的肉桂买卖的控制。

dump [dʌmp]	*v.* 丢弃；乱堆 *n.* 垃圾场；废料堆场
	例 He disposed of the old furniture at the local dump site. 他在当地的垃圾场处理了旧家具。
	用 a nuclear waste dump 核废料储存场

slender ['slendə(r)]	*adj.* 苗条的，纤细的 例 He found that the plant's leaves are long and slender. 他发现这株植物的叶子很细长。 用 her slender figure 她苗条的身材 long, slender fingers 修长纤细的手指
wreck [rek]	*v.* 破坏，摧毁 *n.* 沉船；残骸；遭到严重破坏的东西 例 The car was an absolute wreck after George crashed it into the wall at high speed. 车被George以很快的速度撞到墙上，完全撞坏了。 用 wreck the garden 毁掉花园
distinct [dɪ'stɪŋkt]	*adj.* 明显的；独特的；不同的 例 There is a distinct difference between laziness and reduced motivation. 懒惰和动机低下之间有明显的区别。 用 a distinct smell of gas 一股明显的煤气味 扩 distinctive *adj.* 有特色的；与众不同的
pragmatic [præg'mætɪk]	*adj.* 实际的；实用主义的 例 His approach was pragmatic and he was able to put emotions to one side. 他的方法是务实的，能够把情感放在一边。 用 a pragmatic approach to management problems 对管理问题采取的务实做法
canoe [kə'nuː]	*n.* 独木舟 例 They paddled their canoe gracefully through the winding rivers. 他们优雅地划着独木舟，穿过曲折的河流。 用 paddle the canoe along the coast 划着独木舟沿海岸而行
fabulous ['fæbjələs]	*adj.* 极好的；巨大的；传说的 例 It was a fabulous performance, full of acrobatics and amusing skits. 那是一场精彩绝伦的演出，有许多杂技表演和滑稽的小品。 用 fabulous wealth 巨额财富

Exercise 18

一、中文释义练习

请选择单词正确的中文释义。

_____ 1. disdain   A. 范围   _____ 11. glacier   A. 长寿

_____ 2. recap   B. 妥协   _____ 12. longevity   B. 美学的

_____ 3. annoy   C. 重述   _____ 13. aesthetic   C. 冰川

_____ 4. scope   D. 使恼怒   _____ 14. grind   D. 磨碎

_____ 5. compromise   E. 鄙视   _____ 15. signify   E. 意味

_____ 6. parallel   A. 电缆   _____ 16. spectacular   A. 细菌

_____ 7. phenomenon   B. 复杂的   _____ 17. handicap   B. 障碍

_____ 8. complex   C. 现象   _____ 18. bacteria   C. 驱逐

_____ 9. tranquil   D. 平行的   _____ 19. expel   D. 壮观的

_____ 10. cable   E. 平静的   _____ 20. canoe   E. 独木舟

二、英文释义练习

请选择单词正确的英文释义。

_____ 1. neutron   A. a small piece of matter that carries no electric charge

_____ 2. abound   B. to be very closely involved or connected with sth.

_____ 3. transplant   C. to exist in great numbers or quantities

_____ 4. prejudice   D. an unreasonable dislike of or preference for sth.

_____ 5. entwine   E. to take an organ from one person into another

_____ 6. antique   A. easily or clearly heard, seen or felt

_____ 7. implication   B. to go under the surface of water or liquid

_____ 8. submerge   C. being very old and often highly valuable

_____ 9. dump   D. to get rid of sth. you do not want

_____ 10. distinct   E. a possible effect or result of an action or a decision

standby ['stændbaɪ]	*n.* 备用品；后备人员
	例 The incident was totally under control, but just in case the fire broke out again, the fire team were put on standby. 事故已经完全控制住了，但是为了防止火灾再次发生，消防队员已经进入待命状态。
	用 on standby at the port 在港口待命
occupy ['ɒkjupaɪ]	*v.* 占据，占领
	例 He enjoyed computer programming and learning new computer languages, but it occupied much of his time and he didn't see his family much. 他喜欢计算机编程和学习新的计算机语言，但这占据了他很多时间，他很少见到家人。
	用 occupy half of my time 占用我一半的时间
	扩 occupant *n.* 占有者，占领者 occupation *n.* 职业；占有，占用
disprove [ˌdɪs'pruːv]	*v.* 反驳；证明……虚假
	例 The new evidence disproves his theory completely. 新的证据完全驳倒了他的理论。
	用 disprove the allegation 反驳指控
	扩 prove *v.* 证明 approve *v.* 批准，赞成；满意
edge [edʒ]	*n.* 边缘；优势
	例 He moved closer to the edge of the cliff to try to get a better view of the sea below. 他靠近悬崖边缘，试图更好地看到下面的大海。
	用 on the edge of the cliff 在悬崖边上
	同 brink *n.* 边沿；边缘
parliament ['pɑːləmənt]	*n.* 议会，国会
	例 The new bill was hurriedly rushed through parliament before the deadline. 在截止日期前，新的法案在议会匆匆通过。
	用 win a seat in Parliament 赢得议会中的一个席位

elegant [ˈelɪgənt]	*adj.* 优雅的；简洁的 例 She always looked remarkably elegant—she often wore long stylish dresses and tasteful designer shoes. 她总是看起来非常优雅，经常穿着时尚的长裙和有品位的名品鞋子。 用 an elegant dress 一件优雅的连衣裙 an elegant room 一个雅致的房间 扩 elegance *n.* 高雅；优雅
cylinder [ˈsɪlɪndə(r)]	*n.* 圆柱体，圆筒 例 Deep-sea divers must carry cylinders of oxygen on their backs. 深海潜水员必须背上氧气筒。 用 a wax cylinder 蜡柱 考 Archaeologists discovered cylinders made of clay, with inscriptions on them saying that fats were boiled with ashes. 考古学家发现了一些由黏土制成的圆柱体，上面刻有铭文，说将脂肪和灰烬放在一起煮。
consist [kənˈsɪst]	*v.* 由……组成 例 His weekends were always busy, as they consisted of studies, homework activities and learning swimming, piano and football. 他在周末总是很忙，包括做功课、写家庭作业以及学习游泳、钢琴和足球。 用 consist of 由……组成 consist in 在于，存在于 考 The first approach would consist of focusing on road transport solely through pricing. 第一种方法会包含只通过定价来集中于道路运输。
reserve [rɪˈzɜːv]	*v.* 预约，预订；保留 *n.* 预留；自然保护区 例 It's a very popular concert, so if you want to attend it's important to call beforehand and reserve a place. 这是非常受欢迎的音乐会，所以如果你想参加，提前打电话预订座位是很重要的。 用 reserve a table for three for eight o'clock 预订8点钟三人餐位 同 book *v.* 预约，预订 扩 reservation *n.* 保留；预订，预约 reservoir *n.* 水库，蓄水池 考 It is particularly valuable in regions where natural groundwater reserves have been polluted, or where seawater is the only water source available. 这在那些天然地下水储备被污染的地区，以及海水是唯一可用水资源的地区尤其宝贵。

consequence
['kɒnsɪkwəns]

n. 结果；意义；后果

例 As a consequence of his poor study habits and sheer laziness, he performed badly in the examinations.
由于糟糕的学习习惯和懒惰，他在考试中表现很差。

用 have serious consequences for the industry 对行业造成严重后果

扩 consequential *adj.* 结果的；随之发生的

考 have far-reaching consequences 有深远的影响
The unintentional consequence has been to halt the natural eradication of underbrush, now the primary fuel for megafires.
意料之外的结果是阻止了林下灌木丛的自然衰败，而它们是目前大型火灾的主要燃料。

ditch
[dɪtʃ]

n. 沟渠 *v.* 丢弃；摆脱；紧急降落

例 The farmer dug a ditch to channel water away from the crop fields.
农民挖了一条沟把农田里的水引走。

用 ditch the sofa bed 把沙发床扔掉

pinpoint
['pɪnpɔɪnt]

v. 查明；精确找到；准确描述

例 It was not possible for the detectives to pinpoint the exact time the crime was committed.
侦探们确定犯罪行为发生的确切时间是不可能的。

用 pinpoint on the map the site of the medieval village
在地图上准确找出那个中世纪村庄的位置

考 By pinpointing which genetic traits made it possible for mammoths to survive the icy climate of the tundra, the project's goal is to return mammoths, or a mammoth-like species, to the area.
通过找到哪些基因特质使猛犸象能够在冻土带的冰冻气候中生存，该项目的目标是将猛犸象或类似猛犸象的物种带回这一区域。

slope
[sləʊp]

n. 斜坡；倾斜；斜率

例 That particular ski slope is very steep and only recommend for very professional sportsmen.
那个滑雪坡道非常陡峭，只推荐给非常专业的运动员。

用 ski slopes 滑雪斜坡 a steep slope 陡坡

考 It was something about measuring the slope of the shore, but of course we didn't need it because we were measuring wind direction, and we'd brought the compass for that.
这适用于测量海岸坡度，但我们当然不需要它，因为我们带了指南针来测量风向。

auditorium [ˌɔːdɪˈtɔːriəm]	*n.* 观众席；礼堂
	例 The auditorium filled with applause as the performers took their final bow. 当表演者最后鞠躬时，礼堂里充满了掌声。
	用 a high school auditorium 一所中学的礼堂
	扩 auditory *adj.* 听觉的
	考 The auditorium, stage and dressing rooms for the actors are all below ground level. 礼堂、舞台和演员的化妆间都在地下。

acquisition [ˌækwɪˈzɪʃn]	*n.* 获得；收购；习得
	例 The company went through a successful merger and acquisition. 这家公司进行了成功的兼并与收购。
	用 theories of child language acquisition 幼儿语言习得的理论

delta [ˈdeltə]	*n.* 三角洲
	例 The river delta formed where the river met the sea, creating a rich and fertile ecosystem. 河流三角洲在河流入海口形成，构成了富饶肥沃的生态系统。
	用 the Nile Delta 尼罗河三角洲
	考 Up to now, people have blamed this loss of delta land on the two large dams at Aswan in the south of Egypt, which hold back virtually all of the sediment that used to flow down the Nile. 到目前为止，人们一直在指责埃及南部阿斯旺的两座大坝，认为它们造成了三角洲土地的流失，这两座大坝几乎将所有原来顺尼罗河直下的淤泥都阻挡住了。

condemn [kənˈdem]	*v.* 谴责；定罪
	例 Most rational, moral people condemn violence of any sort. 大多数理性、有道德的人会谴责任何形式的暴力。
	用 be condemned as lacking integrity 被指责为不够正直
	同 sentence *v.* 判决

departure [dɪˈpɑːtʃə(r)]	*n.* 离开，出发；违背
	例 His approach to the situation was a huge departure from the norm. 他处理这种情况的方法与一般方法大不相同。
	用 arrivals and departures 到站和离站班次

grant [ɡrɑːnt]	*v.* 授予，允许；承认，同意 *n.* 补助金
	例 He received a generous grant to complete his PhD studies. 他获得了一笔慷慨的资助以完成博士学业。
	用 take sth. for granted 认为……理所当然

ample ['æmpl]	*adj.* 丰富的；足够的
	例 There was ample room in the plane for the whole family to sit together. 飞机上有足够的空间让全家人坐在一起。
	用 ample proof 充足的证明 ample space 宽敞的空间
	同 plenty of 大量的，充足的
evoke [ɪ'vəʊk]	*v.* 引起，唤起
	例 The movie evoked a whole range of emotions in the audience: some laughed, some cried and some felt shocked. 这部电影唤起了观众各种各样的情感，有些人笑了，有些人哭了，有些人感到非常震惊。
	用 evoke public sympathy 引起公众的同情
outgoing [ˌaʊt'gəʊɪŋ]	*adj.* 外向的，开朗的
	例 She was an extrovert, outgoing person with a great sense of humour and ability to connect with new people. 她是一个外向开朗的人，有很强的幽默感，并且有能力与陌生人建立联系。
	用 an outgoing personality 外向的性格
betray [bɪ'treɪ]	*v.* 背叛，辜负；流露，显露出
	例 When a friend tells you a very personal secret it's important not to betray their trust. 当朋友告诉你一个非常私人的秘密时，重要的是不要辜负他们的信任。
	用 betray his colleagues 出卖他的同事
fraternal [frə'tɜːnl]	*adj.* 兄弟的；友好的
	例 The twin brothers shared a strong fraternal bond, always supporting and caring for each other. 这对双胞胎有着强烈的兄弟情谊，总会支持和照顾对方。
	用 the fraternal assistance of our colleagues 同事间兄弟般的帮助
	考 Alternatively, by comparing the experiences of identical twins with those of fraternal twins, who come from separate eggs and share on average half their DNA, researchers can quantify the extent to which our genes affect our lives. 另一方面，通过比较同卵双胞胎与异卵双胞胎——后者来自两个不同的受精卵且拥有平均来说约为一半的相同基因——的经历，研究人员就可以量化地得出我们的基因到底在何种程度上影响着我们的生活。

urgent ['ɜːdʒənt]	*adj.* 紧急的；急迫的 例 She was in urgent need of treatment but the nearest hospital was far from her home. 她急需接受治疗，但最近的医院离她家也很远。 用 an urgent appeal for information 紧急呼吁提供信息 扩 urgency *n.* 紧急；紧迫性
chain [tʃeɪn]	*n.* 链子，链条；一连串；束缚，枷锁；连锁商店 例 She wore a beautiful necklace that was a fine gold chain with a heart on it. 她戴着一条漂亮的金项链，上面有一颗心。 用 a chain of events 一连串事件 a short length of chain 一截短链条 考 staff from a chain of themed restaurants 一家连锁主题餐厅的员工
biology [baɪ'ɒlədʒi]	*n.* 生物；生物学 例 Biology is a fascinating subject and is now taught in schools at all ages. 生物学是一门吸引人的学科，目前各年龄段学生都在学习。 用 a degree in biology 生物学学位 扩 biological *adj.* 生物的；生物学的
decline [dɪ'klaɪn]	*n./v.* 下降；衰退；拒绝 例 There has been a decline in the use of desktop computers and laptops since the advent of smartphones. 由于智能手机的出现，台式机和笔记本电脑的使用有所下降。 用 a sharp decline 急剧下降 a gradual decline 逐渐下降 economic decline 经济衰退 decline an invitation 拒绝邀请 同 fall *n./v.* 下降 decrease *n./v.* 减少 refuse *v.* 拒绝 反 rise *n./v.* 上升 increase *n./v.* 上升 accept *v.* 接受
accurate ['ækjərət]	*adj.* 准确的，精确的 例 Accurate information is essential if we are to make good judgements. 如果我们要做出正确判断，准确的信息至关重要。 用 an accurate description 准确的描述 an accurate calculation 准确的计算 考 highly accurate timekeeping instruments 高度精确的计时工具
regime [reɪ'ʒiːm]	*n.* 政权，政体；管理体制 例 The regime of the Roman Empire took several decades to fall. 罗马帝国的政权几十年后衰落了。 用 military regime 军事政权

drill [drɪl]	*n.* 钻，钻机；训练，演习 *v.* 钻孔；训练
	例 It really bothers me when I hear the sound of roadworks and drills in the early hours of the morning or late at night. 当我在凌晨或深夜听到道路施工和钻机的声音时，我的确很受困扰。
	用 a fire drill 一次消防演习
axis ['æksɪs]	*n.* 轴；轴线；坐标轴
	例 The Earth revolves about its axis that joins the North and South Poles. 地球绕着连接南北极的地轴旋转。
	用 the vertical axis 纵坐标轴 the horizontal axis 横坐标轴 an axis of symmetry 对称轴
monopoly [mə'nɒpəli]	*n.* 垄断；垄断者
	例 The company has a virtual monopoly in world markets. 这家公司实际上垄断了世界市场。
	用 a monopoly on television broadcasting 对电视节目播放的垄断
	考 Recent years have seen the end of the virtual monopoly of cork as the material for bottle stoppers, due to concerns about the effect it may have on the contents of the bottle. 由于担心栓皮对瓶中液体的影响，近几年来其完全作为瓶塞材料的情况已经走到尽头。
kettle ['ketl]	*n.* 水壶；锅
	例 The tea kettle whistled, signaling that the water had reached a boiling point. 茶壶发出呼啸声，表明水已经达到沸点。
	用 an electric kettle 电水壶
innocent ['ɪnəsnt]	*adj.* 无辜的，无罪的；天真的
	例 The accused man declared himself innocent of the crimes. 被指控者声称自己没有犯罪。
	用 an innocent young child 一个天真的小孩子
deflect [dɪ'flekt]	*v.* （使）转向；（使）偏斜
	例 She skillfully deflected the opponent's attacks during the fencing match. 在击剑比赛中，她巧妙地挡开了对手的进攻。
	用 deflect the first punch 挡开第一拳
	扩 reflect *v.* 反射；反映；反思

corridor ['kɒrɪdɔː(r)]	*n.* 走廊
	例 Everyone lined up along the corridor waiting to enter the audition room. 每个人都沿着走廊排好队，等待进入试音室。
	用 at the end of the corridor 在走廊尽头
hinder ['hɪndə(r)]	*v.* 阻碍，妨碍
	例 The lack of resources hindered their ability to complete the project on time. 缺乏资源阻碍了他们按时完成这一项目。
	用 a situation that hinders economic growth 妨碍经济发展的局面
gear [gɪə(r)]	*n.* 齿轮；器械；设备，用具
	例 The mountaineer checked his gear, ensuring that he had everything necessary for the challenging ascent. 登山运动员检查了他的装备，以确保他有完成具有挑战性的攀登所必需的一切。
	用 change gear 换挡　fishing gear 钓鱼用具
forfeit ['fɔːfɪt]	*v.* 丧失，被没收 *n.* 罚金，没收物 *adj.* 没收的，丧失的
	例 They had to forfeit the game due to a lack of players, conceding victory to the opposing team. 由于队员不足，他们不得不放弃比赛，把胜利让给了对方。
	用 forfeit your deposit 不退还定金
allocate ['æləkeɪt]	*v.* 分配，分派，划拨
	例 Every employee was allocated seven free tickets for the concert. 每个员工都有七张音乐会的免费票。
	用 be allocated to those who apply first 分配给那些先申请的人
	扩 allocation *n.* 分配
	考 Some of the more obvious rewards that managers allocate include pay, promotions, autonomy, job scope and depth, and the opportunity to participate in goal-setting and decision-making. 一些由管理者们分配的更为明显的奖励包括薪酬、晋升、自主权、工作范围和深度，以及参与目标设定和决策的机会。
eccentric [ɪk'sentrɪk]	*adj.* 古怪的，反常的 *n.* 古怪的人
	例 The eccentric old man always wore white suits with very pointy shoes and a hat with a feather in it. 这位古怪的老人总是穿着白色西装和尖头的鞋子，戴着一顶插有羽毛的帽子。
	用 eccentric clothes 奇怪的穿搭

ongoing
['ɒŋɡəʊɪŋ]

adj. 持续存在的；仍在进行的

例 The solution had not been found but discussions were ongoing.
解决方法还没有找到，但讨论还在继续进行。

用 an ongoing debate 一场持续的辩论

---

community
[kə'mjuːnəti]

n. 社区；群落；团体

例 The school provides a strong sense of community for the students and teachers alike.
学校为学生和老师等人提供了一种强烈的社区意识。

用 the international community 国际社会

---

impact
['ɪmpækt] *n.*
[ɪm'pækt] *v.*

n. 巨大影响；撞击，冲撞 *v.* 产生影响；冲击，撞击

例 We need to properly assess the impact of environmental pollution.
我们需要正确评估环境污染的影响。

用 the environmental impact of tourism 旅游业在环境方面的影响

---

abandon
[ə'bændən]

v. 抛弃；放弃

例 They made the difficult decision to abandon the sinking ship and seek safety on lifeboats.
他们做出艰难决定，放弃正在下沉的船，到救生艇上寻求安全。

用 force many drivers to abandon their vehicles
迫使许多驾驶者弃车步行

考 Administration introduced rules demanding that the meat industry abandon practices associated with the risk of the disease spreading.
管理部门出台了规定，要求肉类行业放弃有疾病传播风险的做法。

---

procedure
[prə'siːdʒə(r)]

n. 程序；步骤

例 The medical procedure was complicated and expensive, but highly successful.
治疗过程非常复杂并且价格昂贵，但是非常成功。

用 maintenance procedures 维修程序
quite a simple procedure 相当简单的流程

考 Procedures such as capturing and moving at-risk or dangerous individuals are bolstered by knowledge gained in zoos about doses for anaesthetics, and by experience in handling and transporting animals.
像找到并且转移处于风险中或有危险的动物这样的措施，就是得到了从动物园中获得的有关麻醉剂量的知识，以及帮助和转移动物的经验的支持。

encode [ɪnˈkəʊd]	*v.* 把……译成密码；给……编码 例 The genes in the DNA sequence are encoded in a very complex way. DNA序列中的基因以一种非常复杂的方式编码。 用 encode information meaningfully 有意义地编码信息
plot [plɒt]	*n.* 阴谋，密谋；情节；图表 *v.* 密谋；标记；计划 例 The detective carefully analysed the clues to unravel the intricate plot of the mystery novel. 侦探仔细分析了线索，揭开了推理小说错综复杂的情节。 用 uncover a plot 揭穿阴谋
amorphous [əˈmɔːfəs]	*adj.* 无定形的；无组织的 例 The abstract painting had an amorphous shape, leaving room for interpretation. 这幅抽象画没有确定的形状，留下了可供解读的空间。 用 an amorphous mass of cells with no identity at all 不知何物的杂乱一团的细胞 考 Meis (1992) points out that the tourism industry involves concepts that have remained amorphous to both analysts and decision makers. Meis于1992年指出，旅游业所牵扯到的一些概念对于分析家和决策者来说仍是无法确切定义的。

Exercise 19

一、中文释义练习

请选择单词正确的中文释义。

_____ 1. standby   A. 边缘

_____ 2. occupy   B. 备用品

_____ 3. edge   C. 占据

_____ 4. elegant   D. 观众席

_____ 5. auditorium   E. 优雅的

_____ 11. chain   A. 轴

_____ 12. decline   B. 走廊

_____ 13. drill   C. 训练

_____ 14. axis   D. 下降

_____ 15. corridor   E. 链条

_____ 6. acquisition   A. 习得

_____ 7. slope   B. 三角洲

_____ 8. delta   C. 斜坡

_____ 9. ample   D. 背叛

_____ 10. betray   E. 丰富的

_____ 16. gear   A. 阴谋

_____ 17. eccentric   B. 社区

_____ 18. community   C. 程序

_____ 19. procedure   D. 古怪的

_____ 20. plot   E. 齿轮

二、英文释义练习

请选择单词正确的英文释义。

_____ 1. disprove   A. to find and show the exact position of sth.

_____ 2. reserve   B. to ask for a seat be available at a future time

_____ 3. pinpoint   C. to express very strong disapproval of sb.

_____ 4. condemn   D. to agree to give sb. what they ask for

_____ 5. grant   E. to show that sth. is wrong or false

_____ 6. accurate   A. put into letters or symbols to send secret messages

_____ 7. monopoly   B. the complete control of trade in particular goods

_____ 8. hinder   C. able to give completely correct information

_____ 9. allocate   D. to make it difficult for sb. to do sth.

_____ 10. encode   E. to give sth. officially to sb. for a particular purpose

replenish [rɪ'plenɪʃ]	v. 补充；重新装满
	例 After an exhausting climb up the mountain they had a very good sleep to replenish their energy. 在全力爬上山后，他们睡了个好觉，以便恢复充沛的精力。
	用 replenish food and water supplies 补充食物和水
weave [wiːv]	v. 编织；纺织；编造 n. 织物；织法
	例 Workers in the factory weave silk thread into beautiful cloth. 这家工厂的工人把丝线织成漂亮的布。
	用 weave a narrative 编故事
embarrass [ɪm'bærəs]	v. 使窘迫，使尴尬；妨碍
	例 He often embarrasses her by making jokes about her in front of friends and colleagues. 他经常在朋友和同事面前拿她开玩笑，令她难堪。
	用 embarrass the prime minister 使首相难堪
propound [prə'paʊnd]	v. 提出；提议；考虑
	例 Her new book expands upon the theory propounded in her first book. 她的新书详述了她在第一本书中提出的理论。
	用 propound a general theory of the vocal sounds that animals make 提出一个有关动物发声的通用理论
perspective [pə'spektɪv]	n. 观点，视角；远景；透视图
	例 Travelling to different countries gives you unique perspectives on life that can be very valuable. 去不同国家旅行会带给你独特的生活视角，这是非常有价值的。
	用 see the issue from a different perspective 以不同角度看待这件事
	同 viewpoint n. 观点
	考 Let's consider the benefits of maps from a geographer's perspective. 让我们从地理学家的视角来考虑地图带来的好处。

distribute [dɪ'strɪbjuːt]	*v.* 分配；分类；分发
	例 The teacher distributed the examination papers to the whole class. 老师把试卷分发给了全班同学。
	用 distribute food to the earthquake victims 向地震灾民分发食品
	扩 distribution *n.* 分配；分发

notable ['nəʊtəbl]	*adj.* 值得注意的，显著的；著名的
	例 The gardens are notable for their incredible collection of flowers. 这些花园以其令人难以置信的花卉收藏而闻名。
	用 a notable achievement 一项显著的成就 the most notable feature 最明显的特征
	扩 notably *adv.* 显著地，尤其

redundant [rɪ'dʌndənt]	*adj.* 多余的；冗长的；被解雇的
	例 He had worked in the company since he was twenty-one years old, so when he was made redundant last year, he felt very sad. 他从21岁起就在这家公司工作，所以当他去年被解雇时，他感到很难过。
	用 redundant employees 被裁掉的员工

exceed [ɪk'siːd]	*v.* 超过；胜过
	例 You should never exceed the dose of medicine prescribed by your doctor. 你的用药不能超过医生开的剂量。
	用 exceed expectations 超出预期
	扩 excess *n.* 超过；过量 excessive *adj.* 过度的；过多的

echo ['ekəʊ]	*n.* 回声，回音 *v.* 发出回声；附和，重复
	例 The cave was huge and when they shouted there was an echo which filled the air. 山洞很大，当他们呼喊时，回声在那里回荡。
	用 the echo of footsteps running down the corridor 沿走廊跑的脚步回声
	考 Blind people, without even being aware of the fact, are actually using echoes of their own footsteps and of other sounds, to sense the presence of obstacles. 即使没有意识到这一事实，盲人实际上通过使用他们自己的脚步声或其他声音的回声来感知障碍的存在。

slice [slaɪs]	*n.* 薄片，片；小块；部分 *v.* 切，割，划
	例 She cut a thin slice of birthday cake for each guest at the party. 她为聚会上的每位客人切了一小块生日蛋糕。
	用 four slices of bread 四片面包 potato slices 土豆片

chorus ['kɔːrəs]	*n.* 副歌；合唱团；合唱曲
	例 The chorus sang in perfect harmony, adding depth and richness to the musical performance. 合唱团唱得非常和谐，为音乐演出增添了深度和多样性。
	用 the Hallelujah Chorus 哈利路亚合唱曲 the chorus of her song 她歌曲的副歌

fuse [fjuːz]	*n.* 保险丝，熔丝；导火线，引信 *v.* 熔合，结合；熔化
	例 The electrician replaced the blown fuse to restore power to the house. 电工更换了烧坏的保险丝，使房子恢复供电。
	用 change a fuse 换保险丝

abate [ə'beɪt]	*v.* 减轻，减少；废除；消除
	例 After the storm, the wind began to abate, and the rain subsided. 暴风雨过后，风开始减弱，雨也停了。
	用 show no signs of abating 没有减弱的迹象

discern [dɪ'sɜːn]	*v.* 识别；辨别
	例 I am trying to discern the best approach to solving a problem at work. 我试图找出在工作中解决问题的最佳方法。
	用 discern a number of different techniques in her work 在她的作品中看出许多不同的创作手法
	同 detect *v.* 探察；觉察；发现 distinguish *v.* 辨别

unpredictable [ˌʌnprɪ'dɪktəbl]	*adj.* 不可预知的；出乎意料的
	例 His moods were constantly changing and very unpredictable. 他的情绪总是在变化，难以预测。
	用 unpredictable weather 变幻莫测的天气
	同 unexpected *adj.* 出乎意料的
	反 predictable *adj.* 可预测的
	扩 predict *v.* 预测
	考 unpredictable noise 不可预测的噪音

feeble ['fiːbl]	*adj.* 衰弱的，虚弱的；微弱的
	例 The elderly man's feeble voice struggled to be heard in the noisy room. 老人微弱的声音挣扎着在嘈杂的房间里被听到。
	用 a feeble old man 一位衰弱的老人 a feeble attempt to explain 无力的试图解释

deliberately [dɪ'lɪbərətli]	*adv.* 故意地；谨慎地
	例 She didn't like one of her cousins so she deliberately left him off the guest list for the party. 她不喜欢自己的一个堂兄弟，因此她故意将其排除在聚会的宾客名单之外。
	用 deliberately ambiguous 故意模棱两可
	同 intentionally *adv.* 故意地 on purpose 故意地
	扩 deliberate *adj.* 故意的
isolate ['aɪsəleɪt]	*v.* 隔离；孤立
	例 It's important to isolate yourself if you feel you have symptoms of a potentially contagious illness. 如果你觉得自己有潜在传染性疾病的症状，那么将自己隔离开来是很重要的。
	用 isolate the country from the rest of Europe 使国家与其他欧洲国家隔离开来
	扩 isolation *n.* 隔离；孤立
conversation [ˌkɒnvə'seɪʃn]	*n.* 对话；交谈，会话
	例 She was a great lover of conversation and enjoyed the reunion dinners with her old classmates. 她很喜欢交流，喜欢和老同学们一起聚会吃饭。
	用 a telephone conversation 电话交谈
bloom [bluːm]	*n.* 花，花朵；（肤色的）红润 *v.* 开花，绽放；繁荣，兴旺
	例 The flowers bloomed in vibrant colours, filling the garden with a delightful fragrance. 鲜花绽放出鲜艳的色彩，使花园充满了令人愉悦的香味。
	用 the bloom in her cheeks 她面颊上的红润光泽
steam [stiːm]	*n.* 蒸汽，水蒸气；雾气 *adj.* 蒸汽的
	例 The hot steam rose from the teapot, filling the room with a pleasant aroma. 滚烫的蒸汽从茶壶里冒出来，房间里充满了宜人的香气。
	用 the introduction of steam in the 18th century 18世纪蒸汽动力的采用
	考 When primitive automobiles first began to appear in the 1800s, their engines were based on steam power. 当原始的汽车初次出现在19世纪时，它们的引擎是基于蒸汽动力的。

enclose [ɪnˈkləʊz]	v. 包围，围住；(随信) 附上
	例 The beautiful temple garden was enclosed by a high wall. 这座美丽的寺庙花园被一道高墙环绕着。
	用 a dark enclosed space 一个黑暗的封闭空间
	扩 enclosure n. 占领；围绕

sip [sɪp]	n. 一小口 v. 小口喝
	例 She took a leisurely sip of her hot tea, savouring the warmth and delicate flavours. 她悠闲地喝了一口热茶，品尝着茶的温暖和清香。
	用 take a sip of drink 喝一小口饮料

twig [twɪg]	n. 小枝，嫩枝；血管小支，神经小支 v. 顿悟，突然明白
	例 The bird carefully collected twigs and sticks and weaved them together to build a nest. 这只鸟小心翼翼地收集树枝和木条，把它们编织在一起搭了一个窝。
	用 pull out a twig 抽出一根小枝

plateau [ˈplætəʊ]	n. 高原；稳定期，停滞期
	例 The mountain road levelled off and they saw that they were on the plateau. 山路变平了，他们发现自己到了高原上。
	用 reach a plateau 到达停滞期

implement [ˈɪmplɪment]	v. 实施，执行；实现
	例 They promised to implement a new system to control financial operations in the company. 他们承诺实施新的制度来管理公司的财务运作。
	用 implement reforms 实施改革
	同 carry out 执行
	考 It's true there are new regulations for mercury emissions from power plants, but these will need billions of dollars to implement, and increase costs for everyone. 确实存在有关发电厂汞排放的新规定，但这需要数十亿美元来实施，并且增加每个人的成本。

culminate [ˈkʌlmɪneɪt]	v. 结束；到达顶点；到子午线
	例 After months of hard work, the project will culminate in a grand exhibition. 经过几个月的努力工作，这个项目将在一个盛大展览中达到高潮。
	用 culminate in success 取得成功

legislation [ˌledʒɪsˈleɪʃn]	*n.* 立法；法律
	例 The new legislation will provide better security for personal information and data. 新的立法会更好地保障个人信息和数据的安全。
	用 an important piece of legislation 一条重要的法规
	考 Linguistic issues, it is argued, cannot be solved by logic and legislation. 有人认为，语言问题不能通过逻辑和立法来解决。
schedule [ˈʃedjuːl]	*n.* 计划表；时间表 *v.* 安排；预定；计划
	例 We are currently working on a very tight schedule in order to finish the project on time. 为了按时完成项目，我们目前正按照非常紧张的时间表工作。
	用 a tight schedule 紧凑的日程 a train schedule 列车时刻表
fatigue [fəˈtiːg]	*n.* 疲乏，厌倦；疲劳 *adj.* 疲劳的
	例 After a long day at work, she felt a deep sense of fatigue and eagerly sought rest. 经过一整天的工作，她感到非常疲劳，急切地想休息一下。
	用 physical and mental fatigue 身体和精神的疲劳
	考 Apparently, unpredictable noise produces more fatigue than predictable noise, but it takes a while for this fatigue to take its toll on performance. 显然，非可预测性噪音比可预测性噪音会让人更疲劳，不过疲劳导致工作上的错误还需要一段时间。
instruction [ɪnˈstrʌkʃn]	*n.* 指令；教导；用法说明
	例 His method of instruction was old-fashioned and slightly boring. 他的教学方法过于老旧了，并且有些乏味。
	用 follow the instructions 按照说明操作 carry out one's instruction 执行某人的命令
	扩 instruct *v.* 教学；指导；下指令
	考 The purpose of instruction is to make us even more different from one another, and in the process of being educated we can learn from the achievements of those more gifted than ourselves. 教育的目的在于使我们更加与众不同，而在受教育的过程中，我们可以从比我们更有天赋的人的成就中学有所得。
replay [ˈriːpleɪ] *n.* [ˌriːˈpleɪ] *v.*	*n.* 重放；重演 *v.* 重放；重现，重演
	例 The teacher replayed the section of the video that the students had missed. 老师重新播放了学生们错过的那一段视频。
	用 a replay of the wedding on video 重放婚礼录像

simulate ['sɪmjuleɪt]	*v.* 模仿；假装
	例 Computer programmes can accurately simulate the chess playing strategies of professionals. 计算机程序可以准确模拟专业棋手的下棋策略。
	用 simulate a full year of the globe's climate 模拟全年地球的气候
	扩 simulation *n.* 模仿；模拟

squeeze [skwiːz]	*v.* 挤压；压榨
	例 Cut the lemon in half and squeeze the juice over the fish before baking. 将柠檬切成两半，在烤鱼之前把柠檬汁挤在鱼上。
	用 squeeze the trigger of a gun 扣动枪的扳机

confirm [kən'fɜːm]	*v.* 确认；证实；批准
	例 You must confirm your attendance to the conference by the first Monday of next month. 你必须在下个月的第一个周一前确认自己是否参加会议。
	用 confirm my suspicion 证实我的猜疑

hesitate ['hezɪteɪt]	*v.* 犹豫；不愿意
	例 Don't hesitate to ask me if you have any further questions on the matter. 如果关于这件事你还有进一步的疑问，请不要犹豫，问我就可以。
	用 do not hesitate to contact me 请尽管和我联系
	扩 hesitation *n.* 犹豫

digest [daɪ'dʒest] *v.* ['daɪdʒest] *n.*	*v.* 消化；理解，领悟 *n.* 文摘；摘要
	例 I find that I don't digest meat very easily, so I eat a largely vegetarian diet. 我发觉自己无法很好地消化肉类，因此我以素食为主。
	用 digest plants 消化植物 digest the information 理解这一信息
	扩 digestion *n.* 消化；领悟
	类 bite *v.* 咬，咬住 swallow *v.* 吞，吞咽
	考 Soil is also an ally against climate change: as microorganisms within soil digest dead animals and plants, they lock in their carbon content, holding three times the amount of carbon as does the entire atmosphere. 土壤同样可以帮助我们对抗气候变化：由于土壤中的微生物消化死去的动物和植物，它们可以留住动植物的碳成分，保存相当于整个大气层三倍的碳含量。

brilliant
['brɪliənt]

adj. 明亮的；巧妙的；杰出的

例 The light from the lamp was a brilliant white and he thought it was too bright for night-time reading before bed.
灯光是明亮的白色，他认为这对于晚上入睡前的阅读来说太亮了。

用 a brilliant performance 一场出色的表演
brilliant sunshine 明媚的阳光

考 As the fruit matures, the coconut water gradually solidifies to form the brilliant white, fat-rich, edible flesh or meat.
随着果实成熟，椰子汁逐渐凝固，形成亮白色的、富含脂肪的、可食用的果肉。

confront
[kən'frʌnt]

v. 面对；面临；处理，解决

例 She decided to confront her boss directly about the problem.
她决定直面自己的老板来解决问题。

用 be confronted with 遇到

burgeon
['bɜːdʒən]

v. 萌芽，发芽；迅速发展 *n.* 芽；嫩枝

例 As car prices go down, car dealers are expecting sales to burgeon.
随着汽车价格下降，汽车经销商们期望销量迅速增长。

用 burgeoning demand 迅速增加的需求

arrest
[ə'rest]

v. 逮捕，拘留；阻止，中止

例 Policeman have the power to arrest people who break the law.
警察有权力逮捕违反法律的人。

用 arrest the company's decline 阻止公司的衰落

overuse
[ˌəʊvə'juːs] *n.*
[ˌəʊvə'juːz] *v.*

n./v. 过度使用

例 The mechanism had become ineffective from overuse and needed replacing.
由于过度使用，机械装置已经失效，需要更换。

用 the overuse of chemicals in agriculture
农业中对化学物质的过度使用

反 underuse *v.* 未充分利用

cosmic
['kɒzmɪk]

adj. 宇宙的

例 The study of cosmic laws underlines most astrophysics research.
对宇宙规律的研究是大多数天体物理学研究的基础。

用 cosmic radiation 宇宙辐射

compel [kəm'pel]	*v.* 强迫，迫使 例 She felt compelled to help the stranger, from a sense of moral virtue and empathy. 出于道德和同理心，她觉得必须帮助那个陌生人。 用 compel cyclists to wear a helmet 强制骑车人戴头盔 考 Some researchers say the results constitute compelling evidence that telepathy is genuine. 一些研究人员说，研究结果有力地证明了心灵感应是真实的。
latitude ['lætɪtjuːd]	*n.* 纬度；界限；活动范围 例 He noted the latitude and longitude, and then made a mark on the map. 他记下纬度和经度，并在地图上进行了标记。 用 lines of latitude 纬线 考 Hence, the calendars that were developed at the lower latitudes were influenced more by the lunar cycle than by the solar year. 因此，在低纬度地区编制的历法更多受到月运周期的影响，而非太阳年的影响。
immense [ɪ'mens]	*adj.* 巨大的，广大的 例 She was under immense pressure to resign after the company lost so much money. 在公司亏损很多钱之后，她承受着巨大的辞职压力。 用 a project of immense importance 一项极其重要的工程 考 immense technological progress in the domain of chemistry 化学领域的巨大科技进步
revenue ['revənjuː]	*n.* 收入；收益 例 The company had a significant yearly revenue from car sales, but very little profit due to high staff costs. 这家公司每年的汽车销售收入很可观，但由于员工成本高，利润非常少。 用 a slump in oil revenues 石油收入的下跌
jet [dʒet]	*n.* 喷气式飞机 例 The powerful jet engines propelled the plane swiftly through the sky. 强大的喷气发动机推动飞机在天空中快速飞行。 用 her private jet 她的私人喷气式飞机 考 the subsequent development of the jet aircraft in the 1950s 喷气式飞机在20世纪50年代的后续发展

bibliography
[ˌbɪbliˈɒgrəfi]

n. 参考书目；文献目录

例 The bibliography should be written at the very end of your research paper.
参考书目应该写在你研究论文的最后。

用 the full bibliography printed at the end of the third volume
印在第三卷最后的完整参考书目

Exercise 20

一、中文释义练习

一、中文释义练习

请选择单词正确的中文释义。

_____ 1. weave	A. 合唱团	
_____ 2. distribute	B. 回声	
_____ 3. notable	C. 显著的	
_____ 4. echo	D. 编织	
_____ 5. chorus	E. 分配	

_____ 11. legislation	A. 疲劳	
_____ 12. fatigue	B. 立法	
_____ 13. replay	C. 挤压	
_____ 14. squeeze	D. 重放	
_____ 15. hesitate	E. 犹豫	

_____ 6. fuse	A. 开花	
_____ 7. bloom	B. 蒸汽	
_____ 8. steam	C. 一小口	
_____ 9. sip	D. 实施	
_____ 10. implement	E. 保险丝	

_____ 16. confront	A. 宇宙的	
_____ 17. burgeon	B. 喷气式飞机	
_____ 18. cosmic	C. 收入	
_____ 19. revenue	D. 面对	
_____ 20. jet	E. 萌芽	

二、英文释义练习

请选择单词正确的英文释义。

_____ 1. propound	A. to build a wall or fence around sth.	
_____ 2. redundant	B. to become less strong; to make sth. less strong	
_____ 3. abate	C. that cannot be predicted because it changes a lot	
_____ 4. unpredictable	D. to suggest an idea or explanation of sth. for people	
_____ 5. enclose	E. lose a job because there is no more work available	

_____ 6. plateau	A. the distance of a place north or south of the equator	
_____ 7. schedule	B. a plan that lists work and when you do each thing	
_____ 8. simulate	C. to be made to look like sth. else	
_____ 9. digest	D. an area of flat land that is higher than the land around it	
_____ 10. latitude	E. to change into substances that your body can use	

aquatic
[ə'kwætɪk]

adj. 水生的；水栖的

例 He was attracted to most activities that involved water—so it was not a surprise that he decided to take up aquatic sports at a professional level.

他对大多数与水有关的活动都很感兴趣，因此他决定从事专业的水上运动并不令人意外。

用 aquatic plants 水生植物

扩 aquarium *n.* 水族馆

类 carnivore *n.* 食肉动物　herbivore *n.* 食草动物
primate *n.* 灵长类动物

perish
['perɪʃ]

v. 死亡；毁灭；腐烂

例 Rubber can perish when exposed to changing temperatures and damp conditions.

橡胶暴露在不断变化的温度中和潮湿的环境中会发生腐烂。

用 perish in the first frosts of autumn 在秋天的第一场霜冻时衰落

反 survive *v.* 生存

primary
['praɪməri]

adj. 主要的；初级的；基本的

例 The primary stage of education is usually one in which children learn basic social skills, languages and maths.

教育的初级阶段通常是孩子们学习基本社会技能、语言和数学的阶段。

用 primary causes 首要原因

同 main *adj.* 主要的

扩 primarily *adv.* 主要地

domain
[dəʊ'meɪn]

n. 领域；产业

例 He possessed impressive people-skills and a business-mind, but the academic university domain was really not for him.

他拥有令人印象深刻的人际能力和商业头脑，但大学学术领域真的不适合他。

用 in the domain of art 在艺术领域

pottery
['pɒtəri]

n. 陶器；陶土，黏土；陶艺

例 The artist created intricate pottery pieces with great skill and craftsmanship.
这位艺术家以高超的技巧和工艺制作出复杂的陶器。

用 a piece of pottery 一件陶制品
become interested in sculpting and pottery
变得对雕刻和制陶感兴趣

考 They are also looking at whether the types of pottery used, and other aspects of their material culture, were distinctive to specific regions or were more similar across larger areas.
他们同样关注人们使用的陶器种类，以及他们物质文化的其他方面，是特定区域独有的还是在更大的区域内类似的。

---

opera
['ɒprə]

n. 歌剧；歌剧团，歌剧院

例 The opera singer's powerful voice resonated through the grand theatre, captivating the audience.
歌剧演唱家强有力的声音在大剧院里回荡，使观众着迷。

用 go to the opera 去看歌剧 an opera singer 歌剧演员

---

resolve
[rɪ'zɒlv]

v. 决定；分解；解决

例 They attempted to resolve their differences by going to see a counsellor to talk everything over.
他们找了一位顾问，谈论了所有事情，试图解决他们的分歧。

用 resolve an issue 解决问题

扩 resolution *n.* 决心；解决

---

noteworthy
['nəʊtwɜːði]

adj. 值得注意的；显著的

例 I found nothing particularly interesting or noteworthy about the presentation.
我没有发现演讲中有什么特别有趣或值得注意的地方。

用 the most noteworthy feature of the list 清单上最值得关注的特点

---

glide
[glaɪd]

v./n. 滑行，滑动

例 The graceful swan glided across the calm lake, leaving a trail of ripples in its wake.
优雅的天鹅在平静的湖面上滑翔，在它的身后留下一道涟漪。

用 glide over the ice 在冰上滑行

---

furnish
['fɜːnɪʃ]

v. 为（房间）配备家具；提供，供应

例 They have completed renovations on the house and now need to furnish it.
他们已经完成了房子的翻新，现在需要置办一些家具。

用 was furnished with antiques 摆放着古董

---

venue ['venjuː]	*n.* 地点，场所 例 The concert venue was filled with excited fans eagerly waiting for the show to start. 音乐会场地里挤满了兴奋的歌迷，他们急切地等待着演出开始。 用 the change of venue for this event 比赛易地进行 考 With the growing interest in conservation during the 19th century, it was converted back into an arena for the staging of bullfights, thereby returning the structure to its original use as a venue for public spectacles. 在19世纪，随着人们对保护古迹的兴趣不断高涨，它又被重新改回成一座用来上演斗牛比赛的竞技场，就此恢复了这座建筑作为公开表演的场所的最初用途。
surgeon ['sɜːdʒən]	*n.* 外科医生 例 The path towards becoming a qualified surgeon involves years of specialist training. 要想成为一名合格的外科医生需要经过多年的专业训练。 用 a brain surgeon 一名脑外科医生 扩 surgery *n.* 外科手术
giant ['dʒaɪənt]	*adj.* 巨大的 *n.* 巨人；大公司 例 A tsunami is a giant wave at sea sometimes caused by earthquakes. 海啸是海上的巨浪，有时是由地震引起的。 用 the multinational oil giants 跨国大石油公司
assess [ə'ses]	*v.* 测评，评估 例 She attempted to assess the situation as best as she could in order to decide what the best course of action would be. 她尝试着尽可能地评估形势，以便确定最好的行动方案。 用 assess the effects of these changes 评估变化带来的效果 同 evaluate *v.* 评估 estimate *v.* 估计 扩 assessment *n.* 评估；评价
participate [paː'tɪsɪpeɪt]	*v.* 参与，参加；分享 例 The team leader encouraged all the members to participate in the gala performance. 团队负责人鼓励每个人都参加节日演出。 用 participate in the discussion 参加讨论 扩 participant *n.* 参加者，参与者 participants in the online debate 在线讨论的参与者们 考 children who participate in Western-style schooling 接受西方教育模式的儿童

defence [dɪˈfens]	*n.* 防卫，防护；辩护；答辩
	例 In his defence he claimed that he was mentally impaired at the time of the incident. 在他的辩护中，他声称自己在事件发生时精神存在问题。
	用 natural defence mechanisms 天生的防御机制

undersea [ˈʌndəsiː]	*adj.* 水下的；海面下的；海底的
	例 The undersea tunnel at the aquarium is an exciting part of the experience at Sea World. 水族馆的海底隧道是海洋世界体验中一个令人兴奋的部分。
	用 undersea exploration 海底探险 undersea cables 海底电缆

suicide [ˈsuːɪsaɪd]	*n.* 自杀
	例 The suicide rate amongst young male adults has increased in recent years. 年轻成年男性的自杀率近年来有所上升。
	用 commit suicide 自杀
	扩 suicidal *adj.* 自杀的；自杀性的

expedition [ˌekspəˈdɪʃn]	*n.* 探险，远征；探险队
	例 I've always been a fan of watching documentaries about expeditions into remote locations like the North Pole. 我一直很喜欢看有关去北极这种遥远地方探险的纪录片。
	用 an expedition to the North Pole 一场前往北极的探险

therapy [ˈθerəpi]	*n.* 治疗，疗法
	例 People who suffer psychological problems can benefit from regular counselling therapy. 有心理问题的人可以从定期的咨询治疗中获益。
	用 undergo some sort of drug therapy 接受某种药物治疗
	考 The sports injury treatment service operates on a paying basis, as does the nutritional therapy service. 运动损伤治疗服务和营养治疗服务都是付费开展的。

shutter [ˈʃʌtə(r)]	*n.* 百叶窗；（照相机的）快门
	例 The photographer adjusted the camera shutter speed to capture the fast-moving subject. 摄影师调整了相机的快门速度以捕捉快速移动的物体。
	用 open the shutters and gaze out over village roofs 打开百叶窗朝村里的房顶望去

prestigious [preˈstɪdʒəs]	*adj.* 有声望的；受尊敬的 例 She won a highly prestigious award for her art work. 她的艺术作品获得了极具影响力的奖项。 用 a prestigious university 一所名牌大学 扩 prestige *n.* 威望；名誉
density [ˈdensəti]	*n.* 密度；浓度；密集 例 The region has a very high population density which contributes to the high traffic volume. 该地区人口密度非常高，这使当地的交通量很大。 用 population density 人口密度 low density forest 低密度森林
retain [rɪˈteɪn]	*v.* 保持；保留；保存；记住 例 The best way to retain lots of new vocabulary is to learn it in small chunks. 记住大量新词汇的最好方法是以小的组块进行学习。 用 a soil that retains moisture 保持水分的土壤
static [ˈstætɪk]	*adj.* 静态的；静止的；静电的 例 Demand decreased considerably and then the market levelled off and became fairly static for the rest of the quarter. 需求大幅下降，随后市场趋于平稳，在该季度剩余的时间里没有什么变化。 用 a static population level 稳定的人口水平 扩 stationary *adj.* 静止的；固定的
diploma [dɪˈpləʊmə]	*n.* 学位证书；文凭 例 He spent three years completing his postgraduate diploma in teaching. 他花了三年时间获得了教学方面的研究生文凭。 用 a two-year diploma course 两年制的文凭课程
discard [dɪˈskɑːd]	*v.* 抛弃；放弃；丢弃 例 When you have opened the box, discard the packaging in a responsible manner. 当你打开箱子，需要以负责任的方式把包装丢掉。 用 discarded newspapers 乱扔的报纸
ascend [əˈsend]	*v.* 上升，通往高处；攀登 例 The marble stairs in the wonderful hotel ascended in a graceful curve from the main lobby. 这家豪华酒店的大理石楼梯以优美的曲线从大堂向上延伸。 用 in ascending order 按由低到高的顺序

invoke
[ɪnˈvəʊk]

v. 行使（法权）；援引（法律）；引起；使想起；提出

例 If he could not convince the company to give him his severance package, he would have to invoke legal action.
如果他不能说服公司给他离职赔偿金，他将采取法律行为。

用 invoke several eminent scholars to back up her argument
让几位有名的学者支持她的论点

扩 evoke v. 产生；唤起

influence
[ˈɪnfluəns]

n. 影响；影响力 v. 影响；改变

例 Playing computer games excessively can be a negative influence on young children.
玩太多电脑游戏对小孩子有负面影响。

用 the influence of the climate on agricultural production
气候对农业生产的影响

扩 influential adj. 有影响力的

考 Another issue is the extent to which the technology influences or even controls the workforce.
另一个问题是技术在多大程度上影响甚至控制劳动力。

principle
[ˈprɪnsəpl]

n. 道德原则；行为准则；原理

例 She has very strong principles and always sticks to the rules, and believes in telling the truth, working hard and being responsible at all times.
她有很强的原则性，总是遵守规则，并且总是相信讲真话，工作努力，有责任心。

用 three fundamental principles of teamwork 团队合作的三个基本原则

cater
[ˈkeɪtə(r)]

v. 迎合；满足需要

例 TV programmes should cater for a wide range of tastes and age groups.
电视节目应当适应人们的不同品味和年龄段。

用 novels which cater to the mass-market 迎合大众市场的小说

chronic
[ˈkrɒnɪk]

adj. 慢性的；长期的

例 He had a chronic illness, so he had to take special care of his diet at all times and take some pills every day.
他患有慢性疾病，所以需要时刻特别关注饮食，并每天服药。

用 the country's chronic unemployment problem
该国长期存在的失业问题
chronic lung disease 慢性肺病

扩 chronicle n. 编年史；年代记 synchronous adj. 同期的；同步的

outline ['aʊtlaɪn]	*n.* 概览；轮廓；大纲 *v.* 概述；略述；描绘 例 All students must submit the outline for their final dissertation by next Friday. 所有学生都要在下周五前提交论文大纲。 用 outline our proposals to the committee 向委员会概要性地介绍我们的提案
revise [rɪ'vaɪz]	*v.* 修改；校订；复习 例 Her tutor told her to revise the dissertation one more time before the final submission. 她的导师让她在最终提交论文前再修改一次。 用 a revised edition of a textbook 课本的修订版 扩 revision *n.* 修正；复习；修订本
spot [spɒt]	*n.* 地点，场所 *v.* 看见，注意到 例 She spotted a rare bird perched on a branch, quickly reaching for her camera to capture the moment. 她发现一只罕见的鸟栖息在树枝上，迅速伸手拿起相机捕捉到这一刻。 用 an ideal picnic spot 一个理想的野餐地点 考 There is scientific proof that the bluestones stood in the same spot until approximately 1600 BCE. 有科学证据表明这些青石一直到公元前1600年都处在同一个地方。
van [væn]	*n.* 小型货车；面包车；车厢 例 They rented a spacious van to transport their belongings during the move. 他们租了一辆宽敞的货车在搬家时运输财物。 用 a furniture van 一辆运家具的货车 a luggage van 一节装运行李的车厢
psychology [saɪ'kɒlədʒi]	*n.* 心理学；心理状态 例 He was drawn to the social sciences, so chose to study clinic psychology at master's level. 他被社会科学所吸引，因此在硕士阶段选择了临床心理学。 用 social psychology 社会心理学 扩 psychological *adj.* 心理的；精神的 考 the rich resources for studying human psychology 用于研究人类心理学的丰富资源

moth [mɒθ]	*n.* 飞蛾，蛾 例 The moth fluttered around the porch light on a summer evening. 在一个夏天的晚上，飞蛾在门廊的灯周围飞舞。 用 remove the moth 赶走飞蛾
foliage ['fəʊliɪdʒ]	*n.* 枝叶，叶子 例 The trees' vibrant foliage displayed stunning autumn colours. 树木鲜艳的叶子呈现出令人惊叹的秋日色彩。 用 dense green foliage 茂密的绿叶 healthy green foliage 有益健康的绿叶 考 The stems that are left behind might then grow in size and develop more foliage and larger crowns or tops that produce more coverage for wildlife; they have a better chance to regenerate in a less crowded environment. 留下来的树木随即就有可能增长尺寸、长出更多的枝叶和更大的树冠或树顶，从而为野生生物提供更多荫蔽；在一个不再那么拥挤的环境里，它们有更好的机会复兴壮大。
dye [daɪ]	*n.* 染料；染色 *v.* 给……染色 例 It has recently become fashionable to dye your hair light colours, like blonde and light brown. 最近流行把头发染成浅色，比如金色和浅棕色。 用 dye her hair blonde 把她的头发染成金黄色 考 the man who invented synthetic dyes 发明合成染料的人
combat ['kɒmbæt]	*n./v.* 战斗；搏斗 例 They were very well trained but had little real combat experience. 他们受过很好的训练，但是没什么实战经验。 用 combat troops 作战部队
hurdle ['hɜːdl]	*n.* 障碍；栏架，跨栏 *v.* 克服；跳过 例 The biggest hurdle in reaching her goal was getting her parents to agree with her decision. 实现她目标的最大障碍是要让父母同意她的决定。 用 the next hurdle 下一个难关 考 Securing sufficient numbers of the organism in question, isolating and characterising the compounds of interest, and producing large quantities of these compounds are all significant hurdles. 获得大量尚在讨论中的微生物，分离并鉴定人们关注的化合物，对这些化合物进行大规模生产都有巨大的困难。

testimony ['testɪməni]	*n.* 证词；证言；证据 例 His incredible exam results are testimony to his hardwork and dedication to the course, as well as his keen understanding of the subject area. 他优异的考试成绩证明了自己的努力和付出，以及对这一学科领域的敏锐理解。 用 refuse to give testimony 拒绝作证
encase [ɪn'keɪs]	*v.* 围绕；包装 例 The nuclear fuel was manufactured in the facility and properly encased in special metal containers. 核燃料在该设备中进行制造，并妥善地装在特殊的金属容器中。 用 be encased in concrete and steel 由钢筋混凝土包围着 考 The fruit is encased in a fleshy husk. 果实被包裹在肉质的外壳里。
supplement ['sʌplɪmənt] *n.* ['sʌplɪment] *v.*	*n.* 增补（物），补充（物）*v.* 增补，补充 例 The vitamin supplement seemed to give her increased energy. 维生素的补充似乎可以让她更具活力。 用 dietary supplements 补充饮食 扩 supplementary *adj.* 补充的；增加的
gradual ['grædʒuəl]	*adj.* 逐渐的，渐进的；平缓的 例 Losing weight can be a slow, gradual process that involves a lot of patience. 减重是一个缓慢、渐进的过程，需要很多耐心。 用 a gradual change in the climate 气候的逐渐变化 扩 gradually *adv.* 逐渐地
entitle [ɪn'taɪtl]	*v.* 给予权利，给予资格；命名 例 He has worked incredibly hard this year, with good results; I believe he is entitled to a good year-end bonus. 他今年工作异常努力，并且获得了很好的结果；我相信他会获得非常不错的年终奖金。 用 be entitled to your pension 有资格领取养老金 考 Silk quickly grew into a symbol of status, and originally, only royalty were entitled to have clothes made of silk. 丝绸很快成为一种地位的象征，最初，只有皇室人员有权拥有丝绸制作的服饰。

trigger
['trɪɡə(r)]

n. （枪的）扳机；起因 v. 触发；引起

例 Sleepwalking and strange dreams are often triggered by memories of negative things from our past.
梦游和奇怪的梦境通常由我们过去的消极记忆引发。

用 squeeze the trigger 扣动扳机
the trigger for the strike 引起罢工的原因

考 The problem with novelty, however, is that it tends to trigger the brain's fear system.
然而，创新的问题在于它往往会触发大脑的恐惧系统。

recruit
[rɪ'kruːt]

v. 征募；聘用 n. 招聘；新成员

例 As the company grew they estimated that they needed to recruit a lot of new staff.
随着公司发展，他们估计需要招聘很多新员工。

用 recruit several new members to the club
招募了几名新成员进入俱乐部

Exercise 21

一、中文释义练习

请选择单词正确的中文释义。

_____ 1. pottery   A. 滑行   _____ 11. discard   A. 抛弃

_____ 2. opera   B. 陶器   _____ 12. influence   B. 迎合

_____ 3. noteworthy   C. 巨大的   _____ 13. cater   C. 地点

_____ 4. glide   D. 显著的   _____ 14. outline   D. 影响

_____ 5. giant   E. 歌剧   _____ 15. spot   E. 概览

_____ 6. expedition   A. 治疗   _____ 16. van   A. 围绕

_____ 7. participate   B. 密度   _____ 17. dye   B. 小型货车

_____ 8. therapy   C. 探险   _____ 18. hurdle   C. 障碍

_____ 9. density   D. 参与   _____ 19. encase   D. 扳机

_____ 10. diploma   E. 学位证书   _____ 20. trigger   E. 染色

二、英文释义练习

请选择单词正确的英文释义。

_____ 1. perish   A. an area of knowledge or activity

_____ 2. domain   B. found or happening below the surface of the sea

_____ 3. venue   C. a place where people meet for an organized event

_____ 4. undersea   D. to die, especially in a sudden violent way

_____ 5. retain   E. to keep sth.; to continue to have sth.

_____ 6. chronic   A. a thing that is added to sth. else to complete it

_____ 7. revise   B. to change your opinions or plans

_____ 8. foliage   C. a thing that shows that sth. else exists or is true

_____ 9. testimony   D. the leaves of a tree or a plant

_____ 10. supplement   E. lasting for a long time and difficult to cure

inherit [ɪn'herɪt]	*v.* 继承；遗传
	例 He inherited many good qualities from his parents, including diligence and community spirit. 他继承了父母的许多优秀品质，包括勤奋和社区精神。
	用 an inherited disease 遗传病
	考 Shipbuilding in ancient Rome, however, was more of an art relying on estimation, inherited techniques and personal experience. 但是在古罗马，造船更像是一门依托于估算、技术传承与个人经验的艺术。

sway [sweɪ]	*v.* 摇摆，摇晃；说服，使动摇 *n.* 摇摆，摆动；影响，控制
	例 Your arguments do not sway her: she is insistent on leaving. 你的观点打动不了她，她坚持要离开。
	用 sway in the wind 在风中飘摇
	考 The work of the philosopher and scientist Aristotle, in the fourth century BC, is especially noteworthy, as his ideas held sway for nearly 2,000 years. 哲学家和科学家亚里士多德在公元前4世纪的这一著作格外值得关注，因为他的思想已经影响了人们接近2,000年。

calculate ['kælkjuleɪt]	*v.* 计算；预测，估计
	例 He calculated that he could afford to buy a new car if he saved 30% of his salary each month. 他计算得出，如果每个月把工资存下30%，就能买得起一辆新车。
	用 calculate how much time the assignment will take 算一下花多少时间完成分配的任务
	扩 calculation *n.* 计算
	考 He witnessed a Venus transit but was unable to make any calculations. 他见到了金星凌日现象，但并没能进行任何计算。

rational ['ræʃnəl]	*adj.* 合理的；理性的
	例 He was too upset about the situation to think in a rational way. 他对这种情况感到太沮丧了，以至于无法理智地思考。
	用 a rational argument 一个合理的论点

harness [ˈhɑːnɪs]	*v.* 给（马等）上挽具；控制，利用 *n.* 马具；背带，保护带
	例 They planned to harness the power of the sea to generate electricity. 他们计划利用海洋的力量来产生电能。
	用 a safety harness 安全带
equator [ɪˈkweɪtə(r)]	*n.* 赤道
	例 Countries that lie south of the equator tend to be hotter and are often home to many fascinating plants and animals. 位于赤道以南的国家往往更加炎热，这里通常是许多迷人的植物和动物的家园。
	用 near the equator 位于赤道附近
	扩 equal *adj.* 相等的 equation *n.* 等式，方程式
authentic [ɔːˈθentɪk]	*adj.* 真正的；真实的；可信的
	例 I don't know if the painting is authentic or an excellent fake. 我不知道这幅画是真迹还是优质的仿品。
	用 an authentic account of life in the desert 对沙漠生活的真实描述
	反 inauthentic *adj.* 不真实的，假的
ceramic [səˈræmɪk]	*n.* 陶瓷制品，陶瓷器 *adj.* 陶瓷的
	例 The delicate ceramic vase in the exhibition hall was an exquisite work of art. 展厅里那只精美的陶瓷花瓶是一件精美的艺术品。
	用 a collection of Chinese ceramics 中国陶瓷收藏品 a ceramic bowl 一个瓷碗
succumb [səˈkʌm]	*v.* 屈服，屈从；病情加重
	例 Despite his best efforts, he couldn't resist the temptation and eventually succumbed to it. 尽管他尽了最大努力，但还是抵挡不住诱惑，最终屈服了。
	用 succumb to the temptation 经不住诱惑
imitate [ˈɪmɪteɪt]	*v.* 模仿；仿造
	例 Some people say that the best way to learn excellent pronunciation is to imitate what native speakers say and how they say it. 有些人说，学习地道发音最好的方法是模仿母语人士说什么以及如何说。
	用 provide a model for children to imitate 给孩子提供了模仿的范例
	同 mimic *v.* 模仿
	扩 imitation *n.* 模仿

herb [hɜːb]	*n.* 药草，香草；草本植物
	例 She added fresh basil, a fragrant herb, to enhance the flavour of the pasta sauce. 她加入了新鲜的罗勒，一种芬芳的香草，以增强意大利面酱的味道。
	用 an herb garden 药草园
	考 aromatic herbs 草本香料植物

negative ['negətɪv]	*adj.* 消极的；否定的
	例 The experience was challenging, but certainly more positive than negative. 这段经历具有挑战性，但肯定积极作用大于消极影响。
	用 a fairly negative attitude to the theory 对该理论相当消极的态度
	反 positive *adj.* 积极的

process ['prəʊses]	*n.* 过程；进程；步骤 *v.* 加工；处理
	例 Applying for a new visa is a long and sometimes painstaking process, and you need to have all the right documents. 申请新的签证是一个漫长的、有时很辛苦的过程，你需要准备好所有需要的文件。
	用 the mental processes 思维过程 the ageing process 老化过程
	考 make AI's decision-making process easier to comprehend 让人工智能的决策过程更易于理解

dedicate ['dedɪkeɪt]	*v.* 致力于；献身于；把（书、戏剧、音乐作品等）献给
	例 She dedicated the final song at the performance to her family. 她把演出中的最后一首歌献给了自己的家人。
	用 dedicate her life to scientific studies 献身于科学研究
	同 devote *v.* 奉献
	扩 dedication *n.* 奉献，献身

widespread ['waɪdspred]	*adj.* 普遍的，广泛的；分布广的
	例 David gained widespread popularity after he appeared on national television as the winner of the contest. David作为比赛胜出者出现在国家电视台后，获得了广泛的关注。
	用 widespread damage 广泛的损坏 widespread support 广泛的支持

postcode ['pəʊstkəʊd]	*n.* 邮政编码
	例 A postcode allows the mail to be sorted more quickly and efficiently. 邮政编码可以使邮件被更快速、更高效地分类。
	用 type your street address and postcode 输入街道地址和邮政编码

displace [dɪs'pleɪs]	*v.* 取代；置换；转移；免职
	例 Many people believe that physical, printed books will be soon completely displaced by electronic devices and tablets. 许多人认为实体纸质书将很快被电子设备和平板电脑完全取代。
	用 displaced workers 被辞退的工人
monument ['mɒnjumənt]	*n.* 纪念碑；历史遗迹；不朽作品
	例 A monument dedicated to the saint was erected in the centre of the city. 纪念伟人的纪念碑矗立在市中心。
	用 an ancient monument 古代遗迹
	扩 monumental *adj.* 不朽的；纪念碑的
	考 the intricately carved monument 雕刻精致的纪念碑
concise [kən'saɪs]	*adj.* 简明的，简洁的
	例 It's important to write a concise overview when you write a short essay in an examination. 当你在考试中写一篇短文时，写一个简洁明了的概述是很重要的。
	用 a concise summary 简明扼要的总结 clear concise instructions 言简意赅的说明
	反 redundant *adj.* 多余的；冗长的 complex *adj.* 复杂的
	扩 concisely *adv.* 简明地；简洁地
disturb [dɪ'stɜːb]	*v.* 打扰；妨碍
	例 He really couldn't study when there was a lot of noise or distractions that disturbed his concentration. 当有很多噪音和干扰来分散注意力时，他真的无法学习。
	用 disturb the sleeping patients 惊扰睡着的病人
	扩 turbine *n.* 涡轮机
undergo [ˌʌndə'gəʊ]	*v.* 经历，经受；忍受
	例 He had to undergo surgery for his cardiovascular issue. 他因心血管问题不得不进行手术治疗。
	用 undergo repairs 接受检修
	考 Theme parks are undergoing other changes, too, as they try to present more serious social and cultural issues, and move away from fantasy. 主题公园也在发生其他变化，因为它们期望呈现更加严肃的社会和文化问题，而不再仅仅关注虚幻的事物。

desperate
['despərət]

adj. 不顾一切的；绝望的

例 He had spent months looking for a job and was beginning to get desperate.

他已经花了几个月时间找工作，并且开始感到绝望。

用 face a desperate shortage of clean water 面临清洁水源的严重短缺

考 Bingham made desperate attempts to prove this belief for nearly 40 years.

Bingham在将近40年的时间里用尽一切方法试图证明他的观点。

destination
[ˌdestɪ'neɪʃn]

n. 目的地，终点

例 It took many hours for him to get there after the long journey, but finally he arrived at his destination, exhausted, relieved and very happy.

经过长途旅行，他花了好几个小时才到达那里，但最终他到达了目的地，筋疲力尽，如释重负，非常高兴。

用 arrive at the destination 到达目的地 tourist destination 旅游目的地

考 Large merchant ships would approach the destination port and, just like today, be intercepted by a number of towboats that would drag them to the quay.

和现在一样，大型商船在靠近目标港口的时候会由一些牵引船拖进码头。

censor
['sensə(r)]

v. 审查；检查

例 Many television companies censor out bad language for the sake of children.

许多电视公司为了儿童的利益而删减不良语言。

用 censor the news 对新闻报道进行审查

扩 censorship *n.* 审查；审查制度

twist
[twɪst]

v. 使弯曲；扭动，拧；旋转 *n.* 转动，扭动；转折，突然变化

例 The story was particularly interesting because of the surprising twist at the end.

由于故事结尾令人意外的反转，这个故事非常有趣。

用 twist her arms behind her back 把她的胳膊扭到背后

symbol
['sɪmbl]

n. 象征；符号；标志

例 Making the letter V with your fingers is seen as a symbol of victory or peace.

用手指比出字母V被视为胜利或和平的象征。

用 the chemical symbol for copper 铜的化学符号

扩 symbolic *adj.* 象征的；象征性的

silt
[sɪlt]

n. 淤泥，泥沙 v.（使）淤塞

例 The river carried fine particles of silt, depositing them along its banks.
河流带着泥沙颗粒，沿着河岸沉积下来。

用 silt up 淤积

acid
['æsɪd]

n. 酸 adj. 酸的；酸性的

例 Be careful not to spill the acid; it can be hazardous.
小心不要把酸洒出来，这可能很危险。

用 acid rain 酸雨

matrix
['meɪtrɪks]

n. 矩阵；模型；发源地

例 The diagram was drawn in the form of a matrix to show the relationship of elements.
这张图是以矩阵的形式画出的，以体现元素间的关系。

用 a matrix of paths 纵横交错的小路
the matrix of their culture 他们文明的发源地

assert
[ə'sɜːt]

v. 坚持；断言；主张；声称

例 She tried to assert herself and get him to understand her point of view.
她试图说明自己的观点，并获得他的理解。

用 assert my authority from the beginning 一开始就维护我的权威

prey
[preɪ]

n. 猎物，捕获物；受害者 v. 捕食；欺凌

例 The predator silently stalked its prey through the dense jungle foliage.
捕食者在茂密的丛林中安静地跟踪猎物。

用 easy prey for birds 容易被鸟类捕食

考 The creatures that particularly interest us are the many insects that secrete powerful poison for subduing prey and keeping it fresh for future consumption.
令我们非常感兴趣的生物是一些昆虫，它们分泌强力的毒药来捕杀猎物并使其保持新鲜以备之后食用。

certificate
[sə'tɪfɪkət]

n. 证书；执照；文凭

例 To apply for a place at the college you must supply your original degree certificates and complete the online application form.
为了申请该学院的一个席位，你必须提供学位证书原件并填写在线申请表。

用 a birth certificate 出生证明

扩 certification n. 证明

prohibit [prə'hɪbɪt]	*v.* 阻止，禁止
	例 Most countries have prohibited smoking in public places in an effort to promote a healthier population. 大多数国家都禁止在公共场所吸烟，以促进人口健康。
	用 prohibit many people from taking up this sport 令许多人放弃从事这项运动
	同 forbid *v.* 禁止 prevent *v.* 防止；阻止
associate [ə'səʊʃɪeɪt] *v.* [ə'səʊʃɪət] *n.&adj.*	*v.* 联想；联系；交往 *n.* 伙伴，同事 *adj.* 联合的；准的，副的
	例 My mother doesn't really like the kinds of people I associate with. 我妈妈不喜欢我交往的那类人。
	用 associate with 与……联系
	反 dissociate *v.* 否认关系；与……无关
	扩 association *n.* 联系；联盟
confine [kən'faɪn]	*v.* 限制，局限 *n.* 边界；限制
	例 Can we please confine our discussion to the central matter in question? 我们能不能把讨论集中在问题的核心上？
	用 be confined to the Glasgow area 局限于格拉斯哥地区
	同 restrict *v.* 限制
compound ['kɒmpaʊnd] *n.&adj.* [kəm'paʊnd] *v.*	*n.* 化合物；混合物 *adj.* 复合的；混合的 *v.* 合成；混合
	例 You should first understand the distinction between compound interest and simple interest. 你应当首先理解复利和单利的区别。
	用 organic compounds 有机化合物
attain [ə'teɪn]	*v.* 达到，实现；获得
	例 True happiness is difficult to attain just through money alone. 仅仅靠金钱是很难获得真正的幸福的。
	用 attain my pilot's licence 拿到我的飞行员执照
	扩 attainable *adj.* 可达到的；可得到的
retail ['riːteɪl]	*n./v.* 零售 *adv.* 以零售方式
	例 There are hundreds of different retail outlets near our office. 我们办公室附近有数百家不同的零售店。
	用 department stores and other retail outlets 百货商店和其他零售专营店
	扩 retailer *n.* 零售商；零售店

interior [ɪn'tɪəriə(r)]	*n.* 内部；本质 *adj.* 内部的；本质的
	例 The interior of the hotel was designed in the style of a European Renaissance palace. 酒店的内部设计带有欧洲文艺复兴时期宫殿的风格。
	用 an expedition into the interior of Australia 一次深入澳大利亚腹地的探险 the interior of a building 楼房的内部
	反 exterior *adj.* 外部的
	考 interior designer 室内设计师
deforestation [ˌdiːˌfɒrɪ'steɪʃn]	*n.* 滥伐森林
	例 Deforestation has resulted in significant damage to the natural environment and impacted the ecosystem. 森林砍伐给自然环境带来了巨大危害并影响了生态系统。
	用 a history of deforestation 森林砍伐的历史
wax [wæks]	*n.* 蜡；蜡烛 *v.* 给……上蜡
	例 She carefully applied a layer of wax to her car to protect the paint and give it a glossy shine. 她仔细地在车上涂了一层蜡，以保护车漆，使其闪闪发光。
	用 floor wax 地板蜡 wax polish 上光蜡；蜡光剂
acclaim [ə'kleɪm]	*v./n.* 称赞；欢呼
	例 The conference that they hosted was acclaimed as a considerable success, after receiving much academic praise. 他们主办的会议在获得了许多学术赞誉后，被誉为一次相当成功的会议。
	用 a highly acclaimed performance 受到高度赞扬的表现
seep [siːp]	*v./n.* 渗透；渗漏
	例 Water began to seep through the cracks in the old, worn-out, wooden bucket. 水开始从那只破旧木桶的裂缝里渗出来。
	用 an oil seep 一次石油渗漏
temporary ['temprəri]	*adj.* 暂时的，临时的
	例 He decided to take on a temporary job after finishing university, just to earn a little money. 他决定大学毕业后找一份临时工作，只是为了赚点钱。
	用 a temporary agreement 一份临时协议

barrier
['bæriə(r)]

n. 障碍物，屏障；界线

例 Problems with finding childcare are the biggest barrier to women in Sweden finding work.
寻找儿童托管的问题是瑞典女性寻求工作的最大障碍。

用 stand behind barriers 站在障碍物后面

同 obstacle *n.* 障碍

考 These barriers don't just make it harder to cross the road: they divide communities and decrease opportunities for healthy transport.
这些路障并不仅仅是令过马路这件事本身更困难：它们还将不同人群划分开来，并降低了健康交通出行的机会。

magnetic
[mæg'netɪk]

adj. 有磁性的；有吸引力的

例 A compass was used in navigation as the needle always points to magnetic North.
指南针被用于航海，因为指针总是指向磁北。

用 magnetic materials 磁性材料

concrete
['kɒŋkriːt]

adj. 具体的；有形的；混凝土制的 *n.* 具体物；混凝土

例 He had a very concrete goal in mind and was determined to achieve it.
他心中有一个非常具体的目标，并决心实现它。

用 concrete floor 混凝土地面

反 abstract *adj.* 抽象的

考 Teaching concrete skills such as how to write an effective introduction to an essay then praising students' effort in getting there is probably a far better way of improving confidence than telling them how unique they are, or indeed how capable they are of changing their own brains.
教授具体的技能，例如怎么写出一篇论文的精炼简介，然后再夸奖学生努力达成了目标，这可能在提升学生自信方面是更好的做法，远远优于去告诉学生他们多么与众不同或多么有能力改变他们自己的大脑这类行为。

supervise
['suːpəvaɪz]

v. 监督；管理；指导

例 One of the senior students was asked to supervise the class while the teacher was taking a one-day training course.
当老师参加为期一天的培训课程时，一个高年级学生被要求监督这个班。

用 supervise building work 监理建筑工程

扩 supervision *n.* 监督；管理

考 supervise and support library staff 管理和帮助图书馆工作人员

script
[skrɪpt]

n. 脚本；剧本；笔迹 *v.* 写脚本；写剧本

例 Movie actors usually have to memorise their script before going on camera and acting.
电影演员在拍摄和表演前通常要记住他们的剧本。

用 an error in the original script 最初脚本中的错误

recreation
[ˌriːkriˈeɪʃn]

n. 娱乐；消遣

例 There are excellent facilities for sport and recreation in my city.
我所在的城市有很好的体育和娱乐设施。

用 the increasing use of land for recreation 越来越多的土地用于娱乐

扩 recreational *adj.* 娱乐的；消遣的

考 Well, since we managed to extend the recreation ground, we've spent some time talking to local people about how it could be made a more attractive and useful space.
既然我们设法扩建了游乐场，我们也就花了一些时间和当地人讨论如何使它成为一个更有吸引力和更有用的空间。

Exercise 22

一、中文释义练习

一、中文释义练习

请选择单词正确的中文释义。

_____ 1. inherit	A. 计算	_____ 11. desperate	A. 矩阵
_____ 2. sway	B. 利用	_____ 12. censor	B. 限制
_____ 3. calculate	C. 合理的	_____ 13 matrix	C. 绝望的
_____ 4. rational	D. 继承	_____ 14. prohibit	D. 审查
_____ 5. harness	E. 摇摆	_____ 15. confine	E. 禁止
_____ 6. equator	A. 药草	_____ 16. wax	A. 称赞
_____ 7. herb	B. 经历	_____ 17. acclaim	B. 具体的
_____ 8. disturb	C. 打扰	_____ 18. seep	C. 监督
_____ 9. undergo	D. 赤道	_____ 19. concrete	D. 蜡烛
_____ 10. postcode	E. 邮政编码	_____ 20. supervise	E. 渗透

二、英文释义练习

请选择单词正确的英文释义。

_____ 1. authentic	A. existing or happening over a large area
_____ 2. succumb	B. to not be able to fight an attack or an illness
_____ 3. widespread	C. a building to remind people of a famous person
_____ 4. monument	D. known to be real and genuine and not a copy
_____ 5. symbol	E. an object representing a more general quality or situation
_____ 6. twist	A. an object like a fence that prevents people
_____ 7. certificate	B. a thing consisting of two or more separate things
_____ 8. compound	C. an official document used to prove the facts are true
_____ 9. deforestation	D. to bend or turn sth. into a particular shape
_____ 10. barrier	E. the act of cutting down the trees in an area

cite
[saɪt]

v. 引用，援引

例 When you write academic essays it's essential to cite your sources accurately.
写学术文章时，准确地引用资料来源是很重要的。

用 cite a poem 引用一首诗

同 quote *v.* 引用

mediocre
[ˌmiːdiˈəʊkə(r)]

adj. 中等的；普通的；平凡的

例 He was not a particularly good musician, but he wasn't terrible either; most people described him as a mediocre performer.
他不是一个特别好的音乐家，但也并不差，大多数人认为他是一名普通的表演者。

用 a mediocre musician 一位平庸的音乐家

fertile
['fɜːtaɪl]

adj. 富饶的，肥沃的；能生育的，可繁殖的

例 The rain fell heavily for the entire spring, and the soil became fertile for crops.
整个春天都有很大的雨，土壤变得肥沃，适于种植作物。

用 a fertile region 一片富饶的地区 fertile soil 肥沃的土壤

vary
['veəri]

v. 相异，不同；变化，多样化

例 Marriage customs and traditions vary in different regions of the county.
婚姻习俗和传统在这个国家的不同地区有所不同。

用 vary considerably in quality 质量差异很大

扩 variety *n.* 多样化；种类 variation *n.* 变化；变异 variant *n.* 变体

考 It can vary greatly from one person to another.
人与人之间的差异很大。

approximately
[əˈprɒksɪmətli]

adv. 大约；近似地

例 We evolved from apes approximately seven million years ago.
我们大约于七百万年前由猿类进化而来。

用 take approximately six hours 大约花了六个小时

扩 approximate *adj.* 大概的，大约的

superior
[suːˈpɪəriə(r)]

adj. 更好的，更高的；上级的；优秀的，出众的 *n.* 上级，上司

例 His taste was superior to anyone's, and he enjoyed all the finest wines, meats and cheeses, and never opted for inferior foods.
他的品位比任何人都高，他喜欢所有最好的葡萄酒、肉类和奶酪，从不选择劣质食品。

用 superior intelligence 更高的智商 superior status 更高的地位

slim
[slɪm]

adj. 苗条的，纤细的；修长的

例 With regular exercise and a healthy diet, she managed to maintain a slim physique.
依靠规律的锻炼和健康的饮食，她成功地保持了苗条的身材。

用 a slim figure 苗条的体形 a slim volume of poetry 一本薄薄的诗集

boost
[buːst]

v. 使增长，推动；宣扬，推广 *n.* 推动，促进；广告，宣扬

例 The new marketing campaign helped boost sales significantly.
新的营销活动极大地促进了销售。

用 boost his confidence 提升他的信心

考 The growth mindset is not simply about boosting students' morale.
成长性思维不仅仅和提升学生的士气有关。

observe
[əbˈzɜːv]

v. 观察；观察到，注意到；遵守

例 She observed a distinct change in his behaviour after the medication.
她观察到服药后他的行为有明显的变化。

用 observe the behaviour of babies 观察婴儿的行为

扩 observation *n.* 观察

phase
[feɪz]

n. 时期，阶段

例 Adolescence is usually an interesting but challenging phase in life.
青春期通常是人生中一个有趣但充满挑战的阶段。

用 during the first phase 在第一阶段
the initial phase of the project 项目的初始阶段

同 stage *n.* 阶段

insurance
[ɪnˈʃʊərəns]

n. 保险；保险费

例 Tax and national insurance are automatically deducted from your salary.
税收和居民保险自动从你的工资中扣除。

用 an insurance broker 保险经纪人 insurance premiums 保险费

考 They also provide insurance in case you have an accident, though we hope you won't need that, of course.
他们也为你提供保险，以防你发生事故，尽管我们当然希望你用不上它。

combine [kəm'baɪn]	v.（使）联合，结合；使合并
	例 When making a cake you've got to combine all the ingredients in a bowl. 做蛋糕时，你必须把所有原料都放在一个碗里。
	用 combine the eggs with a little flour 把鸡蛋和少量面粉混合
	扩 combination n. 联合；结合
shelter ['ʃeltə(r)]	n. 庇护；避难所 v. 保护；躲避，避难
	例 As the storm broke out they sought shelter under the huge tree. 暴风雨来临时，他们在那棵大树下躲避。
	用 take shelter from the storm 躲避暴风雨 a night shelter for the homeless 无家可归者夜间收容所
cohesive [kəʊ'hiːsɪv]	adj. 连接的；凝聚的；结合的
	例 Cohesive devices are words that connect our utterances and phrases together when we speak. 衔接手段是指我们说话时，将我们的表达和词组等连接在一起的那些词。
	用 a cohesive group 一个紧密团结的群体
adventure [əd'ventʃə(r)]	n. 冒险（经历）；冒险精神 v. 冒险
	例 Travel to new places was inspiring to him and fulfilled his passion for adventure. 去新的目的地旅行能够让他感到振奋，并且满足他对冒险的热情。
	用 adventure stories 历险故事
subscribe [səb'skraɪb]	v. 订阅；捐款；赞成；签订
	例 He subscribed to the *National Geographic* for an entire year membership. 他订阅了《国家地理》一整年的会员。
	用 subscribe to several sports channels 付费收看几个体育频道
	扩 subscription n. 捐款；订阅
elevate ['elɪveɪt]	v. 提升；升高
	例 Within a few years he was elevated to the position of secretary general of international affairs at his company. 几年内他被提升到公司国际事务秘书长的职位。
	用 elevate blood pressure 使血压升高
	同 raise v. 提升
	扩 elevator n. 电梯；升降机 elevation n. 高处；高地；海拔 lever n. 杆，杠杆

profit
['prɒfɪt]

n. 利润；利益 *v.* 获利；获益

例 Technology industries are currently making an enormous profit.
技术行业正在创造巨大利润。

用 a rise in profits 收益增长 a drop in profits 收益减少

扩 profitable *adj.* 有利可图的；有利润的

类 cost *n.* 成本 revenue *n.* 收入 income *n.* 收入
budget *n.* 预算 expense *n.* 花费，费用 expenditure *n.* 经费，开支

考 arson for profit 纵火谋利

criticise
['krɪtɪsaɪz]

v. 批评；评论

例 He was not a very motivating manager because he always criticised
the employees.
他不是一个善于激励他人的管理者，因为他总是批评员工。

用 criticise them severely 严厉地批评他们

扩 criticism *n.* 批评；评论

automatic
[ˌɔːtə'mætɪk]

adj. 自动的；无意识的

例 Most cars today have automatic gears and are no longer manual.
现在大多数汽车都是自动挡，不再是手动挡了。

用 automatic doors 自动门

考 a semi-automatic process 半自动化过程

impetus
['ɪmpɪtəs]

n. 动力；促进；冲力

例 The sudden decline in the market has provided an impetus for
change across the organisation.
市场的突然衰退促进了整个组织的变革。

用 the primary impetus behind the economic recovery
经济复苏的主要推动力

compatible
[kəm'pætəbl]

adj. 兼容的；能共处的

例 The couple separated because they realised they were not really
compatible.
这对夫妇分开是因为他们意识到彼此并不合得来。

用 compatible software 可兼容的软件
compatible blood groups 相容的血型

反 incompatible *adj.* 不兼容的；无法共存的

lenient
['liːniənt]

adj. 仁慈的，宽大的，宽容的

例 The lenient judge gave the first-time offender a light sentence.
仁慈的法官对初犯从轻判刑。

用 a lenient fine 从宽罚款

engrave
[ɪnˈɡreɪv]

v. 雕刻；铭记

例 They always engrave the names of the winners of the annual contest into the plaque on the base of the trophy.
他们总会把年度竞赛获胜者的名字刻在奖杯底座的牌匾上。

用 be engraved with his name 刻有他的名字

扩 grave *adj.* 严重的；重大的

nostalgia
[nɒˈstældʒə]

n. 怀旧，念旧

例 The old photograph filled her with nostalgia, reminding her of cherished memories from the past.
这张旧照片使她充满了怀旧之情，让她想起过去的美好回忆。

用 a sense of nostalgia 怀旧感

考 No wonder that people who stroll around exhibitions are filled with nostalgia; the evidence in museums indicates that life was so much better in the past.
难怪参观展览的人会充满怀旧情绪；博物馆中的证据表明过去的生活比现在的好得多。

item
[ˈaɪtəm]

n. 项目，条款；一件商品；一则（新闻）

例 The shopping list included essential items like bread, milk, and eggs.
购物清单包括面包、牛奶和鸡蛋等必需物品。

用 the next item on the agenda 议程的下一项

circle
[ˈsɜːkl]

n. 圆，圆形物；循环，周期 *v.* 旋转；环绕；画圆

例 Crop Circles are thought to be made by alien space craft landing in fields by night.
麦田怪圈被认为是由夜间降落在田间的外星宇宙飞船造成的。

用 draw a circle 画一个圆圈

dispose
[dɪˈspəʊz]

v. 安排；处理

例 You should dispose of all paper waste in the basket provided.
你应该把所有废纸放在提供的纸篓里处理掉。

用 the difficulties of disposing of nuclear waste 处理核废料的困难

扩 disposal *n.* 处理；安排

delinquency
[dɪˈlɪŋkwənsi]

n. 犯罪，不良行为

例 The authorities worked to reduce youth delinquency by providing educational and mentorship programs.
当局通过提供教育辅导项目来减少青少年犯罪。

用 an increase in juvenile delinquency 青少年犯罪的增加

overlook [ˌəʊvəˈlʊk]	*v.* 忽略；不予理会；俯瞰
	例 Most of his data analysis was very detailed, but he had overlooked one key factor—the decline in customer satisfaction in the summer period. 他的大部分数据分析都非常详细，但他忽略了一个关键因素，即夏天客户满意度的下降。 用 overlook an important fact 忽略一个重要事实 同 miss *v.* 忽略
grid [ɡrɪd]	*n.* 网格；栅栏；电力网
	例 The city streets were laid out in a grid pattern, making navigation straightforward. 城市街道呈网格状布局，使导航非常方便。 用 New York's grid of streets 纽约棋盘式的街道布局 the national grid 国家电网
fund [fʌnd]	*n.* 基金，专款；资金 *v.* 投资；资助
	例 From the proceeds of the charity event we made a contribution to the famine fund. 我们从慈善活动的收益中捐了一笔钱给饥荒基金。 用 government funds 政府资金 a disaster relief fund 赈灾专款
interval [ˈɪntəvl]	*n.* 间隔，间隙；幕间休息，中场休息
	例 In cinemas in the past you could always buy ice creams or popcorn during the interval. 在过去的电影院，你总是可以在幕间休息时买冰淇淋或爆米花。 用 an interval of 20 minutes 间隔20分钟 考 occur at random intervals 以随机的间隔发生
perplex [pəˈpleks]	*v.* 使困惑；使复杂
	例 The complex problem perplexed him considerably and he couldn't think of a solution. 这个复杂的问题令他非常困惑，他无法想出好的解决办法。 用 a perplexing problem 一个令人不解的问题 同 confuse *v.* 使困惑
helix [ˈhiːlɪks]	*n.* 螺旋，螺旋状
	例 The DNA molecule is a double helix, carrying genetic information. DNA分子呈双螺旋结构，携带遗传信息。 用 the first double helix model of DNA 第一个DNA双螺旋结构

specimen
['spesɪmən]

n. 样品，样本；标本

例 The biology teacher showed a slideshow of the specimens he had collected from the lake.
生物老师放映幻灯片，展示了他从湖中收集的标本。

用 bring back specimens of rock from the moon
从月球带回了岩石标本

同 sample *n.* 样品；样本

考 dental specimens from the majority of prehistoric Americans
多数史前美洲人的牙齿样本

archaeology
[ˌɑːkiˈɒlədʒi]

n. 考古学

例 Michael was a course tutor in the archaeology department of the university.
Michael是这所大学考古系的课程导师。

用 increase their understanding of biology, archaeology and geology
提高他们对生物学、考古学和地质学的理解

扩 archaeological *adj.* 考古的；考古学的
archaeological excavations 考古发掘
archaeological evidence 考古实证
one of the region's most important archaeological sites
该地区最重要的考古遗址之一

考 In today's class I'm going to talk about marine archaeology, the branch of archaeology focusing on human interaction with the sea, lakes and rivers.
在今天的课堂上，我将讲述海洋考古学，它是考古学的一个分支，侧重于人类与海洋、湖泊和河流的相互作用。

institution
[ˌɪnstɪˈtjuːʃn]

n. 机构；制度；建立

例 The academic institution was famous for producing some of the best medical scientists in the country.
这所学术机构以培养出一些国内最优秀的医学科学家而闻名。

用 an educational institution 教育机构 a financial institution 金融机构

bucket
['bʌkɪt]

n. 桶；一桶（的量）

例 He filled the bucket with water to water the plants in the garden.
他把桶装满水，给花园里的植物浇水。

用 a plastic bucket 一个塑料桶

mess
[mes]

n. 混乱；困境

例 His hair was in a real mess after playing basketball this afternoon.
今天下午打完篮球后，他的头发乱糟糟的。

用 be in a mess 陷入混乱

cassette [kə'set]	*n.* 盒式磁带；胶片盒 例 In the past, people enjoyed music by playing cassette tapes on portable players. 过去，人们通过在便携式播放器上播放盒式磁带来欣赏音乐。 用 his two albums released on cassette 他以磁带形式发行的两张专辑
chest [tʃest]	*n.* 胸部，胸膛；箱子，盒子 例 In all pirate stories, there is a treasure chest full of gold coins and other spoils of battle. 在所有海盗故事中，都有一个装满金币和其他战利品的宝箱。 用 chest infection 胸部感染
paralyse ['pærəlaɪz]	*v.* 使瘫痪；使麻痹 例 The effect of the drug is to paralyse the nerves before an operation. 这种药的作用是在手术前使神经麻痹。 用 become paralysed by a stroke 因中风而瘫痪 扩 paralysis *n.* 瘫痪；麻痹
brochure ['brəʊʃə(r)]	*n.* 小册子，资料手册 例 The travel agency provided a colourful brochure with vacation packages. 这家旅行社提供了一本色彩鲜艳的小册子，上面有度假指南。 用 a travel brochure 一本旅游手册
component [kəm'pəʊnənt]	*n.* 组成部分；组件 *adj.* 组成的；构成的 例 The teacher required that the student include every component of the project in order to receive a satisfactory grade. 老师要求学生把项目的每一部分都写进去，以获得满意的分数。 用 the components of a machine 机器部件
appropriate [ə'prəʊpriət]	*adj.* 适当的；恰当的；合适的 例 The appropriate course of action in this difficult situation is to remain calm and try not to panic. 在这种困难情况下，应该采取的做法是保持冷静，尽量不要恐慌。 用 an appropriate method 一个恰当的方法 反 inappropriate *adj.* 不适合的 考 appropriate responses to signals from other civilisations 对来自其他文明的信号给予合适的回应

command [kə'mɑːnd]	*v.* 命令；指挥 *n.* 命令，指令；指挥
	例 The general issued the command for the men to retreat. 将军发布了命令，让人们撤退。
	用 obey the captain's commands 服从船长的命令
controversy ['kɒntrəvɜːsi]	*n.* 争论；争议
	例 The judge's decision about the cases provoked controversy. 法官对这些案件的判决引起了争议。
	用 arouse controversy 引起争论
	同 debate *n.* 辩论；争论
	扩 controversial *adj.* 有争议的
complain [kəm'pleɪn]	*v.* 抱怨；控诉；投诉
	例 He is normally very quick to complain when he experiences bad customer service. 当他遇到非常糟糕的客户服务时，他通常会立即投诉。
	用 complain to the manager about this 就这件事向经理投诉
	扩 complaint *n.* 抱怨；投诉
inevitable [ɪn'evɪtəbl]	*adj.* 必然的；不可避免的
	例 It is inevitable that the environment will suffer badly if we do not take action now. 如果我们现在不采取行动，环境将不可避免地受到严重损害。
	用 an inevitable consequence of the decision 这个决定的必然后果
	同 unavoidable *adj.* 不可避免的

Exercise 23

一、中文释义练习

请选择单词正确的中文释义。

_____ 1. mediocre   A. 富饶的

_____ 2. fertile   B. 大约

_____ 3. approximately   C. 苗条的

_____ 4. slim   D. 时期

_____ 5. phase   E. 中等的

_____ 11. engrave   A. 铭记

_____ 12. dispose   B. 网格

_____ 13. grid   C. 使困惑

_____ 14. perplex   D. 处理

_____ 15. bucket   E. 桶

_____ 6. insurance   A. 凝聚的

_____ 7. cohesive   B. 提升

_____ 8. elevate   C. 动力

_____ 9. automatic   D. 保险

_____ 10. impetus   E. 自动的

_____ 16. chest   A. 胸部

_____ 17. command   B. 争论

_____ 18. component   C. 抱怨

_____ 19. controversy   D. 命令

_____ 20. complain   E. 组成部分

二、英文释义练习

请选择单词正确的英文释义。

_____ 1. observe   A. protection from rain, danger or attack

_____ 2. shelter   B. able to exist or be used together without problems

_____ 3. subscribe   C. to pay regularly in order to receive or use sth.

_____ 4. compatible   D. an affectionate feeling for the past

_____ 5. nostalgia   E. to watch sb. carefully, especially to learn about them

_____ 6. overlook   A. to see sth. wrong or bad but decide to ignore it

_____ 7. interval   B. suitable or correct for the particular circumstances

_____ 8. archaeology   C. unable to feel or move all or part of the body

_____ 9. paralyse   D. the study of cultures and history of the past

_____ 10. appropriate   E. a period of time between two events

colleague ['kɒliːɡ]	*n.* 同事，同僚 例 The boss introduced us to our new work colleagues during the dinner. 老板在宴会上把我们介绍给新同事。 用 a colleague of mine 我的一位同事
epidemic [ˌepɪ'demɪk]	*n.* 传染病；（疾病的）流行 例 A flu epidemic always hits the northern hemisphere between the months of October and January every year. 每年十月到（次年）一月之间，流感总会在北半球爆发。 用 the outbreak of a flu epidemic 流感的爆发
independent [ˌɪndɪ'pendənt]	*adj.* 独立的；单独的 例 She had a very independent attitude and always wanted to do things by herself. 她有非常独立的性格，总是想独自做事情。 用 be financially independent 经济上独立
proponent [prə'pəʊnənt]	*n.* 支持者；建议者 例 He was a big proponent of improving environmental policies. 他是环境改善政策的大力支持者。 用 a leading proponent 一个主要拥护者 同 advocate *n.* 支持者，倡导者 supporter *n.* 支持者 反 opponent *n.* 反对者
trend [trend]	*n.* 趋势，倾向 例 This month, share prices are continuing on their downward trend. 这个月，股票价格继续呈下降趋势。 用 economic trend 经济趋势
vapour ['veɪpə(r)]	*n.* 蒸汽；烟雾 例 The vapours that come off gasoline can be toxic if inhaled. 汽油散发的蒸气如果被吸入是有毒的。 用 water vapour 水蒸气

transparent [træns'pærənt]	*adj.* 透明的；显然的
	例 The glass was not totally transparent so it was impossible to see through clearly. 玻璃并不完全透明，因此无法透过它看清楚。
	用 a transparent attempt to buy votes 明显收买选票的企图
	考 Architects love it because large panels can be bolted together to make transparent walls, and turning it into ceilings and floors is almost as easy. 建筑师们喜欢它，因为大面板可以被固定在一起以形成透明的墙壁，并且把它变成天花板和地板几乎同样容易。
resign [rɪ'zaɪn]	*v.* 辞职；顺从
	例 After years of service, he decided to resign from his position and pursue new opportunities. 工作多年后，他决定从当前岗位辞职，去寻求新的机会。
	用 resign as manager 辞去经理职务
accomplish [ə'kʌmplɪʃ]	*v.* 完成；实现；达到
	例 To accomplish great things, in addition to dream, we must also act. 要想成就伟业，除了梦想，我们还必须付诸行动。
	用 accomplish their mission 完成他们的任务
	考 try harder to accomplish the task 更努力地完成任务
designate ['dezɪgneɪt]	*v.* 命名；指定；指派；标明
	例 The committee decided to designate her as the spokesperson for the project. 委员会决定指定她为该项目的发言人。
	用 be designated as prime minister 被任命为首相 be designated a no-smoking area 被确定为无烟区 a designated nature reserve 一片指定的自然保护区
	考 When he types in an identifier for a particular space object, the database draws a purple line to designate its orbit. 当他输入某个特定太空物体的标识符后，数据库给出了一条紫色的线来指示其轨道。
gist [dʒɪst]	*n.* 主旨；要点
	例 He didn't really understand the film, but he got the general gist of the plot. 他并没有真正理解这部电影，但是他大致了解了剧情的要点。
	用 get the gist of an argument 理解辩论的主旨

horizon [həˈraɪzn]	*n.* 地平线；视野；眼界；范围
	例 The mountains could be seen going off in the distance on the horizon. 从地平面看去，这些山在远处逐渐消失。
	用 broaden my horizons 开阔我的眼界
	扩 horizontal *adj.* 水平的
lifespan [ˈlaɪfspæn]	*n.* 寿命；有效期
	例 The lifespan of a dog is around fifteen years maximum. 狗的寿命最长可达15年左右。
	用 the lifespan of a tiger 老虎的寿命
lever [ˈliːvə(r)]	*n.* 杠杆；控制杆；手段，方法
	例 With a swift pull of the lever, the trapdoor opened, revealing a hidden passage. 随着杠杆的迅速拉动，门打开了，露出一条隐藏的通道。
	用 pull the lever 拉动操纵杆
crane [kreɪn]	*n.* 起重机，吊车 *v.* 探头看，伸长（脖子）
	例 The construction site used a towering crane to lift heavy materials to different levels. 施工现场使用了一台高耸的起重机将重物吊到不同的高度。
	用 be lifted away by a huge crane 被一台巨大起重机吊走
	考 In this stage, the lifting frame was fixed to a hook attached to a crane, and the hull was lifted completely clear of the seabed and transferred underwater into the lifting cradle. 在这一阶段，起吊架被固定在一个绑在起重机上的挂钩上，船体被升起，完全脱离海底并在水下被转移至升降篮中。
enforce [ɪnˈfɔːs]	*v.* 实施，执行；强制
	例 The role of the police is to enforce the laws to make sure that society functions in a relatively harmonious way. 警察起到的作用是执行法规，以确保社会以一种比较和谐的方式运行。
	用 enforce the law 执法
linear [ˈlɪniə(r)]	*adj.* 直线的，线性的；连续的
	例 The graph displayed a linear relationship between time and distance travelled. 该图显示了时间和距离之间的线性关系。
	用 linear relationship 线性关系 linear arrangements 线形布局

paradox
['pærədɒks]

n. 悖论；自相矛盾

例 An interesting paradox in the country's success was its rapid growth despite still having an underdeveloped financial system.
在该国的成功中存在一个有趣的悖论，即尽管金融体系仍不发达，但经济却实现了快速增长。

用 the paradox of exercise 锻炼的矛盾之处

扩 paradoxical *adj.* 矛盾的，似非而是的

考 an explanation for this paradox 对这个悖论的解释

---

persevere
[ˌpɜːsə'vɪə(r)]

v. 坚持

例 If you cannot do something at first, you must persevere and keep trying.
如果你起初做不到某件事，你必须坚持并不断尝试。

用 the ability to persevere despite obstacles and setbacks
在困难和挫折面前坚持的能力

---

adhere
[əd'hɪə(r)]

v. 依附，黏着；遵守；坚持

例 It's important that all school children adhere to the rules at all times.
所有的学生在任何时候都遵守规则是很重要的。

用 adhere to the surface of the red cells 附着在红细胞表面上

扩 adherent *adj.* 附着的；黏着的 adherence *n.* 坚持；遵守

---

intuition
[ˌɪntjuˈɪʃn]

n. 直觉；本能

例 Her intuition told her that something was wrong, but she couldn't quite put her finger on it.
她的直觉告诉她有些地方不对，但她不能确切地指出来。

用 allow our intuition to guide us 让直觉指引我们

扩 intuitional *adj.* 直觉的

考 As the chapters will illustrate, mathematics is not restricted to the analytical and numerical; intuition plays a significant role.
正如本章将说明的，数学并不局限于分析和数值；直觉扮演着重要角色。

---

cortex
['kɔːteks]

n. 皮质；皮层；（尤指）大脑皮层

例 The prefrontal cortex controls most of our conscious decision-making.
前额叶皮层控制着我们大部分的意识决策。

用 auditory cortex 听觉皮层

考 the orbital cortex 眶额皮层

overweight [ˌəʊvəˈweɪt]	*adj.* 超重的；过重的 例 He spent years eating fatty, high-cholesterol foods and doing little exercise, and was distinctly overweight as a result of this. 多年来，他一直食用高脂肪、高胆固醇的食物，很少运动，因此明显超重。 用 overweight baggage 超重的行李
publish [ˈpʌblɪʃ]	*v.* 出版，发行（书、杂志等） 例 She had dedicated her life to writing detective fiction, and was about to publish her seventh novel. 她一生致力于写侦探小说，并即将出版她的第七部小说。 用 write and publish the poem 创作并发表这首诗 publish reference books 出版工具书 考 His recently published research answers the question of whether automation, AI and robotics will mean a "jobless future" by looking at the causes of unemployment. 他近期发表的研究通过分析造成失业的各种原因，回答了关于自动化、AI和机器人技术是否会意味着一个"没有工作的未来"这个问题。
infringe [ɪnˈfrɪndʒ]	*v.* 违反，违背（法规）；侵犯（权益） 例 It is important to respect intellectual property rights and not infringe upon others' creative work. 尊重知识产权、不侵犯他人的创造性工作是很重要的。 用 infringe his copyright 侵犯他的著作权
episode [ˈepɪsəʊd]	*n.* （电视剧的）一集；（人生的）一段经历；片段，插曲 例 The third episode in the second season of the series, is definitely the most exciting one. 这部电视剧的第二季第三集肯定是最激动人心的一集。 用 forget the whole episode 忘掉整段经历
simultaneous [ˌsɪmlˈteɪniəs]	*adj.* 同时的；同时发生的 例 Simultaneous interpretation involves listening to a language and translating it at the same time. 同声传译是在听一种语言的同时翻译它。 用 simultaneous interpretation 同声传译
instrument [ˈɪnstrəmənt]	*n.* 仪器；工具；乐器；手段 例 It's good for children to learn to play a musical instrument in school. 孩子们在学校学习演奏一种乐器是有好处的。 用 surgical instruments 外科手术器械 optical instruments 光学仪器

deserve [dɪˈzɜːv]	*v.* 应受，应得 例 She had studied hard and felt she deserved to do well in the final examination. 她学习非常努力，认为自己应该在期末考试中取得好成绩。 用 deserve to win 应当获胜
telepathy [təˈlepəθi]	*n.* 心灵感应 例 Some say that you can communicate messages from one person's mind to another's using telepathy. 有人说你可以通过心灵感应把一个人的想法传达给另一个人。 用 use telepathy 利用心灵感应
fade [feɪd]	*v.* 褪色；逐渐变暗；逐渐消失 例 The colours of the sunset gradually faded, leaving behind a serene twilight sky. 落日的余晖渐渐褪去，留下一片宁静的暮色。 用 a girl in a faded dress 一个穿褪色连衣裙的女孩
ingenuity [ˌɪndʒəˈnjuːəti]	*n.* 独创性；心灵手巧 例 Creativity and ingenuity are talents required to be a good programmer today. 创造力和独创性是当今优秀程序员需要的才能。 用 ingenuity in making toys 在做玩具方面有创造力 考 the ingenuity and artistry of ancient civilisations 古代文明的智慧与艺术
layout [ˈleɪaʊt]	*n.* 布局，设计；安排；陈列 例 The layout of the new apartments was appealing and offered a lot of space. 新公寓的布局很吸引人，提供了很大的空间。 用 the layout of streets 街道的布局
corrode [kəˈrəʊd]	*v.* 腐蚀，侵蚀；损害，破坏 例 The old metal fence began to rust and corrode due to prolonged exposure to moisture. 旧的金属栅栏由于长期暴露在湿气中，开始生锈和腐蚀。 用 corrode buildings 腐蚀建筑 扩 corrosion *n.* 腐蚀，侵蚀
contrive [kənˈtraɪv]	*v.* 谋划，策划；设计，发明 例 She tried to contrive a plan to surprise her friend on her birthday. 她试图想出一个计划，在她朋友生日那天给她一个惊喜。 用 contrive a plan to do it 精心策划要做这件事

wholesaler [ˈhəʊlseɪlə(r)]	*n.* 批发商
	例 The store owner purchased goods from the wholesaler to stock up on inventory for the season. 店主从批发商那里购买货物，以备当季使用。
	用 fruit and vegetable wholesalers 水果和蔬菜批发商
	扩 wholesale *n.* 批发 *adj.* 批发的
	考 I don't much like the fact, either, that they've travelled an average of 2,000 refrigerated kilometres to my plate, that their quality is so poor, because the varieties are selected for their capacity to withstand such substantial journeys, or that 80% of the price I pay goes to wholesalers and transport companies, not the producers. 我还不愿意看到，它们平均要经历2,000千米的冷藏旅途才能放在我的盘子上，以及它们的质量如此之差，因为对其种类的选择取决于它们能否扛得住如此长途跋涉的运输，还有我所支付价钱中的80%都给了批发商和运输公司，而不是它们的生产者。
compose [kəmˈpəʊz]	*v.* 组成，构成；创作（音乐），作曲
	例 Mozart composed many piano works when he was just a young boy. 莫扎特在年纪很小时就创作了许多钢琴作品。
	用 compose the committee 组成委员会
	扩 composition *n.* 成分；构成；作品；创作
	考 New Zealand is a small country with a visitor economy composed mainly of small businesses. 新西兰是一个小国家，游客经济主要由小型商家所组成。
brink [brɪŋk]	*n.* 边缘
	例 Scientists are on the brink of a fantastic new discovery in space—they believe there is a new planet in the solar system that has not been seen before. 科学家们即将有一项有关太空的了不起的新发现，他们相信太阳系中有一颗以前从未被发现的新行星。
	用 on the brink of making a new discovery 很快会有新发现
optimistic [ˌɒptɪˈmɪstɪk]	*adj.* 乐观的；乐观主义的
	例 After rehearsing a lot for the contest, she was very optimistic about her chances of winning. 在为比赛进行了大量练习之后，她对获胜的机会非常乐观。
	用 very optimistic about the outcome of the talks 对会谈的结果很乐观

deprive [dɪ'praɪv]	*v.* 使丧失，剥夺 例 When they did not select him to play in the basketball team he felt he had been deprived of an opportunity to participate. 当他们没有选他参加篮球队时，他觉得自己被剥夺了参与的机会。 用 be deprived of their basic rights 剥夺了他们的基本权利 考 With every bit of wilderness that disappears, we deprive ourselves of potential medicines. 随着每一片荒野的消失，我们都会失去潜在的药物。
turbine ['tɜːbaɪn]	*n.* 涡轮；涡轮机 例 Hot water is converted into electricity through a huge turbine engine. 热水通过一个巨大的涡轮发动机转化成电能。 用 gas turbines 燃气涡轮机 考 Nearly one fifth of all the electricity generated worldwide is produced by turbines spun by the power of falling water. 全世界近五分之一的电力是由利用落水动力旋转的涡轮机产生的。
propel [prə'pel]	*v.* 推进；驱使；激励 例 The boat was propelled through the water by an advanced engine and propellor mechanism. 这艘船由先进的发动机和螺旋桨装置推动着在水中前行。 用 mechanically propelled vehicles 机动车辆 扩 propeller *n.* 螺旋桨；推进器 考 wind power and ship propellers 风力和船舶螺旋桨
reluctant [rɪ'lʌktənt]	*adj.* 不情愿的；勉强的 例 My son didn't really like school and was always reluctant to get ready in the mornings. 我儿子不太喜欢上学，早上总是不愿意做好准备。 用 reluctant agreement 勉强同意
parallax ['pærəlæks]	*n.* 视差 例 This technique approximates the parallax that can be observed on uneven surfaces. 这种技术近似于在不平的表面上观察到的视差。 用 parallax correction 视差校正 考 examples of different ways in which the parallax principle has been applied 关于视差原理不同应用方式的举例

enable [ɪ'neɪbl]	*v.* 使能够；使成为可能
	例 The evidence they provided to the police should enable them to solve the mystery this week. 他们向警方提供的证据应该能使他们在本周解开这个谜。
	用 enable doctors to detect the disease early 使医生们尽早查出疾病
	扩 unable *adj.* 不可以的，不能的
numerous ['njuːmərəs]	*adj.* 许多的，很多的
	例 There are numerous different kinds of protected birds and plants at the national park. 国家公园里有许多不同种类受保护的鸟类和植物。
	用 on numerous occasions 在很多场合
ethereal [ɪ'θɪəriəl]	*adj.* 优雅的；轻飘的；超凡的
	例 The ethereal music seemed to transport the listeners to another world. 空灵的音乐似乎把听众带到了另一个世界。
	用 ethereal music 优雅的音乐 the prettiest, most ethereal romantic heroine in the movies 那些电影中最美丽、最优雅浪漫的女主角
heyday ['heɪdeɪ]	*n.* 全盛期
	例 She was a fantastic singer in her heyday, back in the 1970s. 在20世纪70年代，她作为一位出色的歌手达到了自己的全盛时期。
	用 the heyday of Italian cinema 意大利电影的全盛期
	考 at the very beginning of the heyday of the middle class 在中产阶级的全盛期刚开始的时候
construct [kən'strʌkt] *v.* ['kɒnstrʌkt] *n.*	*v.* 建造；组成，创建 *n.* 构想；概念
	例 There are plans to construct a new bridge across the river. 有计划在这条河上建一座新桥。
	用 construct a theory 创立一种理论 a well-constructed novel 一本构思巧妙的小说
	扩 construction *n.* 建设；建筑物
	考 His idea was to relocate the poor workers who lived in the inner-city slums to newly constructed suburbs, and to provide cheap rail travel for them to get to work. 他的想法是将住在内城贫民窟里的贫困工人们转移到新建的郊区去住，并为他们提供廉价的铁路交通供其通勤使用。

obstacle

['ɒbstəkl]

n. 障碍；干扰；障碍物

例 The new mother faced an obstacle of providing time for her newborn baby while having a time-consuming job.

这位新妈妈面临的一个难题是，花时间工作的同时还要留出空来照顾孩子。

用 overcome all the obstacles 排除一切障碍

考 They hunt at night, and cannot use light to help them find prey and avoid obstacles.

他们在夜间捕猎，无法利用光亮帮助自己找寻猎物和避开障碍物。

Exercise 24

一、中文释义练习

请选择单词正确的中文释义。

_____ 1. epidemic   A. 指定   _____ 11. instrument   A. 边缘

_____ 2. designate   B. 传染病   _____ 12. telepathy   B. 涡轮

_____ 3. horizon   C. 寿命   _____ 13. corrode   C. 腐蚀

_____ 4. lifespan   D. 地平线   _____ 14. brink   D. 心灵感应

_____ 5. lever   E. 杠杆   _____ 15. turbine   E. 仪器

_____ 6. linear   A. 侵犯   _____ 16. propel   A. 推进

_____ 7. persevere   B. 直觉   _____ 17. reluctant   B. 视差

_____ 8. adhere   C. 直线的   _____ 18. parallax   C. 不情愿的

_____ 9. intuition   D. 依附   _____ 19. numerous   D. 全盛期

_____ 10. infringe   E. 坚持   _____ 20. heyday   E. 许多的

二、英文释义练习

请选择单词正确的英文释义。

_____ 1. resign   A. to officially leaving your job from an organization

_____ 2. gist   B. the main or general meaning of a piece of writing

_____ 3. transparent   C. the outer layer of an organ in the brain

_____ 4. paradox   D. allowing sb. to see through sth.

_____ 5. cortex   E. a person or situation that has two opposite features

_____ 6. episode   A. buy large quantities of goods, sell in smaller amounts

_____ 7. ingenuity   B. an event or a situation in sb.'s life or a novel

_____ 8. wholesaler   C. the ability to invent things in clever new ways

_____ 9. deprive   D. a situation that makes it difficult for you to do sth.

_____ 10. obstacle   E. to prevent sb. from having or doing sth. important

mingle ['mɪŋgl]	v. （使）混合；交际
	例 At the party, guests had the opportunity to mingle and socialize with each other. 在聚会上，客人们有机会互相交流和社交。
	用 feel a kind of happiness mingled with regret 感到既高兴又遗憾

feature ['fiːtʃə(r)]	n. 特色，特征；容貌 v. 以……为特色；由……主演；以……为主要组成；起作用
	例 Teamwork is a key feature of the training programme. 团队合作是该培训项目的一个重要特点。
	用 geographical features 地理特征 the most striking feature 最显著的特征

dome [dəum]	n. 穹顶，圆屋顶
	例 The magnificent dome adorned the grand cathedral, its intricate details captivating visitors. 宏伟的圆顶装饰着大教堂，其复杂的细节吸引着游客。
	用 the dome of St Paul's Cathedral 圣保罗大教堂的穹顶

skeleton ['skelɪtn]	n. 骨架，骨骼；梗概；（楼房或计划的）构架，框架
	例 Bones of the dinosaur skeleton helped archaeologists determine the extinct animal's height and weight. 恐龙骨骼化石帮助考古学家确定这种已灭绝动物的身高和体重。
	用 a dinosaur skeleton 恐龙骨架 the concrete skeleton of the factory 厂房的混凝土结构

remote [rɪ'məut]	adj. 遥远的；偏僻的；远程的
	例 The old man lived in a very remote location in the countryside. 那位老人住在乡下一个非常偏远的地方。
	用 in the remote past 在遥远的过去

marble ['mɑːbl]	n. 大理石；大理石雕像
	例 The elegant statue was carved from exquisite white marble. 这座优雅的雕像是用精美的白色大理石雕刻而成的。
	用 a slab of marble 一块大理石板 a marble sculpture 一座大理石雕像

bias
['baɪəs]

n. 偏见；偏爱；偏误

例 She was not objective at all—she had a clear bias against people from certain places.

她一点也不客观，对来自某些地方的人有明显的偏见。

用 bias against 对……有偏见

同 prejudice *n.* 偏见

locomotive
[ˌləʊkə'məʊtɪv]

n. 机车，火车头 *adj.* 移动的，运动的

例 The powerful locomotive pulled the long train, chugging steadily along the tracks.

有力的火车头拉着长长的火车，沿着轨道平稳行进。

用 a diesel locomotive 一辆柴油机车

考 This might involve trying to see every locomotive of a particular type, using published data that identifies each one, and ticking off each engine as it is seen.

这包括通过使用每一类火车已发布的数据，试着认识某一类型的所有火车，并且认识看到的每一个火车引擎。

cereal
['sɪərɪəl]

n. 谷类食物；谷类植物

例 She poured milk over her favorite cereal, enjoying a nutritious and delicious breakfast.

她把牛奶倒在最喜欢的麦片上，享受着一顿营养又美味的早餐。

用 have a bowl of cereal every morning 每天早上吃一碗麦片粥

the cereal-growing districts 生产谷类植物的地区

cabin
['kæbɪn]

n. 小木屋；船舱；机舱

例 The cabin provided a comfortable retreat in the mountains, and was equipped with great facilities.

这间小屋提供了舒适的山间静修处，并配备了很棒的设施。

用 a log cabin 一间小木屋

haul
[hɔːl]

v. 拖，拉，拽；费力前进，艰难地走

例 The workers helped haul heavy crates onto the truck, ready for transportation.

工人们帮忙把沉重的板条箱拖上卡车，准备运输。

用 haul the car out of the stream 把轿车从河里拉出来

考 How, then, did prehistoric builders without sophisticated tools or engineering haul these boulders, which weigh up to four tons, over such a great distance?

那么，并没有发达工具或工程技术的史前建造者们是如何将这些重量高达4吨的巨大石块拖拽了如此遥远的距离呢？

endanger [ɪnˈdeɪndʒə(r)]	*v.* 危及，使处于险境
	例 Smoking endangers your health and the health of those around you. 吸烟危害你和你周围人的健康。
	用 endangered species 濒危物种
	考 list endangered ocean species 列出濒临灭绝的海洋物种

spin [spɪn]	*v./n.* 快速旋转；转身
	例 The skilled gymnast executed a flawless double spin in the contest. 这位技能娴熟的体操运动员在比赛中完成了完美的双周旋转动作。
	用 spin a wheel 转动轮子
	考 the spinning wheel 纺车

effect [ɪˈfekt]	*n.* 影响；效果；作用
	例 The effects of global warming are being felt by people all across the globe. 全球各地的人们都感受到了全球变暖的影响。
	用 the effect of heat on metal 热对金属产生的影响
	扩 effective *adj.* 有效的 efficient *adj.* 高效的 efficiently *adv.* 高效地 efficiency *n.* 效率
	考 the effects of emotion, imagination and the unconscious on learning 情绪、想象力和无意识对学习的影响

synchronous [ˈsɪŋkrənəs]	*adj.* 同步的；同时的
	例 Online communication is a lot more effective now as we have synchronous real-time video calling utilities for meetings. 现在在线交流更加有效，因为我们有了会议的实时同步视频通话工具。
	用 synchronous sound effects 同步音效
	扩 synchronise *v.* 同步；同时发生；校准
	考 Synchronous sound effects are those sounds which are synchronised or matched with what is viewed. 同步音效是那些与观看内容同步或匹配的声音。

inspire [ɪnˈspaɪə(r)]	*v.* 鼓舞；启示；产生灵感
	例 He was deeply inspired by the countryside and painted a series of works dedicated to the landscapes there. 他深受乡村生活的启发，创作了一系列作品，描绘那里的景色。
	用 inspire the kids 鼓舞孩子们
	扩 inspiration *n.* 灵感；鼓舞人心的事
	考 Writers and artists have also been inspired by the stoics. 作家和艺术家也受到了斯多葛学派的启发。

function ['fʌŋkʃn]	*n.* 功能，作用；宴会，典礼 *v.* 运转，起作用
	例 The main function of the heart is to pump blood around the body. 心脏的主要功能是把血液注入到全身各处。
	用 a venue for weddings and other functions 婚礼和其他宴会活动的场所
	考 Each of these three functions utilizes a different circuit in the brain. 这三种功能的每一个都用到不同的大脑回路。

substitute ['sʌbstɪtjuːt]	*n.* 代替品；代替者 *v.* 用……代替，取代
	例 You can substitute butter for oil in this recipe to make it healthier. 在这份食谱中，你可以用黄油代替油，来使其更加健康。
	用 a meat substitute 肉食替代品
	扩 substitution *n.* 替代；替代物
	考 Silbo is a substitute for Spanish, with individual words recoded into whistles which have high and low-frequency tones. Silbo是西班牙语的替代品，每个单词都被重新编码成带有高低频音调的口哨声。

lend [lend]	*v.* 借给，借出；贷款
	例 Some people do not like to lend others money because they fear they will not get it back. 有些人不喜欢借钱给别人，因为他们担心以后拿不回这笔钱。
	用 lend the car to a friend 把车借给一位朋友
	同 loan *v.* 贷款

synthesis ['sɪnθəsɪs]	*n.* 综合；合成
	例 Proteins are essential to the synthesis of muscles and body tissue. 蛋白质对肌肉和身体组织的合成是至关重要的。
	用 a synthesis of traditional and modern values 传统与现代价值观的结合
	扩 synthetic *adj.* 合成的；综合的 synthetic fertiliser 合成肥料

insight ['ɪnsaɪt]	*n.* 洞察力；洞悉
	例 His insights into the complex political situation were invaluable for the negotiations. 他对复杂政治形势的洞察对谈判而言是无价的。
	用 a writer of great insight 一位有深刻洞察力的作家

vague [veɪg]	*adj.* 不清楚的；模糊的
	例 His vague explanation left us confused about his intentions. 他含糊的解释使我们对他的意图感到困惑。
	用 have a vague idea where the place was 大概知道那个地方的位置

gesture ['dʒestʃə(r)]	*n.* 姿态；手势
	例 The teacher was upset when the student made a rude gesture at her in class. 当那个学生在课堂上对老师做出粗鲁的手势时，老师很生气。
	用 communicate entirely by gesture 完全用手势交流

disability [ˌdɪsə'bɪləti]	*n.* 残疾；无能力；无资格
	例 It's difficult for people with disabilities to find certain kinds of work. 身患残疾的人很难获得某些特定类型的工作。
	用 people with severe learning disabilities 具有严重学习障碍的人
	扩 disable *v.* 使无能力；使残疾

tactic ['tæktɪk]	*n.* 策略，手法；战术
	例 She was nervous about the outcome so she decided on a stalling tactic to delay negotiations. 她为结果而紧张，因而决定采取拖延策略来延迟谈判。
	用 a change of tactic 改变策略

sketch [sketʃ]	*n.* 素描，速写；草图，略图 *v.* 画素描；简述，概述
	例 She was not very good at painting, but was excellent at sketching with a pencil. 她不太擅长绘画，但擅长用铅笔素描。
	用 a sketch map of the area 一幅这个地区的草图

arithmetic [ə'rɪθmətɪk]	*n.* 算术，算法；计算；数据
	例 The basic skills of reading, writing and arithmetic are as important in education today, as they were in the past. 阅读、写作和算术等基本能力在现今的教育中与过去一样重要。
	用 mental arithmetic 心算
	类 mathematics *n.* 数学 algebra *n.* 代数 geometry *n.* 几何 equation *n.* 方程 coordinate system 坐标系

attribute [ə'trɪbjuːt] *v.* [ˈætrɪbjuːt] *n.*	*v.* 把……归因于；认为是……所作 *n.* 属性；特质
	例 He attributed his successes to the strong influence and teachings of his father. 他把自己的成功归功于父亲的强大影响和教导。
	用 attribute to 归因于
	考 We can, perhaps, attribute mediocre results to an inadequate placebo effect. 或许，我们可以将平庸的结果归结于安慰剂效应的不足。

imperative [ɪmˈperətɪv]	*adj.* 必要的；紧急的；表示命令的 *n.* 必要的事；紧迫的事 例 It's imperative that you study the Highway Code when you are doing your driving theory test. 当你要进行驾驶理论考试时，学习公路法规是非常必要的。 用 an imperative tone 命令的语调 be imperative to continue the treatment 必须继续治疗
exploit [ɪkˈsplɔɪt]	*v.* 开发，开采；利用；剥削，压榨 例 It's a good thing to exploit every opportunity we are given to learn new things. 利用我们得到的每一个机会学习新事物是件好事。 用 exploit the rainforests for hardwood 为获取硬木材而开发雨林
hinge [hɪndʒ]	*n.* 铰链；合页 *v.* 装铰链 例 We had to take the front door off its hinges to get our new bed into the house. 我们不得不把前门从合页上卸下来才把新的床搬进屋子里。 用 well-oiled hinges 上好油的合页
novice [ˈnɒvɪs]	*n.* 初学者，新手 例 As a novice in the kitchen, he followed the recipe carefully to avoid mistakes. 作为厨房新手，他仔细地按照菜谱操作，以免出错。 用 a complete novice at skiing 一个滑雪新手
rim [rɪm]	*n.* （圆形物体的）边沿；（篮球的）篮筐 例 The basketball bounced on the rim before finally going through the net, scoring a point. 篮球在篮筐上弹跳，最后进网，获得一分。 用 spectacles with gold rims 金框眼镜
polish [ˈpɒlɪʃ]	*v.* 抛光，磨光；改进，润色 *n.* 抛光；上光剂 例 He polished his new bike with a special all-weather protection polish. 他用一种特殊的全天候保护上光剂把他的新自行车擦亮了。 用 furniture polish 家具上光漆
anchor [ˈæŋkə(r)]	*n.* 锚；精神支柱，顶梁柱 *v.* 抛锚；使固定 例 The heavy anchor kept the ship steady during the storm. 沉重的锚使船在暴风雨中保持稳定。 用 drop anchor 抛锚 the anchor of the family 全家的顶梁柱

reap
[riːp]

v. 收获，获得；收割

例 People often say "you reap what you sow", to mean that the efforts you put into something, are rewarded accordingly.
人们常说"一分耕耘，一分收获"，意思是你付出努力，就会得到相应的回报。

用 reap the benefits of being fitter 获得身体更健康带来的好处

同 harvest v. 收获

类 output n. 产量 barn n. 谷仓 warehouse n. 仓库 prolific adj. 多产的

reiterate
[riˈɪtəreɪt]

v. 重申，反复说

例 He had to reiterate his point multiple times before it was fully understood.
他不得不多次重申他的观点，大家才完全理解。

用 reiterate an argument 重申观点

dilute
[daɪˈluːt]

v. 稀释，冲淡；降低

例 The cleaning detergent is incredibly strong, so it's better to dilute it with water before use.
这种清洁剂效果很强，所以最好在使用前用水稀释。

用 dilute the quality of education 降低教育质量

laboratory
[ləˈbɒrətri]

n. 实验室，研究室

例 The laboratory in the university had all the latest scientific equipment.
这所大学的实验室拥有全部最新的科学仪器。

用 a research laboratory 研究实验室

考 an excellent laboratory for testing theories of economic growth
检验经济增长理论的优秀实验室

deficit
[ˈdefɪsɪt]

n. 赤字，亏损；不足，缺乏

例 They had a financial meeting to discuss the budget deficit.
他们开了一个财务会议，讨论预算赤字问题。

用 trade deficit 贸易逆差
cut the federal budget deficit for the next fiscal year
削减下一财年的联邦预算赤字

hedge
[hedʒ]

n. 树篱；防范手段 v. 包围，限制

例 The tall, thick hedge that surrounded the garden provided privacy for the property.
花园周围又高又厚的树篱为房子提供了隐私。

用 buy gold as a hedge against inflation
购买黄金以抵消通货膨胀造成的损失

solid ['sɒlɪd]	*adj.* 固体的；可靠的 *n.* 固体；立方体 例 Water becomes solid and turns to ice when it reaches zero degrees. 水在达到零摄氏度时会变成固体，结成冰。 用 solid evidence 确凿的证据 扩 solidify *v.* 使凝聚；固化
prosper ['prɒspə(r)]	*v.* 繁荣，兴旺，蓬勃发展 例 After putting more time, energy and money into marketing, the business started to prosper. 在把更多时间、精力和资金投入到营销方面后，业务开始快速发展。 用 continue to prosper 持续繁荣发展 同 thrive *v.* 繁荣，兴旺 扩 prosperity *n.* 繁荣 prosperous *adj.* 繁荣的
prominent ['prɒmɪnənt]	*adj.* 突出的，显著的；杰出的 例 She was a prominent figure in the national fashion industry. 她是国内时尚业的杰出人物。 用 a prominent politician 一位杰出的政治家
foresee [fɔː'siː]	*v.* 预见；预知 例 He did not blame himself, because it was impossible to foresee the events. 他没有责怪自己，因为事情是不可能预知的。 用 foresee potential problems 预见潜在问题 同 predict *v.* 预测 forecast *v.* 预测 考 reference to an unforeseen problem arising from ignoring the climate 提到由于忽视气候而导致的一种不可预见的问题
render ['rendə(r)]	*v.* 致使，使成为，使变得；提供；递交 例 The report contained so many errors and untrue facts that it was rendered useless. 这篇报告有许多错误和不实信息，这使其毫无用处。 用 render it ineffective 使其失效
obsession [əb'seʃn]	*n.* 痴迷；困扰；令人着迷的人（或事物） 例 You should be careful not to let this interest of yours become an overriding obsession. 你应该小心不要让自己的兴趣成为压倒一切的痴迷。 用 one's obsession with 对……的痴迷 考 New research suggests that this obsession with efficiency is misguided. 新的研究表明，这种对效率的痴迷是错误的。

modest
['mɒdɪst']

adj. 谦虚的，谦逊的；适度的

例 She was noted for being modest and was not the type of person to show off about her achievements.
她以谦虚著称，不是那种会炫耀自己成就的人。

用 a modest reform 一场温和的改革

反 radical *adj.* 激进的

扩 modesty *n.* 谦虚，谦逊

stride
[straɪd]

n. 大步；步伐；进展 *v.* 大步走，阔步走

例 The wrestler walked into the ring with a strong and confident stride.
摔跤手迈着有力而自信的大步走进了拳击场。

用 stride across the snowy fields 大步穿过被白雪覆盖的旷野

aisle
[aɪl]

n. 走廊，过道

例 They walked down the grocery store aisle, carefully selecting items for their shopping list.
他们走过杂货店的过道，仔细挑选购物清单中的商品。

用 an aisle seat 紧靠过道的座位

Exercise 25

一、中文释义练习

请选择单词正确的中文释义。

_____ 1. dome   A. 谷类食物
_____ 2. locomotive   B. 机车
_____ 3. cereal   C. 大理石
_____ 4. cabin   D. 船舱
_____ 5. marble   E. 圆屋顶

_____ 11. sketch   A. 边沿
_____ 12. imperative   B. 合页
_____ 13. hinge   C. 必要的
_____ 14. rim   D. 锚
_____ 15. anchor   E. 概述

_____ 6. spin   A. 快速旋转
_____ 7. inspire   B. 综合
_____ 8. function   C. 不清楚的
_____ 9. synthesis   D. 功能
_____ 10. vague   E. 鼓舞

_____ 16. solid   A. 预见
_____ 17. foresee   B. 实施
_____ 18. render   C. 走廊
_____ 19. obsession   D. 固体的
_____ 20. aisle   E. 痴迷

二、英文释义练习

请选择单词正确的英文释义。

_____ 1. skeleton   A. happening or existing at the same time
_____ 2. endanger   B. the ability to see and understand the truth
_____ 3. synchronous   C. to put sb. in a situation where they could be harmed
_____ 4. substitute   D. the structure of bones that supports the body
_____ 5. insight   E. a thing you use instead of the one you normally use

_____ 6. tactic   A. the particular method you use to achieve sth.
_____ 7. arithmetic   B. to develop in a successful way
_____ 8. polish   C. dealing with the adding or multiplying of numbers
_____ 9. dilute   D. to make a liquid weaker by adding water to it
_____ 10. prosper   E. rubbing a surface to make it smooth and shiny

contrast ['kɒntrɑːst] *n.* [kən'trɑːst] *v.*	*n./v.* 对比，对照
	例 I love the contrast between the golden corn fields and the light blue cloudless sky.
	我喜欢金黄的玉米田和淡蓝色无云天空之间的对比。
	用 show a striking contrast with sth. 与某事物形成显著的对比

empathy ['empəθi]	*n.* 同情；同理心；共情
	例 She lacked empathy and didn't usually consider other people's feelings.
	她缺乏同理心，不能总是考虑到他人的感受。
	用 empathy for other people's situations 对他人所处境况的同情

immerse [ɪ'mɜːs]	*v.* 沉浸；使陷入
	例 She got a pile of books from the library and immersed herself in French literature in order to widen her vocabulary.
	为了扩充自己的词汇量，她从图书馆拿了一堆书，沉浸于法国文学中。
	用 immerse herself in her work 沉浸在她的工作中

foster ['fɒstə(r)]	*v.* 促进；培养；抚育
	例 The school aims to foster an environment of motivation and encouragement amongst staff and students.
	学校希望在教职人员和学生中建立一个充满激励和鼓励的环境。
	用 foster better relations 促进更好的关系
	考 foster a warm and damp environment 培养温暖潮湿的环境

refund ['riːfʌnd] *n.* [rɪ'fʌnd] *v.*	*n.* 退款；偿还金额 *v.* 退款；退还，偿还
	例 Now if you buy things online and they arrive in poor condition or are damaged, you can usually get a refund.
	现在，如果你在网上购买商品，而收到时它们状况不佳或者出现损坏，你通常可以得到退款。
	用 a tax refund 税款退还

orchestra [ˈɔːkɪstrə]	*n.* 管弦乐队 例 The symphony orchestra filled the concert hall with beautiful melodies and harmonies. 交响乐团使音乐厅充满了优美的旋律和和声。 用 play the flute in the school orchestra 在校管弦乐队里吹长笛 考 As a composer, she has received commissions from numerous orchestras, other performers and festivals in several countries. 作为一名作曲家，她收到了来自一些国家的众多管弦乐队、其他表演者和各种音乐节的创作佣金。
entity [ˈentəti]	*n.* 实体；存在 例 The United Nations is an international entity, or organization, consisting of 193 member states, that aims to improve global cooperation. 联合国是一个国际实体，或者说组织，由193个成员国组成，旨在促进全球合作。 用 a separate entity 一个独立实体
miracle [ˈmɪrəkl]	*n.* 奇迹 *adj.* 神奇的 例 The unexpected recovery of the patient was hailed as a medical miracle. 这位病人的意外康复被誉为医学中的奇迹。 用 an economic miracle 经济方面的奇迹
boundary [ˈbaʊndri]	*n.* 边界；范围；分界线 例 There was a clear boundary between the road and the edge of the cliff. 道路和悬崖边缘之间有一条清晰的分界线。 用 national boundaries 国界 boundary disputes 边界争端
refine [rɪˈfaɪn]	*v.* 精炼，提纯；改善 例 She practiced a lot to refine her dance movements for the performance. 她为演出进行了大量练习，来改进自己的舞蹈动作。 用 the process of refining oil 炼油的流程 扩 refinery *n.* 精炼厂，提炼厂
impede [ɪmˈpiːd]	*v.* 阻碍，妨碍；阻止 例 He had no torch, but the darkness did not impede his progress. 他没有手电筒，但黑暗并没有妨碍他前进。 用 be impeded by severe weather 因天气恶劣而停下来 同 hamper *v.* 妨碍，阻碍

illusion [ɪ'luːʒn]	*n.* 幻觉，错觉 例 I thought that the river was really deep then I realised it was a kind of illusion, because of the way the light was on the water. 我以为河水很深，然后我意识到这是一种错觉，这是由光线照在水面上的方式造成的。 用 an optical illusion 视觉错觉 distinguish between illusion and reality 区分幻想与现实
agile ['ædʒaɪl]	*adj.* 敏捷的，灵活的 例 The agile gymnast effortlessly performed stunning routines on the balance beam. 敏捷的体操运动员轻松地在平衡木上表演令人惊叹的动作。 用 an agile mind 敏捷的思维
mortgage ['mɔːgɪdʒ]	*n.* 按揭，抵押贷款 *v.* 抵押 例 They applied for a mortgage to purchase their dream home. 他们申请抵押贷款来购买他们梦想中的房子。 用 a mortgage on the house 一项房产按揭 monthly mortgage repayments 每月偿还的按揭贷款
counterpart ['kaʊntəpɑːt]	*n.* 职位（或作用）相当的人；对应的事物 例 The British ambassador's counterpart in Russia was in agreement with the proposal. 英国驻俄罗斯大使对这一提议表示赞同。 用 his counterpart in Italy 在意大利与他对应的人 扩 counterproductive *adj.* 有相反效果的
wedge [wedʒ]	*n.* 楔子；楔形物 *v.*（将……）楔入，插入 例 He used a wedge to keep the door open while he carried in the heavy boxes. 他把沉重的箱子搬进去时，用一个楔子卡住了门。 用 hammer the wedge into the crack in the stone 用锤子把楔子砸入石缝里
modify ['mɒdɪfaɪ]	*v.* 修改；修饰；更改 例 The design of the rally car had to be modified in order that the vehicle could drive longer distances on rough terrain. 拉力赛车的设计必须进行修改，以便车辆能够在崎岖的道路上行驶更长距离。 用 modify their diet 调节他们的饮食 扩 modification *n.* 修改，更改

pump [pʌmp]	*n.* 抽水机，泵；打气筒 *v.*（用泵）抽出，注入，输送
	例 He used a bicycle pump to inflate the tires before embarking on a long ride. 在开始长途骑行前，他用自行车打气筒给轮胎打了气。
	用 a petrol pump 汽油泵
	考 Produce grown using this soil-free method, on the other hand—which relies solely on a small quantity of water, enriched with organic nutrients, pumped around a closed circuit of pipes, towers and trays—is "produced up here, and sold locally, just down there". 而另一方面，用这种无土栽培的方法——也就是完全依靠少量的水，其中添加了一些有机营养元素，通过一套管道、塔架和托盘组成的封闭式回路输送灌溉——所培育出来的农产品，则是"在上面这里生产，在本地售卖，直接送到下面那里"。

profound [prə'faʊnd]	*adj.* 深厚的；意义深远的；巨大的
	例 The lecture gave profound insights into the topic that he had not considered before. 这场演讲对他之前没有考虑过的问题进行了深刻的洞悉。
	用 profound changes 巨大变化

impair [ɪm'peə(r)]	*v.* 损害；削弱；减少
	例 Tiredness can seriously impair your ability to drive a car safely. 疲劳会严重损害你安全驾驶汽车的能力。
	用 permanently impaired hearing 永久性听力损伤

sledge [sledʒ]	*n.* 雪橇 *v.* 乘雪橇；用雪橇搬运
	例 The team used a sturdy sledge to transport supplies across the snowy terrain. 队伍使用结实的雪橇在雪地上运送物资。
	用 travelled 2,000 kilometres by sledge 乘雪橇穿越2,000千米

loan [ləʊn]	*n.* 贷款；借款 *v.* 借出
	例 They had a real struggle paying back the huge loan they took out to put their son through university. 他们挣扎于努力偿还供儿子读大学而支付的巨额贷款。
	用 bank loans with low interest rates 银行低息贷款 take out a loan 取得贷款 repay a loan 偿还贷款
	考 There is a restricted loan time on these so that they are not missing from the shelves for too long. 它们被借出的时间是有限制的，因此不会在书架上消失太久。

leak [liːk]	*v.* 泄露；渗漏 *n.* 漏洞；裂缝；泄漏
	例 There was a water leak somewhere in the roof of the house, and water came seeping down through the ceiling. 房顶上有漏水的地方，水通过天花板渗了下来。
	用 a leaking pipe 渗漏的管道 a leaked document 泄密的文件
	同 disclose *v.* 揭露；公开
	扩 leakage *n.* 泄漏；透露
apparent [ə'pærənt]	*adj.* 显然的；表面上的
	例 Her unhappiness was very apparent, although she tried to hide it. 她的不开心是很明显的，尽管她试图掩饰。
	用 my apparent lack of enthusiasm 我明显缺乏热情
	同 obvious *adj.* 明显的
	考 apparent biological purpose 明显的生物学目的
transit ['trænzɪt]	*n.* 运输；经过，通过 *v.* 经过，穿过
	例 When you fly from Beijing to Madrid, you can transit in Dubai, Moscow or Amsterdam, depending on which airline you fly with. 当你从北京飞往马德里，你会经过迪拜、莫斯科或是阿姆斯特丹，这取决于你所选择的航线。
	用 the transit of goods between two countries 两国间的货物运输
	考 Venus in transit 金星凌日
detain [dɪ'teɪn]	*v.* 拘留，扣押；耽搁
	例 The police detained the suspect for several days for questioning. 警察拘留了犯罪嫌疑人几天进行审问。
	用 be detained for questioning 被拘捕接受问询
destruction [dɪ'strʌkʃn]	*n.* 破坏，毁灭，摧毁
	例 The level of destruction caused by the floods was enormous. 洪水造成的破坏程度是巨大的。
	用 the destruction of rainforests 对热带雨林的破坏
	扩 destruct *v.* 破坏
bay [beɪ]	*n.* 海湾，湖湾
	例 The boat sailed peacefully in the calm waters of the bay. 小船在海湾平稳的水面上平静地航行。
	用 a magnificent view across the bay 海湾对面的壮观景象
spray [spreɪ]	*n.* 喷雾；水花，飞沫 *v.* 喷射，喷洒
	例 He sprayed an insect repellant over his body to ward off mosquitoes. 他在身上喷了驱虫剂以驱除蚊子。
	用 a can of insect spray 一罐杀虫喷雾

ascribe
[ə'skraɪb]

v. 归因于；归咎于

例 She ascribed her success in music to the influence of her father.
她将自己在音乐上的成功归因于父亲的影响。

用 ascribe to 归因于

同 attribute *v.* 归因于

estimate
['estɪmeɪt] *v.*
['estɪmət] *n.*

v. 估计，估量；判断 *n.* 估计，估价；判断

例 I estimate that the new construction will cost the company over a million dollars.
我估计新建筑将给公司带来一百多万美元的开支。

用 a rough estimate of the amount of wood you will need
粗略估计一下你所需要的木材量

扩 underestimate *v.* 低估 overestimate *v.* 高估

ripe
[raɪp]

adj. 成熟的

例 The fruit was perfectly ripe, exuding a sweet aroma and offering a burst of juicy flavour.
水果完全成熟，散发出甜美的香气，并产生了多汁的口味。

用 four ripe tomatoes 四个成熟的西红柿

handout
['hændaʊt]

n. 传单，宣传材料；讲义

例 The teacher listed all the important reading materials in a handout she gave to the class.
老师把所有重要的阅读材料都列在了发给班级的讲义上。

用 distribute handouts 分发讲义

类 coursebook *n.* 教材 curriculum *n.* 课程

suspense
[sə'spens]

n. 焦虑，悬念；悬而不决

例 I love watching thriller and horror movies because I enjoy the sense of suspense that builds up.
我喜欢看惊悚和恐怖电影，因为我喜欢由此产生的悬疑感。

用 a tale of mystery and suspense 一个神秘而充满悬念的故事

扩 suspend *v.* 暂停；延缓

catastrophe
[kə'tæstrəfi]

n. 大灾难；灾祸

例 Countries are taking great environmental steps to avoid a climate catastrophe.
各国正在采取重要的环境措施，以避免气候灾难。

用 an environmental catastrophe 一场环境灾难

同 disaster *n.* 灾难

扩 catastrophic *adj.* 灾难性的 catastrophic effects 灾难性的影响

evolve [ɪ'vɒlv]	*v.* 发展；进化
	例 It's interesting to consider that we likely evolved from lifeforms in the sea billions of years ago. 有趣的是，我们很可能是从数十亿年前的海洋生物进化而来的。
	用 evolve into a major chemical manufacturer 发展成一家大型化工厂
	扩 evolution *n.* 进化；发展

diverse [daɪ'vɜːs]	*adj.* 不同的，多种多样的
	例 A multi-cultural and diverse workforce is proven to make teams more effective. 具备多元文化和多样性的员工们被证明能够使团队协作更有效。
	用 people from diverse cultures 不同文化背景的人

digital ['dɪdʒɪtl]	*adj.* 数字的，数码的
	例 We are living in the middle of an exciting digital revolution, and are witnessing so many new technological advances. 我们生活在一场令人兴奋的数字革命中，正在目睹许多新的技术进步。
	用 a digital camera 一台数码照相机

dock [dɒk]	*n.* 码头，船坞 *v.* （使船）进港，停靠码头
	例 The ship slowly approached the dock, ready to unload its cargo and begin its next voyage. 船慢慢靠近码头，准备卸货，开始下一次航行。
	用 dock workers 码头工人

acknowledge [ək'nɒlɪdʒ]	*v.* 承认，认可
	例 She felt that her success had been finally acknowledged when they handed her the award. 当他们给她颁奖时，她感觉自己的成功终于得到了承认。
	用 a generally acknowledged fact 一个公认的事实
	考 The book also acknowledges that our attitude towards bacteria is not a simple one. 这本书同样承认我们对于细菌的态度并不是一个简单的话题。

contract ['kɒntrækt] *n.* [kən'trækt] *v.*	*n.* 合同；合约 *v.* （使）收缩；感染（疾病）
	例 The Human Resources department will prepare two copies of contract for you. 人力资源部会为你准备两份合同。
	用 sign a contract 签订合同
	扩 contraction *n.* 收缩；缩减

mansion ['mænʃn]	*n.* 大厦，宅邸；公寓楼
	例 The wealthy entrepreneur owned a grand mansion with a stunning view. 这位富有的企业家拥有一座风景优美的大厦。
	用 an eighteenth-century mansion in Sydney 悉尼一座18世纪的大厦
prolong [prə'lɒŋ]	*v.* 延长；拖延
	例 If you eat healthy foods you will certainly prolong your life. 如果你的饮食很健康，那么显然你的寿命会被延长。
	用 prolonged the war 拉长了战事
	同 extend *v.* 延长；延伸
cement [sɪ'ment]	*n.* 水泥；胶合剂 *v.* 粘合；巩固，加强
	例 The construction workers mixed cement to create a solid foundation for the building. 建筑工人搅拌水泥，为大楼打下坚实的基础。
	用 a cement floor 水泥地板
	考 Cement is high carbon, but concrete is not. 水泥是高碳的，但是混凝土不是。
sore [sɔː(r)]	*adj.* 疼痛的；痛苦的；恼火的 *n.* 伤处，痛处
	例 Her sore muscles ached for days after a strenuous workout at the gym. 在健身房剧烈锻炼后，她的肌肉酸痛了好几天。
	用 have a sore throat 嗓子疼
monotonous [mə'nɒtənəs]	*adj.* 单调乏味的；无变化的
	例 He found learning vocabulary terribly boring and monotonous. 他觉得学习词汇非常无聊和单调。
	用 monotonous work 单调乏味的工作
	同 dull *adj.* 单调的 repetitious *adj.* 重复的
	扩 monopoly *n.* 垄断 monologue *n.* 独白 monolingual *adj.* 使用一种语言的
ritual ['rɪtʃuəl]	*n.* 仪式；惯例；礼制
	例 Some religions have very elaborate rituals and ceremonies. 有些宗教有非常复杂的仪式和庆典。
	用 religious rituals 宗教仪式
buckle ['bʌkl]	*n.* 搭扣，锁扣 *v.* 扣紧；使弯曲；（腿、膝）发软
	例 She fastened the seatbelt buckle before starting the car. 她在发动汽车前系好了安全带扣。
	用 a belt with a large brass buckle 一根有很大黄铜扣的皮带

monologue [ˈmɒnəlɒɡ]	*n.* 独白；长篇大论
	例 She always talked so much, and often she would launch into long monologues about her opinions on issues. 她总是滔滔不绝，经常就一些问题长篇大论讲述自己的观点。
	用 a long monologue about life in America 滔滔不绝地讲述在美国的生活
captain [ˈkæptɪn]	*n.* 队长；首领；船长
	例 The captain of the winning team held the trophy high in the air above his head. 获胜队的队长将奖杯高高地举过头顶。
	用 captain of the hockey team at school 学校曲棍球队的队长

Exercise 26

一、中文释义练习

请选择单词正确的中文释义。

_____	1.	immerse	A. 促进
_____	2.	foster	B. 沉浸
_____	3.	orchestra	C. 管弦乐队
_____	4.	boundary	D. 边界
_____	5.	refine	E. 精炼

_____	6.	illusion	A. 幻觉
_____	7.	agile	B. 敏捷的
_____	8.	modify	C. 修改
_____	9.	profound	D. 雪橇
_____	10.	sledge	E. 深厚的

_____	11.	leak	A. 泄露
_____	12.	apparent	B. 归因于
_____	13.	bay	C. 悬念
_____	14.	ascribe	D. 海湾
_____	15.	suspense	E. 显然的

_____	16.	spray	A. 独白
_____	17.	dock	B. 码头
_____	18.	cement	C. 喷雾
_____	19.	monologue	D. 水泥
_____	20.	buckle	E. 搭扣

二、英文释义练习

请选择单词正确的英文释义。

_____	1.	empathy	A. the ability to understand another person's feelings
_____	2.	refund	B. to delay or stop the progress of sth.
_____	3.	impede	C. a sum of money that is paid back to you
_____	4.	pump	D. being moved or carried from one place to another
_____	5.	transit	E. a machine that is used to force liquid out sth.

_____	6.	estimate	A. to make sth. last longer than before
_____	7.	evolve	B. an official written agreement
_____	8.	contract	C. to develop gradually to a more complicated form
_____	9.	prolong	D. never changing and therefore boring
_____	10.	monotonous	E. a judgement without having the exact figures

feedback ['fi:dbæk]	*n.* 反馈；回复
	例 It's important to give students regular feedback on their progress. 定期给学生反馈他们的进步是很重要的。
	用 give you feedback on the test 对你的测验进行反馈
	扩 drawback *n.* 缺点，劣势
comparative [kəm'pærətɪv]	*adj.* 比较的；相对的，比较而言的
	例 I believe that a comparative study is required to understand why some companies in the e-learning industry are performing better than others. 我认为需要进行一项比较研究来了解为什么一些网络学习行业的公司比其他公司表现好。
	用 comparative linguistics 比较语言学 a comparative study of the educational systems of two countries 两国教育制度的比较研究
porcelain ['pɔ:səlɪn]	*n.* 瓷；瓷器
	例 The delicate porcelain teacups added an elegant touch to the table setting. 精致的瓷茶杯为餐桌摆设增添了优雅的装点。
	用 a porcelain figure 一尊瓷像
	考 porcelain and glass 陶瓷和玻璃
arthritis [ɑ:'θraɪtɪs]	*n.* 关节炎
	例 The elderly woman managed her arthritis pain with regular exercise and medication. 这位老妇人通过定期锻炼和药物治疗来控制关节炎疼痛。
	用 have a touch of arthritis in the wrist 手腕有轻微关节炎
cascade [kæ'skeɪd]	*n.* 小瀑布；倾泻 *v.* 倾泻；大量落下
	例 The waterfall cascaded gracefully down the rocks, creating a mesmerizing sight. 瀑布从岩石上优雅地倾泻而下，形成了一幅迷人的景象。
	用 a cascade of rainwater 暴雨如注

eclipse
[ɪˈklɪps]

n. 日食，月食；黯然失色

例 The moon blocked the sun, creating a stunning solar eclipse visible from certain parts of the world.
月亮挡住太阳，造成了在世界上某些地方可以看到的令人惊叹的日食。

用 an eclipse of the sun 日食 an eclipse of the moon 月食

考 astronomical phenomena such as solstices, equinoxes and eclipses
天文现象比如冬至（夏至）、春分（秋分）、日食（月食）

shortcoming
[ˈʃɔːtkʌmɪŋ]

n. 缺点；短处

例 She was a highly motivated and hard-working team player, but her main shortcoming was that she had a terrible temper when she felt stressed.
她是一个非常积极和努力的团队成员，但她的主要缺点是当她感到压力时，脾气就会很糟糕。

用 a result of the shortcomings of both partners
双方缺点所带来的后果

同 defect *n.* 缺点，欠缺 drawback *n.* 缺点
disadvantage *n.* 缺点；不利 demerit *n.* 缺点

反 advantage *n.* 优点，优势 merit *n.* 优点，好处

agency
[ˈeɪdʒənsi]

n. 代理，中介；代理处，经销处

例 It's easier to hire the services of an agency when you apply for a student visa.
申请学生签证时，聘请中介机构进行服务会更加容易。

用 a local travel agency 一家当地旅行社

spasm
[ˈspæzəm]

n. 痉挛；抽搐

例 She experienced a sudden spasm of pain in her back, causing her to wince.
她突然感到背部一阵剧痛，使她整个人畏缩起来。

用 a muscle spasm 肌肉痉挛 send his leg into spasm 使他的腿痉挛

sponsor
[ˈspɒnsə(r)]

n. 赞助者；主办者 *v.* 赞助；倡议；主办

例 A new sponsor is leading the team this year and is looking for additional benefactors.
今年有一位新的主办者领导这个团队，并正在寻找更多赞助商。

用 attract sponsors 吸引赞助者

扩 sponsorship *n.* 赞助；发起

intensive [ɪn'tensɪv]	*adj.* 加强的；集中的
	例 His course was tough and intensive and he found it hard to study so much in such a short time. 他的课程难度和强度都很大，他发现很难在如此短的时间内学习这么多内容。
	用 an intensive language course 速成语言课程 two weeks of intensive training 两周的强化训练
	扩 intense *adj.* 强烈的；紧张的 intensively *adv.* 强烈地；集中地
	考 As a consequence, each vehicle would be used more intensively, and might need replacing sooner. 因此，每一辆汽车将会被更密集地使用，并且可能会需要更早被置换。
instinct ['ɪnstɪŋkt]	*n.* 本能，直觉；天性
	例 I believe it is a natural human instinct to be curious about the lives and relationships of others. 我认为对他人的生活和人际关系感到好奇是人的自然本能。
	用 maternal instinct 母性本能
	扩 instinctive *adj.* 本能的；天生的
parasite ['pærəsaɪt]	*n.* 寄生虫
	例 Malaria comes from a parasite that is injected into the bloodstream from the mosquito. 疟疾来自蚊子将一种寄生虫注射到血液中。
	用 a vast range of parasites 各种各样的寄生虫
	扩 parallel *adj.* 平行的 parallax *n.* 视差 parachute *n.* 降落伞
	考 a larval parasite imported from Singapore 一种来自新加坡的寄生虫幼虫
military ['mɪlətri]	*adj.* 军事的；军队的 *n.* 军队；军人
	例 After multiple promotions and medals he had reached the peak of his military career. 在多次获得晋升和勋章之后，他达到了军事生涯的顶峰。
	用 military intelligence 军事情报 military uniform 军服
	类 armament *n.* 武器，军备 cannon *n.* 加农炮；大炮 weapon *n.* 武器，兵器 fleet *n.* 舰队 navy *n.* 海军 troop *n.* 军队
	考 In every era, the stadium has acquired new value and uses: from military fortress to residential village, public space to theatre and most recently a field for experimentation in advanced engineering. 在每一个时代里，体育场都获得了新的价值和用途：从军事堡垒到住宅村落，从公共空间到演艺剧院，最近还成为先进工程技术的实验场地。

theme
[θiːm]

n. 主题；题目

例 This year's theme at the annual conference was the importance of technology in language learning.
今年年会的主题是科技在语言学习中的重要性。

用 the theme of the conference 会议的主题

scatter
['skætə(r)]

v. 分散；散开；散播

例 She scattered the wild flower seeds over the fresh soil.
她把野花的种子撒在新鲜的土壤上。

用 scatter the grass seed over the lawn 把草籽撒到草坪上

同 disperse *v.* 散播；传播

aspect
['æspekt]

n. 方面；朝向；样子，外观

例 Climate and weather are important aspects of our lives.
气候和天气是我们生活中的重要方面。

用 all aspects of city life 城市生活的各个方面

考 These two unique aspects, one political, the other natural make food production highly vulnerable and different from any other business.
这两个独特的方面，一是人为的，另一个则是自然的，使粮食生产非常容易受到影响并且与其他行业不同。

optimum
['ɒptɪməm]

adj. 最佳的；最适宜的 *n.* (the ~) 最佳结果；最好的条件

例 The hot summer weather enables the grapes to reach their optimum ripeness.
炎热的夏季天气使葡萄达到最佳成熟度。

用 the optimum use of resources 对资源的充分利用

考 For instance, crops would be produced all year round, as they would be kept in artificially controlled, optimum growing conditions.
例如，作物可以全年生产，因为它们处于人工控制的最佳生长环境中。

cave
[keɪv]

n. 洞穴，山洞；地窖

例 The explorers cautiously ventured into the dark cave, eager to uncover its mysteries.
探险者们小心翼翼地冒险进入黑暗洞穴，渴望揭开它的奥秘。

用 the entrance of the cave 洞口

考 The caves were first explored in 1887 by a local Maori chief, Tane Tinorau, and an English surveyor, Fred Mace.
这些洞穴于1887年由当地毛利人首领Tane Tinorau和英国测量员Fred Mace首次探索。

temple ['templ]	*n.* 庙宇，寺庙；神殿 例 The ancient temple stood as a testament to the rich cultural heritage of the region. 这座古庙是该地区丰富文化遗产的证明。 用 go to temple on Saturdays 每周六去寺庙 考 The complex in which it was built was the size of a city in ancient Egypt and included a temple, courtyards, shrines, and living quarters for the priests. 它所搭建其中的整个建筑群达到了一座古埃及城市的规模，包括一座寺庙、几处庭院、若干神龛，还有神职人员的生活区域。
intelligence [ɪn'telɪdʒəns]	*n.* 智力，才智；情报 例 He was obviously a man of very high intelligence, but he lacked common sense at times. 他显然是一个非常聪明的人，但他有时会缺乏常识。 用 a person of high intelligence 一个拥有高智商的人 扩 intelligent *adj.* 聪明的；智能的 考 Social intelligence is the ability to understand and manage people in a business setting. 社交智力是在商业情境下理解他人并与他人打交道的能力。
audition [ɔː'dɪʃn]	*n./v.* 试镜，试演，试唱 例 She prepared rigorously for the audition, hoping to land the lead role. 她为试镜做了严谨的准备，希望能获得主演角色。 用 an audition for a Broadway musical 一部百老汇音乐剧的试演
blank [blæŋk]	*adj.* 空白的，空的；茫然的 *n.* 空白；空格 例 The writer stared at the blank page, waiting for inspiration before starting to write. 作家盯着空白页，等待灵感，然后开始写作。 用 a blank sheet of paper 一张空白的纸 考 My mind just goes blank when I read anything about chemicals. 当我读到任何关于化学的内容时，我的大脑就会一片空白。
rival ['raɪvl]	*n.* 对手；竞争者 *v.* 与……相匹敌，比得上 例 He was nervous about the boxing match, as this time he would be up against his biggest rival in the field. 他对这场拳击比赛很紧张，因为这次他将在拳击场上面对他最大的竞争对手。 用 our biggest economic rivals 我们最大的经济竞争对手

municipal [mjuːˈnɪsɪpl]	*adj.* 市政的；市的
	例 The municipal office for registering for your tax returns is located in the city's central financial building. 市政税务申报大厅位于该市的中央金融大厦。
	用 municipal councils 市政委员会　municipal workers 市政工作者
constitute [ˈkɒnstɪtjuːt]	*v.* 组成，构成；建立
	例 The universities constitute a reservoir of extensive knowledge of research for the country. 大学是一个国家广泛研究知识的地方。
	用 constitute less than 7 percent of its total population 构成总人口的不到7%
	同 make up 组成，构成
	扩 constitution *n.* 宪法；组成
border [ˈbɔːdə(r)]	*n.* 边境，国界
	例 The border between the two countries is heavily guarded. 两国间的边境戒备森严。
	用 a border dispute 边界争端
status [ˈsteɪtəs]	*n.* 地位；状态；情形
	例 People should not see money as the sole criterion of social status. 人们不应该把金钱作为社会地位的唯一衡量标准。
	用 low status jobs 地位低下的工作 have a high social status 拥有高社会地位
	考 But despite an implicit recognition that the spread of good reproductions can be culturally valuable, museums continue to promote the special status of original work. 但是，尽管人们含蓄地承认优秀复制品的传播或许在文化层面有价值，但博物馆依然继续宣传原作品的特殊地位。
flee [fliː]	*v.* 逃离，逃避，逃跑
	例 The frightened animals fled from the approaching forest fire. 受到惊吓的动物逃离了正在逼近的森林大火。
	用 a camp for refugees fleeing from the war 收留战争难民的难民营
consecutive [kənˈsekjətɪv]	*adj.* 连贯的，连续不断的
	例 This is the fifth consecutive weekend that I have spent at the gym. 这已经是我在健身房连续度过的第五个周末了。
	用 eight consecutive days 连续八天

conscious
['kɒnʃəs]

adj. 意识到的；神志清醒的；刻意的

例 As he woke up gradually on the train, he became conscious that people were looking at him.
随着他在火车上逐渐醒来，他意识到人们都在看着他。

用 very conscious of the problems involved 意识到了所涉及的问题

反 unconscious *adj.* 无意识的

扩 subconscious *n.* 潜意识；下意识 *adj.* 潜意识的；下意识的
consciousness *n.* 意识；观念

mature
[mə'tʃʊə(r)]

adj. 成熟的；到期（应该支付）的 *v.* 成熟；到期（应付款）

例 He has a mature attitude to work, and is always making efforts to diplomatically resolve any disputes amongst the team members.
他有成熟的工作态度，总是努力通过委婉的方式解决团队成员间的争论。

用 a mature and sensible attitude 成熟而理智的态度

反 immature *adj.* 不成熟的

扩 maturity *n.* 成熟；完备

intervene
[ˌɪntə'viːn]

v. 干涉，干预

例 When their argument started to get aggressive, I felt I had to intervene to calm things down.
当他们的争论开始变得激烈时，我认为自己需要介入来平息争论。

用 intervene in the dispute 介入纠纷

扩 intervention *n.* 干涉；干预 military intervention 军事干预

elaborate
[ɪ'læbərət] *adj.*
[ɪ'læbəreɪt] *v.*

adj. 精心制作的；详尽的 *v.* 详细阐述

例 The designs covering the temple roof were elaborate and intricate.
寺庙屋顶的设计是精致而复杂的。

用 an elaborate computer system 精密的计算机系统
elaborate on a statement 详述观点

扩 elaborately *adv.* 精巧地
an elaborately decorated room 一间精心装饰的房间

amateur
['æmətʃə(r)]

n. 业余爱好者 *adj.* 业余的

例 He was only an amateur but he displayed promise; his teachers were sure he'd end up being a real pro.
他只是个业余爱好者，但表现得很有发展前景，他的老师确信他最终会成为一个真正的专业人员。

用 open to both amateurs and professionals
对业余选手和职业选手都开放

反 professional *adj.* 职业的；专业的

column
['kɒləm]

n. 圆柱；专栏；列队

例 The romans were famous for building temples with different styles of columns.
罗马人以建造拥有不同风格柱子的庙宇而闻名。

用 the financial column 财经专栏

类 biweekly n. 双周刊 adj. 两周一次的
bimonthly n. 双月刊 adj. 两个月一次的 columnist n. 专栏作家
editor n. 编辑 encyclopedia n. 百科全书
headline n. 标题 journal n. 期刊

degenerate
[dɪ'dʒenəreɪt]

v. 退化；恶化；堕落

例 The debate began reasonably and calmly but quickly degenerated into chaos after everyone started to passionately argue.
辩论开始时有条理而冷静，但在大家开始激烈争论后，很快陷入了混乱。

用 degenerate quickly 迅速恶化

同 deteriorate v. 恶化，变坏

扩 generate v. 产生；形成 generation n. 代；一代人；产生
generator n. 发电机

instalment
[ɪn'stɔːlmənt]

n.（分期付款的）一期付款；（连载故事的）一节，（电视剧的）一集

例 She decided to pay back the loan in small instalments each month.
她决定以每月进行小额分期的方式偿还贷款。

用 the final instalment on the loan 贷款的最后一期付款

vent
[vent]

n. 通风口，排气口 v. 表达，发泄；排放（烟、煤气等）

例 The decorator opened the window to vent out the strong smell of gloss paint.
装修工打开窗户，以排出亮面漆的强烈气味。

用 vent her frustration 发泄她的沮丧

overwhelm
[ˌəʊvə'welm]

v. 淹没；压倒

例 He was overwhelmed with the amount of work he was given—the only thing he could do was try to organize his time as best as he could.
他被分配给他的工作量压得喘不过气来，他唯一能做的就是尽自己所能安排好时间。

用 overwhelm the weakened enemy 击溃脆弱的敌军

扩 overwhelming adj. 压倒性的，不可阻挡的

cluster [ˈklʌstə(r)]	*n.* 群；簇；丛；串 例 There was a small cluster of people standing in the hallway outside the exhibition room. 有一小群人站在展览室外的走廊上。 用 a cluster of stars 星团　a cluster of spectators 一群旁观者 考 this cluster of cells 这些细胞
newsletter [ˈnjuːzletə(r)]	*n.* 时事通讯；内部通讯，简讯 例 A weekly newsletter is sent by email to all subscribers, outlining the events, plans and activities of the school. 每周时事通讯会通过电子邮件发送给所有订阅者，概述学校的事件、计划和活动。 用 receive a quarterly newsletter 收到内部通讯季刊
carve [kɑːv]	*v.* 雕刻；切，割 例 The sculptor carved intricate designs into the woodwork of the temple eaves. 这位雕刻家在神庙屋檐的木制品上雕刻了复杂的图案。 用 be carved into the shape of a flower 雕成花朵状
groove [gruːv]	*n.* 凹槽；音乐节奏 例 The carpenter carefully fitted the well-crafted table leg into the groove in the table top. 木匠小心地把精心制作的桌腿装进桌面的凹槽里。 用 a jazz groove 爵士乐节奏
conjunction [kənˈdʒʌŋkʃn]	*n.* 结合；连接；同时发生 例 The conjunction of heavy winds and rains caused the delays in shipping. 暴雨和大风同时出现，造成了航运的延误。 用 the conjunction of low inflation and low unemployment 低通货膨胀与低失业率同时出现
illustrate [ˈɪləstreɪt]	*v.*（用示例、图画等）阐明，解释；给（书）加插图 例 He used amusing storytelling methods of illustrating his point during the presentation. 他在演讲中使用了有趣的讲故事的方法来阐述他的观点。 用 an illustrated textbook 一本有插图的课本 扩 illustration *n.* 说明；例证；图解

abolish [ə'bɒlɪʃ]	*v.* 废除，废止；取消 例 They officially abolished slavery in the late 1800s, but some countries continued the practice for many years afterwards. 他们在19世纪末正式废除了奴隶制，但一些国家在之后的许多年里继续实行这一制度。 用 abolish racially discriminatory laws 废除带有种族歧视的法律
radical ['rædɪkl]	*adj.* 激进的；根本的，彻底的 例 The new CEO is proposing radical changes to the way the company is structured. 新任CEO提出对公司的组织结构进行彻底改革。 用 the need for radical changes in education 对教育进行彻底变革的需要
proceed [prə'siːd]	*v.* 继续进行，接着做；行进，前往 例 After successfully passing the first-stage interview, the company decided to proceed with the candidate's application. 在成功通过第一阶段面试后，公司决定继续候选人的申请。 用 proceed slowly along the street 沿着街道缓缓行进
benchmark ['bentʃmɑːk]	*n.* 基准；标准 例 The boss established some reasonable benchmarks to measure employee performance for the coming quarter. 老板制定了一些合理的标准，用来在下季度衡量员工的表现。 用 a benchmark for the economy 衡量经济发展的基准 扩 bench *n.* 工作台；长凳

Exercise 27

一、中文释义练习

请选择单词正确的中文释义。

_____ 1. feedback   A. 反馈

_____ 2. porcelain   B. 本能

_____ 3. intensive   C. 加强的

_____ 4. sponsor   D. 瓷器

_____ 5. instinct   E. 赞助者

_____ 11. border   A. 干预

_____ 12. status   B. 边境

_____ 13. flee   C. 连贯的

_____ 14. consecutive   D. 逃离

_____ 15. intervene   E. 地位

_____ 6. cave   A. 市政的

_____ 7. temple   B. 庙宇

_____ 8. intelligence   C. 智力

_____ 9. rival   D. 洞穴

_____ 10. municipal   E. 对手

_____ 16. column   A. 阐明

_____ 17. degenerate   B. 退化

_____ 18. carve   C. 专栏

_____ 19. illustrate   D. 标准

_____ 20. benchmark   E. 雕刻

二、英文释义练习

请选择单词正确的英文释义。

_____ 1. comparative   A. to throw or drop things in different directions

_____ 2. cascade   B. a large amount of water falling or pouring down

_____ 3. parasite   C. empty, with nothing written or printed on it

_____ 4. scatter   D. a small animal that lives on or inside another

_____ 5. blank   E. studying things to find out how similar they are

_____ 6. conscious   A. a long narrow cut in the surface of sth. hard

_____ 7. elaborate   B. being carefully prepared and organized

_____ 8. amateur   C. aware of sth. or noticing sth.

_____ 9. groove   D. a person who takes part in a sport for enjoyment

_____ 10. abolish   E. to officially end a law, a system or an institution

thorough [ˈθʌrə]	*adj.* 彻底的；十分的 例 He recommended they perform a thorough investigation of the incident. 他建议他们对这一事件进行彻底调查。 用 carry out a thorough investigation 展开全面的调查 扩 thoroughly *adv.* 彻底地，完全地
iterative [ˈɪtərətɪv]	*adj.* 迭代的；重复的，反复的 例 The team used an iterative approach, making incremental improvements to the product. 团队使用迭代的工作方法，对产品进行逐步的改进。 用 an iterative process 一个迭代的过程
cardiovascular [ˌkɑːdiəʊˈvæskjələ(r)]	*adj.* 心血管的 例 Regular exercise is beneficial for improving cardiovascular health and reducing the risk of heart disease. 经常运动有利于改善心血管健康，降低患心脏病的风险。 用 serious risk of cardiovascular and respiratory disease 患心血管和呼吸道疾病的高度风险
canyon [ˈkænjən]	*n.* 峡谷 例 The hikers marveled at the breathtaking views as they stood on the edge of the vast canyon. 徒步旅行者站在巨大峡谷的边缘，惊叹于那令人叹为观止的景色。 用 the Grand Canyon 大峡谷 考 Cusco lies on a high plateau at an elevation of more than 3,000 metres, and Bingham's plan was to descend from this plateau along the valley of the Urubamba river, which takes a circuitous route down to the Amazon and passes through an area of dramatic canyons and mountain ranges. 库斯科位于海拔超过3,000米的高原，Bingham的计划是沿着乌鲁班巴河的山谷一路向下，绕路到达亚马孙并在途中穿过一片巨大的峡谷和山脉。

critical ['krɪtɪkl]	*adj.* 重要的，决定性的；批评的；评论的 例 She was good at remembering facts and figures but her critical analysis skills were limited. 她在记忆事实和数字方面很出色，但批判性分析能力有限。 用 a critical factor in the election campaign 竞选活动的关键因素 同 important *adj.* 重要的 crucial *adj.* 重要的，关键的
appreciate [ə'priːʃieɪt]	*v.* 欣赏；感激；理解 例 It's very hard to appreciate foreign poetry in translated versions. 欣赏经过翻译的国外诗歌是很困难的。 用 appreciate foreign literature 欣赏外国文学 扩 appreciation *n.* 欣赏；感激；理解
constrain [kən'streɪn]	*v.* 强迫，迫使；限定，约束 例 Children at the school are constrained to work according to strict guidelines in order to get through the end-of-year examinations. 为了通过期末考试，学生们不得不在严格的学科指导下学习。 用 feel constrained to accept it 感到不得不接受 扩 constraint *n.* 约束；限制 strain *n.* 拉力；压力 *v.* 拉紧
circumstance ['sɜːkəmstəns]	*n.* 环境；条件；情况 例 He wanted to go to university overseas but his financial circumstances were strained, and he couldn't afford it. 他想去国外读大学，但是他的经济状况非常紧张，无法支付这笔开支。 用 changing social and political circumstances 正在变化的社会和政治环境
spacious ['speɪʃəs]	*adj.* 宽敞的；广阔的 例 The new apartment was large and spacious with a lot of sunlight coming in through the huge windows. 新公寓又大又宽敞，大量阳光透过巨大的窗户照进来。 用 a spacious kitchen 一间宽敞的厨房
pesticide ['pestɪsaɪd]	*n.* 杀虫剂，农药 例 The farmer used a pesticide to protect crops from harmful insects. 农民使用杀虫剂保护庄稼不受害虫侵害。 用 vegetables grown without the use of pesticides 种植过程中未使用杀虫剂的蔬菜 crops sprayed with pesticide 喷洒过杀虫剂的庄稼

taxonomy
['tæk'sɒnəmi]

n. 分类学；分类法

例 Biologists study the taxonomy of living organisms to understand their classification and relationships.
生物学家研究生物体的分类学，以了解它们的分类和关系。

用 plant taxonomy 植物分类学 a taxonomy of smells 气味的分类法

---

gadget
['gædʒɪt]

n. 小器具，小玩意儿

例 He loved collecting the latest tech gadgets to stay up-to-date with technology.
他喜欢收集最新的科技产品，以跟上科技的步伐。

用 kitchen gadgets 厨房小用品

---

salvage
['sælvɪdʒ]

n./v. 打捞；抢救；海上救助

例 They salvaged most of the treasure from the sunken ship.
他们从沉船中打捞出了大部分财宝。

用 a salvage company 一家打捞公司

---

despise
[dɪ'spaɪz]

v. 轻视，鄙视

例 She loved pets and despised seeing any form of cruelty to animals.
她喜欢宠物，鄙视任何对动物的虐待行为。

用 secretly despise his work 暗地里瞧不起他的工作

---

dreadful
['dredfl]

adj. 糟糕的，讨厌的；极端的；可怕的

例 The dreadful storm caused widespread damage and disruption.
这场可怕的风暴造成了大范围的破坏和损失。

用 the dreadful news 坏消息

---

probe
[prəʊb]

v. 调查；探查；搜寻 *n.* 探究，调查；探针；探测器

例 The scientist used a specialized probe to investigate the composition of the distant planet.
科学家使用了一种专门的探测器来研究那颗遥远行星的构成。

用 probe into his background 调查他的背景

考 The space probe, Voyager I, launched in 1977, had sent back spectacular images of Jupiter and Saturn and then soared out of the Solar System on a one-way mission to the stars.
1977年发射的太空探测器"旅行者1号"发回了木星和土星的壮观照片，然后飞出太阳系开始它的单程旅行，飞往其他恒星执行任务。

---

ultraviolet
[,ʌltrə'vaɪələt]

adj. 紫外线的

例 It is said that ultraviolet light kills all number of germs and bacteria.
据说紫外光能杀死所有的病菌和细菌。

用 ultraviolet rays 紫外线

geography [dʒi'ɒgrəfi]	*n.* 地理；地理学；地形，地貌
	例 He was especially interested in physical geography and the study of land features such as volcanoes. 他对自然地理学以及火山等陆地特征的研究非常感兴趣。
	用 a degree in geography 地理学学位
	扩 geographic *adj.* 地理的；地理学的

batch [bætʃ]	*n.* 一批 *v.* 分批处理
	例 The bakery prepared a fresh batch of delicious cookies and bread. 面包店准备了一批新鲜又美味的饼干和面包。
	用 deliver the goods in batches 分批交付货物
	考 The picture is made more complicated by the fact that these crystals occur in batches. 这些晶体总是成批出现，使情况更加复杂。

slum [slʌm]	*n.* 贫民窟，棚屋区
	例 The impoverished community lived in overcrowded slums, struggling to meet basic needs. 这个贫困的社区位于拥挤的贫民窟里，努力满足基本需求。
	用 a slum area of this city 这座城市中的一个贫民区
	考 The area within consisted of poorly built, overcrowded slums and the streets were full of horse-drawn traffic. 环内的区域里有着建造简陋、拥挤不堪的贫民窟，街道上遍布着作为交通工具的马车。

resort [rɪ'zɔːt]	*v.* 求助于，诉诸 *n.* 度假胜地；诉诸，求助
	例 His intense work schedule caused him to resort to drinking lots of coffee to stay awake. 高强度的工作安排使他不得不喝很多咖啡来保持清醒。
	用 a popular holiday resort 一个受欢迎的度假胜地

climax ['klaɪmæks]	*n.* 高潮；顶点；极点
	例 The film was long and ended with an incredibly dramatic and moving climax. 这部电影很长，以令人难以置信的充满戏剧性而又感人的高潮结束。
	用 come to a climax 达到极点

apparatus [ˌæpə'reɪtəs]	*n.* 装置，设备；仪器
	例 Astronauts have special breathing apparatus in their space suits. 宇航员有放置在宇航服里的特殊呼吸装置。
	用 a piece of laboratory apparatus 一件实验室仪器

mortal ['mɔːtl]	*adj.* 致死的；终将死亡的
	例 The fact that all life is mortal is something that scientists continue to study and try to understand. 所有生命都是终将死亡的，这件事是科学家们持续研究和试图理解的。
	用 a mortal wound 一个致命的伤口
	反 immortal *adj.* 不死的；不朽的
	扩 mortality *n.* 死亡率；必死性
grab [græb]	*v.* 抓住；利用；吸引
	例 She quickly reached out to grab the daughter's arm as she almost tripped over. 她迅速伸手抓住女儿的手臂，差点被绊倒。
	用 manage to grab her hand 设法抓住她的手
	考 They had nothing to grab onto, so multiple areas of their brains were activated. 他们没有可抓取的信号，所以他们大脑的多个区域都被激活了。
code [kəʊd]	*n.* 代码；密码；编码 *v.* 把……编码
	例 He could not enter his home because he had forgotten the door code. 由于忘记了开门密码，他无法进入自己的家。
	用 the genetic code 遗传密码
	考 Researchers have also found that different types of laughter serve as codes to complex human social hierarchies. 研究者们还发现：不同类型的笑可以像密码一样代表复杂的人类社会阶层。
comprehensive [ˌkɒmprɪ'hensɪv]	*adj.* 综合的，全面的；有理解力的
	例 The book gives a very comprehensive overview of the history of the country. 这本书对这个国家的历史作了非常全面的概述。
	用 a comprehensive study 全面的研究 a comprehensive guide to the region 介绍该地区的一本全面指南
artistry ['ɑːtɪstri]	*n.* 艺术性；艺术技巧
	例 Ancient crafts from the Tang Dynasty show an incredible mastery of artistry. 唐代的古代工艺品显示出令人难以置信的高超技艺。
	用 play the piece with effortless artistry 游刃有余地演奏这首乐曲
	扩 artist *n.* 艺术家 artistic *adj.* 艺术的；有美感的 artisan *n.* 工匠

deposit
[dɪˈpɒzɪt]

n. 存款；押金；沉淀物 *v.* 沉淀；放下，放置；付（押金）；将（钱）存入银行

例 Passengers who cancel their reservations will lose their deposit.
取消预订的乘客将失去押金。

用 pay a deposit 付押金

反 withdrawal *n.* 取款

考 And I have to tell you there's also a deposit of £250, which is returnable of course as long as there's no damage.
我需要告诉你同样有250英镑押金，当然这是可退还的，只要不发生损坏。

disrupt
[dɪsˈrʌpt]

v. 扰乱；打乱；使中断

例 Flights have recently been disrupted by unfavourable weather conditions.
近期航班因天气状况不佳而中断。

用 disrupt agricultural production 干扰农业生产

locate
[ləʊˈkeɪt]

v. 位于；确定……的位置；定居

例 The castle is located on the western side of the mountain, just north of the river.
城堡位于山的西侧，河的北边。

用 locate their headquarters in Beijing 把总部设在北京

扩 location *n.* 位置，地点

spectacle
[ˈspektəkl]

n. 精彩的表演；壮观的景象；[pl.]眼镜

例 This year's annual gala performance was an incredible spectacle.
今年的年度晚会表演呈现出令人难以置信的壮观场面。

用 a pair of spectacles 一副眼镜

drainage
[ˈdreɪnɪdʒ]

n. 排水系统；排水

例 The city implemented an effective drainage system to prevent flooding during heavy rains.
该市落实了有效的排水系统，以防止暴雨期间发生洪水。

用 a drainage system 排水系统

考 Research also indicates that green roofs can be integrated with drainage systems on the ground, such as street trees, so that the water is managed better and the built environment is made more sustainable.
研究也表明，绿色屋顶还可以与地面上的排水系统相融合，例如街边行道树，这样可以更好地利用水源，构建起来的环境也更有利于可持续发展。

infrastructure [ˈɪnfrəstrʌktʃə(r)]	*n.* 基础设施；公共建设
	例 They have improved the transport infrastructure significantly over the past few years. 在过去几年间，他们显著改善了交通基础设施。
	用 investment in infrastructure 对基础设施的投资
	考 Improvements to infrastructure can have a major impact on risk for farmers. 基础设施的改善对降低农民面临的风险有很大作用。
compile [kəmˈpaɪl]	*v.* 编译；编制；汇编
	例 His book is an interesting attempt to compile information, stories and facts about people's experiences during the revolution in Cuba. 他的书是一种有趣的尝试，试图整理古巴革命期间与人们经历有关的信息、故事和事实。
	用 compile a dictionary 编制一部词典
evaluate [ɪˈvæljueɪt]	*v.* 估计；评价；评估
	例 When you finish a project it is important to have a clear process to evaluate how successful it is and why. 当你完成一个项目时，重要的是要有一个清晰的流程来评估它有多成功以及背后的原因。
	用 evaluate the effectiveness of different drugs 评估不同药物的疗效
	扩 evaluation *n.* 评价；评估
	考 Grossmann argues that even when we aren't able to change the situation, we can still evaluate these experiences from different perspectives. Grossmann指出：即使在不能改变场合时，我们也仍然可以从不同的角度来评估这些体验。
inflation [ɪnˈfleɪʃn]	*n.* 通货膨胀，通胀率
	例 The country faced high inflation, leading to rising prices and economic instability. 该国面临高通货膨胀，导致物价上涨，经济不稳定。
	用 curb inflation 抑制通货膨胀
	反 deflation *n.* 通货紧缩
moist [mɔɪst]	*adj.* 潮湿的；湿润的
	例 When planting seeds it's best to ensure the soil is moist but not too wet. 播种时，最好确保土壤湿润，但不要太潮湿。
	用 warm moist air 温暖潮湿的空气
	考 keep the soil moist 保持土壤潮湿

philosophy
[fə'lɒsəfi]

n. 哲学；哲理；生活的信条（或态度）

例 He studied philosophy at university, and spent much of his time thinking about theories of life, being and time.
他在大学学习哲学，大多数时间在思考有关生命、存在和时间的理论。

用 a professor of philosophy 一位哲学教授

扩 philosopher *n.* 哲学家

literacy
['lɪtərəsi]

n. 读写能力

例 The level of literacy amongst rural children is slightly lower than urban children, but the new educational policies should address that discrepancy.
农村儿童的识字率略低于城市儿童，但新的教育政策应该可以解决这一差异。

用 basic literacy skills 基本的读写技巧

扩 literal *adj.* 文字的；字面的 literate *adj.* 有读写能力的；有学问的
illiterate *adj.* 不识字的；文盲的

考 The effects of maternal literacy programmes can be seen very quickly.
孕产妇文化学习项目的效果可以很快被看到。

precaution
[prɪ'kɔːʃn]

n. 预防措施，防备

例 You should wear a safety helmet when cycling, just as a precaution in case you have an accident.
骑自行车时你应该戴安全头盔，以防发生事故。

用 precautions against fire 防火措施

discriminate
[dɪ'skrɪmɪneɪt]

v. 歧视；区别；辨别

例 It is unethical to discriminate against people because of their race or gender.
因种族或性别而歧视他人是不道德的。

用 unable to discriminate between letters and numbers
不能辨别字母与数字

扩 discrimination *n.* 歧视 gender discrimination 性别歧视

overdue
[,əʊvə'djuː]

adj. （到期）未付的，未还的；早该发生的

例 He was charged a small fee by the credit card company for an overdue payment.
信用卡公司因逾期付款而向他收取了一笔小的费用。

用 an overdue payment 逾期的欠款
an overdue library book 逾期未还的图书

circulate [ˈsɜːkjəleɪt]	*v.* 循环；散发，传播 例 The rumour circulated throughout the office and soon everyone knew about it. 谣言在办公室中传播开来，很快每个人都知道了。 用 circulate throughout the building 在整座大楼里循环
quantity [ˈkwɒntəti]	*n.* 量，数量 例 A huge quantity of people are now applying for jobs in the technology industry. 现在有大量的人在申请技术领域的工作。 用 be cheap to produce in large quantities 低成本大批量生产 考 Throughout the first three-quarters of the 20th century, the quantity of freshwater consumed per person doubled on average; in the USA, water withdrawals increased tenfold while the population quadrupled. 在20世纪的前四分之三，人均淡水消耗量平均翻了一倍；在美国，取水量增加了十倍而人口翻了两番。
strategy [ˈstrætədʒi]	*n.* 战略；策略 例 Their strategy was mapped out and planned very carefully. 他们的策略是经过精心设计和规划的。 用 marketing strategy 营销策略 the government's economic strategy 政府的经济策略 扩 strategic *adj.* 策略的；战略的 考 However, the underlying lessons apply anywhere—the effectiveness of a strong brand, a strategy based on unique experiences and a comprehensive and user-friendly website. 然而，其背后的经验却可放之四海而皆准——一个强有力品牌的效应，一项基于独特体验的策略，以及一个全面而十分照顾用户体验的网站。
transmit [trænzˈmɪt]	*v.* 传输；传播；发射 例 The signals from mobile phones used to be transmitted through electromagnetic radiation. 手机信号过去是通过电磁辐射传输的。 用 signals transmitted from a satellite 从卫星传送来的信号 扩 transmission *n.* 传输；传播；发射 考 Perception is not simply a product of what your eyes or ears transmit to your brain. 直觉并不是简单的由眼睛或耳朵获得并传到大脑的信息。

mutual ['mjuːtʃuəl]	*adj.* 共同的；相互的，彼此的
	例 After working together for so many years, a deep mutual respect had developed between them. 在一起工作了许多年之后，他们之间产生了深厚的相互尊重。
	用 mutual respect 相互尊重 mutual understanding 相互理解
	扩 mutually *adv.* 相互地；共同地
	考 mutually beneficial or mutually destructive 互相有益或互相伤害
sustain [sə'steɪn]	*v.* 维持；使稳定持续；支撑；供养
	例 The expedition did not have the supplies to sustain themselves for the winter ahead. 探险队没有足够的补给来支撑自己度过即将到来的冬天。
	用 a period of sustained economic growth 经济持续增长的时期
	同 maintain *v.* 维持
	扩 sustainable *adj.* 可持续的 sustainable development 可持续发展
replicate ['replɪkeɪt]	*v.* 复制；再生，自我复制
	例 They are working on computer-generated speech that perfectly replicates the human voice. 他们正在研究能够完美复制人类声音的计算机生成语音。
	用 replicate the experiment 复制该实验
	扩 replication *n.* 复制；折叠

Exercise 28

一、中文释义练习

请选择单词正确的中文释义。

_____ 1.　canyon　　　　A. 欣赏
_____ 2.　appreciate　　　B. 打捞
_____ 3.　circumstance　C. 环境
_____ 4.　taxonomy　　　D. 分类学
_____ 5.　salvage　　　　E. 峡谷

_____ 6.　despise　　　　A. 高潮
_____ 7.　batch　　　　　B. 抓住
_____ 8.　climax　　　　C. 一批
_____ 9.　mortal　　　　D. 鄙视
_____ 10.　grab　　　　　E. 致死的

_____ 11.　ultraviolet　　A. 排水系统
_____ 12.　deposit　　　　B. 紫外线的
_____ 13.　spectacle　　C. 存款
_____ 14.　drainage　　　D. 基础设施
_____ 15.　infrastructure　E. 壮观景象

_____ 16.　inflation　　　A. 循环
_____ 17.　literacy　　　B. 歧视
_____ 18.　discriminate　C. 传输
_____ 19.　circulate　　　D. 读写能力
_____ 20.　transmit　　　E. 通货膨胀

二、英文释义练习

请选择单词正确的英文释义。

_____ 1.　cardiovascular　A. a chemical used for killing insects
_____ 2.　constrain　　　B. ask questions in order to find out hidden information
_____ 3.　pesticide　　　C. to force sb. to do sth. or behave in a particular way
_____ 4.　probe　　　　　D. a poor area where houses are in bad condition
_____ 5.　slum　　　　　E. connected with the heart and the blood vessels

_____ 6.　code　　　　　A. something done in advance to avoid danger
_____ 7.　apparatus　　　B. not paid, done or returned by the required time
_____ 8.　compile　　　　C. produce a book by bringing together different articles
_____ 9.　precaution　　　D. the tools needed for a particular activity or task
_____ 10.　overdue　　　　E. a system of words or numbers representing a message

blast [blɑːst]	*n.* 爆炸，爆破；强劲气流，疾风 *v.* 炸毁，爆破
	例 The explosion sent a powerful blast of air and debris in all directions. 爆炸向四面八方喷射出强烈的空气和碎片。
	用 a bomb blast 炸弹爆炸 the wind's icy blasts 凛冽的狂风

fragile [ˈfrædʒaɪl]	*adj.* 脆弱的；易碎的
	例 The thin glass of the decorative vase was exceptionally fragile; you had to handle it with great care when moving it or cleaning it. 那只装饰性花瓶的薄玻璃非常易碎，当你移动或清洗它的时候，必须非常小心。
	用 fragile glass 易碎的玻璃

retrieve [rɪˈtriːv]	*v.* 找回，取回；检索数据
	例 Although the hard drive was broken, they said that a specialist computer engineer might be able to retrieve some of the data. 虽然硬盘损坏了，但他们说专业的计算机工程师也许能找回一些数据。
	用 retrieve her comb from the floor 从地上捡起她的梳子
	同 recover *v.* 找回；恢复

conflict [ˈkɒnflɪkt] *n.* [kənˈflɪkt] *v.*	*n.* 冲突，矛盾；斗争 *v.* 冲突，抵触
	例 He is a very diplomatic person to work with, and usually avoids conflict with team members. 他是个非常善于处理关系的人，通常会避免与团队成员发生冲突。
	用 a conflict between two cultures 两种文化间的冲突 break up conflicts 解决冲突
	考 For this reason, bilingual people often perform better on tasks that require conflict management. 由于这一原因，使用双语的人在那些需要冲突管理的任务中表现更好。

agenda [əˈdʒendə]	*n.* 议程；工作事项；日程表
	例 The agenda for the meeting was communicated to the team yesterday. 会议议程于昨天传达给了团队。
	用 top of the agenda 首要事项

coherent [kəʊ'hɪərənt]	*adj.* 连贯的，一致的 例 His argument was logical and coherent but I still didn't agree with his opinion on the issue. 他的论证逻辑清晰，内容连贯，但我仍然不同意他在这个问题上的观点。 用 a coherent narrative 条理清楚的叙述 扩 coherence *n.* 连贯性
ethnic ['eθnɪk]	*adj.* 种族的；民族的 例 There are a lot of ethnic groups in my country, each with their own distinctive customs, traditions, music and art. 我国有很多少数民族，每个民族都有自己独特的风俗、传统、音乐和艺术。 用 ethnic tensions 种族间的紧张形势
charity ['tʃærəti]	*n.* 慈善；赈济；慈善机构 例 More and more companies are engaging in corporate social responsibility and giving money to charity. 越来越多的公司正在承担企业社会责任，并向慈善机构捐款。 用 a charity concert 一场慈善音乐会
scratch [skrætʃ]	*v.* 挠，抓 *n.* 划痕，划伤 例 The cat stretched lazily, using its claws to scratch the post and sharpen them. 那只猫懒洋洋地伸着懒腰，用爪子抓着柱子，将它们磨得锋利。 用 scratch my hands and face 划破我的双手和脸 from scratch 从零开始 考 The teams in Brazil and China have now used this knowledge to reintroduce these changes from scratch while maintaining or even enhancing the desirable traits of wild strains. 巴西和中国的团队目前已经运用这一知识以从零开始重新诱发这些改变，同时保留甚至加强一些人类想要的野生植株的特性。
orbit ['ɔːbɪt]	*n.* 轨道；范围 *v.* 绕轨道运行，环绕……运行 例 We know that the satellite is now in stable orbit around the earth. 我们知道卫星目前稳定地绕地球运行。 用 the earth's orbit around the sun 地球环绕太阳的轨道 a space station in orbit round the moon 绕月球运行的一个航天站 扩 orbital *adj.* 轨道的

tissue
['tɪʃuː]

n. （人、动植物细胞的）组织；纸巾

例 As a top athlete, he hardly has any fatty tissue.
作为一名优秀运动员，他几乎没有什么脂肪组织。

用 a box of tissues 一盒纸巾 nerve tissue 神经组织

类 cell *n.* 细胞 muscle *n.* 肌肉 bacterium *n.* 细菌

考 Humans with comparative levels of adipose tissue would be considered obese and would be likely to suffer from diabetes and heart disease.
如果是人类有着同等水平的脂肪组织，势必会被视为肥胖并且极有可能遭受糖尿病和心脏病的困扰。

glossary
['glɒsəri]

n. 术语表；词汇表

例 There is a comprehensive glossary of terms you need to learn for studying finance.
为了学习金融，你需要学习这个全面的术语词表。

用 a glossary of terms 术语词汇表

intricate
['ɪntrɪkət]

adj. 错综复杂的；难理解的

例 The elaborate carvings and designs on the temple walls were intricate.
寺庙墙壁上的精致雕刻和图案错综复杂。

用 intricate patterns 复杂的图案

meteorology
[ˌmiːtiə'rɒlədʒi]

n. 气象学；气象状态

例 Meteorology is becoming an increasingly important branch of science as we are looking more into space for answers.
气象学正成为一个越来越重要的科学分支，因为我们正在更多地探索太空寻求答案。

用 interactive meteorology 交互气象学

扩 meteorological *adj.* 气象的

考 Diels also hopes to see the birth of "interactive meteorology"—not just forecasting the weather but controlling it.
Diels同样希望看到"交互气象学"的产生，也就是不仅仅预测天气，而是可以控制它。

wrap
[ræp]

v. 包，裹；缠绕

例 She wrapped the gift in attractive shiny paper and tied a bow around it.
她用漂亮闪亮的纸把礼物包了起来，还系了一个蝴蝶结。

用 individually wrapped chocolates 单块包装的巧克力

flourish
['flʌrɪʃ]

v. 繁荣；旺盛；茁壮成长

例 Wild plants flourish along the banks of certain rivers, where there is plenty of water, ample sunlight and rich, nourishing soil.
野生植物沿着某些河流的河岸旺盛生长，那里有大量的水、充足的阳光和丰富、有营养的土壤。

用 flourish in a damp climate 在潮湿气候下长势茂盛

同 thrive *v.* 繁荣，兴旺 prosper *v.* 繁荣，兴旺

individual
[ˌɪndɪ'vɪdʒuəl]

adj. 个人的；个别的；单独的 *n.* 个人，个体

例 A good teacher can adapt and modify lessons to suit individual learning needs of students.
一个好的老师可以调整和修改课程以满足学生们的个体学习需求。

用 individual tuition 个别指导

扩 individualism *n.* 个人主义 individually *adv.* 个别地；单独地

考 Their objective is to make AI technologies more trustworthy and transparent, so that organisations and individuals understand how AI decisions are made.
他们的目标是使得AI技术更值得信赖也更透明，这样无论组织还是个人都能了解到人工智能的算法结论是如何得出的。

timber
['tɪmbə(r)]

n. 木材，原木

例 The carpenter selected high-quality timber to build a sturdy and beautiful dining table.
木匠选用优质木材制作了一张结实美观的餐桌。

用 a small timber building 小型木质建筑
contracts to cut timber 树木砍伐合同

考 Recent years have seen the emergence of tall buildings constructed almost entirely from timber.
近些年来，已经出现了几乎完全是由木材构建的高楼大厦。

withdraw
[wɪð'drɔː]

v. 撤退；收回；提取（银行账户中的款）；（从活动或组织中）退出

例 The troops decided to withdraw from the border following the resolution.
根据这项决议，军队决定从边境撤退。

用 withdraw from the EU 退出欧盟

扩 withdrawal *n.* 撤退

考 Although population, industrial output and economic productivity have continued to soar in developed nations, the rate at which people withdraw water from aquifers, rivers and lakes has slowed.
尽管发达国家的人口、工业产值和经济生产率依然在激增，人们从含水层、河流及湖泊中取水的速率却下降了。

span
[spæn]

n. 时间跨度，持续时间；范围

例 The life span of a tadpole is only a few days, before it starts transforming into a frog.
在蝌蚪开始变成青蛙之前，它的寿命只有几天。

用 attention span 注意力持续时间
be completed within a specific time span 在规定期限内完成

扩 lifespan *n.* 寿命

organ
[ˈɔːgən]

n. 器官；机构

例 The heart and the brain are two of the most important organs in the human body.
心脏和大脑是人体中两个最重要的器官。

用 an organ transplant 器官移植

facilitate
[fəˈsɪlɪteɪt]

v. 使容易，使便利；促进，推动

例 The new software was designed to facilitate efficient communication and collaboration among team members.
新软件旨在促进团队成员之间的高效沟通和协作。

用 facilitate the development of tourism 促进旅游业的发展

扩 facility *n.* 设施，设备

考 In conditions of good visibility, seamen in the Mediterranean often had the mainland or islands in sight, which greatly facilitated navigation.
在良好的可视度条件下，在地中海区域航行的水手们经常可以看见大陆或岛屿，这极大地帮助了水手们导航。

artificial
[ˌɑːtɪˈfɪʃl]

adj. 人造的；虚伪的

例 These organic candies contain no artificial flavours or preservatives.
这些有机糖果不含人造香料和防腐剂。

用 artificial intelligence 人工智能 artificial light 人造光

扩 superficial *adj.* 肤浅的；表面的

考 Artificial dyes continue to play a crucial role today.
如今人工染料依然扮演着重要角色。

irritation
[ˌɪrɪˈteɪʃn]

n. 恼怒；刺激

例 If you use too much of that dishwasher detergent, you might find that you get a mild irritation on the skin of your hands.
如果你使用太多洗碗机清洁剂，你可能会发现手的皮肤有轻微刺激。

用 cause irritation to sensitive skins 对敏感皮肤造成刺激

扩 irritate *v.* 刺激；激怒

tolerate ['tɒləreɪt]	*v.* 忍受；默许 例 She refused to tolerate his behaviour any longer, and sent him out of the classroom. 她再也不能容忍他的行为，把他赶出了教室。 用 the ability to tolerate pain 对疼痛的忍受力 扩 tolerance *n.* 宽容；容忍
chase [tʃeɪs]	*v.* 追逐；追赶 例 The police were trying to chase the criminals through the winding streets of the old town. 警察正试图在老城区曲折的街道中追捕罪犯。 用 chase the job 竞争岗位
intestine [ɪn'testɪn]	*n.* 肠；肠管 例 The nutrients from the food are absorbed in the small intestine during the digestion process. 食物中的营养成分在消化过程中被小肠吸收。 用 loops of intestine 一圈圈肠管
commence [kə'mens]	*v.* 开始，着手 例 The ceremony commenced with a heartfelt speech, marking the beginning of a new chapter. 仪式以诚挚的致辞开始，标志着新篇章的开启。 用 commence at the beginning of October 十月初开始
fascinate ['fæsɪneɪt]	*v.* 使着迷，深深吸引 例 She was fascinated by all things related to fantasy and magic. 她对一切与幻想和魔法有关的事物都很着迷。 用 be fascinated by foreign cultures 被异国文化吸引 扩 fascinating *adj.* 迷人的；有吸引力的 考 Moore became fascinated with this stone sculpture, which he thought had a power and originality that no other stone sculpture possessed. Moore迷上了这座石雕，他认为它具有其他石雕所不具备的力量和独创性。
metropolitan [ˌmetrə'pɒlɪtən]	*adj.* 大都市的；本土的 例 He moved to the bustling metropolitan city to pursue career opportunities and a vibrant lifestyle. 他搬到了熙熙攘攘的大都市，追求职业机会和充满活力的生活方式。 用 the New York metropolitan area 纽约市区

adapt [ə'dæpt]	*v.* 适应；调整，使适合；改编 例 When you moved to another country it can be hard to adapt to a new lifestyle and culture. 当你搬到另一个国家时，适应新的生活方式和文化会是比较困难的。 用 be specially adapted for use by disabled people 经过特别改装供残疾人使用 扩 adaptive *adj.* 适应的 adaptation *n.* 改写；适应 考 And yet most of us have had the experience of having to adjust to sleeping in the mountains or the countryside because it was initially "too quiet", an experience that suggests that humans are capable of adapting to a wide range of noise levels. 我们大多数人都有过这样的经历：如果在深山或者乡村睡觉，必须做一些调整才能睡得着，因为这些地方起初"太安静"了，这一例子说明人类有能力去适应不同程度的各种噪声。
prescribe [prɪ'skraɪb]	*v.* 规定；开药方 例 The doctor prescribed a course of antibiotics to help him fight the illness. 医生开了一个疗程的抗生素来帮助他对抗疾病。 用 twice the prescribed dose of sleeping tablets 所开剂量两倍的安眠药 扩 prescription *n.* 处方，药方
alluvial [ə'luːviəl]	*adj.* 冲积的 例 The fertile alluvial soil was ideal for agricultural cultivation. 肥沃的冲积土壤非常适合农业耕种。 用 rich alluvial soils 肥沃的冲积土壤
supreme [su'priːm]	*adj.* 最高的；极其的 例 He was so tired and bored that it required a supreme effort to stay awake. 他又疲惫又厌烦，需要极大的努力来保持清醒。 用 a supreme effort 最大努力
optical ['ɒptɪkl]	*adj.* 光学的；视力的；视觉的 例 Telescopes and microscopes are examples of optical instruments. 望远镜和显微镜都是光学仪器的例子。 用 optical effects 视觉效果 考 invaluable to the optical industry 在光学产业中非常宝贵

despoil
[dɪˈspɔɪl]

v. 掠夺，剥夺；夺取

例 Many ancient tombs in Egypt have been despoiled by thieves.
埃及的许多古墓被窃贼洗劫一空。

用 despoil sb. of his right 剥夺某人的权利

intrigue
[ɪnˈtriːg]

v. 引发兴趣，引发好奇；密谋 *n.* 密谋，阴谋；秘密关系

例 The intricate plot of the novel intrigued readers, keeping them captivated until the end.
小说错综复杂的情节引起了读者的兴趣，使他们一直着迷到结尾。

用 a web of intrigue in the academic world 学术界关系复杂的网络

考 This might sound off-putting, but it supports Harrison's concept of the building—that the person approaching is intrigued and wonders what will be inside.
可能听起来没什么意思，但是它代表了Harrison的建筑理念，人们走进这里会好奇里面到底是什么。

jaw
[dʒɔː]

n. 颌；下巴

例 The dentist examined the patient's jaw to assess the alignment of the teeth.
牙医检查病人的下颌以评估牙齿的排列情况。

用 a strong square jaw 一副结实的方下巴

考 The average captive animal will have a greater life expectancy compared with its wild counterpart, and will not die of drought, of starvation or in the jaws of a predator.
一般圈养动物会比野生动物活得更久，并且不会死于干旱、饥饿或是捕食者。

curiosity
[ˌkjʊəriˈɒsəti]

n. 好奇；好奇心

例 Children often have a very strong sense of curiosity—they're always exploring new things and interested in life around them.
孩子们通常有很强的好奇心，他们总是在探索新事物，对周围的生活充满兴趣。

用 satisfy my curiosity 满足我的好奇心

扩 curious *adj.* 好奇的

考 The primary reason for the search is basic curiosity—the same curiosity about the natural world that drives all pure science.
搜寻活动的主要原因是基本的好奇心，与驱使着一切自然科学发展的对自然世界的好奇心一样。

democratic [ˌdeməˈkrætɪk]	*adj.* 民主的；有民主精神的 例 She was a very democratic boss—she always asked team members their opinions and got their feedback before making decisions. 她是一个非常民主的老板，她总是在做决定前征求团队成员的意见并得到他们的反馈。 用 democratic participation 民主参与 扩 democracy *n.* 民主
bachelor [ˈbætʃələ(r)]	*n.* 学士；单身汉 例 He claimed that he didn't want to get married and was happy as a bachelor. 他声称自己不想结婚，单身生活非常快乐。 用 a bachelor degree in chemistry 化学学士学位
visible [ˈvɪzəbl]	*adj.* 明显的；看得见的 例 If you live on the ground floor it's best not to tempt thieves by leaving valuables visible through the window. 如果你住在一楼，最好不要把贵重物品放在透过窗户能看到的地方，以免引起小偷的注意。 用 visible benefits 显而易见的好处 反 invisible *adj.* 无形的；看不见的
clarity [ˈklærəti]	*n.* 清楚，明晰；透明 例 His presentation was well-delivered and informative, but a bit confusing in places and lacking clarity. 他的演讲表达流畅，内容丰富，但有些地方有点混乱，不够清晰。 用 a lack of clarity in the law 法律上不明确 扩 clarify *v.* 使清楚；澄清
landscape [ˈlændskeɪp]	*n.* 风景，景色；乡村风景画 例 The view of the landscape from the hotel window was magnificent and certainly part of the hotel's charm. 从酒店窗户看到的景色非常壮观，这也是该酒店的魅力之一。 用 typical features of the English landscape 典型的英国风景特征 考 One of its original works is a series of fuzzy landscapes, depicting trees and sky. 它的原创作品之一是一系列朦胧风景画，描绘的是树木与天空。

subtle
['sʌtl]

adj. 微妙的；精细的；淡的；敏锐的

例 He was not always direct, and often expressed his views in subtle ways, expecting others to get the hint.
他并不总是非常直接，经常以委婉的方式表达自己的观点，希望别人领会他的暗示。

用 subtle colours 淡淡的色彩

---

canal
[kə'næl]

n. 运河，水道

例 The boat glided smoothly along the picturesque canal, offering a serene and relaxing journey.
船沿着风景如画的运河平稳滑行，带来一段宁静而放松的旅程。

用 an irrigation canal 一条灌溉渠 the Suez Canal 苏伊士运河

考 Our brains run at slow biochemical processing speeds on the power of a light bulb, and their size is restricted by the dimensions of the human birth canal.
我们的大脑以一种低生物化学处理速度、用相当于一个灯泡的耗能运行着，而其尺寸也被人类生育通道的尺寸所限制着。

---

capable
['keɪpəbl]

adj. 有能力的；能胜任的

例 He's a very capable manager—he's organized, disciplined and patient with all team members.
他是一位很有能力的管理者，他有条理，自律，对所有团队成员都很有耐心。

用 a very capable teacher 一位很有能力的教师

反 incapable *adj.* 无能力的；不能胜任的

扩 capability *n.* 能力，才能

---

omit
[ə'mɪt]

v. 忽略；省略；遗漏

例 He got a low score because he omitted several key details from the final research report.
他的分数很低，因为在最终研究报告中，几个关键细节缺失了。

用 omit the salt in this recipe 去掉食谱中的盐

扩 omission *n.* 省略；遗漏

---

finite
['faɪnaɪt]

adj. 有限的；限定的

例 Every computer has a finite amount of memory space, so you have to be careful about your storage.
每个计算机的内存空间都是有限的，所以你必须小心使用存储空间。

用 a finite number of possibilities 有限的可能性

反 infinite *adj.* 无限的

ventilation
[ˌventɪ'leɪʃn]

n. 通风，通风系统

例 The room had excellent ventilation, allowing fresh air to circulate and maintain a comfortable environment.
这个房间的通风状况很好，新鲜空气可以流通，保持舒适的环境。

用 ventilation system 通风系统

扩 vent *n.* 通风口 *v.* 排放

Exercise 29

一、中文释义练习

请选择单词正确的中文释义。

_____ 1. retrieve   A. 慈善   _____ 11. tolerate   A. 忍受
_____ 2. conflict   B. 冲突   _____ 12. intestine   B. 使着迷
_____ 3. charity   C. 复杂的   _____ 13. commence   C. 肠
_____ 4. scratch   D. 挠   _____ 14. fascinate   D. 大都市的
_____ 5. intricate   E. 找回   _____ 15. metropolitan   E. 开始

_____ 6. meteorology   A. 气象学   _____ 16. irritation   A. 冲积的
_____ 7. wrap   B. 跨度   _____ 17. alluvial   B. 刺激
_____ 8. flourish   C. 缠绕   _____ 18. optical   C. 有能力的
_____ 9. span   D. 器官   _____ 19. jaw   D. 下巴
_____ 10. organ   E. 繁荣   _____ 20. capable   E. 光学的

二、英文释义练习

请选择单词正确的英文释义。

_____ 1. fragile   A. logical and well organized and easy to understand
_____ 2. agenda   B. trees that are grown to be used for making things
_____ 3. coherent   C. curved path followed by a planet
_____ 4. orbit   D. a list of items to be discussed at a meeting
_____ 5. timber   E. can be easily broken or damaged

_____ 6. artificial   A. made or produced to copy something natural
_____ 7. prescribe   B. the quality of being expressed clearly
_____ 8. despoil   C. to steal something valuable from a place
_____ 9. clarity   D. a long passage dug in the ground and filled with water
_____ 10. canal   E. to tell someone to take a particular medicine

multiple ['mʌltɪpl]	*adj.* 数量多的；多种多样的 *n.* 倍数
	例 He attempted to complete the puzzle multiple times but still couldn't do it, however hard he tried.
	他试了好几次，依然无法完成拼图，无论他有多努力。
	用 multiple copies of documents 各种文件的大量副本
	a multiple entry visa 多次入境签证
	扩 multiply *v.* 乘；增加
feasible ['fiːzəbl]	*adj.* 可行的；可能的；可实行的
	例 It was not feasible to continue running the business on such low profits.
	利润如此之低，继续经营这项业务是不可行的。
	用 a feasible plan 一个可行的计划
	考 While the original aim was to raise the hull if at all feasible, the operation was not given the go-ahead until January 1982, when all the necessary information was available.
	尽管最初的目标是在一切可行的情况下打捞起整个船体，但这一操作直到1982年1月所有需要的信息都完备的时候才被允许执行。
impel [ɪm'pel]	*v.* 推动；驱使；激励
	例 They were impelled to investigate the matter further to discover more evidence.
	他们被迫进一步调查此事，以发现更多的证据。
	用 feel impelled to investigate further 感觉需要进一步调查
	扩 impress *v.* 给……留下印象 impressive *adj.* 有印象的；印象深刻的
tunnel ['tʌnl]	*n.* 隧道；通道
	例 The train rushed through the dark tunnel, its headlights piercing through the blackness.
	火车冲过黑暗的隧道，车头灯划破黑暗。
	用 a railway tunnel 铁路隧道
	考 tunnel construction 隧道建设

occupation [ˌɒkjuˈpeɪʃn]	*n.* 职业；消遣；占领，占用
	例 I believe that being a civil engineer is an interesting and rewarding occupation, especially at this time of great development. 我相信土木工程师是一个有趣而有收获的职业，尤其是在这个有巨大发展的时代。
	用 look for an occupation 找工作 a dangerous occupation 一份危险的工作
incorporate [ɪnˈkɔːpəreɪt]	*v.* 包含；使并入；组成公司
	例 The company planned to incorporate new technology to streamline its operations. 公司计划采用新技术来简化其运营工作。
	用 incorporate a number of major improvements 包含许多重大改进
	考 Fly ash, a byproduct of coal-burning power plants, can be incorporated into concrete mixes to make up as much as 15 to 30% of the cement, without harming the strength or durability of the resulting mix. 粉煤灰是发电厂燃烧煤炭的副产物，可以在混凝土搅拌中替代最高可达15%～30%的水泥，而不会影响到混合后产物的强度和耐用性。
neurological [ˌnjʊərəˈlɒdʒɪkl]	*adj.* 神经学的；神经系统的
	例 His moods were diagnosed as due to a neurological problem in his brain. 他的情绪被诊断为由脑部神经系统问题引起。
	用 neurological damage 神经损伤
	考 neurological studies of the brain 关于大脑的神经科学研究
foam [fəʊm]	*n.* 泡沫，气泡
	例 The waves crashed against the shore, leaving behind white frothy foam on the sands. 海浪拍打着海岸，在沙滩上留下白色的泡沫。
	用 shaving foam 剃须泡沫膏 a foam mattress 泡沫橡胶床垫
	考 And the walls had a layer of foam around them too, to increase the insulation. 这些墙面也有一层泡沫环绕，以增强绝缘。
spread [spred]	*v.* 扩散，传播；伸展开；铺开 *n.* 传播，散布；扩展
	例 A network of railways has spread over the whole country. 铁路网络遍布整个国家。
	用 spread a cloth on a table 在桌上铺桌布

compress [kəmˈpres]	*v.* 压缩；压紧
	例 Divers often take oxygen tanks of air which is highly compressed so that it can be breathed for a long time under water. 潜水员经常带氧气罐，里面的空气被高度压缩，这样就可以在水下呼吸很长时间。
	用 compressed air 压缩空气
terminal [ˈtɜːmɪnl]	*n.* 终点；终点站；航站楼 *adj.* 终点的；末端的
	例 Flights from Amsterdam airport to international destinations all leave from terminal 3. 从阿姆斯特丹机场飞往国际目的地的航班都从3号航站楼起飞。
	用 a railway terminal 铁路终点站
	扩 terminate *v.* 结束，终结
durable [ˈdjʊərəbl]	*adj.* 耐用的，持久的
	例 The new material used in making bags is not only waterproof, but highly durable and resistant to damage. 制作袋子使用的新材料不仅防水，而且非常耐用，不易损坏。
	用 durable plastics 耐用塑料 negotiations for a durable peace 为持久和平而进行的谈判
	扩 duration *n.* 持续；持续时间
premise [ˈpremɪs]	*n.* 前提，假设
	例 It is not difficult to deduce the conclusion from the premise. 从这一假设推断出结论并不难。
	用 a false premise 一个错误的前提
conform [kənˈfɔːm]	*v.* 遵守，遵从；相一致，相符合
	例 He was an unruly boy and refused to conform to many of the school rules. 他是一个不守规矩的孩子，拒绝遵守学校的很多规则。
	用 conform to the local customs 遵从当地风俗
	同 comply *v.* 遵守，依从
suspicious [səˈspɪʃəs]	*adj.* 可疑的；怀疑的；多疑的
	例 She was very suspicious of his motives for giving the boss gifts and constantly praising him all the time. 她非常怀疑他送给老板礼物并总是赞扬老板的动机。
	用 a suspicious look 怀疑的神情
	扩 suspicion *n.* 怀疑

convict [kən'vɪkt] *v.* ['kɒnvɪkt] *n.*	*v.* 定罪，证明有罪 *n.* 罪犯，服刑囚犯 例 The convict managed to escape from prison by digging a tunnel under the walls. 这名罪犯在墙下挖了一条地道，设法逃出了监狱。 用 a convicted murderer 已定罪的谋杀犯
indifference [ɪn'dɪfrəns]	*n.* 漠不关心；冷淡 例 He had lost his enthusiasm for the project and displayed an attitude of complete indifference. 他已经对这个项目失去了热情，表现出一种完全漠不关心的态度。 用 a matter of complete indifference to me 对我来说完全无关紧要 扩 indifferent *adj.* 漠不关心的
daunt [dɔːnt]	*v.* 使胆怯，使气馁；威吓 例 Despite the challenges, she faced them head-on, refusing to let them daunt her spirit. 尽管有这些挑战，她还是勇敢面对，不让自己胆怯。 用 feel daunted by the task ahead 对面前的任务信心不足 考 The ship's crew had the daunting task of repairing the rudder at sea, and only succeeded at the second attempt. 船员们不得不在海上修理船舵，并在第二次尝试中才取得成功。
agent ['eɪdʒənt]	*n.* 代理人，代理商；经纪人 例 The agent negotiated the deal on behalf of her client to try to get her the best deal possible. 代理人代表她的客户就这笔交易进行谈判，试图为她争取尽可能好的结果。 用 an insurance agent 保险经纪人
autonomy [ɔː'tɒnəmi]	*n.* 自治，自治权；独立自主 例 If children are given more autonomy it's surprising how much they can learn by self-discovery. 如果给孩子们更多的自主权，他们通过自我发现学到的东西会令人吃惊。 用 local autonomy 地方自治 同 independence *n.* 独立 扩 autonomous *adj.* 自治的；有自主性的
diminish [dɪ'mɪnɪʃ]	*v.* 减少，缩减，降低；贬低 例 His career opportunities in the country were rapidly diminishing. 他在这个国家的职业机会迅速减少。 用 diminish the cost of production 降低生产成本

realm [relm]	*n.* 领域；范围；王国
	例 He made outstanding contributions to the realm of foreign affairs. 他在外交领域做出了杰出的贡献。
	用 in the realm of literature 在文学领域内
	同 field *n.* 领域

intermittent [ˌɪntəˈmɪtənt]	*adj.* 间歇的；断断续续的
	例 The signal on his mobile phone kept cutting out, and he could only hear his friend talking in intermittent bursts. 他的手机信号一直中断，只能断断续续听到朋友在讲话。
	用 intermittent bursts of applause 一阵阵的掌声

preliminary [prɪˈlɪmɪnəri]	*adj.* 初步的，开始的，预备的 *n.* 准备工作，初步行动
	例 After a few preliminary remarks, the judge announced the winners. 在一些铺垫性的点评之后，裁判公布了优胜者。
	用 preliminary results 初步结果 preliminary findings 初步发现
	考 In a preliminary talk, the teacher introduces them to the material to be covered, but does not "teach" it. 在事先进行的谈话中，老师向他们介绍了会涉及的材料，但并没有"教授"这些内容。

symptom [ˈsɪmptəm]	*n.* 症状；征兆
	例 Typical symptom of anxiety is bad dreams and the inability to sleep well. 焦虑的典型症状是做噩梦和睡眠质量差。
	用 flu symptoms 流感症状 symptoms of depression 抑郁症状

charter [ˈtʃɑːtə(r)]	*n.* 宪章，章程；特许状，许可证 *v.* 租用；特许成立，给予特权
	例 The school obtained a charter to operate independently and tailor its curriculum. 这所学校获得了独立运作和定制课程的许可。
	用 the European Union's Social Charter of workers' rights 保障工人权利的欧盟社会宪章

appeal [əˈpiːl]	*n.* 呼吁；上诉；吸引力 *v.* 呼吁；启发；上诉；有吸引力
	例 He was not sure how to convince his boss to give him a pay rise, so he chose to appeal to his sense of sympathy for his struggles. 他不知如何说服老板给他加薪，所以他选择去唤起老板对他努力工作的同情。
	用 lose their appeal 不再吸引人
	扩 appealing *adj.* 吸引人的；有感染力的

fraction ['frækʃn]	*n.* 分数，小数；小部分
	例 She was only able to solve a fraction of the complex math problem before the time ran out. 在时间用完之前，她只解决了这道复杂数学题的一小部分。
	用 have a grasp of decimals, percentages and fractions 掌握小数、百分数和分数
	考 It is cheap to run, too, consuming a tiny fraction of the electricity used by some techniques. 运转起来也很便宜，只需消耗另一些技术所需电力的九牛一毛。
delegate ['delɪgət] *n.* ['delɪgeɪt] *v.*	*n.* 代表；成员 *v.* 授权；委托；委派
	例 Many managers find it difficult to delegate work to employees and end up doing too much themselves. 很多管理者发现很难把工作授权给员工，结果最终自己做了太多。
	用 delegates from 20 countries 来自20个国家的代表
	扩 delegation *n.* 代表团；委托
dormitory ['dɔːmətri]	*n.* 宿舍，学生宿舍
	例 She lived in the college dormitory, and chose not to rent a flat off campus. 她住在大学宿舍，并没有选择在校外租公寓。
	用 dormitory building 宿舍楼
spine [spaɪn]	*n.* 脊柱；书脊
	例 The spine provides support and protection to the delicate spinal cord. 脊柱为脆弱的脊髓提供支撑和保护。
	用 injuries to his spine 他脊柱的创伤
	考 the vast turning propeller of a ship, the ribcage of a whale or the spine of a fish 船上巨大的旋转螺旋桨、鲸的胸腔或鱼的脊骨
proportion [prə'pɔːʃn]	*n.* 比例；占比；部分
	例 The proportion of women in the workforce increased considerably in the past ten years. 在过去十年中，劳动力中女性的比例大幅提高。
	用 a large proportion of the earth's surface 地球表面的大部分
	扩 proportional *adj.* 成比例的
	考 the estimated proportion of children in New Zealand with auditory problems 新西兰存在听觉问题儿童的预估比例

conceal [kən'siːl]	*v.* 隐藏；隐瞒
	例 She tried to conceal her anger, but he could see from her expression that she was furious. 她试图隐藏自己的愤怒，但他可以从她的表情看出她很生气。
	用 conceal his disappointment 掩饰他的失望
ignite [ɪg'naɪt]	*v.* 点燃，燃烧；引发，激起
	例 The match struck against the rough surface to ignite the candle's wick, casting a warm glow. 火柴擦着粗糙的表面点燃了蜡烛芯，发出温暖的光芒。
	用 ignite their anger 激起了他们的怒火
	考 The brothers added features such as a key-based ignition in the cabin, eliminating the need for the operator to manually ignite the boiler. 这群兄弟们增加了一些新特点，例如驾驶舱内的钥匙点火装置，这样司机就无须手动去点燃车上的锅炉。
aviation [,eɪvi'eɪʃn]	*n.* 航空；飞机制造业
	例 He studied aviation in university but he never passed the exam to become a pilot. 他在大学里学的是航空，但他从没有通过飞行员考试。
	用 civil aviation 民用航空 military aviation 军用航空
heal [hiːl]	*v.* 治愈；痊愈
	例 The traditional medicine she used was known for being effective in healing basic ailments. 她使用的传统药物以治疗常规疾病有效而为人所知。
	用 heal your cuts and scratches 治好割伤和擦伤
	类 injure *v.* 受伤 wound *n.* 伤口 scar *n.* 疤痕 disease *n.* 疾病
intense [ɪn'tens]	*adj.* 强烈的；激烈的；紧张的
	例 Competition for the job was extremely intense, and George didn't feel confident he would be shortlisted. 这份工作的竞争非常激烈，George对自己能进入最终候选名单没有信心。
	用 intense competition 激烈的竞争
havoc ['hævək]	*n.* 大破坏；浩劫
	例 The hurricane wreaked havoc on the small coastal village. 飓风给这个沿海小村庄造成了严重破坏。
	用 wreak havoc on crops 严重危害农作物

triumph ['traɪʌmf]	*n.* 巨大成功；伟大胜利
	例 She had trained for months to compete in the marathon and felt a great sense of triumph when she completed the race. 为了参加马拉松比赛，她训练了好几个月，完成比赛时，她感到一种巨大的成就感。
	用 one of the greatest triumphs of modern science 现代科学最重大的成就之一
trunk [trʌŋk]	*n.* 树干；躯干
	例 They were surprised because the tree trunk was hollow inside. 他们很吃惊，因为树干里面是空的。
	用 rest on the trunk 在树干上休息
	考 Immature coconut flowers are tightly clustered together among the leaves at the top of the trunk. 未成熟的椰花紧密地聚集在树干顶端的叶子中。
stimulate ['stɪmjuleɪt]	*v.* 刺激；鼓舞，激励
	例 They injected billions of dollars to stimulate the economy. 他们投入了数十亿美元来刺激经济。
	用 stimulate a passion for learning 激发学习热情
subordinate [sə'bɔːdɪnət] *adj.&n.* [sə'bɔːdɪneɪt] *v.*	*adj.* 从属的，下级的；次要的 *n.* 下级；从属 *v.* 使处于次要地位
	例 He was a gentle and diplomatic manager, always knowing how to appeal to his subordinates by bringing out their best side and motivating them. 他是一位举止得体、善于交际的管理者，总是知道如何通过发挥下属好的一面并激励他们来获得欣赏。
	用 the relationship between subordinates and superiors 上下级关系
abnormal [æb'nɔːml]	*adj.* 反常的，异常的
	例 His behaviour was considered abnormal by psychologists, and he found it difficult to interact with other pupils and make friends. 他的行为被心理学家们认为是不正常的，并且他发现很难与其他学生交流和交朋友。
	用 abnormal levels of sugar in the blood 血糖值不正常
	反 normal *adj.* 正常的
predecessor ['priːdəsesə(r)]	*n.* 前任；前辈
	例 In her inauguration speech she expressed warm admiration for her predecessor. 她在就职演说中对她的前任表达了相当的敬佩。
	用 face the same kind of problems as his predecessor 面临与前任同样的问题

arrogant ['ærəgənt]	*adj.* 傲慢的，自大的 例 His arrogant behavior alienated many of his colleagues and they ended up avoiding him. 他傲慢的行为疏远了许多同事，最终他们都避免与之相处。 用 a typically arrogant assumption 典型的自大假设 扩 arrogance *n.* 傲慢，自大
transfer [træns'fɜ:(r)] *v.* ['trænsfɜ:(r)] *n.*	*v./n.* 转移；转换 例 I need to transfer money from my current bank account to my friend's account so that we can pay for the airline tickets. 我需要将钱从我的银行账户转给我的朋友，这样我们就可以支付机票费用了。 用 transfer the patient to another hospital 将患者转去另一家医院 扩 transference *n.* 转移；转让 考 High achievers have been found to use self-regulatory learning strategies more often and more effectively than lower achievers, and are better able to transfer these strategies to deal with unfamiliar tasks. 人们发现相比低成就者，高成就者会更频繁而有效地使用自我调节的学习策略，并更能够在不熟悉的任务中使用这些策略。
deploy [dɪ'plɔɪ]	*v.* 部署，调度；利用 例 The military decided to deploy troops to the eastern front of the conflict zone. 军方决定把部队部署到冲突地区的东部前线。 用 deploy missiles along the border 在边境部署导弹
yield [ji:ld]	*v.* 出产；屈服；放弃 *n.* 产量；收益 例 One beehive can yield enough honey to fill almost a hundred jars. 一个蜂箱就能够产出足够的蜂蜜来装满一百个罐子。 用 trees that no longer yield fruit 不再结果实的树 yield to 让步于
artefact ['ɑ:tɪfækt]	*n.* 手工艺品；人工制品 例 The museum had a huge collection of ancient artefacts, including jade and bronzes from the Ming Dynasty. 这个博物馆收藏了大量古代文物，包括明朝的玉器和青铜器。 用 repair broken religious artefacts 修补破损的宗教手工艺品
perimeter [pə'rɪmɪtə(r)]	*n.* 外缘，周边；周长 例 We would go jogging around the perimeter of Chaoyang Park every other day. 我们每隔一天就会绕着朝阳公园的周边慢跑。 用 the perimeter of the airport 机场周边

Exercise 30

一、中文释义练习

请选择单词正确的中文释义。

_____ 1. impel   A. 前提

_____ 2. tunnel   B. 泡沫

_____ 3. foam   C. 耐用的

_____ 4. durable   D. 推动

_____ 5. premise   E. 隧道

_____ 11. spine   A. 治愈

_____ 12. conceal   B. 点燃

_____ 13. ignite   C. 减少

_____ 14. heal   D. 脊柱

_____ 15. diminish   E. 隐藏

_____ 6. indifference   A. 漠不关心

_____ 7. daunt   B. 使胆怯

_____ 8. realm   C. 症状

_____ 9. symptom   D. 领域

_____ 10. fraction   E. 小部分

_____ 16. trunk   A. 刺激

_____ 17. stimulate   B. 手工艺品

_____ 18. transfer   C. 树干

_____ 19. perimeter   D. 周长

_____ 20. artefact   E. 转移

二、英文释义练习

请选择单词正确的英文释义。

_____ 1. feasible   A. to behave in the same way as other people in a group

_____ 2. incorporate   B. that is possible and likely to be achieved

_____ 3. terminal   C. to include sth. so that it forms a part of sth.

_____ 4. conform   D. feeling that sb. has done sth. wrong or illegal

_____ 5. suspicious   E. a building in airport where passengers arrive and leave

_____ 6. intermittent   A. a person chosen to represent a group of people

_____ 7. delegate   B. stop and start often over a period of time irregularly

_____ 8. aviation   C. the designing, building and flying of aircraft

_____ 9. predecessor   D. the total amount of crops or profits that are produced

_____ 10. yield   E. a person who did a job before someone else

音频

pilot ['paɪlət]	*n.* 飞行员；领航员 *adj.* 试点的 *v.* 驾驶；领航；试验，试行
	例 The skilled pilot maneuvered the airplane safely through turbulent weather conditions. 熟练的飞行员驾驶飞机安全渡过了不稳定的天气环境。
	用 an airline pilot 民航飞行员 a pilot study 试验性研究
	考 This weight, together with that of the fuel, pilot and four crew, approached the helicopter's maximum payload, and there were times when it was clearly right on the edge of the helicopter's capabilities. 这个重量，再加上燃料、飞行员和四名机组人员，已接近该架直升机的最大承重量，有时载重量明显达到了飞机承重能力的极限。
medium ['miːdiəm]	*adj.* 中等的；中号的 *n.* 方法，手段；媒介，媒体
	例 The online medium is probably the most common way of conducting business in the world today. 线上媒体或许是当今世界最普遍的业务形式。
	用 a man of medium height 一个中等身材的男子
	同 average *adj.* 平均的；中等的
	扩 media *n.* 媒体 mass media 大众传媒
	考 the current digital medium 当前的数字媒介
barrel ['bærəl]	*n.* 桶；一桶（的量）；枪管
	例 The distillery stored the whiskey in oak barrels, allowing it to age and develop rich flavours. 酿酒厂将威士忌储存在橡木桶中，使其变陈并产生丰富口味。
	用 a beer barrel 啤酒桶 a wine barrel 葡萄酒桶 oak barrels 橡木桶
bubble ['bʌbl]	*n.* 气泡，泡沫
	例 The children blew soap bubbles, chasing after them with sheer delight. 孩子们吹着肥皂泡，兴高采烈地追逐着泡泡。
	用 champagne bubbles 香槟酒的泡沫

restrict
[rɪˈstrɪkt]

v. 限制；约束；限定

例 We restrict the number of students in each class to twelve, in order that each student gets a lot of teacher attention.
我们将每个班的学生人数限制在12人以内，以使每个学生得到老师足够的关注。

用 restrict public access to the hills 限制公众进入山区

扩 restriction *n.* 限制；约束

superfluous
[suːˈpɜːfluəs]

adj. 多余的；不必要的

例 To save on costs they are cutting out superfluous managers from the organisation.
为了节省开支，他们正在裁掉组织中多余的管理者。

用 many superfluous belongings 很多无用的物品

同 unnecessary *adj.* 不必要的

impose
[ɪmˈpəʊz]

v. 强加；强制实行

例 The authorities imposed new restrictions on vehicles so that they could reduce the air pollution in major cities.
当局对车辆施加了新的限制，以减少大城市的空气污染。

用 impose additional financial burdens on many people
给很多人增加额外经济负担

inaugurate
[ɪˈnɔːgjəreɪt]

v. 为……举行就职典礼；为……举行落成仪式；开始，开创

例 They celebrated the moon landing which inaugurated a new era in space exploration.
他们庆祝登陆月球，这开创了太空探索的新纪元。

用 inaugurate as President in January 于一月份就任总统

candidate
[ˈkændɪdeɪt]

n. 候选人；应试者

例 He was an ideal candidate for the job—he was motivated, dedicated and highly skilled.
他是这份工作的理想人选，他有上进心、敬业、技术熟练。

用 one of the leading candidates 主要候选人之一

decompose
[ˌdiːkəmˈpəʊz]

v. 分解；腐烂，腐败

例 Organic waste left in the open will decompose over time, returning nutrients to the soil.
留在露天的有机废物会随着时间的推移而分解，将营养物质归还给土壤。

用 be decomposed by microorganisms 被微生物完全分解

扩 compose *v.* 组成；创作

renew [rɪ'njuː]	*v.* 延长 (执照、合同的) 有效期; 更新, 更换; 重新开始
	例 In most countries every ten years you have to renew your driving licence. 在大多数国家, 每十年要更换一次驾照。
	用 renew my passport 续签护照
	扩 renewable *adj.* 可再生的; 可更新的
transaction [træn'zækʃn]	*n.* 交易, 买卖, 业务
	例 The bank processed the financial transaction swiftly and securely, ensuring the funds were transferred. 银行迅速而安全地处理了这笔金融交易, 确保了资金的转移。
	用 financial transactions between companies 公司之间的财务往来 commercial transactions 商业交易
	考 That is mainly because the costs of all this damage are what economists refer to as externalities: they are outside the main transaction, which is for example producing and selling a field of wheat, and are borne directly by neither producers nor consumers. 这主要因为这些代价是经济学家们所说的 "外部经济效应", 它们不在如生产或出售一块地里的小麦那样的主要交易过程之中, 而且它们也不是由生产者和消费者直接来承担的。
jury ['dʒʊəri]	*n.* 陪审团; 评判委员会
	例 Generally, the jury consisted of citizens from all walks of life. 通常, 陪审团由来自各行各业的公民组成。
	用 members of the jury 陪审团成员
contend [kən'tend]	*v.* 主张; 竞争; 处理, 对付
	例 The company was too small to contend against the growing competition. 这家公司太小了, 无法应对日益激烈的竞争。
	用 have to contend with violence 需要应对暴力
	同 maintain *v.* 主张; 认为
destiny ['destəni]	*n.* 命运, 定数, 天命
	例 He believed strongly in destiny, and felt that things in life always turned out the way they were intended to, somehow. 他坚定地相信命运, 觉得生活中的事情总会在一定程度上以它们想要的方式发生。
	用 be in control of his own destiny 掌握着他自己的命运
	同 fate *n.* 命运

exaggerate [ɪɡ'zædʒəreɪt]	*v.* 夸张，夸大 例 He didn't lie, but often he exaggerated the truth enormously. 他并没有说谎，但他经常对事实进行夸大。 用 exaggerate the difficulties 夸大困难 扩 exaggeration *n.* 夸大，夸张
detour ['diːtʊə(r)]	*n./v.* 绕道，绕行，迂回 例 Due to road construction, they had to take a detour to reach their destination. 由于道路施工，他们不得不绕道到达目的地。 用 make a detour around the flooded fields 绕道避开被洪水淹没的田野
embryo ['embriəʊ]	*n.* 胚胎；胚芽；初期 *adj.* 胚胎的；初期的 例 At seven weeks old an embryo in the womb is a recognisable human baby. 七周大的胚胎在子宫里是一个可辨认的婴儿形象。 用 human embryos 人的胚胎 the embryo of an idea 一种想法的雏形 考 Early embryos of many species develop ancestral features. 许多物种的早期胚胎都具有祖先的特征。
engine ['endʒɪn]	*n.* 引擎，发动机 例 Manufacturing activities are the main engine of economic growth in the country. 制造业活动是这个国家经济增长的主要引擎。 用 a steam engine 蒸汽机
concentrate ['kɒnsntreɪt]	*v.* 集中（注意力）；（使）浓缩 例 He always found it hard to concentrate on his studies during the summer—it was hot and stuffy and it made him feel tired and distracted. 他发现在夏天总是很难集中精力学习，天气闷热，他感到疲惫，时常分心。 用 concentrate on 聚焦于；集中于 concentrate resources on the most run-down areas 把资源集中用于最衰败的地区 扩 concentration *n.* 集中；专注 考 Background noise in the classroom becomes a major distraction, which can affect their ability to concentrate. 背景噪音成了教室中的主要干扰，这会影响学生们集中注意力的能力。

splash [splæʃ]	v.（液体）飞溅，泼溅；拍打戏水
	例 The kids giggled as they played and splashed in the pool. 孩子们在池塘里玩耍和戏水时发出阵阵笑声。
	用 splash around in the pool for a while 在水池里玩耍一会儿
nurture ['nɜːtʃə(r)]	v./n. 养育；培养；培植
	例 It's important to nurture a sense of responsibility and social awareness in children from a young age. 从小培养孩子的责任感和社会意识是很重要的。
	用 children nurtured by loving parents 受到慈爱父母养育的孩子
	同 foster v. 培养
escalate ['eskəleɪt]	v. 加剧；增加；增强
	例 They engaged in high-level negotiations to avoid the conflict escalating. 他们进行了高层谈判，以避免冲突升级。
	用 the escalating costs of health care 逐渐增加的医疗费用
	扩 escalator n. 自动扶梯
architect ['ɑːkɪtekt]	n. 建筑师；创造者，设计师
	例 Along with civil engineers and urban planners, architects are in great demand in the province at the moment. 与土木工程师和城市规划师一样，目前建筑师在该省也有很大需求。
	用 the principal architect 主设计师
emerge [ɪ'mɜːdʒ]	v. 出现；浮现；显露；兴起
	例 The problems started to emerge after he started working with the new team. 在他开始与新团队一起工作后，问题开始出现了。
	用 emerged from the lake 从湖水中浮出来 emerging markets of South Asia 正在兴起的南亚市场
	扩 emergency n. 紧急状况，突发事件
	考 Excellence does not emerge without appropriate help. 没有恰当的帮助，很难成就优秀。
plague [pleɪg]	n. 瘟疫，传染病；灾害 v. 困扰，折磨
	例 The deadly plague ravaged the city, causing widespread fear and panic. 致命的瘟疫在这座城市中肆虐，引起了广泛的担心和恐慌。
	用 an outbreak of plague 瘟疫的爆发 be under threat from a plague of rats 面临着鼠疫的威胁

arouse [əˈraʊz]	*v.* 引起；唤醒；激发
	例 He tried to arouse the students' interest in the subject by telling exciting stories. 他试图通过讲述令人兴奋的故事来唤起学生对这门课的兴趣。
	用 arouse one's interest 引起某人的兴趣 arouse one's curiosity 引起某人的好奇心
	扩 arousal *n.* 引起；唤起；激励
	考 We're going to see a revival of that production, which aroused a lot of interest. 我们将要看的是这出剧的新版演出，它引起了人们很大的兴趣。
improvise [ˈɪmprəvaɪz]	*v.* 即兴创作；临时做
	例 With limited resources, she had to improvise and create a makeshift shelter in the wilderness. 由于资源有限，她不得不在荒野中搭建了一个临时住所。
	用 improvise a harness 临时做一副马具
	考 A suggested method for transport engineers is to improvise design solutions and get instant feedback about how they would work from their own experience of them, or model designs at full scale in the way choreographers experiment with groups of dancers. 向交通工程师们建议一个方法：即兴给出一些设计方案，然后自己亲身去进行体验以获得即时的反馈，或者像舞蹈设计师用一群舞者来实验动作效果那样全方面地模拟设计方案。
elicit [ɪˈlɪsɪt]	*v.* 引发，引起
	例 The psychological test uses a series of pictures to elicit responses from children. 心理测试使用一系列图片来引发孩子们的反应。
	用 elicit no response from him 得不到他的回复
lifetime [ˈlaɪftaɪm]	*n.* 一生；寿命；有效期
	例 Through hard work and determination he achieved an incredible amount in his lifetime. 通过努力工作和决心，他一生中取得了令人难以置信的成就。
	用 a lifetime of experience 毕生的经验
pledge [pledʒ]	*n.* 誓言；保证，承诺 *v.* 保证；发誓
	例 They made a solemn pledge to support each other through thick and thin. 他们郑重承诺要同甘共苦互相支持。
	用 a pledge that there will be no job losses this year 保证今年不会削减工作职位

enormous [ɪ'nɔːməs]	*adj.* 庞大的，巨大的
	例 She made enormous efforts to overcome her anxiety, but still needed counselling. 她做了巨大努力来克服焦虑，但仍然需要心理辅导。
	用 an enormous amount of time 大量的时间
dynamic [daɪ'næmɪk]	*adj.* 充满活力的；动态的；动力的 *n.* 动态；动力
	例 He was a positive, dynamic and energetic leader who loved innovation projects. 他是一个积极、有活力、精力充沛的领导者，喜欢创新项目。
	用 fluid dynamics 流体力学 group dynamics 小组互动
	反 static *adj.* 静止的 still *adj.* 静止的
drastically ['dræstɪkli]	*adv.* 彻底地；剧烈地
	例 In the past two years things have started to go drastically wrong with the economy. 在过去两年间，经济出现了严重的问题。
	用 reduce drastically 显著减少
	扩 drastic *adj.* 显著的 a drastic shortage of food 食物的极度短缺
prospect ['prɒspekt]	*n.* 前景；预期；将要发生的事；景色
	例 The prospect of going to university in another country made him feel incredibly nervous. 将要去另一个国家上大学这件事使他感到非常紧张。
	用 an exciting prospect 令人兴奋的前景
	扩 prospective *adj.* 预期的；可能的
	考 In order to encourage them to see that working in a hotel could be worthwhile and rewarding, with good prospects, they introduced a management programme. 为了能让他们知道在酒店工作是值得的和有回报的，而且前景不错，他们引进了管理制度。
inject [ɪn'dʒekt]	*v.* 注入；注射
	例 They injected him with a type of steroid which helped the heart beat stronger and gave him energy and strength. 他们给他注射了一种类固醇，使他的心脏跳动更有力，并带给他能量和力量。
	用 be injected into the muscle 注射到肌肉里
	扩 injection *n.* 注入；注射
	考 When iron element was injected back into the affected trees, they immediately recovered. 当铁元素被重新注入受影响的树的时候，这些树马上恢复了。

insert
[ɪn'sɜːt] v.
['ɪnsɜːt] n.

v. 插入，嵌入；添加 n.（书报的）插页，广告附加页

例 Please insert your name and contact details into the online form provided.
请将您的姓名及联络资料填入提供的网上表格中。

用 insert the thermometer 插入温度计

microscope
['maɪkrəskəʊp]

n. 显微镜

例 The bacteria samples were taken to the laboratory and studied carefully under the microscope.
细菌样本被送往实验室，在显微镜下进行细致研究。

用 look through a microscope at plant cells 在显微镜下观察植物细胞

repertoire
['repətwɑː(r)]

n. 全部节目；全部技能

例 The comedian had a fantastic repertoire of jokes that he told with great confidence.
这位喜剧演员有一整套绝妙的笑话，他讲这些笑话很有信心。

用 a pianist with a wide repertoire 一位能演奏很多曲目的钢琴师

考 build a repertoire of creative problem-solving skills
具备创造性解决问题的能力

articulate
[ɑː'tɪkjuleɪt] v.
[ɑː'tɪkjələt] adj.

v. 明确表达；清晰发音 adj. 善于表达的；口齿清楚的

例 He could not articulate himself properly to explain what was on his mind.
他无法清晰得当地表达，来说明自己的想法。

用 articulate her thoughts 表明她的想法

assemble
[ə'sembl]

v. 集合，聚集；装配，组装

例 They sell a lot of furniture that you have to assemble yourself at home.
他们出售很多需要你自己在家里进行组装的家具。

用 assemble evidence 收集证据 assemble data 收集数据

考 A team there carefully assembled the 1,200 tonnes of steel, painstakingly fitting the pieces together to an accuracy of just 10 mm to ensure a perfect final fit.
那里的团队仔细装配了1,200吨钢铁部件，竭尽全力地以细致到仅为10毫米的精确度将零件组装在一起，以确保完美的最终合并。

scene
[siːn]

n. 场面；场景；景象

例 She enjoyed the view of the magnificent scene of the waterfall through the windows.
她很喜欢透过窗户看到的壮观的瀑布景色。

用 the scene of the accident 事故现场

innate [ɪ'neɪt]	*adj.* 先天的；固有的；与生俱来的
	例 There are some parenting skills which are surly innate, but many have to be learned and practiced. 有些育儿技能显然是天生的，但很多仍然需要通过学习和实践获取。
	用 the innate ability to learn 天生的学习能力
	同 inborn *adj.* 天生的 inherent *adj.* 固有的；内在的
virtual ['vɜːtʃuəl]	*adj.* 虚拟的；实质上的
	例 The city came to a virtual standstill when they hosted the football match. 当他们举办足球比赛时，这座城市实际上陷入了停顿。
	用 a virtual monopoly in this area of trade 实质上垄断了这种贸易
	扩 virtually *adv.* 实质上；实际上
pregnant ['pregnənt]	*adj.* 怀孕的；富有意义的
	例 An elephant is pregnant for usually eleven months before giving birth. 大象在生产前通常会怀孕11个月。
	用 be pregnant with the third child 怀了第三个孩子
	扩 pregnancy *n.* 怀孕
diversity [daɪ'vɜːsəti]	*n.* 多样性；差异
	例 Globalisation has brought about the need for us to embrace diversity, as cities become increasingly cosmopolitan. 随着城市变得越来越国际化，全球化趋势使我们需要拥抱多样性。
	用 the biological diversity of the rainforests 热带雨林的生物多样性
	扩 biodiversity *n.* 生物多样性 diversify *v.* 使多样化
	考 Because of their tremendous breeding potential and genetic diversity, many pests are known to withstand synthetic chemicals and bear offspring with a built-in resistance to pesticides. 由于它们巨大的繁殖潜力和遗传多样性，人们知道很多害虫可以抵抗合成化学物，并且能够繁衍具备天生抗杀虫剂特质的后代。
abuse [ə'bjuːs] *n.* [ə'bjuːz] *v.*	*n./v.* 滥用；虐待
	例 Verbal abuse can be as bad as physical abuse and can lead to psychological problems. 言语虐待可以和身体虐待一样糟糕，并能够导致心理问题。
	用 drug abuse 嗜毒 alcohol abuse 酗酒
	同 insult *v.* 侮辱；辱骂

consignment
[kən'saɪnmənt]

n. 委托；运送；装运的货物

例 In preparation for the annual office gala performance, the director ordered a huge consignment of decorations.
为了准备一年一度的办公室晚会表演，导演订购了一大批装饰品。

用 a consignment of medicines 运送的一批药物

nourish
['nʌrɪʃ]

v. 滋养，养育；培养，助长

例 Vitamin A and vitamin D nourish and protect the skin.
维生素A和维生素D能滋养和保护皮肤。

用 nourish the talents of our children 培养孩子们的才能

考 More recently, we have found that indiscriminate use of fertilisers hurts the soil itself, turning it acidic and salty, and degrading the soil they are supposed to nourish.
最近，我们发现滥用化肥对土壤本身也有很大伤害，使其变成酸性且含盐度高，并且使那些本想被其滋养的土壤出现退化。

regulate
['regjuleɪt]

v. 调节；管理；规定

例 Governments often introduce policies to regulate financial markets, so that they do not spiral out of control.
政府经常出台政策来调节金融市场，从而使其运转不要失控。

用 regulate the temperature of the room 调节室内温度

扩 regulation *n.* 规则；控制；管理

考 regulate our immune systems 调节我们的免疫系统

Exercise 31

一、中文释义练习

请选择单词正确的中文释义。

_____ 1. medium   A. 中等的

_____ 2. barrel   B. 气泡

_____ 3. restrict   C. 桶

_____ 4. bubble   D. 分解

_____ 5. decompose   E. 限制

_____ 6. jury   A. 陪审团

_____ 7. exaggerate   B. 溅落

_____ 8. detour   C. 绕行

_____ 9. engine   D. 夸大

_____ 10. splash   E. 引擎

_____ 11. escalate   A. 引起

_____ 12. arouse   B. 巨大的

_____ 13. elicit   C. 引出

_____ 14. enormous   D. 前景

_____ 15. prospect   E. 加剧

_____ 16. inject   A. 集合

_____ 17. articulate   B. 注入

_____ 18. assemble   C. 滥用

_____ 19. pregnant   D. 怀孕的

_____ 20. abuse   E. 明确表达

二、英文释义练习

请选择单词正确的英文释义。

_____ 1. superfluous   A. a person whose job is designing buildings

_____ 2. transaction   B. unnecessary or more than you need or want

_____ 3. embryo   C. an animal in early stages of development before birth

_____ 4. architect   D. to make or do something using whatever is available

_____ 5. improvise   E. a piece of business that is done between people

_____ 6. pledge   A. all the plays that a performer knows and can perform

_____ 7. dynamic   B. having a lot of energy and a strong personality

_____ 8. repertoire   C. to keep an animal or a plant alive and healthy

_____ 9. diversity   D. a range of things that are very different from each other

_____ 10. nourish   E. to formally promise to give or do something

esteem
[ɪ'stiːm]

n./v. 尊重，尊敬

例 She was praised for her excellent contribution to the team project; it really boosted her self-esteem.
她因为对团队项目的杰出贡献而受到表扬，这真的增强了她的自尊心。

用 a highly esteemed scientist 一位深受敬重的科学家

---

tube
[tjuːb]

n. 管，管子；管状物

例 The dentist used a small tube to suck out excess saliva during the dental procedure.
牙医在做牙科手术时用一根小管子吸出多余的唾液。

用 a bike's inner tube 自行车内胎 a tube of toothpaste 一管牙膏

考 Peer inside and you see the tubes are completely hollow, the roots of dozens of strawberry plants dangling down inside them.
向其中窥视一下你就能发现：这些管道是完全中空的，数十株草莓的根部悬垂其中。

---

analogy
[ə'nælədʒi]

n. 类比；类推；类似

例 The biology teacher drew an analogy between the human heart and a pump.
生物老师把人的心脏类比为一个水泵。

用 learning by analogy 用类比法学习

扩 analogous *adj.* 相似的，类似的

---

revive
[rɪ'vaɪv]

v. 恢复，复兴；使苏醒

例 The vet managed to revive the injured bird with the help of medicines.
兽医在药物的帮助下设法救活了受伤的小鸟。

用 revive the region's economy 复苏这个地区的经济

扩 revival *n.* 复兴；复苏

---

preserve
[prɪ'zɜːv]

v. 保存；保护；维持

例 It is important to preserve old buildings and historical sites.
保护古老建筑和历史遗迹是很重要的。

用 preserve his reputation 维护他的名声

pursue [pə'sjuː]	*v.* 追求；执行；从事；追赶
	例 It is important to pursue a goal that is realistic and achievable, rather than a dream which is ideal but not attainable. 重要的是追求一个现实的、可实现的目标，而不是一个理想但无法实现的梦想。
	用 pursue an objective 追求目标
	扩 pursuit *n.* 追求；追赶；工作
peripheral [pə'rɪfərəl]	*adj.* 外围的；次要的
	例 Fund-raising and charitable donations are peripheral to the company's main business. 募捐和慈善捐赠是这家公司主营业务外的周边事务。
	用 some peripheral information 一些辅助信息 the peripheral nervous system 周围神经系统
	反 central *adj.* 中心的；核心的
	考 One way of learning about a job is "legitimate peripheral participation"—a novice stands next to experts and learns by observation. 了解一种职业的方式之一就是"适度外围参与"，即一个新手站在专家们身旁，通过观察来学习。
genetic [dʒə'netɪk]	*adj.* 遗传的；基因的
	例 Some people claim that anxiety and depression are actually genetic disorders of the mind. 有些人认为焦虑和抑郁实际上是遗传性的精神障碍。
	用 genetic and environmental factors 遗传和环境因素 genetic abnormalities 基因异常
	扩 gene *n.* 基因
devastate ['devəsteɪt]	*v.* 毁灭；毁坏
	例 The wild fires devastated vast tracts of land and forests in California. 野火摧毁了加利福尼亚的大片土地和森林。
	用 devastate much of the old part of the city 毁掉旧城的一大片地方
flexible ['fleksəbl]	*adj.* 灵活的；柔韧的；易弯曲的
	例 I am pleased that our company have began flexible working hours for employees. 我很高兴我们公司开始让员工实行弹性工作时间。
	用 a more flexible approach 一个更灵活的方法 be flexible enough to cater for the needs of everyone 足够变通以满足每个人的需求
	反 inflexible *adj.* 不可弯曲的；顽固的
	扩 flexibility *n.* 灵活性；机动性

mystery
['mɪstri]

n. 谜；神秘

例 Agatha Christie was famous for her mystery and detective novels.
Agatha Christie以她的悬疑和侦探小说而闻名。

用 remain a mystery 依然是个谜
the mysteries of outer space 外层空间之谜

扩 mysterious *adj.* 神秘的
the mysterious mass extinction of the dinosaurs 神秘的恐龙大灭绝

考 A 2014 study by Shi Ping Liu and colleagues sheds light on this mystery.
一份2014年由刘世平及其同事完成的研究解释了这个秘密。

---

commute
[kə'mjuːt]

v. 通勤，上下班往返 *n.* 通勤的路程

例 The commute to work was horrific—crowded subways and unreliable timetables.
拥挤的地铁和不可靠的时间表使上班的通勤非常可怕。

用 commutes from Oxford to London every day
每天上下班往返于牛津与伦敦之间
have a short commute to work 上班路程很近

---

highlight
['haɪlaɪt]

v. 突出；强调；使显著 *n.* 最精彩部分；最重要的事

例 The teacher highlighted the main points of the paragraph in order to illustrate the logic of writing an argumentative essay.
老师强调了这段话的要点，以说明写议论文的逻辑。

用 highlight the importance 强调重要性

考 highlight some differences between past and future job losses
强调过去和未来失业现象的差异

---

bully
['bʊli]

v. 威吓，欺侮；威胁，胁迫 *n.* 恃强凌弱者

例 The school took action to address the issue of bullying among students.
学校采取行动解决学生之间的欺凌问题。

用 the school bully 学校里横行霸道的学生
victims of bullying 遭受欺凌的人

考 Their movement might be somewhat restricted, but they have a safe environment in which to live, and they are spared bullying and social ostracism by others of their kind.
它们的活动会受到一定程度的限制，但它们有安全的生存环境，更少受到物种中其他个体的攻击和排斥。

---

encircle
[ɪn'sɜːkl]

v. 包围；围绕；环绕

例 It takes the earth 365 days to encircle the sun in its orbit.
地球绕太阳公转一周需要365天。

用 be encircled by a coral reef 被一片珊瑚礁围绕

pamphlet ['pæmflət]	n. 小册子，活页
	例 They distributed a pamphlet with information about the upcoming event.
	他们分发了小册子，上面有关于即将到来的活动的信息。
	用 a pamphlet about skiing 一本关于滑雪的小册子

fragment ['frægmənt]	n. 碎片；片段
	例 After he broke my grandmother's vase, we kept finding small fragments of pottery all over the place.
	在他打碎了我祖母的花瓶后，我们在各种地方都能找到陶器的碎片。
	用 a fragment of the conversation 谈话中的只言片语
	扩 fragmentation n. 分裂；破碎

strand [strænd]	n. 缕，串；岸，滨 v. 使滞留，使困在；搁浅
	例 She had a habit of twisting strands of hair around her finger while she was thinking or daydreaming.
	她有一个习惯，当她思考或做白日梦的时候，会把一缕缕头发缠绕在手指上。
	用 a strand of wool 一缕羊毛 a few strands of dark hair 几缕黑发
	考 the insertion of strands of extinct animal DNA
	插入已灭绝物种的DNA片段

imply [ɪm'plaɪ]	v. 意味；暗示
	例 He didn't directly say that he didn't like her new dress, but he implied it with his phrasing.
	他没有直接说不喜欢她的新衣服，但他的措辞暗示了这一点。
	用 the implied criticism in his voice 他暗中批评的语气
	同 suggest v. 暗示
	扩 implication n. 含义；含蓄

obligation [ˌɒblɪ'geɪʃn]	n. 义务；职责
	例 An obligation of being an employee is following standard operational procedures and the company behavioural code.
	员工有义务遵守标准操作程序和公司的行为准则。
	用 a moral obligation to protect the environment
	道德上有责任保护环境
	考 under obligation to those shareholders to maximize profits
	有义务为股东创造最多利润

temperate
['tempərət]

adj. 温和的；适度的；有节制的

例 The climate in most of Northern Europe is temperate and neither extremely hot nor extremely cold.
北欧大部分地区气候温和，既不太热也不太冷。

用 keep a temperate climate throughout the year 全年气候温和

---

penalty
['penəlti]

n. 罚款，罚金；处罚

例 The penalty for driving too fast is a speeding ticket with a heavy fine and points on your licence.
超速驾驶的惩罚是一张超速罚单，有很重的罚款并在驾照上记分。

用 impose a penalty 予以惩罚

---

contrary
['kɒntrəri]

adj. 相反的 n. 相反；反面

例 Contrary to their expectations, the weather was dreadful and rained the whole time.
与他们的预期相反，天气很糟糕，一直在下雨。

用 on the contrary 相反地

---

interchange
['ɪntətʃeɪndʒ] n.
[ˌɪntə'tʃeɪndʒ] v.

n./v. 交换，互换

例 Information is efficiently interchanged between members across the different departments of the organisation.
信息在组织不同部门的成员间高效流转。

用 a continuous interchange of ideas 不断的思想交流

---

eligible
['elɪdʒəbl]

adj. 合格的，合适的；符合条件的

例 She has been working in the company for over 30 years, so she is eligible for early retirement.
她已经在这家公司工作了30多年，因此有资格提前退休。

用 be eligible to vote 有资格投票

反 ineligible adj. 不合格的

---

underlie
[ˌʌndə'laɪ]

v. 成为……的基础；为……的起因

例 The attitude of both partners, and their different approaches to business, were the two main issues that underlie the problems.
合作伙伴双方的态度，以及他们不同的经营方式，是导致问题的两个主要原因。

用 the fundamental issue which underlies the conflict
引起冲突的根本问题

扩 underlying adj. 潜在的；根本的
underlying assumption 潜在假设，基本假设

crude [kruːd]	*adj.* 粗略的，大概的；粗糙的，粗制的；天然的，自然的 *n.* 原油
	例 The early prototypes were fairly rough and crude compared to the final product. 与最终产品相比，早期的原型相当粗糙和原始。
	用 crude oil 原油 crude wooden boxes 粗制的木盒子 an important but crude way of assessing the risk of heart disease 评估心脏病风险的一种重要却粗略的方法
dramatically [drə'mætɪkli]	*adv.* 剧烈地，明显地；戏剧性地
	例 The weather in sub-tropical climates can change dramatically and it often suddenly starts to rain in torrents. 亚热带气候的天气变化显著，经常突然下起倾盆大雨。
	用 increase dramatically 显著增长
	扩 dramatic *adj.* 巨大的；生动的；戏剧性的 a dramatic increase 显著增长
	考 During the industrial revolution and population explosion of the 19th and 20th centuries, the demand for water rose dramatically. 在19和20世纪的工业革命和人口爆炸期间，对水资源的需求快速增长。
superficial [ˌsuːpə'fɪʃl]	*adj.* 表面的；浅薄的，肤浅的
	例 She made a superficial analysis without delving into the underlying issues. 她做了肤浅的分析，没有深入研究深层问题。
	用 a superficial analysis 粗略的分析 a superficial understanding of the historical context 对历史背景肤浅的理解
	扩 artificial *adj.* 人造的，人工的；矫揉造作的
	考 a superficial understanding 一个浅显的理解
switch [swɪtʃ]	*n.* 开关；转换 *v.* 改变；转换；替换
	例 He became very tired of his major after only a few months and put in an application to switch subjects half way through the first semester. 仅仅几个月后他就厌倦了自己的专业，并在第一个学期进行到一半时申请换专业。
	用 a light switch 电灯开关
	考 need to switch to a different occupation within the next 10–15 years 需要在未来10到15年之间换一份工作

rectangle ['rektæŋgl]	*n.* 矩形，长方形
	例 The table had a sleek design with a smooth, polished rectangle-shaped top. 桌子的设计很时尚，桌面是光滑平整的矩形形状。
	用 the rectangle books on the shelf 书架上那些长方形的书
	扩 rectangular *adj.* 矩形的，长方形的
discourse ['dɪskɔːs] *n.* [dɪs'kɔːs] *v.*	*n.* 演讲，论述；话语，语篇 *v.* 论述，讲述
	例 In the presentation she gave a lengthy discourse about the project aims. 在报告中，她对这个项目的目的进行了长篇论述。
	用 discourse analysis 语篇分析
negotiate [nɪ'ɡəʊʃieɪt]	*v.* 谈判，商议；交涉
	例 It's important to learn to negotiate a good salary when you are applying for a job. 当你申请工作时，学会协商一份好的薪水是很重要的。
	用 negotiating skills 谈判技巧
	扩 negotiation *n.* 谈判
legacy ['leɡəsi]	*n.* 遗产
	例 After her aunt passed away she received a sizeable legacy in the will. 姑姑去世后，她在遗嘱中得到了一大笔遗产。
	用 receive a legacy 得到一笔遗产
entire [ɪn'taɪə(r)]	*adj.* 全部的；整个的；全体的
	例 His unruly behaviour disturbed the entire class and annoyed the teacher. 他不守规矩的行为扰乱了整个班级，也惹恼了老师。
	用 in the entire country 在整个国家
	同 whole *adj.* 全部的
comet ['kɒmɪt]	*n.* 彗星
	例 The comet streaked across the night sky, leaving a brilliant trail behind. 彗星划过夜空，留下一条灿烂的轨迹。
	用 Halley's Comet 哈雷彗星
	考 He also described celestial phenomena such as haloes—that is, bright circles of light around the sun, the moon and stars—and comets. 他还描述了一些天文现象，比如光晕——即围绕太阳、月亮和恒星的明亮光圈，以及彗星。

acquaintance [əˈkweɪntəns]	*n.* 认识，了解；相识的人，泛泛之交
	例 She made a number of new acquaintances at the social gathering. 她在社交聚会上结识了许多新朋友。
	用 an old acquaintance of his 他的一位老相识

albeit [ˌɔːlˈbiːɪt]	*conj.* 虽然，尽管
	例 It was a beautiful, romantic day by the river, albeit slightly cold due to the autumn breeze. 那是在河边度过的美丽浪漫的一天，虽然由于秋风，天气有些冷。
	用 albeit reluctantly 尽管很勉强
	同 although *conj.* 尽管；虽然

sculpture [ˈskʌlptʃə(r)]	*n.* 雕塑，雕像
	例 He was an excellent artist, though he concentrated mainly on oil painting and was not very skilled at sculpture. 他是一位优秀的艺术家，尽管他主要专注于油画，不太擅长雕塑。
	用 study painting and sculpture 学习绘画和雕塑

vibrant [ˈvaɪbrənt]	*adj.* 充满活力的，充满生机的
	例 The city streets came alive at night with vibrant lights, music, and bustling activity. 夜晚，城市街道上有明亮的灯光、活跃的音乐和热闹的活动。
	用 a vibrant city 一座充满生机的城市 Shakespeare's vibrant language 莎士比亚那充满活力的语言
	考 If the trend continues, it could create new jobs and a more vibrant and sustainable local food economy—alongside many other benefits. 如果这个趋势继续下去，就有可能创造新的工作机会和一种更加生机勃勃、更可持续发展的本地食物经济——以及带来许多其他好处。

arch [ɑːtʃ]	*n.* 拱门；拱顶；拱形物
	例 The grand arch marked the entrance to the majestic palace, evoking a sense of awe. 气派的拱门标志着宏伟宫殿的入口，令人肃然起敬。
	用 go through the arch 穿过拱门
	考 Brick walls were then constructed, and finally a brick arch was added to create a tunnel. 接下来筑起砖墙，最后再加盖砖拱，这样就建成了一条隧道。

comply [kəmˈplaɪ]	*v.* 遵守；遵从
	例 All owners of heavy goods vehicles have one month to comply with the new driving regulations announced last month. 所有重型货车车主有一个月时间调整以遵守上个月公布的新驾驶规则。
	用 comply with the UN resolution 遵守联合国决议
mammal [ˈmæml]	*n.* 哺乳动物
	例 Mammals are usually warm-blooded animals that are covered in fur, and sometimes have tails. 哺乳动物通常是恒温动物，全身长有皮毛，有些会长有尾巴。
	用 the function of a mammal's fur 哺乳动物皮毛的功能
	扩 mammalian *adj.* 哺乳动物的
	考 Play is a crucial part of development in most young mammals. 游戏是多数年幼哺乳动物成长中的重要部分。
battery [ˈbætri]	*n.* 电池，蓄电池；一组，一系列
	例 The battery of the old smartphone needed frequent recharging. 旧智能手机的电池需要经常充电。
	用 replace the batteries 更换电池 a rechargeable battery 充电电池
correspond [ˌkɒrəˈspɒnd]	*v.* 符合，相一致；通信
	例 Infant school in the UK generally corresponds to first grade in the USA. 英国的幼儿学校一般相当于美国的一年级。
	用 correspond every week 每周通信
	扩 corresponding *adj.* 相应的；对应的
concept [ˈkɒnsept]	*n.* 概念；观念
	例 The concept of individual responsibility was alien to him. 个人责任的概念对他来说是陌生的。
	用 the concept of social class 社会等级的概念
unveil [ˌʌnˈveɪl]	*v.* 揭开；除去面纱；显露
	例 At the end of the ceremony the CEO unveiled the plans for the new office building. 典礼的最后，CEO公布了新办公大楼的计划。
	用 unveil his new strategy 公布他的新策略
	同 reveal *v.* 揭示
	反 veil *v.* 遮盖，掩饰

velocity [vəˈlɒsəti]	*n.* 速度，速率 例 The car accelerated quickly, reaching a high velocity on the open highway. 汽车迅速加速，在开阔的公路上达到了很高速度。 用 the velocity of light 光速 gain velocity 加速 lose velocity 减速 考 It collects images from digital cameras running at 50 frames a second and breaks down each part of a swimmer's performance into factors that can be analysed individually—stroke length, stroke frequency, average duration of each stroke, velocity, start, lap and finish times, and so on. 系统采用摄影频率为50帧/秒的数码相机收集影像，然后将游泳运动员的每个动作都分解成可单独分析的因素，例如划距、划频、每个划水动作的平均持续时间、速率、出发时间、往返时间和结束时间等。
property [ˈprɒpəti]	*n.* 所有物，财产；房地产；特性，性质 例 Lost property should be handed in to the reception desk in the hotel lobby. 遗失物品应当被交回酒店大堂服务台。 用 damage other people's property 损坏他人的财物
bulk [bʌlk]	*n.* 主体，大部分；（大）体积，大（量） 例 The bulk of the population is concentrated in the major cities. 大部分人口集中生活在大城市里。 用 bulk buying 大量购买 考 bulk cargo 大宗货物

Exercise 32

一、中文释义练习

请选择单词正确的中文释义。

_____	1. tube	A.	管子
_____	2. peripheral	B.	通勤
_____	3. genetic	C.	遗传的
_____	4. mystery	D.	外围的
_____	5. commute	E.	谜

_____	11. superficial	A.	彗星
_____	12. legacy	B.	雕塑
_____	13. albeit	C.	尽管
_____	14. comet	D.	表面的
_____	15. sculpture	E.	遗产

_____	6. highlight	A.	成为基础
_____	7. fragment	B.	合格的
_____	8. interchange	C.	强调
_____	9. eligible	D.	交换
_____	10. underlie	E.	碎片

_____	16. battery	A.	概念
_____	17. correspond	B.	电池
_____	18. concept	C.	大块
_____	19. unveil	D.	一致
_____	20. bulk	E.	揭开

二、英文释义练习

请选择单词正确的英文释义。

_____	1. analogy	A. single thin piece of thread, wire or hair
_____	2. flexible	B. able to change to suit new conditions or situations
_____	3. pamphlet	C. have to do something because it is your duty
_____	4. strand	D. comparing one thing with another with similar features
_____	5. obligation	E. a very thin book containing particular information

_____	6. penalty	A. to surround sb./sth. completely in a circle
_____	7. encircle	B. to try to reach an agreement by formal discussion
_____	8. negotiate	C. things that are owned by somebody
_____	9. comply	D. a punishment for breaking a law, rule or contract
_____	10. property	E. to obey a rule or an order to meet particular standards

Answer Keys

Exercise 01

一、中文释义练习

1–5	CEABD	6–10	AEDBC
11–15	CBAED	16–20	ABDEC

二、英文释义练习

1–5	DCAEB	6–10	CEADB

Exercise 02

一、中文释义练习

1–5	BCEAD	6–10	ABCED
11–15	EDCAB	16–20	ACBDE

二、英文释义练习

1–5	ACBDE	6–10	EBACD

Exercise 03

一、中文释义练习

1–5	DCEAB	6–10	BDACE
11–15	BDCEA	16–20	AEDBC

二、英文释义练习

1–5	BCADE	6–10	DABCE

Exercise 04

一、中文释义练习

1–5	CBEDA	6–10	DEABC
11–15	ECBAD	16–20	AEDBC

二、英文释义练习

1–5	BECAD	6–10	BDCAE

Exercise 05

一、中文释义练习

1–5	ACBED	6–10	ACEBD
11–15	CDAEB	16–20	ECDBA

二、英文释义练习

1–5	ABCED	6–10	EABCD

Exercise 06

一、中文释义练习

1–5	EBDCA	6–10	AEDBC
11–15	DACBE	16–20	EBADC

二、英文释义练习

1–5	BEACD	6–10	DBEAC

Exercise 07

一、中文释义练习

1–5	CEBDA	6–10	CEADB
11–15	CBADE	16–20	BACED

二、英文释义练习

1–5	CAEBD	6–10	DCAEB

Exercise 08

一、中文释义练习

1–5	CBADE	6–10	EDACB
11–15	BAECD	16–20	BECDA

二、英文释义练习

1–5	CDABE	6–10	ACEDB

Exercise 09

一、中文释义练习

　　1–5　AEBDC　　　　6–10　BCAED
　　11–15 DEBCA　　　　16–20 BACDE

二、英文释义练习

　　1–5　AEBDC　　　　6–10　BAEDC

Exercise 10

一、中文释义练习

　　1–5　EBADC　　　　6–10　AEDBC
　　11–15 ECBAD　　　　16–20 DABEC

二、英文释义练习

　　1–5　DCAEB　　　　6–10　ACEDB

Exercise 11

一、中文释义练习

　　1–5　ABCDE　　　　6–10　ABCDE
　　11–15 AEDBC　　　　16–20 CBDAE

二、英文释义练习

　　1–5　ACBED　　　　6–10　ECBAD

Exercise 12

一、中文释义练习

　　1–5　ADCEB　　　　6–10　DBCEA
　　11–15 BEDCA　　　　16–20 CBEAD

二、英文释义练习

　　1–5　EBDAC　　　　6–10　CBDAE

Exercise 13

一、中文释义练习

　　1–5　EACDB　　　　6–10　DCAEB
　　11–15 BCEAD　　　　16–20 EDBAC

二、英文释义练习

　　1–5　ECABD　　　　6–10　EDCAB

Exercise 14

一、中文释义练习

　　1–5　EBADC　　　　6–10　ACEBD
　　11–15 ACEBD　　　　16–20 BAEDC

二、英文释义练习

　　1–5　EDACB　　　　6–10　AECBD

Exercise 15

一、中文释义练习

　　1–5　DEBCA　　　　6–10　ABDCE
　　11–15 DEBAC　　　　16–20 CAEDB

二、英文释义练习

　　1–5　BCEAD　　　　6–10　BACED

Exercise 16

一、中文释义练习

　　1–5　ACEBD　　　　6–10　ADCEB
　　11–15 EACBD　　　　16–20 BEADC

二、英文释义练习

　　1–5　BECAD　　　　6–10　EBADC

Answer Keys

Exercise 17

一、中文释义练习

1-5	ADCEB	6-10	CEDBA
11-15	DECAB	16-20	BDAEC

二、英文释义练习

1-5	DBEAC	6-10	DABEC

Exercise 18

一、中文释义练习

1-5	ECDAB	6-10	DCBEA
11-15	CABDE	16-20	DBACE

二、英文释义练习

1-5	ACEDB	6-10	CEBDA

Exercise 19

一、中文释义练习

1-5	BCAED	6-10	ACBED
11-15	EDCAB	16-20	EDBCA

二、英文释义练习

1-5	EBACD	6-10	CBDEA

Exercise 20

一、中文释义练习

1-5	DECBA	6-10	EABCD
11-15	BADCE	16-20	DEACB

二、英文释义练习

1-5	DEBCA	6-10	DBCEA

Exercise 21

一、中文释义练习

1-5	BEDAC	6-10	CDABE
11-15	ADBEC	16-20	BECAD

二、英文释义练习

1-5	DACBE	6-10	EBDCA

Exercise 22

一、中文释义练习

1-5	DEACB	6-10	DACBE
11-15	CDAEB	16-20	DAEBC

二、英文释义练习

1-5	DBACE	6-10	DCBEA

Exercise 23

一、中文释义练习

1-5	EABCD	6-10	DABEC
11-15	ADBCE	16-20	ADEBC

二、英文释义练习

1-5	EACBD	6-10	AEDCB

Exercise 24

一、中文释义练习

1-5	BADCE	6-10	CEDBA
11-15	EDCAB	16-20	ACBED

二、英文释义练习

1-5	ABDEC	6-10	BCAED

Exercise 25

一、中文释义练习

1-5	EBADC	6-10	AEDBC
11-15	ECBAD	16-20	DABEC

二、英文释义练习

1-5	DCAEB	6-10	ACEDB

Exercise 26

一、中文释义练习

1-5	BACDE	6-10	ABCED
11-15	AEDBC	16-20	CBDAE

二、英文释义练习

1-5	ACBED	6-10	ECBAD

Exercise 27

一、中文释义练习

1-5	ADCEB	6-10	DBCEA
11-15	BEDCA	16-20	CBEAD

二、英文释义练习

1-5	EBDAC	6-10	CBDAE

Exercise 28

一、中文释义练习

1-5	EACDB	6-10	DCAEB
11-15	BCEAD	16-20	EDBAC

二、英文释义练习

1-5	ECABD	6-10	EDCAB

Exercise 29

一、中文释义练习

1-5	EBADC	6-10	ACEBD
11-15	ACEBD	16-20	BAEDC

二、英文释义练习

1-5	EDACB	6-10	AECBD

Exercise 30

一、中文释义练习

1-5	DEBCA	6-10	ABDCE
11-15	DEBAC	16-20	CAEDB

二、英文释义练习

1-5	BCEAD	6-10	BACED

Exercise 31

一、中文释义练习

1-5	ACEBD	6-10	ADCEB
11-15	EACBD	16-20	BEADC

二、英文释义练习

1-5	BECAD	6-10	EBADC

Exercise 32

一、中文释义练习

1-5	ADCEB	6-10	CEDBA
11-15	DECAB	16-20	BDAEC

二、英文释义练习

1-5	DBEAC	6-10	DABEC

Index

descend / 166
deserve / 262
designate / 258
desperate / 240
despise / 301
despoil / 317
destination / 240
destiny / 334
destruction / 282
detach / 92
detain / 282
deteriorate / 139
detour / 335
detrimental / 183
devastate / 344
deviation / 81
device / 181
devote / 27
diagnose / 38
diagram / 124
dialect / 82
diameter / 111
diesel / 37
digest / 220
digital / 284
dilemma / 114
dilute / 274
dimension / 127
diminish / 325
diploma / 229
disability / 272
disappoint / 114
discard / 229
discern / 216
discharge / 85
discipline / 62
disclose / 101
discount / 121
discourse / 349

discover / 154
discrepancy / 161
discriminate / 306
disdain / 193
disguise / 55
dismal / 183
dismantle / 187
dismiss / 136
disorder / 188
disparage / 94
dispense / 82
disperse / 25
displace / 239
dispose / 251
disprove / 203
dispute / 113
disrupt / 304
disseminate / 159
dissertation / 49
dissolve / 154
distil / 167
distinct / 201
distinguish / 160
distort / 157
distract / 105
distribute / 215
disturb / 239
ditch / 205
diverge / 176
diverse / 284
diversity / 340
divorce / 120
dock / 284
document / 144
domain / 225
dome / 268
dominate / 120
dopamine / 113
dormitory / 327

dose / 127
draft / 183
drainage / 304
dramatically / 348
drastically / 338
drawback / 41
dreadful / 301
drift / 47
drill / 209
dubious / 63
dull / 106
dump / 200
duplicate / 34
durable / 324
dwell / 124
dwindle / 158
dye / 232
dynamic / 338
eccentric / 210
echo / 215
eclipse / 289
ecology / 30
ecosystem / 13
edge / 203
edible / 186
effect / 270
efficiency / 52
elaborate / 294
elastic / 156
elbow / 67
elderly / 21
elect / 60
elegant / 204
element / 33
elevate / 249
elicit / 337
eligible / 347
eliminate / 145
eloquently / 157

embark / 65
embarrass / 214
embassy / 102
embed / 57
embody / 50
embrace / 14
embryo / 335
emerge / 336
eminent / 80
emission / 142
emotion / 31
empathy / 278
emphasis / 175
empirical / 187
emulate / 79
enable / 265
encase / 233
encircle / 345
enclose / 218
encode / 212
encompass / 138
encounter / 191
endanger / 270
endeavour / 102
endorse / 59
endure / 190
enervation / 194
enforce / 259
engage / 101
engender / 165
engine / 335
engrave / 251
engross / 180
enhance / 190
enlarge / 72
enlighten / 15
enormous / 338
enrich / 188
enrol / 94

paraphrase / 133

parasite / 290

parcel / 48

parliament / 203

participate / 227

particle / 49

passive / 37

pastime / 37

pasture / 138

patent / 169

patriotic / 171

patronage / 188

peculiar / 155

pedal / 178

pedestrian / 187

penalty / 347

penetrate / 128

pension / 164

perception / 99

perfume / 191

peril / 153

perimeter / 330

peripheral / 344

perish / 225

permanent / 20

perpetual / 101

perplex / 252

persevere / 260

persist / 25

perspective / 214

pervasive / 62

pesticide / 300

pharmacy / 51

phase / 248

phenomenon / 194

philosophy / 306

physiology / 23

pile / 148

pilot / 332

pine / 131

pinpoint / 205

pitch / 196

pitfall / 141

placebo / 175

plagiarism / 65

plague / 336

plank / 49

plateau / 218

plausible / 80

pledge / 337

plot / 212

plough / 26

polish / 273

poll / 44

porcelain / 288

portfolio / 191

postcode / 238

postpone / 120

pottery / 226

poverty / 98

pragmatic / 201

praise / 48

precaution / 306

precede / 145

precedent / 37

predator / 125

predecessor / 329

pregnant / 340

prejudice / 197

preliminary / 326

premier / 89

premise / 324

premium / 86

prescribe / 316

preserve / 343

prestigious / 229

presume / 73

pretend / 53

prevail / 61

prey / 241

primary / 225

primitive / 127

principal / 175

principle / 230

priority / 51

privilege / 112

probe / 301

procedure / 211

proceed / 297

process / 238

proclaim / 173

prodigious / 195

proficiency / 13

profile / 88

profit / 250

profound / 281

prohibit / 242

prolong / 285

prominent / 275

prompt / 173

prone / 132

propel / 264

proper / 39

property / 352

proponent / 257

proportion / 327

propose / 163

propound / 214

prospect / 338

prosper / 275

protein / 164

prototype / 53

protrude / 134

provision / 29

psychiatric / 170

psychic / 133

psychology / 231

publicise / 93

publish / 261

pulse / 106

pump / 281

purchase / 160

pursue / 344

qualify / 84

quality / 113

quantity / 307

quota / 153

radical / 297

rage / 175

random / 70

rational / 236

rationale / 169

realm / 326

reap / 274

recap / 193

recede / 69

receptive / 38

recession / 75

recipe / 152

reciprocal / 105

reclaim / 187

recommend / 100

recover / 15

recreation / 245

recruit / 234

rectangle / 349

rectify / 98

recycle / 72

redundant / 215

refine / 279

reflect / 17

refrain / 146

refresh / 156

refuge / 170

refund / 278

regardless / 98